The Governance of Place
Space and planning processes

Edited by

ALI MADANIPOUR, ANGELA HULL and PATSY HEALEY
University of Newcastle upon Tyne, UK

Ashgate

Published by
Ashgate Publishing Limited
Gower House
Croft Road
Aldershot
Hampshire GU11 3HR
England

Ashgate Publishing Company
131 Main Street
Burlington, VT 05401-5600 USA

Ashgate website: http://www.ashgate.com

British Library Cataloguing in Publication Data
The governance of place : space and planning processes
    1. City planning 2. Public spaces
    I. Madanipour, Ali II. Hull, Angela III. Healey, Patsy, 1940-
    3 07.1'2

Library of Congress Catalog Card Number: 00-132797

ISBN 0 7546 1086 1

Reprinted 2002

Printed in Great Britain by Biddles Limited, Guildford and King's Lynn

Contents

List of Figures and Tables   vii
List of Contributors   viii
Acknowledgements   x

1   Introduction   1
       Ali Madanipour, Patsy Healey and Angela Hull

PART ONE: CONCEPTS OF SPACE
Concepts of Space   19
Ali Madanipour

2   How Should We Think About Place in a Globalising World?   23
       Nigel Thrift

3   A New Approach to Identifying Localities: Representing
       'Places' in Britain   51
       Mike Coombes and Colin Wymer

4   Imagined Value: The Poetics and Politics of Place   69
       Jean Hillier

5   The Integrated Metropolis: A Strategy for the Networked,
       Multi-Centred City   102
       Tony Lloyd-Jones, Bill Erickson, Marion Roberts and
       Stephen Nice

6   Urban Futures? Integrating Telecommunications into
       Urban Planning   124
       Stephen Graham and Simon Marvin

7   Multiple Meanings of Space and the Need for a Dynamic
       Perspective   154
       Ali Madanipour

PART II: CHANGING GOVERNANCE PROCESSES
Changing Governance Processes   171
Angela Hull

8   The Need to Zoom Out: Understanding Planning Processes in a
     Post-Corporatist Society   178
     Maarten Hajer

9   Structures and Processes in Strategic Spatial Plan Preparation:
     The Participatory Agenda   203
     Angela Hull and Geoff Vigar

10   The Influence of New Institutional Processes in Shaping Places:
     The Cases of Lyon and Nîmes (France 1981–95)   223
     Alain Motte

11   Metropolitan Development as a Complex System: A New
     Approach to Sustainability   239
     Judith Innes and David Booher

12   Towards a More Place-focused Planning System in Britain   265
     Patsy Healey

13   Shaping Urban Areas into the Twenty-first Century: The Roles
     of the Planning Process   287
     Ted Kitchen

Index   309

List of Figures and Tables

Figure 3.1   Facets of localities   55
Figure 3.2   Inputs to the synthetic data for the localities definition   63
Figure 3.3   Map of Sudbury (East Anglia); synthetic data   65
Figure 3.4   Sudbury (East Anglia); localities and urban areas   65
Figure 5.1   Travel time constraints and the multi-centred metropolis:
             how the '100-mile city' has developed   108
Figure 8.1   The Dutch discursive space   193
Figure 8.2   Institutional preferences   194
Figure 10.1 Lyon general plan   227
Figure 10.2 Urban Projects of the Plan d'Ordonnancement de Nîmes   231
Figure 12.1 The evolution of regulatory purposes in the British
             planning system and its practices   273
Figure 12.2 Emerging regulatory forms for planning systems
             compared   275
Figure 12.3 Forms of planning as developed in Britain   276
Figure 13.1 Consequences of over-riding economic base
             considerations   290
Figure 13.2 Possible policy responses   291
Table 13.1   Changes experienced by English local planning
             authorities in the two years up to 31 December 1996   298
Table 13.2   The history and immediate future of the British urban
             planning process   306

List of Contributors

David Booher, Institute of Urban and Regional Development, University of California, Berkeley.

Mike Coombes, Centre for Urban and Regional Development Studies (CURDS), Department of Geography and Northeast Regional Research Laboratory, University of Newcastle.

Bill Erickson, School of Urban Development and Planning, University of Westminster, London.

Stephen Graham, Centre for Urban Technology (CUT), School of Architecture, Planning and Landscape, University of Newcastle.

Maarten Hajer, Department of Political Science, University of Amsterdam.

Patsy Healey, Centre for Research in European Urban Environments (CREUE), School of Architecture, Planning and Landscape, University of Newcastle.

Jean Hillier, Department of Urban and Regional Planning, Curtin University, Perth, Western Australia.

Angela Hull, Centre for Research in European Urban Environments (CREUE), School of Architecture, Planning and Landscape, University of Newcastle.

Judith Innes, Institute of Urban and Regional Development, University of California, Berkeley.

Ted Kitchen, School of Urban and Regional Studies, Sheffield Hallam Univerity.

Tony Lloyd-Jones, School of Urban Development and Planning, University of Westminster, London.

Ali Madanipour, Centre for Research in European Urban Environments (CREUE), School of Architecture, Planning and Landscape, University of Newcastle.

Simon Marvin, Research Centre for Sustainable Urban and Regional Futures, University of Salford.

Alain Motte, Institute of Regional Management, University of Aix-Marseille.

Stephen Nice, Burns and Nice Consulting Engineers, London.

Marion Roberts, School of Urban Development and Planning, University of Westminster, London.

Nigel Thrift, Department of Geography, University of Bristol.

Geoff Vigar, Centre for Research in European Urban Environments (CREUE), School of Architecture, Planning and Landscape, University of Newcastle.

Colin Wymer, School of Architecture, Planning and Landscape and Northeast Regional Research Laboratory, University of Newcastle.

Acknowledgements

The earlier versions of most papers in this book were first delivered at a conference entitled *Shaping Places: Conceptions and Directions for Spatial Planning*, which marked the 50th Anniversary of the Department of Town and Country Planning, University of Newcastle upon Tyne, in October 1996. Since then, new papers have been added and much alteration has been made to a number of papers. Some papers were subsequently published in journals. Nigel Thrift's paper was published in *Scottish Geographical Magazine* under the title 'Cities without modernity, cities with magic', and is published here with the kind permission of the Royal Scottish Geographical Society. Judith Innes and David Booher's paper was published in *Economic Development Quarterly* under the title 'Metropolitan Development as a Complex System', and is published here with the kind permission of Sage Publications Inc. The paper by Tony Lloyd-Jones, Bill Erickson, Marion Roberts and Stephen Nice was published in *Journal of Urban Design* and is published here with kind permission. Patsy Healey's paper is an amended version of 'Collaborative Planning in a Stakeholder Society' which appeared in *Town Planning Review*, and is published here with kind permission.

Chapter One

Introduction

Ali Madanipour, Patsy Healey and Angela Hull

The Argument

There seems to be common agreement among observers about some of the major changes that have occurred in western societies. Global economic and technological change has caused social and political upheavals at local and national levels, forcing people, organisations and governments to find new responses to these major challenges. As telecommunications and transport technologies enable resources and people to move around the world at ever faster speeds, the institutions designed for smaller scales and slower modes of operation find it increasingly hard to cope. As the growth and decline of economies can depend on the decisions of a global network of investors, national governments and local authorities seem to lose some of their control over their territories. The competition among urban regions in the global marketplace to attract resources and the rising significance of regions in political terms, especially in the European Union, pose a new challenge to national and local authorities. Another challenge to these traditional sources of authority comes from an ever more sophisticated populace, who are concerned for the sustainability of the environment, are sceptical of the rule of experts and demand better services, more participation in their own affairs and are less responsive to the traditional forms of legitimacy and social control. A further challenge comes from those who find themselves increasingly marginalised in the economic and social transition out of the industrial era, as they witness a proportionate deterioration of their living conditions and are unable or unwilling to participate in political decision making processes and in shared cultural experiences. These challenges clearly show that the relationship between the state and society is moving into new, somewhat unknown directions, where voting behaviour is changing and the traditional channels of representative democracy are bypassed. Spatial planning systems, as one of the significant components of the state-society relations, are facing their share of these challenges and have been under pressure for some time to provide a response.

The redefinition of state-society relation has often meant a pressure for the reduction of the role of state in the economy, which had reached its peak in the post-war welfare state with its corporatist arrangements. This pressure for reduction was either out of necessity, where costs were seen to be no longer affordable, or out of choice, to facilitate innovation and renewal. Cuts in public spending and privatisation of public organisations and services are among the familiar measures of the last three decades taken to change the extent of state intervention. The private sector agencies were invited to fill the gap that is left by the withdrawal of the state from some of its traditional spheres of activity. The private sector contribution may be first and foremost in economic matters, but engagement in decision-making can also be politically significant. What was once a powerful government with a high degree of control over the political economy of a specific territory was to be replaced with a fragmented collection of agencies, engaged in territorial governance. The challenge for spatial planning has been to adjust to this change from government to governance, where political and economic power lies with not one powerful government but a multiplicity of agencies and interests.

This dramatic change of political and economic contexts has brought forward the need for spatial planning systems and practices to go through some substantial changes, so as to assert its position or to define a new role for itself. Spatial planning, therefore, essentially faces a main challenge: how to fit in a new political and economic configuration where many new actors are involved, proving that it is not only engaged in regulating environmental change but also positively contributing to economic development and environmental care (Vigar et al., 2000). It has to define its role as well as its area of engagement to be distinctive from those of other actors. The pressure is such that if it does not, it could either dissolve or become marginalised. This role has increasingly been seen as centred on innovative ways of engaging with governance processes and its area of engagement has been seen to be place and territory. It is on these two topics, the need for new approaches to governance and the need for new approaches to space, that this book concentrates.

Spatial planning systems (land use planning, town and country planning, territorial management, whatever they are called) are all about the way the physical resources of places are used and developed. In this sense, they have a strong emphasis on place, space and territory. Two increasingly interrelated notions are now being widely discussed: the rising significance of territory and the need to transform the planning systems built in the twentieth century so that they meet the conditions of the twenty-first century. Much has been said about the need to reflect new ideas about governance in the design and practices of planning systems, and new experiments abound. In public policy, in Europe and the US, there is an increasingly strong emphasis on territory and place as a focus of governance attention. Although geographers have long argued for the integration of space into social understanding (Soja, 1989; Martin and Sunley, 1996), the economists have started to take into account the importance of territory (Krugman, 1995). But so far, there has been only limited discussion in the planning field on how territory and place should be understood and what the implication of this is for the transformation of spatial planning systems.

Our argument in this book is that the new ways of 'doing governance' need to be linked to new ways of thinking about space, place and territory, if spatial planning systems are really to be transformed into valuable governance activities in the next century. The aims of this book are, therefore, to discuss some of the new ways of understanding space; to explore, in an international context, some of the new ways of engaging in governance processes by spatial planning systems; and take some tentative steps towards bringing these two discursive realms together.

Spatial planning systems, along with the other tools of state intervention in social and economic spheres which were devised in the postwar period, are changing fast. After several shifts of paradigm, there are new pressures to give more emphasis to space and the importance of place-making, this time working through different processes and with a wider community of actors. In the context of this change, this book puts forward a new hypothesis: that this renewed attention to space heralds the start of a new understanding, but one which will only be successful if spatial planning is seen as a socio-spatial process. How we as social beings use and perceive space cannot be divorced from the wider structuring networks of property relations, the forces of production and the government apparatus itself. This leads to two further points: there is a need for a) a multidimensional, complex understanding of space, and b) new ways of negotiating how society should shape and influence the myriad of urban actors who mobilise to transform places. These two points are taken up in the two main parts of the book. The first part introduces various perspectives which together enrich our understanding of space, including a case study from Australia, while the second part brings together case studies from the United Kingdom, France, Netherlands, and the United States as innovatory benchmarks in our search for new processes of spatial planning in a changing governance context. Together the two parts argue for a new balance between the process and substance of spatial planning.

Spatiality and Spatial Planning

After fifty years as a planning theorist, in his search for a '*substantive domain*' that would secure the holders of planning degrees a legitimate professional place amongst other more established professionals, John Friedmann wrote (1998, p.251):

> What, I asked, was our unique competence as planners, the body of knowledge which no one else could legitimately claim as their own? If we were unable to identify such a domain, then, indeed, planning, as a field of professional study, was perhaps not worth saving. My provisional answer was that planners have or should have a grounding in knowledge about the socio-spatial processes that, in interaction with each other, *produce the urban habitat.*

In this assertion, Friedmann was drawing upon Henri Lefebvre (1991), who had argued that the production of space is deeply embedded and centrally located in the overall political, economic and cultural conditions of a society. Space, therefore, becomes a central concept and introducing spatial thinking into planning theory and practice an urgent need. The main message from Ed Soja, in addressing the Association of the Schools of Planning in Bergen, Norway, in the summer of 1999, was that all planners should think spatial and act spatial. Involvement in all areas, including community-based planning, sustainability and social justice need to be spatialised, to arrive at spatial justice and regional democracy.

A similar emphasis on the need for integrating space into planning was made by Manuel Castells, who, also drawing on Lefebvre, argued that the '...defence of the locale, of their meaning, of their uses, is the banner of use value versus exchange value'. That is why the role of planning in a new world would be '...making new spaces, meaningful places with connecting capability' (Cuthbert, 1996, p.8). But has planning been here before? Is there a danger in seeing the integration of spatiality into planning as a return to the past, rather than a new development, a step backwards rather than forwards?

Spatial planning grew out of architecture as its branch dealing with urban design. In Britain, in the early days after the 1947 Town and Country Planning Act, planning had a clear focus on designed urban spaces, requiring the skills of technical experts (architects and engineers) in built form. This was a process by which the experts' analytical and design skills were seen as being able to improve the living environment and, as a by-product, even the inhabitants themselves. The social legitimacy of this approach hinged on the experts' ability as 'doctors of space' to relieve perceived problems and symptoms, but in a vacuum far removed from the economic and political tensions of the time.

However, large scale, state intervention in the city proved to be a complex process and needed administrative management as well as support from new branches of science and technology. As a result, planning as an independent activity emerged, seeing the city as a site of spatial relationships, rather than merely a collection of artefacts. There was a shift of role for the planning task from design to the 'efficient' resource management of land and infrastructure. The 1970s property boom and concomitant recession questioned the ability of planners to manage growth and spread the benefits. The broadening out of the planning task was accompanied by the rise of community pressure groups intent on affirming the political nature of decisions on space management. The slow down of space production in the 1980s drove attention away from the built environment and its qualities and focused attention instead on the process of decision-making. The planning task was redefined in procedural terms as facilitating the efficient release of sites for development in response to market signals. Community reaction to this led to local struggles to protect places valued for their use value rather than their exchange value.

In the 1990s, more gradual structural economic change toward flexible production has in turn brought about a new cycle of space production and new attention to the marketable qualities of the built environment. The intense competition of cities in the global marketplace, the new patterns of consumption of goods and services (including space), as well as the increasing danger of fragmentation of cities and societies, and the mounting environmental problems all demand a more careful treatment of the built environment. To compensate for the previous neglect of the built environment, public policy attention in Britain has now turned its attention to urban space (Urban Task Force, 1999).

Yet this new-found concern is arising in a governmental context where administrative reorganisations have shaken up local state bureaucracies to take on the new market challenges and form new relationships with the private sector and local communities. British government and European Commission programmes are pushing the detailed working out of spatial strategies down to local level. A diversity of local actors are now interacting in ad hoc networks both to promote the marketable qualities of local places which can be commodified and to protect and enhance the qualities of these same places as 'lived-in' environments for local people. The process by which these two objectives and the claims of different communities of interest can be reconciled has yet to be determined.

There is a danger that the return of interest in space by planners could lead to a simplistic response to the new demands for space being created through the current reorganisation of the economy. The shifts of attention in planning, in response to the various cycles of space production, have created imbalances of focus through their failure to address the tensions between conceptions of space as exchange value and everyday meanings attached to the use of space. Also significant have been the tensions between those who use and manage the existing stock or between the development industry, which has the capacity to bring about radical physical change, and those agencies that seek to regulate the use of land and buildings.

To avoid such a danger, first, it is essential that the concept of space be discussed and developed in its complexity. This is the theme of the first part of this book, which addresses a number of perspectives from which space can be studied, and in particular the different perceptions and heuristic tools available to understand the social and psychological attributes people attach to material space. There is an obvious need now for the built environment professionals to relearn the tradition of analysing space. Second, spatial planning, in moving towards a more successful urban development process, has to ensure the integration of these different spatial concerns in the policy-making process either through the 'technical' analysis of the complex understanding of space or through encouraging 'community' participation in decisions which may affect their neighbourhoods. The second part of the book presents innovatory approaches to addressing this challenge in four different countries to help suggest ways in which planners can utilise different representations, symbolic forms, and embedded assumptions about places in the materiality of future spatial strategies. Such cases help us to comprehend the dynamics of specific places as well as to evaluate the different processes employed in managing the governmental regulatory task. Fragmented responsibilities for administrative spaces and the shifting nature of market relations call for a coherent vision and agenda to steer spatial change in line with a diversity of place strategies.

Concepts of Space

But how are we to understand these spaces and places, if we are to integrate new forms of spatiality into spatial planning, rather than relying on the worn out, simplistic concepts of the past? The notions of space, as we explore in Part One, are complex concepts. Our main argument here is that such complexity requires a dynamic, multidimensional approach, which would capture complexity without the need for excessive reductionism. This was a challenge that Coombes and Wymer faced (Chapter Three) when trying to define localities.

Concepts of space are used in different disciplinary discourses, sometimes used interchangeably, and at times used to mean quite different things. The tradition in the planning field has been to treat space and place as unproblematic, as part of an obvious reality, often as a surface on which things happen, a two-dimensional Euclidean 'mosaic' or 'jigsaw' (Graham and Healey, 1999). Much work in the social sciences challenges this assumption. Increasingly, a distinction is being made between the inherent spatiality and temporality of all relations, and the meanings which are given to particular qualities of specific 'places'. In a diverse society, transected by all kinds of relations, with multiple connections in space and time, places are not 'singular' in the meanings given to them. They are given different meanings in different relational contexts. Place and territory thus relate to both a materiality and an identity, as shown by Hillier (Chapter Four). As Madanipour (Chapter Seven) argues, social reality in the city is a sum total of a congregation of people and material objects that create cities and a rich patchwork of meaning that people assign to this material reality. These representations and meanings, however, are not singular but multiple. They are symbolic representations as well as the product of direct experiences.

As Nigel Thrift (Chapter Two) and Tony Lloyd-Jones et al. (Chapter Five) stress, place/territory as a concept reflects a situatedness and fixity. But in our current era of dynamic globalisation, this fixity is in continual tension with movement and mobility. 'Places' are temporary 'fixes' or nodes in flows of ideas, of goods, of people etc. They also exist in a flow of time. They were like something, they are as something now, they could be something else. So the analysis and practice of spatial planning systems needs to take account of place/movement with something more sophisticated than land use-transportation models, and something richer than population projections and time periods for plans. Maybe we need metaphors of flow and mobility, and multiple myths of place to capture this multidimensional, evolving diversity. These new conceptualisations also stress the complexity of the relationships that transect an area and may get drawn into the articulation and assertion of place meanings. This is reflected in everyday experiences of the city – as polynodal, as mosaics of locales with diverse qualities. So we are searching for means with which to understand and describe these dynamic realities, and how what happens in one area links to others – neighbours, 'global' economic and cultural relationships, etc. There is also much interest in recognising the way the richness and diversity of relationships which transect in an area can generate a potential for creativity and innovation, though it may also generate conflict and tension. Some of the tension is beneficial (Hajer, Chapter Eight); but some can generate severe problems. But how are these new ways of thinking about place and territory to be translated into new forms of representation? The limits of the traditional two-dimensional map show how this affects the Development Plan long established as a policy and management tool in spatial planning systems.

Why is all this important? Because the qualities of place and how we think about place are significant for contemporary concerns with the quality of life, economy and environment. Because it becomes politically important when all this is translated into values asserted in arenas of policy and governance. Because what is done in the name of planning policy has real material effects. Because what happens through the translation of conceptions of place into spatial planning policies has effects on values political communities may care about – notably social justice, environmental sustainability and economic competitiveness.

By bringing together a number of what may first appear to be disparate approaches to space, this book argues for a complex understanding of a complex phenomenon. If space is multilayered and has multiple meanings, then a static, single viewpoint is not enough to understand it. Part One stresses that, whatever their significance, single viewpoints and relativist approaches to space are not sufficient to account for the multiplicity of perspectives and interests. If spatial planning is engaged in regulating and transforming space, it must act at the intersection of these perspectives. Bringing statistical data and phenomenological accounts of life into conjunction with the political-economic and cultural-aesthetic perspectives into space, will offer us a much more complex understanding than any of these can offer on their own (Madanipour, 1996).

Potential Problems of Spatiality

Emphasis on spatiality, however, is not unproblematic. A number of potential problems can emerge, either raised by those who are not convinced with the need for integrating spatiality into planning, or by the dangers of overemphasising spatiality at the cost of other concerns.[1] Some may object that space is an abstract notion and can take so many forms and definitions that it does not play a clear role in our understanding and action. It is true that, as Lefebvre argues, '...Space, considered in isolation is an empty abstraction; likewise energy and time' (Lefebvre, 1991, p.12). For our purposes, however, we have used space as a context. Spatiality can therefore offer embeddedness as well as a vehicle of communication and innovation. Rather than functional, instrumental links, there are many other channels that link people to places. By understanding these channels and taking them into consideration, spatial planning can operate more sensitively and efficiently. The question of identity, for example, is one among many, where the sense of identity of individuals and groups is often strongly linked to particular places. The sense of well-being of people, therefore, can draw on their embeddedness in particular localities, rather than necessarily on their social mobility, which so frequently is linked with spatial mobility. Spatiality, therefore, is an essential component of social relations, rather than an epiphenomenon.

Some may object to the emphasis on spatiality by saying that planning should be engaged in human environments as social systems and approaching cities should be mainly approaching social relations, rather than particular spaces or places. Emphasis on spatiality is not in our meaning to narrow down the area of engagement and interest of planners to focus on physical transformation of urban environment without its political, economic and cultural significance. It aims instead to contextualise and concretise knowledge and action, the policy formulation and implementation of the planning process in space and time. In this sense, emphasis on spatiality does not mean to undermine social concerns. It is about embedding the social relations and concerns in a particular context. It is, therefore, not to be taken as a return to environmental determinism and a new ecological fallacy.

Our argument, therefore, does not imply a return to the simplistic assumptions of physical planning of the past, with its environmental determinist outlook and its social engineering intentions, which was once so powerfully criticised by social scientists. The intention here is to create a balance between action and context, between policy and place. It is not meant to equate social problems with the problems related to space and place and therefore misdirect the concerns for social justice. The issue is not to mistake the malfunctioning of social processes, which lead to deprivation and social exclusion, for spatial problems and concentrate all our energies on environmental improvements which benefit primarily young professionals and new technology firms. Instead, our approach needs to be cautiously aware how specific social relations play out spatially and how these distribute power, resources and identities.

Some may argue that space is a commodity in the market and there is not much that spatial planning can do about it. So, the argument goes on, the need to emphasise space becomes redundant. If property markets have a strong role in establishing what uses spaces and places are put to, then what is there for a planner to do? The answer to this argument is to see how planning has emerged in the first place to envision possible futures, to regulate the market and at times to decommodify space. Its role has been to keep in play, through politics and policy, what markets threaten or neglect. These roles of planning would then allow the development of many functions and living experiences which otherwise would be impossible. It is not only the exchange value of space that has the final say in how land is used. There are many other aspects of space, as summed up under the title use value (or symbolic value or experiential value), that should be considered, where spatial planning comes into play.

Another argument may be that space is not the central concern of several areas of planning and therefore should not be extended to such a central position in the spatial planning agenda. Economic development policy, for example, is more interested in particular economic processes rather than particular places. It is not enough to say that these take place in space, because most other human activities take place in space and this does not give planning any particular vantage point about spatiality.

Some may say that space has always been a concern of the planners and that asking for attention to space is not needed. Is it not the case that planning practices have dealt with space and that new practices, such as the use of Geographical Information Systems, have emerged? What we argue here is that first, emphasis on spatiality takes place in a context which has long undermined spatial issues as irrelevant (such as much work by economists, sociologists, and political scientists) and which now needs to be persuaded of the need for a socio-spatial balance. Second, we argue that much of thinking about space has been developed in the past and there is a need for fresh approaches to spatiality for the new generations of spatial planners.

Some argue that space is one dimension that needs attention and time is another, both implicit in any human understanding and experience. After all, these are the two main dimensions in which our actions take place. Ever since the development of the theory of relativity, space-time relations have occupied the minds of many observers as closely interrelated phenomena. It is obvious that spatial planning needs to deal with spatial as well as temporal dimensions of social reality (Madanipour, 1996). Dealing with complex, multiple relations cannot take spatiality or temporality for granted. What needs attention is often specific dimensions of all the different relations. If spatial planning is to innovate, it needs to imagine conditions which deal with difference and the conflicts of interest and perspective, as created in the past or likely to emerge in the future. Is attention to space not undermining the concern with time, with how we approach our past and future? Is it not undermining mobility and speed, which are the hallmarks of our time? What we argue here is not to move towards an obsession with space at the cost of forgetting the time dimension. Instead, asking for a socio-spatial understanding means asking for a balance between space and time, so that both are considered together and none undermines the other. It is important at the same time to realise that both space and time are the context not the aim. Undermining spatial and temporal contexts would mean sinking into abstract or mechanical thinking, uprooted from the concrete context. This would lead to the loss of the capacity of innovation and renewal.

There may be an argument that the emphasis on space comes from a disciplinary bias. Those who are located within the disciplinary boundaries of spatial arts and sciences (such as planning and geography among others) may stress the centrality of space, while those who outside these disciplines may not see the point. The answer is that precisely for this attitude to space, it needs to be taken more seriously. The nineteenth century, according to Michel Foucault, was obsessed with history. Space was, therefore, considered as 'the dead, the fixed, the undialectical, the immobile' (Quoted in Soja, 1989, p.10). With his spatialised thinking, however, Foucault argued for the fundamental importance of space in any form of communal life and any exercise of power (Flynn, 1994; Foucault, 1993). It becomes evident, therefore, that seeing the relevance of space is a call for a balanced judgement, rather than shifting the pendulum to the other extreme. Through a socio-spatial approach, spatiality and temporality can be seen as interrelated.

The appreciation of spatiality embeds the social relations in a context and offers a more sensitive and detailed understanding of these processes. It should be noted, at the same time, that this can be limiting and restrictive, if it goes against a critical assessment of these contexts and relations. Many such contexts can stifle change and prevent the most disadvantaged from possible improvement of their conditions through emancipation from such ties. Emphasis on spatiality can therefore become reactionary and nostalgic, rather than sensitive and innovative. If understanding social phenomena in their socio-spatial contexts are not part of a vision of social justice, the focus on spatiality can be limiting if it only pays attention to spatial management of inequality, rather than tackling inequality itself at its roots.

Shaping Places

The question that needs answering is what sorts of changes are implied by these new conceptions of place and territory? Cities are changing in their materialities and in the mentalities through which they are interpreted. But they are also full of governance institutions which are tied to old conceptions – of governance process and of space and place. Formal planning systems are often to be found embedded in their institutional histories, while around them build up local political practices which embed them in their past still further. But governance processes are being driven to change, and so too are spatial planning systems. Part Two looks at examples where old spatial planning practices are challenged and new ones are struggling to emerge, often with a 'cacophony of voices' (Hajer, Chapter Eight). Many situations can be identified, where the past is hanging on, but there are signs of something new as well.

These dynamics, between hanging on and changing, can be seen in the conceptions of problems and policy agendas, of places and territories which inform the content of planning systems. They can also be seen in ideas about how to go about planning processes. The discussion of planning processes has generated a rich normative debate in planning theory. But these have not always been well-connected to the debates about place-qualities. In concrete situations, shaped by specific institutional dynamics, there may be powerful forces which inhibit making this connection. Healey (Chapter Twelve) and Kitchen (Chapter Thirteen) illustrate this with respect to the UK, while Hajer (Chapter Eight) and Innes and Booher (Chapter Eleven) identify similar disjunctions in the different institutional contexts of the Netherlands and the US. As old conceptions hang on, new practices seem to be evolving rapidly outside the practices of planning systems.

When planners emphasised space in the middle of twentieth century, they used a vocabulary of ideal urban forms. It is well-understood why this is no longer appropriate. Such conceptions were too simplistic in their approach to socio-spatial relations. They ignored the inherent contestability of conceptions of place. This is now very obvious given the contemporary dispersed power context in which planning systems typically operate.

One of the arguments of this book is that policy should recognise the diversity of situations; learn to recognise local specificities (institutional as well as material conditions); and learn to work with the grain of the dynamic complexity. Policy makers, therefore, need to develop adaptive capabilities, rather than searching for 'optimising' ones or off-the-shelf solutions. This should help to recover a consciousness of spatiality and place quality and bring it into an active role in policy discourse. In some circumstances, this can be done by developing strategies collaboratively, in the form of place-focused visions. Enduring orientations, which are widely shared, help to create a 'shared myth' which can aid coordination and mobilisation, while leaving space for initiative and creativity. This is very different to a traditional 'structure plan' approach as evolved in the British planning system.

In other circumstances, emphasis may be on constructing shared ground-rules, which allow agents to experiment and innovate without wading through complex conflicts at every turn. In this situation, visions are not about end-states, but about opening up possibilities. As Judith Innes and David Booher (Chapter Eleven) stress in their paper, '...Don't impose a vision. Let people learn how to get there'. In this sense, structures and formal tools are less important than processes of interaction and learning. It follows that there is no need to plan comprehensively, but instead look out for the 'intersections', as stressed by Madanipour (Chapter Seven).

The chapters in Part Two try to map some of the changes that are happening now or could happen in the future. These chapters emphasise the process of change, to complement the emphasis of Part One on a substantive domain. The importance of argumentative processes then becomes paramount in opening up old agendas, and 'refreshing' them, providing challenges to the old and chances for the new. The importance of linking the evolution of new processes with that of developing new discourses about place qualities is stressed in Part Two. But this also involves generating new ideas about values and positions in relation to values.

In this book we have argued for a fresh approach to space and place in the planning process and take some tentative steps towards bringing spatiality and governance together. Healey (Chapter Twelve) argues that the search for more effective ways of conflict management has led to a pressure to develop an approach to spatial planning as strategic, collaborative place-making. This is a result of the awareness of the political and business elite in cities and regions of the need for promoting places in their search for economic development. She argues that the largely aspatial, performance criteria approach to regulation needs to be replaced with a more collaborative and strategic approach which uses places as a focus of attention. Collaborative development of strategic place-making helps to articulate a shared language which can relate the realities of lived experience with general principles and ideas. This can then feed into investment and regulatory decisions.

Motte (Chapter Ten) shows a way of integrating spatiality into planning processes by examples from Lyon and Nîmes in France, on how a locally developed, shared vision can integrate a locale with the outside pressure for change. The integration of local and global and the process of relocation of institutional relations in places therefore contribute towards integrating space and place. The shared vision of the urban region's development is translated into concrete principles of action, mediated through planning agencies and shaped by political processes. This is a process that can re-embed key stakeholders and their interests in the locality. By relying on the integration of a growing number of urban projects and focusing on a number of places and axes, planning in Lyon becomes a continuous process, which abandons the distinction between elaboration and implementation. The same emphasis is made by Ted Kitchen (Chapter Thirteen) on the need for continuous collaboration and consultation.

Another example of using spatiality to develop a vision of development is produced by Hajer, in his examples from the Netherlands (Chapter Eight). Hajer argues that there is a need for planning to 'zoom out' and concentrate on the social context in which planning debates and processes take place. He shows how in the Netherlands, the traditional role of planning as extending the welfare state (by providing high quality public housing and by keeping market forces in check) was abandoned. What was adopted instead was seeing planning as building the spatial base for economic recovery. The 1990s in the Netherlands, as he shows, witnessed a flourishing of different spatial imaginations for the country as a whole. All the three main trends in strategic planning articulate space as a main component part of their thinking, combining it with concerns for economic development, quality of life and environmental sustainability.

Some have argued that the British planning system has lost its capacity for spatial awareness and imagination (Vigar et al., 2000). This is happening just as, across Europe, more attention is being paid to space, place and territory (Committee on Spatial Development, 1999). We offer this book as a contribution to developing the conceptual and operational tools for a more place-conscious planning for the future.

Note

1   This section partly draws on, and responds to, a debate that took place on Planning Theory email list in July and August 1999, where Ernest Sternberg, Howell Baum, Dwell Myers, Oren Yiftachel, Seymour Mandelbaum and Tridib Banerjee were among contributors.

References

Committee on Spatial Development (1999), *European Spatial Development Perspective: Towards Balanced and Sustainable Development of the Territory of the EU*, Potsdam, Germany.

Cuthbert, A. (1996), 'An Interview with Manuel Castells', *Cities*, Vol. 13 (1), pp.3–9.

Flynn, T. (1994), 'Foucault's Mapping of History', in Gutting, G. (ed.), *The Cambridge Companion to Foucault*, Cambridge University Press, Cambridge, pp.28–46.

Foucault, M. (1993), 'Space, Power and Knowledge', in During, S. (ed.), *The Cultural Studies Reader*, Routledge, London, pp.161–9.

Friedmann, J. (1998), 'Planning Theory Revisited', *European Planning Studies*, Vol. 6 (3), pp.245–53.

Graham, S. and Healey, P. (1999), 'Relational Concepts of Space and Place: Issues for Planning Theory and Practice', *European Planning Studies*, Vol. 7 (5), pp.623–46.

Krugman, P. (1995), *Development, Geography and Economic Theory*, MIT Press, Cambridge, MA.

Lefebvre, H. (1991), *The Production of Space*, Blackwell, Oxford.

Madanipour, A. (1996), 'Urban Design and Dilemmas of Space', *Environment and Planning D; Society and Space*, Vol. 14, pp.331–355.

Martin, R. and Sunley, P. (1996), 'Paul Krugman's Geographical Economics and Its Implications for Regional Development Theory: a Critical Assessment', *Economic Geography*, Vol. 72, pp.259–92.

Soja, E. (1989), *Postmodern Geographies: The Reassertion of Space in Critical Social Theory*, Verso, London.

Urban Task Force (1999), *Towards an Urban Renaissance*, E. and F.N. Spon, London.

Vigar, G., Healey, P., Hull, A. and Davoudi, S. (2000), *Planning, Governance and Spatial Strategy-Making in Britain*, Macmillan, London.

PART ONE
CONCEPTS OF SPACE

Concepts of Space

Ali Madanipour

This part discusses how spaces and places are understood and conceptualised. It is organised in the form of a dialogue between various approaches to the understanding of space. Altogether, these approaches offer a breadth and depth of understanding space and place from a variety of angles: from objective and statistical to subjective and cultural, from the relation between places within cities to connectivity between places across the globe. What is argued here is that it is at the intersection of these perspectives that we will understand places, which is the necessary basis for spatial planning.

The line that connects the chapters in Part One to each other, therefore, is that they all try to make sense of place in complex and ever changing contemporary urban environments. They all argue against various forms of reductionism in their analysis and try to offer a more sophisticated understanding of the meaning of place. They differ in their methodological outlook in ways which, we argue, is often complementary rather than mutually exclusive.

There are at least three strong lines of argument that connect these chapters together.

- They all have a common theme, as they all address space and place. The spatial focus is what brings them together and their different perspectives into space.

- They all argue for going beyond simplistic assumptions and simplified perspectives. What they all share is therefore an attempt to develop and elaborate a particular perspective on space.

- They use different perspectives to approach space. This may seem to break the coherence of the part. In fact, however, as Chapter Seven argues, they should be seen to make sense *together*, rather than separately. What may seem disparate can be complementary.

The different perspectives, therefore, each offer one angle, which needs to be complemented with others, to arrive at a dynamic, complex picture of the subject matter.

Nigel Thrift's chapter challenges four myths, forms of analytical reductionism that hinder, rather than help understanding the place. He argues against the notions that cities are becoming instants in a global space of flows, that cities are becoming homogenised; that cities (or parts of them) are inauthentic; and that one city can be taken as the representative of an era. Instead, he argues that cities have become richer place experiences, with stronger patterns of social interaction and their importance has been boosted as key story-telling nodes for the world as a whole. These, he asserts, are the features of many cities, rather than famous cities such as Los Angeles. He then goes on to outline alternative ways of thinking about the city, providing two examples of the kind of urban activity that can then come to light, trying to situate the body in the city, and seeing the city as a repository of knowledge.

Mike Coombes and Colin Wymer suggest a new quantitative methodology for identifying localities. Their main question is how to identify where one place ends and its neighbours begin. Rather than the traditional, mono-dimensional method of defining localities on the basis of journey-to-work, they argue for a multifaceted approach. Numerous datasets, including journey-to-service data from banking zones, were created. These were then used to devise a completely innovative method of a single Synthetic Dataset, which provides a measure of integration between every pair of neighbourhoods on the basis of a wide range of different types of interactions. Over three hundred localities were defined in Britain, generally including a main town with perhaps some nearby satellite towns and its rural hinterland.

The next chapter by Jean Hillier concentrates on a qualitative methodology in identifying places. She takes us to western Australia, discussing the contested and multiple meanings of place in the development of the North East Corridor, Perth. She focuses on the analysis of the discourses of planning in relation to places. Hillier uses actor network theory to understand place. She criticises the failure of the planners to recognise the limitations of their rational technical discourse, which leaves power relations as unproblematic. Instead, she suggests that an examination of networks enables us to unpack how domains of inquiry and representation are constructed so that certain representations can be made and others cannot. To understand space and place, which are socially constructed, she suggests concentrating on images and identities of those involved. The shaping of place then becomes understood as the outcome of power struggles between the images, aspirations and values of various actant-networks.

Both these chapters in their own way argue against methodological reductionism: Coombes and Wymer against the traditional mono-dimensional datasets and Hillier against the rational technical discourse of planning. The result is the realisation that only one set of data, or one single perspective into understanding, and managing space, is not sufficient. It is this insight that encourages us to see the value of a combined methodology, of using quantitative and qualitative methodologies in our approach to the analysis of space and place.

The next two chapters should also be seen in the light of providing complementary views. While Lloyd-Jones et al. concentrate on the way the various parts of the physical space of a city are interconnected through infrastructure and intra-city networks, Graham and Marvin are interested in the way places are located in a regional and global set of electronically mediated networks. Together, the two chapters show the significance of connectivity in understanding place, through inter-subjective interaction both in places and across space.

The chapter by Tony Lloyd-Jones, Bill Erickson, Marion Roberts and Stephen Nice concentrates on the physical form of the city and argues against reducing the city to its constituent neighbourhoods. Instead, they argue for focusing on connections between these parts. In the light of modern communication and transport technologies, the previous networks and hierarchies of neighbourhoods and districts should be revisited. As the city has grown and movement across space has been made easier, it is the communication network that is the essential building block of the city. The chapter, therefore, argues against the feasibility of conceptualising, and therefore prescribing for, urban villages and mono-centric cities. The authors argue that with the emergence of the polycentric city, the infrastructure network that connects the different parts of the city should be the basis of understanding the urban space and of designing, planning, and managing it.

Stephen Graham and Simon Marvin show that the arrival of the new communication technologies has not undermined but emphasised the importance of cities in a world of fast flows and great volatility. Cities are where face-to-face interactions take place within a high quality physical, service and telecommunication infrastructure. Rather than the demise of the city, the trend is that the new communication technologies become combined with the spiralling use of transport and a strong reliance on face-to-face contacts. The impact seems to be helping a transition from mono-centric, core dominated cities, towards extended, complex polycentric city regions. This, they argue, should lead to a new style of spatial planning which shapes face to face interactions in place in parallel with electronically mediated ones across distance. At the same time, they warn against overstating this need.

The last chapter in part one concludes these arguments and proposes that space should be understood at several intersections: between various concepts of space, such as absolute and relational concepts; between people and objects, which contextualises space; and between place-making and use, which is the ground where space is both contested and is endowed with meaning. These various intersections, it is argued, all contribute towards a social understanding of space. The chapter shows how spatiality has become increasingly more important in managing cities, and argues that a dynamic and multilayered complex approach is needed for understanding and managing space, with its multiple meanings resulting from multiple interests and perspectives. There is a need for spatial planning to go beyond relativism and to act at the intersection of these perspectives. The picture offered by a combination of statistical data and phenomenological accounts of life is more convincing than what any of these approaches can offer alone. Similarly, the understanding of space needs to be placed at the intersection of political and economic concerns. In broad terms, the intersection of political-economic and cultural-aesthetic approaches is where space should be understood and managed. The chapter argues that understanding and managing places is only possible through negotiation between agencies involved at the intersection of these often conflicting interpretations.

Chapter Two

How Should We Think About Place in a Globalising World?

Nigel Thrift

Introduction – Hidden Cities

In this chapter, I want to lay to rest some of the most prevalent myths about modern western cities and, at the same time, I want to provide some of the elements of alternative accounts. In so doing, I am aware that I may appear as a figure, rather like Coleridge's person from Porlock, who punctures the magic of the moment with mundane, even tiresome, observations. But my argument is that the everyday life of the modern city is already shot through with magic and that there is therefore no need to stir more in.

This chapter is organised into three main parts. In the first and briefest part of the paper, I want to explain my theoretical position. This is crucial since it informs the rest of the chapter. Then, in the second part of the chapter, I want to outline some of the myths about the modern western city which have come down to us from the nineteenth century and which we still cannot seem to shake off. In the third part of the chapter, I want to show how, once these myths are set aside, a number of aspects of the modern city start to come into view which had previously remained hidden, aspects which provide new resources for talking and writing 'about cities'. Of course, in pointing to only a set number of these aspects, regrettably I have to ignore much of the remarkable work represented in contemporary geography and, typified by the writings of Bell, Jackson, Ogborn, Pile, Rose and Valentine on the sexual geographies of the city.

Before the discussion proper, it seems sensible to make it clear how I want to see the world, and therefore cities. This 'vision' can be distilled into four main propositions. First, I am a long-run historian. I believe that human practices change slowly and that many of the practices that we assume are 'new' are in fact of considerable antiquity. But I also believe that we do not want to believe this, not only because we only have a short time to live and we want to believe that our time is the most significant time in history, but also because novelty is a value we have been taught to cleave to, and, as a consequence, we have found it difficult to find a language which can describe certain aspects of practice as 'new' and others as 'old': it is all or nothing (Serres, 1995; Serres and Latour, 1995). None of this is meant to imply that I believe in long cycles of history. Rather I assume that history is uneven, open-ended and non-redemptive: there are no foregone conclusions (Bernstein, 1994). So, second, I therefore believe that time is a multiple phenomenon; many times are working themselves out simultaneously in resonant interaction with each other. '...Absolute, calibrated time – like its negation, pure stochasticity – is an illusion, reinforced by our own species-specific dimensional scaling, and self-referentiality' (Davis, 1996, p.65). Third, I am a theorist of practices. That is, my main concern, unlike the bulk of those currently operating in the human sciences, is with the nonrepresentational aspects of human life, the embodied non-cognitive activity in which people engage. That means that my interest is caught up with the world of emotions, desires and imagination, with embodied or practical knowledge, and, more generally, with the infinitude of sensuous real-time encounters through which we make the world and are made in turn. In other words, I want to talk about 'thinking' as forms of doing and inhabiting. Fourth, when I consider how practices are formed, maintained and changed, I think in terms of networks of associations between unlike actors which can exert power for change (even when that change is only intended to hold the network in its current state). These networks are more or less durable over space and through time according to their ability to translate actors to their cause. They are, therefore, always radically incomplete and require constant semiotic-cum-material work to maintain; as Latour (1993, p.63) puts it, '...things do not hold because they are true; they are true because they hold.'

How do these four principles influence how I view city spaces? First, when I look at what is going on in contemporary cities I try to think about how future historians of this era will see these happenings, once the natural enough emphasis upon the uniqueness of our own time is overtaken by our deaths, and once new urban fabric has been tempered by ageing, dereliction and decay. Second, I always try to think of cities as performative, as *in use*, and therefore I see urban landscapes as essentially incomplete and only rarely in the hands of just one network of association. In other words, cities are only ever 'partially connected' multiples (Strathern, 1992). Third, I see cities as bubbling over with human creativity, which means that '...twenty minutes into the future, the radically new development is already being absorbed, being made to respond to the exigencies of specific cultural contexts' (Collins, 1995, p.5).

In turn, these three rules have three consequences. First, I am suspicious of concepts like 'modernity'. Though such concepts may be treated as simply a kind of historical shorthand, I believe that they are ultimately dangerous. Whether 'modernity' is interpreted as one or more periods of expansion in sense of self, a period of constant change and motion, the gradual triumph of ordered and secularised systems, or a new paradigm of spatio-visual experience, it always leaves out too much and, thereby, too often writes the west as 'the stuff of saga, a vast saga of radical rupture, fatal destiny, irreversible good or bad fortune' (Latour, 1993, p.48).

Second, I am also suspicious of concepts like everyday life and lifeworld. The danger of these concepts arises less from their existence than their implicit opposition to another abstract and systematic order which is responsible for oppression. This order is thereby reified, when it is just as anthropologically practised as any other order. As Latour (1993, pp.125–6) famously puts it:

> Take some small business owner hesitatingly going after a few modest shares, some conqueror trembling with fever, some poor scientist tinkering in his lab, a lowly engineer piecing together a few more or less favourable relationships or force, some strutting and fearful politician: turn the critics loose on them, and what do you get? Capitalism, imperialism, science, technology, domination – all equally absolute, systematic, totalitarian. In the first scenario, the actors were trembling, in the second, they are not. The actors in the first scenario could be defeated; in the second they no longer can.

Third, it follows that I am clear that human creativity has not been 'damped down'. Life is fundamentally uncertain and people make their peace with that uncertainty in many 'rational' and 'irrational' kinds of ways. It is only a surprise to intellectuals who want to believe that the Enlightenment project has been carried through, or thwarted, that we live in an era which has seen, for example, a rebirth of evangelical Christianity and paganism, in an age when many people still take astrology seriously and many others at least take note of it, in an age in which many people believe in UFOs and others at least follow *Star Trek*, in an age when near-death experience has its own academic journals and death still has its very definite rituals, in an age in which older religious traditions like New Thought, Theosophy and Spiritualism, stirred and shaken by the psychological and eastern religious organisations of the 1950s and 1960s countercultures have seen a rebirth as New Age, and in an age in which the study of implicit religion which recognises the implicit religiosity of everyday life, has rightly become an important area of research. The whole fabric of everyday life, in other words, is shot through with dreams, fantasies, superstitions, religious yearnings and millenarian movements. Like Probyn, then, (1996, p.19) '...I want to reinvigorate the idea that living is bewildering, strange, and sometimes wonderful [and] I also want to emphasise the magic of ordinary desires'. *The magic has not gone away.*

Having set the context, I am now in a position to begin to identify where I believe some of the current writing on cities has gone wrong. In this way, I hope to be able to foreground what has often been regarded as background. I want to begin this task by setting out some of the myths about current urban societies. Like magic, these myths – which all date back to the nineteenth century or even earlier – are often only half-articulated and half-believed. In a sense, one might well argue that this is what gives them their power since they are only rarely the subject of sustained scrutiny. What I want to do is to clear the ground by bringing them into the full light of day, so sapping their power. Then it becomes possible to consider the city as a partially connected multiplicity, and to begin to describe spaces which disclose new aspects of the contemporary city.

Four Myths

MYTH 1: All Cities Are Becoming Instants in a Global Space of Flows

It is claimed we live in a globalising world and one of the key elements of this world is the existence of a space of flows bought into existence by modern information technologies. This space of flows is: '...the space of information. This proliferating and multidimensional space is virtual, densely webbed and uniformly complex; a vast and sublime realm accessed through the mediations of our imaginative and technical representations' (Davis, 1994, p.86). And, in turn, the existence of the space of flows is changing our apprehension of space, time, and subjectivity. Places move closer together in time, time becomes instantaneous, and the subject becomes decentred, strung out on the wire.

The two main contemporary tellers of this myth are Harvey (1989) and Virilio (1993). For Harvey, the world is in the grip of another round of 'time-space compression':

> the processes that so revolutionise the objective qualities of space and time that we are forced to alter ... how we represent the world to ourselves...space appears to shrink to a 'global village' of telecommunications and a spaceship of earth economic and ecological interdependencies...and as time horizons shorten to

the point where the present is all there is...so we have to learn how to cope with our overwhelming sense of *compression* of our spatial and temporal worlds (Harvey, 1989, p.240).

Thus time-space compression is simultaneously a story of the marked increase in the pace of life brought about by modern transport and telecommunications *and* the upheaval in our experience of space and time that this speed-up brings about as people, images, capital, and information all speed more and more rapidly around the world. The result is that '...time-space compression...exerts its toll on our capacity to grapple with the realities unfolding around us' (Harvey, 1989, p.306), most especially by challenging our sense of identity and our ability to preserve tradition.

Virilio (1993) is willing to go further. For him, Harvey only describes the first effects of speed-up in which physical displacement still presupposes a journey: the individual makes a departure, moves from one location to another, and so arrives. But now, with the 'instant' transmission made possible by electronic technology, a new 'generalised arrival' has occurred, in which the element of a journey across space is lost. The individual can be in two places at once, acting as both transmitter and receiver. Thus we have arrived in a historical period in which there is '...a crisis of the temporal dimension of the present':

> one by one, the perceptive faculties of an individual's body are transferred to machines, or instruments that record images, and sound; more recently the transfer is made to receivers, to sensors and to detectors that can replace absence of tactility over distance. A general use of telecommunications is on the verge of achieving permanent telesurveillance. What is becoming critical here is no longer the concept of three spatial dimensions, but a fourth, temporal dimension – in other words that of the present itself (Virilio, 1993, p.4).

In this new order, cities become interruptions in the space of flows, transient moments in the circulation of capital. Their future is to act as waystations for dominant organisational forces making their wishes known '...through the powerful medium of information technologies' (Castells, 1989, p.6).

Here is a myth, which is overdrawn and overdone, and for at least four reasons. First, these revelations, which are presented as of the hour, are certainly of considerable antiquity. Through history and around the world, innovations in transport and communications have been heralded as proof positive that the world was speeding up, that places were moving closer together in time, that the world was shrinking. For example, in the eighteenth century a number of nervous disorders were thought to be the result of the faster pace of life (Porter, 1993). In the nineteenth century, as the stagecoach was replaced by the train, the telegraph and the telephone, so the theme of the 'annihilation of space and time' became a favourite meditation of many writers (Thrift, 1995). In the twentieth century, the idea surfaced yet again; one author even went so far as to calculate the rate (in minutes per year) at which places were converging on one another, a phenomenon which he christened *'time-space convergence'* (Janelle, 1969). These different variants on the theme of a speeded-up world were nearly always associated with a generalised crisis of identity. From the nervous disorders of the eighteenth century onwards, the acceleration of everyday life has been thought likely to lead to volatile, fragmented, and spread-out people whose identity is in question because of the shallowness of their lives.

Second, this myth is based in a technological determinism which unproblematically reads off the characteristics of the technologies involved onto society. For example, there is little or no sense of technologies as culturally mediated. Thus, whilst it cannot be denied that '...a dynamics of thought is not separable from a physics of traces...the medium...is but the ground floor. One cannot rest there' (Debray, 1996, p.11). Therefore, '...when these technologies are mastered...their functions and cultural resonances change fundamentally' (Collins, 1995, p.16). In the case of the 'new' information technologies, there is manifold evidence that this process is already taking place:

> the bloom of unlimited possibility is already passing from them. The Internet begins to shrink back from its ecstatic characterisation, (a web for democracy, a veritable sea of data, an instrument of expanded perception) and settles down as a very large database-cum-techie salon. The smart idolatry is moving on (Spufford, 1996, p.271).

Again, too often the medium is assumed to be one when it is multiple. Thus work on communications networks too often ignores the *content* of communication – from bank statements to love letters – which illustrate that the medium is in fact a set of different but intersecting elements of a whole range of actor-networks.

Third, this myth places too much of a premium on technologies which conform to dominant cultural stereotypes of what is 'new'. But, as Mark Edwards (1996, p.10) points out:

in a survey last year, Americans were asked which piece of recent technology had most altered their lives. The most common reply was not the Internet, not even the personal computer. First, – by some way – came the microwave, followed by the video recorder.

Then, fourth, cities cannot be seen as places which are leaking away into a space of flows. This is to fundamentally misunderstand the way in which new information technologies have normally acted as a supplement to human communication rather than a replacement. Innovations like the telephone, the fax, and the computer are used to extend the range of human communication, rather than act as a substitute. It is not a case of either/or but both/and. For example, in my work on the City of London (Thrift, 1996), I have shown the way in which the growth of information from new communication technologies has presented fundamental problems of interpretation for workers in the City which have forced greater rather than less face-to-face communication: the City has become, even more than formerly, a key storytelling node for the world as a whole, and, as a result, its importance as a spatially fixed centre has, if anything, been boosted.

MYTH 2: Cities Are Becoming Homogenised

In this myth, cities are depicted as increasingly bleak and interchangeable places. Usually such a view is connected in some way with a rising tide of commodification which acts as a block on creative citizenship.

The rise of shopping malls is often taken as the most visible sign of the landscape as simply a moment in the circulation of commodities. The landscape is increasingly constructed in the image of the commodities. Worst of all, the landscape itself becomes a commercial package through the growth of a 'heritage industry' which packages the past of places to sell them in the present.

Thus places increasingly become infected by the condition of 'placelessness' (Relph, 1981) which apparently characterises sites like shopping malls: '…we are in the midst of a desert of shops, a wasteland of services, a chaos of commerce. If not nowhere, we are in an extremely shallow somewhere' (Casey, 1993, pp.268–9)

However there are some serious problems with this viewpoint. First, the icons of placeless urbanity may not travel. For example, high rise office buildings, which are often regarded as symbols of American invasion, are few and far between in Britain, (even in the United States, high rise CBDs were rare in the late 1960s – only New York, Chicago, Detroit, Philadelphia and Pittsburgh had more than two buildings over twenty-five stories and two of these cities – New York and Chicago – had produced quite specific capitalist vernaculars) (Glass, 1995).

Second, as has now been shown in numerous empirical studies, what may look like similar urban spaces can be used in quite dissimilar ways. Thus a growing literature on shopping malls in Britain shows that although they are growing in number and size, they are simply not used in the same way as in the United States. For example, fewer malls, lower car ownership, and limited opening hours mean that these malls are only rarely used in the same way as by American youth (Thornton, 1995). In any case, British traditions of shopping, which have a long history, are sometimes quite different (Mort, 1995; Glennie and Thrift, 1996).

Third, judgements on placelessness are bedevilled by a lack of historical depth rooted in their narrative of an all-consuming newness. Take the example of the shopping mall (which is usually anchored by one or two department stores, outposts of an earlier mode of retailing). As Savage and Warde (1993, p.143) note in their discussion of malls as icons of placelessness.

> If the shopping mall appears new and placeless today, this is because it has not yet been integrated back into its surrounding urban fabric, either by wear and tear, by feats of imagination or by reputation. Urban dwellers of the nineteenth century regarded innovations such as the subway as a bewildering and new, placeless realm. Today, these have been moulded into their contextual environments.

Fourth, it might even be argued that, if anything, cities have, over time, become richer place experiences. Most cities have offered, over the course of history, an increasing range of experiences which it is possible to use as imaginative resources. For some time the city has had an underground landscape (Williams, 1991; Prendergast, 1992). It has a sky which is often filled with activity. It is made of all kinds of materials that let us sense in new ways; for example glass (Armstrong, 1996). This is to ignore the new means of apprehension, from photography to film to video to CD Rom, which have allowed us to touch the city in new ways, to memorise it, to rewrite it, to make it tactile, '…once more with feeling' (Benjamin, 1969, 1979). And these 'new magics' are chiefly examples chosen from the visual register. The same kind of richness is, *place* writers like Corbin suggest, being invested in other sensory registers too.

It is worth underlining this point: if we could measure the process, perhaps our experience of places has thickened, not thinned.

One example of this process might be the advent of different forms of artificial light which, in turn, have extended our experience of place into the night. As the use of artificial light spread so urban landscapes began to appear that before had only been figments of the imagination. At first it was the glow of gaslight that lit up the city. Then, from the late nineteenth century, it was the gradual spread of electric light. Finally, it was the spread of light attached to mobile objects – cars, aeroplanes, satellites, and so on. The night-time city becomes an active landscape which, furthermore, has become actively peopled.

> Now there is a whole after-hours community – everything from evening classes to supermarkets, night clubs, discos and massage parlours, as well as a great array of maintenance people who service and repair the daytime world while its inhabitants sleep. The defence establishment, the financial markets, broadcasting, transport, communications now work on a 24 hour day schedule (Alvarez, 1995, p.20).

The night-time urban landscape is one in which many people work (for example, 14 per cent of the UK workforce is involved in shifts) and in which, for all the real dangers, many people play. Thus what we have also seen is the growth of a specific 'night life'. Night life is hardly a new invention: the Vauxhall pleasure gardens and the theatres of seventeenth century London were an early manifestation. But night life has now grown to major proportions: theatres, pubs, night-clubs, shops, cafes, restaurants. Thus, Worpole (1995) can write of a '24 hour city' of culture and entertainment.

The point is that this extension of human activity into the night resulting from the profusion of artificial light, provides us with *new* imaginative resources. In particular, it has produced a whole set of alternative technologically-induced landscapes that were simply not there before; edited and highlighted landscapes which have now become 'second nature' to us (some, like Nye (1995), have even talked of a 'technological sublime') and which have radically altered our appreciation of many places.

MYTH 3: Cities (or Parts of Cities) Are Inauthentic

This is a myth that dates from at least the founding fathers of urban studies like Simmel and Wirth and no doubt before. In that work, these writers depicted the city as a mirror of modernity. The city, in opposition to the small-scale tradition-bound community, was the main locale in which new impersonal social relationships, the harsh calculus of the money economy, and social fragmentation would be observed. According to some commentators the same kind of division can be found in Benjamin's work: experience (*erfahrung*) is replaced by instrumental reaction (*erlebnis*).

> In the former state, found in preindustrial societies, experience is based in habit and repetition of actions, without conscious intention. These experiences are bound to traditions, the socially constructed and legitimated ways of acting, which gain their authority by their uniqueness and specificity. In the latter state, found in modern industrial societies, the mass reproduction of commodities and symbols disperses tradition, so that individuals simply react to the stimuli of the environment and develop instrumental ways of thinking in order to cope in such a changed environment (Savage, 1995, p.201).

Nowadays this kind of thinking seems to have been replaced by a different kind, one in which authentic experience can still be found, but now located in the city in a residual sphere called 'everyday life', which, pressed in on all sides by an alienating and monolithic capitalism, is still the last best hope for humankind. Here the authentic 'when' has been replaced by an authentic 'where':

> superior activities leave a 'technical vacuum' between one another which is filled up by everyday life. Everyday life is profoundly related to all activities, and emphasises that with all their differences and their conflicts, it is their meeting place, their bond, their common ground. And it is in everyday life that the sum total of relations which make the human – and every human being – a whole takes its shape and its form. In it are expressed and fulfilled those relations which bring into play the totality of the real, albeit in a certain manner which is always partial and incomplete: friendship, comradeship, love, the need to communicate, play, etc (Lefebvre, 1995, p.97).

Whilst, it might well be necessary to retain some notion of the everyday as a means of promising 'the possibility of other sorts of non-exploitative solidarities' (Taussig, 1992, p.141), it is hard not to avoid the conclusion that Lefebvre's notion of everyday life is ultimately romantic. Much the same has been said of de Certeau's notion of 'tactics' in *The Practice of Everyday Life*. As Ahearne (1995) points out, for all of the understated subtleties of de Certeau's work, figures of indeterminacy and of a bewildering multiplicity are continually converted into visions of '...the night side of societies', '...an obscure sea' or '...the oceanic murmur of the ordinary'. These images work to conceal as much as they reveal and, at worst, can be counted as an uncritical hero worship, changing incomprehension into aesthetic pleasure, to no real political end.

As Lefebvre and de Certeau were well aware, there is no quotidian walled garden to be found in cities, in however liminal a register. But that such a notion can become current stems from the assumption that sometime or somewhere authentic spaces have existed. In fact, outside or inside the city, this assumption has deadly consequences. It distracts attention from the sheer work involved in constructing alternative spaces. It cedes too much to capitalist and other '...distinct specialised, structured activities' (Lefebvre, 1995) by depicting them as somehow asocial. It splits people's lives into acceptable and non-acceptable bits. It erases difference '...in much the same way as do modern European-derived notions of the public and the masses' (Taussig, 1992, p.141). And it thereby provides a licence to ignore much of the outpouring of ethnographic and other research on cities, which shows urban life as ambiguous, fragmented, dilemmatic, and thereby creative.

Let me briefly illustrate this latter point by turning to recent work by British and North American authors on kinship and friendship in cities. One of the things that is remarkable about this work is that it is largely ignored by many writers on cities, in part at least because it simply does not fit their preconceptions about modernity and the city.

What this work shows is that, historically speaking, rather than living in a period when kinship and friendship relationships are being smothered by individualism and privatism we may actually be living at a kind of high water mark of interaction.

Take the example of families.

> Families are now much more complex than at any time in the past. As long as we do not make the silly mistake of conflating household with family, it is arguable that the family and family relations are now, in the 1990s, stronger than at any time in the past (Pahl, 1995, p.179).

We can illustrate this statement through the seminal work of Janet Finch (Finch, 1989; Finch and Mason, 1993). She shows that families are probably more complex than in the past. Though fewer children may be born, longer life, divorce and so on, mean that family relations are often much more extensive. But she also shows that family relationships are still central to most people's lives. Of course, these relationships are not matters of automatic allegiance: they are a product of sustained and thoughtful interaction over long periods of time, often involving all manner of dilemmas, negotiations and compromises, and, even, extensive reading (Giddens, 1992). Further, the increasing geographical distance between family members seems to be of only minor consequence.

Pahl (1995, p.178) notes it more succinctly:

> When family members migrate to America or Australia, they do not necessarily lose contact with those they leave behind. Regular letters can come in a few days; telephoning is becoming progressively cheaper and the cost of air tickets from London to New York is not much more expensive than an ordinary return ticket from London to Aberdeen by train.

Threading through kin networks are friendship networks – the two are not exclusive – which seem as or more concentrated than at any time in the past. (Wellman and Berkowitz, 1988). Indeed, it might be argued that for some communities (such as the lesbian and gay communities) the importance of friendships is so great that they have become the '...families we choose' (Weston, 1991).

To summarise, it seems that a story of greater privatism and individualism – and less and less authenticity – does not really hold.

MYTH 4: One City Tells All

There is a fourth myth, that in each era there is a paradigmatic 'celebrity' city which sums up that era, the place where it all comes together. In recent years, out of many such cities (Chicago, Vienna, New York, Zurich) two cities seem to have been particularly prominent examples. So far as the nineteenth century is concerned, Paris is taken to be the birthplace of all the most significant signs of modernity; department stores, mass leisure, flânerie, urban crowds, and so on, and these historical assets have become one of the means of ensuring the cultural ascendancy of Paris in the twentieth century (see Sheringham, 1996).

Taking up the baton, and pointing to the future, is the city of Los Angeles, 'the capital of the late 20th century' (Scott and Soja, 1986, p.249) where 'it all comes together' (Soja, 1989, p.8). By 1990, Davis was able to note that a so-called LA school had emerged, consciously founded on the Chicago School, who '...have made clear that they see themselves as excavating the outline of a paradigmatic post Fordism, an emergent twenty first century urbanism' (p.84). Meanwhile, social theorists like Baudrillard, Eco and Jameson made pilgrimages to this new cradle of urban civilisation, adding to its mystique and, as with the case of Paris, reproducing its story around the world.

But alighting on one city as a means of telling the tale of an era (and thereby producing that era) is dangerous. Four problems become immediately apparent. First of all, such a choice can nearly always be empirically undone. For example, the choice of Paris as the leading urban edge of the nineteenth century is increasingly being challenged. Thus, the expanding history of consumption and shopping in Britain makes it clear that many of the developments thought to be special to Paris in the mid-nineteenth century were common in Britain before that date. (Glennie and Thrift, 1996). Again, the history of art suggests that many of the key elements of impressionism were also able to be found elsewhere than in Paris (Graham-Dixon, 1996). Second, as these examples make clear, the choice of a paradigmatic city deflects attention from other cities which may be just as significant but remain unexamined as what may well be an exception becomes the norm through which all other cities are measured. For example, were it not for a remarkable series of articles by Walker (1994, 1995, 1996), extraordinary events in San Francisco would have been wiped from the map by the new Angeleno hegemony. Third, it seems unlikely that any city can bear the weight of this kind of interpretative load. Los Angeles is a case in point. The depiction of the city as the site of a utopian or, more normally dystopian, future stretches interpretation beyond what we can know into the realms of myth. At the same time, it can divert attention (although it does not in the case of authors like Soja) from many of the struggles that *are* constantly taking place in the city – over the environment, over homelessness and poverty, over ethnic identity, and so on. '…Rather than address these realities the media draws a portrait of Los Angeles entering a *Blade Runner* epoch' (Acuna, 1996, p.xviii). Fourth, and finally, it can divert attention from the fact that events in cities are often linked to events in other cities. As Gilroy (1993) and others have spent much time working through, even (or especially) in imperial systems cities are points of interconnection, not hermetically sealed objects. What is important, then, is often a city's connectibility to events in other cities which are not necessarily or even preponderantly hierarchical in nature.

Other Cities

Critique is all very well but how, then, are we to understand contemporary cities? There are two problems. The first is that we can be much clearer about the mistakes of the past than we can be sure of the certainties of the future. This perennial problem is heightened by another; we live in a time when a series of root metaphors of western modernity, metaphors like speed-up, which were used to construct, inhabit and understand the urban world, and the world as urban, are beginning to break down. These metaphors have hardly been erased, but their strength is being sapped.

These old metaphors were based in what Gibbons et al. (1994) call 'Type 1' systems of knowledge production which were disciplinary, homogenous and hierarchical in nature. But these metaphors are now being replaced by new ones which are the result of the advent of systems of knowledge production – what Gibbons et al. (1994) call 'Type 2' – which are transdisciplinary, heterogeneous, transient, more socially accountable, and reflexive, and dependent upon a much wider range of producers. These new systems, which have given rise to metaphors of change and flow like 'flexibility', 'adaptability', 'complexity', 'turbulence', the 'labyrinth', and the like, show once again that, '...as Foucault told us (and neo-Kantians long before him) every new science creates its object' (Buck-Morss, 1995, p.116).

The advent of Type 2 knowledge production with its accompanying metaphors of change and flow (Thrift, 1996b) is clearly leading, slowly but surely, towards a view of the urban and urban policy which is substantially different from the view held before. At least four differences seem worth highlighting. First, a particular form of urban theory which sees the city as the stamp of great and unified forces which it is the task of the theorist to delineate and delimit is left behind. Instead, the city is seen as a partially connected multiplicity which we can only ever know partially and from multiple places (Strathern, 1991; Haraway, 1995; Law and Mol, 1996). The city is the living example of the proposition of multiplicity (Law and Mol, 1996).

Second, the habit of downgrading human practices in cities to the everyday, thereby stripping the magic from them, is abandoned. Otherwise too much is lost. Not only are the embodied and performative aspects of practices foregone, but equally the 'domestic' is downgraded by an enforced domestication (Reed, 1996), the 'local' is localised by being opposed to the 'global', and the linguistic (whether spoken or western) is privileged, when so much agency cannot be captured by linguistic re-presentation. (Callon and Law, 1995). In other words:

the multiple as such, unhewn and little unified, is not an epistemological monster, but on the contrary the ordinary lot of situations, including that of the ordinary scholar, regular knowledge, everyday work, in short, our common object. May the aforesaid scientific knowledge strip off its arrogance, its magisterial, ecclesial drapery; may it leave off its martial aggressivity, the hateful claim of always being right; let it tell the truth; let it come down, pacified, toward common knowledge (Serres, 1995, p.5).

Third, the creativity, the sheer inventiveness of the inhabitants of cities, is acknowledged, thereby bringing into view some of the most interesting things that are currently going on in cities, and no longer blocking off the emergent effects that have become trapped in the amber of old theoretical categories.

Fourth, the advisability of taking a heterogenous approach to all kinds of urban policy is made clear since such an approach is much more likely to resist pressures for conformity; to take on the latest trendy policy, to coordinate policy-making in cities; and so on. As Grabher and Stark (1996, p.2) argue:

from an evolutionary perspective, ...although such institutional homogen-isation might foster adaptation in the short run, the consequent loss of institutional diversity will impede adaptability in the long run. Limiting the search for effective institutions and organisational forms to the familiar quadrant of tried and proven arrangements locks [cities] in to exploring known territories at the cost of forgetting (or never knowing) the skills of exploring for new solutions.

It follows that disagreement, redundancy and mistakes are no longer seen as necessarily bad. Indeed, in some cases, quite the reverse:

Institutional friction preserves diversity; it sustains organisational routines that might later be recombined in new organisational forms. Resistance to change, in this sense, can foster change. Institutional legacies embody not only the persistence of the past but also resources for the future. Institutional friction that blocks transition to an already designated future keeps open a multiplicity of alternative paths to the future (ibid., pp.2–3).

In other words, since we cannot know the future, it follows that it is better to have policy that allows cities to be adaptable, rather than optimal.

In the remainder of this paper, I want to note just two emergent areas of research which are attempts to sketch out this 'Type 2' city, a city that is constantly changing (even to stay the same), a city that does not necessarily hold together, a city that is both little and large (since the idea of scale is replaced by the idea of partially connected networks), a city that is, to summarise, a set of diverse, interacting, practical orders in which the interaction is more important than the order. This is the city in which the magic is still there.

In making these choices, I am acutely aware that it may appear as though I am negating other vibrant areas of work on the city. Nothing could be further from my mind. For example, I would, if I had the space and time, have wanted to point to a whole series of other areas of work, including the relationship between the city and the visual register, as found especially in the work of feminist writers like Bruno (1993) and Pollock (1988), the relationship between the city and memory, as found in the work of Samuel (1994) and Boyer (1995), and the relationship between the city and the rise of geographical information systems which sometimes seems to prefigure a mimetic impulse of Borgesian dimensions. And this would still have been to ignore massively important work on ethnic identity, and on environment and 'urban nature' (King, 1996). But choices have to be made. Therefore I will concentrate on: the embodied city (of play) and the learning city (of knowledge, identity and soft capitalism) both of which are concerned with different means of knowing cities.

The Embodied City (Play)

The first element of the 'Type 2' city must be embodiment. Now there is, of course, currently a very large amount of work on the body which cleaves to the view that '…the most radical and expansive gesture against the totalitarian attempt to dominate spatiality is the challenge provided by the creative and imaginative space of the human body' (Woods, 1995, p.109). But it is surprising how little of this work *locates* the body, even though it is difficult to think of the body except as located. There are, I think, two reasons for this state of affairs. One can be found in Grosz's (1996) excellent triad of papers on the body and the city. Too often she writes in an almost overwhelmingly abstract way about something which by definition cannot be framed as abstract. In part, this may be because Grosz regards the city as just one more element of explanation of the social constitution of the body. Yet in the following passage, she gradually moves away from this view towards something more contextual:

> The city in its particular geographical, architectural and municipal arrangements is one particular ingredient in the social construction of the body. It is by no means the most significant (the structure and particularity of, say, the family is more directly and visibly influential); nonetheless the form, structure and norms of the city seep into and alter all the other elements that go into the constitution of complexity. It affects the way the subject sees others (an effect of, for example, domestic architecture as much as smaller family size), the subject's understanding of and alignment with space, different kinds of limited spontaneity (the verticality of the city as applied to the horizontality of the landscape – at least our own) must have effects on the ways we live space and this on our corporeal alignments, compartment and orientations. It also affects the subject's focus of corporeal

exertion – the kind of terrain it must negotiate day to day, the effect this has on its muscular stature, its nutritional context, providing the most elementary focus of material support and sustenance for the body. Moreover the city is also by now the site for the body's cultural saturation, its take-over and transformation by images, representational systems, the mass media, and the arts – the place where the body is representationally re-explored, transformed, contested, reinscribed. In turn, the body (as cultural product) transforms, reinscribes the urban landscape according to its changing (demographic) needs, extending the limits of the city even towards the countryside that borders it. As a hinge between the population and the individual, the body, its distribution, habits, alignments, pleasures, needs, and ideals are the ostentive subject of governmental regulation, and the unity is both a mode for the regulation and administration of subjects but also an urban space in turn reinscribed by the similarities of its occupation and use (Grosz, 1996, p.109).

The second reason is that the body in the city is too often thought of as the individual body, rather than an 'intersubjective' body occupying a space with other bodies which necessarily responds in a variety of sensuous and differently skilled ways according to prevailing cultural notions of body, space and time. And this is to ignore the presence of other objects (to which Merleau-Ponty was so keen to draw attention) which are the missing terms of this tactile collection (Crossley, 1996; Thrift, 1996).

Are there any authors who have genuinely attempted to situate the body in the city?

I can think of three. The first is Henri Lefebvre whose 'rhythmanalysis' is an attempt to capture the interactive temporality of the city as, amongst other things, the to and fro of a crowd of crowded bodies. Thus when Lefebvre (1995) looks out of his window onto crowded streets he remarks:

What this window which opens onto one of the most lively streets of Paris shows, what appears *spectacular*, would it be this *feeling* of spectacle? To attribute this rather derogatory character to this *vision* (as dominant feature) would be unjust and would bypass the *real*, that is, of meaning. The characteristic features are really temporal and rhythmical, not visual. To extricate and to listen to the rhythms requires attentiveness and a certain amount of time. Otherwise it only serves as a *glance* to enter into the murmurs, noises and cries. The classical term in philosophy, the 'object', is not appropriate to rhythm. 'Objective'? Yes, but a spilling over the narrow framework of objectivity by bringing into it the multiplicity of the *senses* (sensorial and meaningful).

The second author is Torsten Hägerstrand who in his 'time-geography' attempted to produce a musical score of bodies and things. His diagrammatic scores were attempts to describe something that could not be written, but could be seen and felt. Though they produce uncomfortable echoes of Laban's work on worker effort, these scores certainly have an effect. The third and final author is Richard Sennett who has tried to consider bodies in the city as a series of differential mapping of bodies onto spaces and spaces onto bodies via cultural intermediaries like rituals. He sees one of the main problems of current cities as the passive relationship between body and environment and in *Flesh and Stone* he sets out how a more positive relationship might be installed.

In the work of each of these three authors there is, then, a sense that the space of the body (or rather bodies) is important. Most particularly, there is a sense that space is important because it produces what Probyn (1996) calls singularity from the range of specificities (race, class, sexuality, gender) that we inhabit. Cultural geographers have spent considerable time attempting to juggle with the singularity of specificity, most especially in work on sexuality (Bell and Valentine, 1995). Here I want to point to one of the areas that has so far been curiously neglected, the example of dance, an area of study which is becoming increasingly central to work on the city and for obvious reasons (Thomas, 1995; 1996).

The importance of dance becomes self-evident in the light of the concerns of writers like Lefebvre, Hägerstrand and Sennett. This importance can be indexed in five main ways. First, dance represents a conscious formulation of the sensuous inter-bodily movement that we usually take for granted, and so do not write down. Martha Graham called dance 'knowledge itself' because dance '...does not pass through the sign but is itself contextualised in movement' (Franko, 1996, p.37). Of course, some caution needs to be exercised here or dance can be represented as a pure phenomenology of immediate experience (indeed many forms of modern dance, prior to the 1980s, were intended to convey exactly this) but, even so, it cannot be denied that, in part, dance is a gratuitous outpouring of force, an expenditure without return. (Lingis, 1994).

Thus, second, it is important to approach dance as a socially constructed ritual, which, like other forms of artful and skilful moving together in time (McNeill, 1995) act to produce or strengthen connection. Indeed, in certain cases, dance has become a vital part of modern spectacle (and not always to the good, as Wollen (1995) has shown). Third, dance is usually linked to other media, most especially music but also quite often visual display (from special costume to light) and artificial enhancers (such as alcohol and other drugs). Fourth, dance is normally carried out at predetermined sites. These may be concert halls and other formal sites (thus underlining the links between dance and other artistic modes) but for most people, in most of their lives, these sites are more likely to be more mundane settings in which they are quite likely to be participants, '...from street dancing to dance halls, discos and raves, to parties, dinner dances, weddings and church socials' (Thomas, 1995, p.3). Fifth, as these settings make clear, dance is simply a very widespread part of the '...urban commercial sphere' (Mort, 1996), ranging all the way from ballet to modern dance to ballroom dancing to visual theatre, to film and TV and video, to keep fit clubs and raves, and so on. As Thornton (1995) notes, admissions to 'dances' ranks far above admissions to sports, live arts or cinema, for single younger people. In other words, dance is a significant urban economic activity because for so many people it is a crucial part of '...leisure activity, entertainment and sexuality' (McRobbie, 1984).

Why then, given its widespread nature (surely equivalent to the breadth of musical activity found by Finnegan (1989) in Milton Keynes), is there so little work on dance in relation to urban life? Five main explanations come to mind. First, there is the simple fact that issues of sensuous body movement in the city have only just begun to be considered, especially as 'non-representational theories' (Thrift, 1996) have begun to bite. In particular, dance is an instance of *expressive* embodiment: the body is not just inscribed, it is itself a source of inscription which can be used to conjure up virtual 'as if' worlds which can in turn become claims to 'something more' (Pini, 1996). Thus, in the case of dance:

> dance can be considered as the fabrication of a 'different world' of meaning made with the body. It is perhaps the most direct way in which the body – subject sketches out an imaginary sphere. The word 'imaginary' is used here in the sense 'as if', suggesting a field of potential space. The dance is not aimed at describing events (that is, it is not representational) but at evolving a semblance of a world within which specific questions take their meaning (Radley, 1995, p.12).

Second, dance chiefly belongs to the sphere of *play* and therefore lives beyond the rational auspices of purposive means-end systems like work. In western societies, play is often regarded as peripheral to the real business of life because of its gratuitous, free (if one is forced into such a practice, it is no longer play), and non-cumulative nature (Huizinga, 1949; Geertz, 1972; Bateson, 1973; Winnicott, 1971; Bauman, 1993). Play is simply the irrational precursor to the real business of life.

Third, dance, unlike other, more durable aspects of human experience, is comparatively rarely recorded (though one might well argue that it is itself a technology for recording bodily movement). Fourth, dance is nearly always considered in relation to music and it is the music that is privileged (although, recently, much popular music has become subordinated to dance). Of course, musical soundscapes are a crucial element of dance but dance cannot be reduced to them. Then, finally, dance is often regarded as 'high culture' and therefore as of little interest to cultural studies. Yet, even a cursory inspection of contemporary dance practice shows the tenuousness of this judgement: children's ballet classes, square dancing, ceroc, line dancing, morris dance, step dancing, sequence dancing, ice dance... the list goes on and on.

The Learning City of Knowledge, Identity and Soft Capitalism

Cities are often seen as repositories of knowledge, as pedagogic engines. Certainly pedagogic institutions, from school to museums to libraries are scattered through them. It is no surprise then, that there has been an outpouring of work on the educational institutions of the city, sometimes but not only stimulated by writers like Bourdieu and Foucault. For example, we now know that there are cities of science. Writers in the sociology of scientific knowledge have revealed the sheer diversity of institutions and institutional contexts through which 'science' is produced and reproduced, from laboratories to lecture rooms to libraries to public houses.

Then, there have been studies of academic institutions. Not least, there has been a rapid growth of work on the economic, social and cultural effects of universities (which have turned out to be substantial) and equally, of late, the economic, social and cultural effects of students. Then there is work on what makes a city 'creative'. Writers like Ken Worpole and Franco Bianchini have pointed to the cultural creativity that some cities seem to enjoy which, at least in part, seems to be a function of their pedagogic power.

But, in all this, what has not been realised has been that capitalism itself has been receiving a pedagogic boost. The grand myths of urban life tend to support the authorised version of a 'global' capitalism which is interpreted as a vast and monolithic presence, now able to dream global dreams through the advent of the space of flows: cyberspace becomes a metaphor for the flow of capital (Buck-Morss, 1995). This authorised version of global capitalism has been repeated many times since the cultural turn has swept across the social sciences and humanities, most probably because it allows capitalism to be portrayed as something always already accounted for. Its presence can therefore be acknowledged but then everyone can get on to the more interesting, more cultural things.

The irony, of course, is that those who manage capitalism no longer see it in this way, let alone those who study it. Beginning in the 1960s, a new discourse of how capitalism is has come into being. Spun out of the interaction between events, managers and business schools, this discussion interprets the world in which capitalist organisations must survive as profoundly *uncertain*: capitalists don't know what is going on either. The business organisation's 'environment' is framed as multiple, complex and fast-moving, and therefore as ambiguous, fuzzy, plastic or even chaotic. To survive the business organisation must attempt to form an island of superior adaptability able to dance its way out of trouble. (In fact, dancing is a favourite metaphor of the new capitalism). This means three things in particular.

First, in a business world that is increasingly constructed by information, knowledge becomes crucial. Increasingly, knowledge is seen as the key to competitive advantage. Thus, whereas managers:

> used to think that the most precious resource was capital, and that the prime task of management was to allocate it in the most productive way, now they have become convinced that their most precious resource is knowledge and that the prime task of management is to ensure that their knowledge is generated as widely and used as efficiently as possible (Wooldridge, 1995, p.4).

In Drucker's (1982, p.16) famous words, '...Knowledge has become the key economic resource and the dominant, if not the only source of comparative advantage.'

Second, it follows that organisations must foster and preserve their knowledge base. This will be achieved via a number of means. These include the introduction of an emergent 'evolutionary' or 'learning' strategy which is '...necessarily incremental and adaptive but that does not in any way imply that its evolution cannot be, or should not be analysed, managed, and controlled' (Kay, 1993, p.359). Such a strategy will be based on what are seen as the particular capabilities of a business organisation which are then amplified via informal methods of control which rely on a much greater grasp of the issues involved, and which also mean that whole layers of bureaucracy, most of whose time was taken up with oversight, can be shrunk or, in the jargon, 'delayered' (Clarke and Newman, 1993). Another means of fostering knowledge is to pay much greater attention to the skills of the workforce. Thus the organisation pays much closer attention to enhancing formal skills.

It will also probably become involved in experiential learning which involves placing the workforce in situations which demand cooperative responses to the uncertain and unknown (Martin, 1994). Most importantly, the organisation will also pay close attention to the resources of *tacit* (familiar but unarticulated) *knowledge* embodied in its workforce and to the generation of trust, both within its workforce and with other organisations. Work on tacit knowledge has been almost entirely generated from the writings of Michael Polanyi (Botwinick, 1986) (rather than, for example, Heidegger, Merleau-Ponty or Bourdieu) who, in turn, drew on the ideas of Gestalt psychology. Polanyi's (1967, p.20), most famous saying '…we can know more than we can tell' has become a vital part of business discourse, as a way into the problem of mobilising the full bodily resources of workforce. In turn, Polanyi's work has underlined the need to generate *trust* or (as Polanyi often called it) confidence, since '…the overwhelming proportion of our factual beliefs continue…to be held at second hand through trusting others' (Polanyi, 1958, p.208).

Third, the business organisation is mainly therefore seen as a culture which attempts to generate new representations of itself (new metaphors, new traditions) which will allow it to see itself and others in new, more profitable ways.

This, then, is a radically different narrative of political economy in which the capitalist organisation is framed as always in *action*, '…on the move, if only stumbling or blundering along' (Boden, 1994, p.192), but stumbling or blundering along in ways which will allow it to survive and prosper, most particularly through mobilising a culture which will produce traditions of learning (collective memories which will act both to keep the organisation constantly alert and as a reservoir of innovation (Lundvall, 1992; 1994)) and extensive intra-and inter-firm social networks (which will act both as conduits of knowledge and as a means of generating trust). In turn, the manager has to become a kind of charismatic itinerant, a 'cultural diplomat' (Hofstede, 1991), constantly imbuing the business organisation's values and goals, constantly on a mission to explain and motivate. Management is no longer, therefore, seen as a science. Rather it becomes an art form, dedicated to '…the proposition that a political economy of information is in fact coexistent with a theory of culture' (Boisot, 1995, p.7). Capitalism is increasingly a part of the 'humanities' as well as the 'sciences'.

In other words, the rational company man of the 1950s and 1960s, skilled in the highways and by ways of bureaucracy, becomes the reflexive corporate social persona of the 1990s, skilled in the arts of social presentation and 'change management'. And the giant multidivisional corporation of the 1950s and

1960s now becomes a 'leaner', 'networked', 'post-bureaucratic', 'virtual' or even 'post structuralist' organisation, a looser form of business which can act like a net floating on an ocean, able to ride the swell and still go forward because it too is perpetually in transition (Drucker, 1988; Heckscher and Donnellon, 1994; Eccles and Nohria, 1990).

This is a discourse that is aware of its own limits and, it is therefore no surprise that, as each year comes and goes, new management ideas appear, as both a means of meeting uncertainty and satisfying the voracious appetite of this form of capitalism for new ideas and practices. New managerial magic 'spells' – like quality circles, the paperless office, the factory of the future, entrepreneurship, brands, strategic alliances, globalisation, and business-process re-engineering – usually last for only a limited time but, since capitalist firms have the power to realise their fantasies, these spells are often responsible for quite extraordinary rounds of restructuring with serious consequences for workforces.

In a sense, capitalism has returned to its magical past.

How has this new discourse been produced and disseminated? Mainly through an urban pedagogic infrastructure, which, in effect, dates only from the 1960s and which has now grown into a powerful, autopoietic system which produces and distributes business knowledge; which I call the 'capitalist circuit of cultural capital' (Thrift, 1997b). This infrastructure has its own geography of university and business campuses, office buildings, exhibition centres, and the like.

The institutions chiefly responsible for producing business knowledge include the institutions of formal business education, and especially the MBA course, which have produced a large number of academics and students who have acted both to generate and transport the new knowledge. (In the US, admittedly the most extreme example, almost one in four students now majors in business, while the number of business schools has grown fivefold since 1957).

Then there are the set of institutions which are responsible for dissemination. These include management consultants and management gurus. Consultants have acted as a key link between theory and practice and they have often had a vital interest in disseminating the new discourse because of their attempts at authorship. 'Management gurus' like Peter Drucker, Charles Handy, John Kay, Theodore Levitt, Gareth Morgan, John Naisbitt, Tom Peters, Rosabeth Moss Kanter, Kenichi Ohmae, and the like, have become increasingly important as embodiments of new managerialist arguments. These gurus have been responsible for the diffusion of a whole host of the 'business fads' taught on management courses which, jointly and singly, have promoted a new managerial world-view (Huczynski, 1993).

Distribution of the discourse then takes place via a selection of different media, some specialised, some not. The discourse thereby reaches various managerial audiences (though we know remarkably little about these audiences or how they practice the discourse).

In summary, what can be said is that cities are now the sites of a *knowledgeable capitalism* which, through its institutional infrastructure, is intent on producing and disseminating a specific discourse of adaptability and learning. This discourse is not passive for two reasons. First, it is a discourse of constant change and adaptation. Second, it is intent on providing new managerial and worker identities, based on a concept of a person which is broader than before but still radically attenuated (Rose, 1996). Right now, for example, at numerous sites around the world, seminars and workshops are being held which are attempts to ingrain a more 'enterprising' identity by harnessing *belief* (Martin, 1994). In these seminars and workshops:

> the worker is represented as an *individual* in search of *meaning* in work, and working to achieve fulfilment through work. Excellent organisations are those that 'make money for people' by encouraging them to believe that they have control of their own destinies; that, no matter what position they may hold in an organisation, their contribution is vital, not only to the success of the company for which they work but also to the enterprise of their own lives. Peters and Waterman (1982, p.81; p.45) for example, quote approvingly Nietzsche's axiom that 'that he who has a *why* to live for can bear most any *how.*' They argue that 'the fact that...we think we have a bit of discretion leads to much greater commitment' and that 'we desperately need meaning in our lives, and will sacrifice a great deal to institutions that will provide meaning for us. We simultaneously need independence to feel as though we are in charge of our own destinies, and to have the ability to stand out.' In this vision work is a sphere within which the individual constitutes and confirms his or her identity. Excellent organisations get the most out of everyone, not by manipulating group human relations to secure a sense of 'belonging', but by harnessing the psychological stirring of individuals for autonomy and creativity and channelling them into the search for excellence and success (Miller and Rose, 1992, p.26), (Du Gay, 1996, p.60).

In some senses, it is belief itself, rather than what is believed, that is what counts as important. Thus, that recent staple of New Age thought, *The Celestine*

Prophecy (Redfield, 1994) is used as a key text in a number of management seminars. Again the galactic outings of the Starship Enterprise form the material for lessons of management in other seminars. The magic has not gone away – if anything, it is coming back!

Conclusions

In this paper I have attempted to clear some ground in the hope that some new senses of the city might begin to emerge. I have pointed to only two examples of these senses out of many. But hopefully these examples begin to show just how narrow has been our conception of the city – and how rich it could be. Hopefully I might have helped to show why cities retain their magic, notwithstanding the attempt by theorists of modernity to disenchant them.

References

Acuna, R.F. (1996), *Anything But Mexican. Chicanos in Contemporary Los Angeles*, Verso, London.

Ahearne, J. (1995), *Michel de Certeau. Interpretation and its Other*, Polity Press, Cambridge.

Allan, G. (1996), *Kinship and Friendship in Modern Britain*, Oxford University Press, Oxford.

Alvarez, A. (1995), *Night. An Exploration of Night Life, Night Language, Sleep and Dreams*, Cape, London.

Ardener, S. (1995), 'Women Making Money Go Round: Roscas Revisited', in Ardener, S. and Burman, S. (eds), *Money-Go-Rounds: The Importance of Rotating Savings and Credit Associations for Women*, Berg, Oxford, pp.1–19.

Armstrong, I. (1996), 'Transparency: Towards a Poetics of Glass in the Nineteenth Century', in Spufford, F. and Uglow, J. (eds), *Cultural Babbage. Technology, Time and Invention*, Faber and Faber, London, pp.123–48.

Bateson, G. (1977), *Steps to an Ecology of Mind*, Picador, London.

Bauman, Z. (1993), *Postmodern Ethics*, Blackwell, Oxford.

Bell, D. and Valentine, G. (eds), *Mapping Desire*, Routledge, London.

Benjamin, W. (1969), *Illuminations*, Schocken Books, New York.

Benjamin, W. (1979), *One Way Street*, New Left Books, London.

Bernstein, J. (1994), *Foregone Conclusions*, University of California Press, Berkeley, CA.

Bruno, G. (1993), *Streetwalking on a Ruined Map. Cultural Theory and the Films of Elvira Notari*, Princeton University Press, Princeton, NJ.

Buck-Morss, S. (1995), 'Envisioning Capital: Political Economy on Display' in Cooke, L. and Wollen, P. (eds), *Visual Display. Culture Beyond Appearances*, Bay Press, Seattle, WA, pp.110–41.

Callon, M. and Law, J. (1995), 'Agency and the Hybrid Collectif', *South Atlantic Quarterly*, Vol. 94, pp.481–507.

Casey, E.W. (1993), *Getting Back into Place. Towards a Renewed Understanding of the Place-World*, University of Indiana Press, Bloomington, IN.

Collins, J. (1995), *Architectures of Excess. Cultural Life in the Information Age*, Routledge, London.

Crossley, N. (1996), *Intersubjectivity. The Fabric of Becoming*, Sage, London.

Davis, E. (1994), 'Techgnosis, Magic, Memory and The Angels of Information', *South Atlantic Quarterly*, Vol. 92, pp.518–617.

Davis, M. (1990), *City of Quartz. Excavating Los Angeles*, Verso, London.

Davis, M. (1996), 'Cosmic Dancers On History's Stage? The Permanent Revolution in the Earth Sciences', *New Left Review*, No. 217, pp.48–84.

Debray, R. (1996), *Media Manifestations. On the Technological Transmission of Cultural Forms*, Verso, London.

de Certeau, M. (1986), *The Practice of Everyday Life*, University of California Press, Berkeley, CA.

Du Gay, P. (1996), 'Organising Identity. Entrepeneurial Governance and Public Management', in Hall, S. and Du Gay, P. (eds), *Questions of Identity*, Sage, London, pp.151–69.

Finch, J. (1989), *Family Obligations and Social Change*, Polity Press, Cambridge.

Finch, J. and Mason, J. (1993), *Negotiating Family Responsibilities*, Routledge, London.

Finnegan, R. (1989), *The Hidden Musicians*, Cambridge University Press, Cambridge.

Fisher, C.S. (1992), *Calling America. The Social History of the Telephone*, University of California Press, Berkeley, CA.

Geertz, C. (1972), 'Deep Play: Notes on the Balinese Cock Fight', *Dadalus*, 101, pp.1–37.

Gibbons, M. et al. (1994), *The New Production of Knowledge*, Sage, London.

Gilroy, P. (1993), *The Black Atlantic: Modernity and Double Consciousness*, Verso, London.

Glennie, P. and Thrift, N.J. (1996), 'Consumers, Identities, and Consumption Spaces in Early-Modern England', *Environment and Planning A*, Vol. 28, pp.35–46.

Grabher, G. and Stark, D. (1996), 'Organising Diversity: Evolutionary Theory, Network Analysis and Postsocialist Transformations', in Grabher, G. and Stark, D. (eds), *Restructuring Networks: Legacies, Linkages and Localities in Postsocialism*, Oxford University Press, Oxford.

Grosz, E. (1996), *Space, Time and Perversions*, Routledge, London.

Harvey, D. (1989), *The Condition of Postmodernity*, Blackwell, Oxford.

Heelas, P. (1996), *The New Age Movement. The Celebration of the Self and the Sacralization of Modernity*, Blackwell, Oxford.

Holmes, R. (1993), *Dr Johnson and Mr Savage*, Flamingo, London.

Huizinga, J. (1949), *Homo Ludens: A Study of the Play Element in Culture*, Routledge and Kegan Paul, London.

Humphrey, N. (1995), *Soul Searching. Human Nature and Supernatural Belief*, Chatto and Windus, London.

Janelle, D.G. (1969), *Annuals of the Association of American Geographers*.

King, A.D. (ed.) (1996), *Re-Presenting the City. Ethnicity, Capital and Culture in the 21st-Century Metropolis*, Macmillan, Basingstoke.

Latour, B. (1993), *We Have Never Been Modern*, Harvester-Wheatsheaf, Hemel Hempstead.

Law, J. and Mol, A. (1996), 'Decision/s', unpublished paper.

Lefebvre, H. (1995), *Writings on Cities*, Blackwell, Oxford.

Lingis, A. (1994), *Foreign Bodies*, Routledge, New York, NY.

Martin, E. (1994), *Flexible Bodies*, Beacon Press, Boston, MA.

McRobbie, A. (1994), 'Dance and Social Fantasy' in McRobbie, A. and Nava, M. (eds), *Gender and Generation*, Macmillan, London.

Mort, F. (1996), *Cultures of Consumption*, London, Routledge.

Nye, D. (1990), *Electrifying America*, MIT Press, Cambridge, MA.

Nye, D. (1995), *The Technological Sublime*, MIT Press, Cambridge, MA.

Pahl, R. (1995), *After Success. Fin-de-Siecle Anxiety and Identity*, Polity Press, Cambridge.

Pini, M. (1996), 'Dance Classes – Dancing Between Classifications', *Feminism and Psychology*, Vol. 6, pp.411–26.

Prendergast, C. (1992), *Paris and the Nineteenth Century*, Blackwell, Oxford.

Probyn, E. (1996), *Outside Belongings*, Routledge, London.

Redfield, J. (1994), *The Celestine Prophecy*, Bantam, London.

Reed, D. (ed.), *Not at Home. The Suppression of Domesticity in Modern Art and Architecture*, Thames and Hudson, London.

Relph, E. (1981), *Place and Placelessness*, Pion, London.

Rose, N. (1996), *Inventing Our Selves*, Cambridge University Press, Cambridge.

Samuel, R. (1994), *Theatres of Memory*, Verso, London.

Savage, M. (1995), 'Walter Benjamin's Urban Thought: A Critical Analysis', *Environment and Planning D. Society and Space*, Vol. 13, pp.201–16.

Savage, M. and Warde, A. (1993), *Urban Sociology, Capitalism and Modernity*, Macmillan, London.

Scott, A. and Soja, E. (1986), 'Los Angeles: The Capital of the Twentieth Century', *Environment and Planning D. Society and Space*, Vol. 4, pp.249–54.

Sennett, R. (1995), *Flesh and Stone. The Body and the City in Western Civilization*, Allen Lane, London.

Serres, M. (1995), *Genesis*, University of Michigan Press, Ann Arbor, MI.

Serres, M. and Latour, B. (1995), *Conversations on Science, Culture and Time*, University of Michigan Press, Ann Arbor, MI.

Sheringham, M. (ed.) (1996), *Parisian Fields*, Reaktion Books, London.

Social and Community Planning Research (1996), *British Social Altitudes*.

Soja, E. (1989), *Postmodern Geographies*, Verso, London.

Spufford, F. (1996), 'The Difference Engine And The Difference Engine', in Spufford, F. and Uglow, J. (eds), *Cultural Babbage. Technology, Time and Invention*, Faber and Faber, London, pp.266–90.

Srinivon, S. (1995), 'ROSCAs among South Asians in Oxford', in Ardener, S. and Burmna, S. (eds), *Money-go-rounds: The Importance of Rotating Savings and Credit Associations for Women*, Berg, Oxford, pp.199–208.

Stebbins, R.A. (1979), *Amateurs. On the Margin Between Work and Leisure*, Sage, Beverly Hills.

Storper, M. (1992), 'The Limits of Globalisation: Technology Districts and International Trade', *Economic Geography*, Vol. 68, pp.60–93.

Taussig, M. (1992), *The Nervous System*, Routledge, London.

Thomas, H. (1995), *Dance, Modernity and Culture*, Routledge, London.

Thomas, H. (ed.) (1996), *Dance in the City*, Macmillan, London.

Thornton, S. (1995), *Club Cultures*, Polity Press, Cambridge.

Thrift, N. J. (1996a), *Spatial Formations*, Sage, London.

Thrift, N.J. (1996b), 'Old Technological Fears and New Urban Eras: Reconfiguring the Goodwill of Electronic Things', *Urban Studies*, Vol. 33, pp.1463–93.

Thrift, N.J. (1996c), 'The Place of Complexity: Towards a Metaphorical Geography', paper presented to the Centre for the Study of Science and Technology Conference on Complexity, Keele University, November.

Thrift, N.J. (1997), 'The Rise of Soft Capitalism', in Herod, A., Roberts, S. and Toal, G. (eds), *Globalising Worlds*, Routledge, London.

Tickell, A. and Peck, J. (1995), 'Social Regulation After Fordism: Regulation Theory, Neo-Liberalism and The Global-Local Nexus', *Economy and Society*, Vol. 24, pp.357–86.

Virilio, P. (1993), 'The Third Interval: A Critical Transition', in Conley, V.A. (ed.), *Rethinking Technologies*, University of Minnesota Press, Minneapolis, MN, pp.3–12.

Walker, R.A. (1990), 'The Playground of US Capitalism? The Political Economy of The San Francisco Bay Area in the 1980', in Davis, M. et al. (eds), *Fire in the Hearth*, Verso, London, pp.43–82.

Walker, R.A. (1995), 'Landscape and City Life: Four Ecologies of Resistance in San Francisco', *Ecumene*, Vol. 2, pp.33–64.

Walker, R.A. (1996), 'Another Round of Globalisation in San Francisco', *Urban Geography*, Vol. 17, pp.60–94.

Wellman, B. and Berkowitz, S.D. (eds) (1988), *Social Structures. A Network Approach*, Cambridge University Press, Cambridge.

Weston, K. (1991), *Families We Choose: Lesbians, Gays, Kinship*, Columbia University Press, New York.

Williams, R. H. (1991), *Notes on the Underground: An Essay on Technology, Society and the Imagination*, MIT Press, Cambridge MA.

Winnicott, D. (1971), *Playing and Reality*, Harmondsworth, Penguin.

Wollen, P. (1995), 'Tales of Total Art and Dreams of the Total Museum', in Cooke, L. and Wollen, P. (eds), *Visual Display: Culture Beyond Appearances*, Bay Press, Seattle, pp.154–77.

Woods, T. (1995), 'Looking for Signs in the Air: Urban Space and the Postmodern in "In the Country of Last Things"', in Barone, D. (ed.), *Beyond the Red Notebook. Essays on Paul Auster*, University of Pennsylvania Press, Philadelphia, PA, pp.107–128.

Zajonc, A. (1993), *Catching the Light. The Entwined History of Light and Mind*, Oxford University Press, Oxford.

Chapter Three

A New Approach to Identifying Localities: Representing 'Places' in Britain

Mike Coombes and Colin Wymer

Introduction

This chapter is concerned with the identification of individual 'places' – at its simplest, the drawing of the boundaries which indicate where one place ends and its neighbours begin. As discussed in more detail in Introduction and other chapters in Part One, the nature of places is becoming increasingly complex and contested. In some contexts, boundaries represent a way of 'constructing' places by representing a claim about which areas are recognisably distinct (Massey, 1995). For example, choosing to draw a single boundary around the whole of Teesside would mean that the two main towns Middlesborough and Stockton-on-Tees are being grouped together in a way which would run counter to any claim that each is a highly distinct place in its own right. In this chapter, the aim is not to shape places by imposing boundaries but instead to discover the local patterning of social and economic life – and to use statistical techniques to represent this patterning as a set of locality boundaries.

Each part of the country is now increasingly likely to embrace a range of social and economic groups whose connection with that locality – and with each other – may be intimate, or ephemeral, or anywhere between these two extremes. A group of people's attachment to a place is often central to their sense of identity, but unfortunately there is little information on the areas with which most people identify most strongly in Britain at the end of the 1990s. As a result, this chapter's empirical approach to devising a set of locality boundaries can only draw on more indirect reflections of people's identification with their localities.

The reason why this chapter seeks an empirical approach to identifying localities is that no 'off the shelf' set of areas provides consistently defined boundaries which reflect the localised structuring of Britain's economy and society. In the 1960s, Britain was one of the first western European countries to begin rationalising its local government boundaries in response to the increasing mobility of the population. The original proposals for new local government areas by the Royal Commission on Local Government in England (1969) took some account of evidence on commuting patterns and service hinterlands, as well as the different scales at which people identified with local areas. The local government reorganisation which was subsequently implemented in practice unfortunately did not implement this strategy. The boundaries which were then created have recently been partially reviewed, but it is already clear that the new set of boundaries provide no better or more consistent a representation of the current state of localities as social or economic entities. For example, the local authority boundaries of some towns and cities embrace quite large tracts of rural land (e.g. Leeds and Carlisle), whilst those of many comparable cities do not even include the whole of their own built-up area (e.g. Leicester and Norwich). It is clear that the problem is not merely one of the geography of the country evolving, but it is also that defining local government boundaries in Britain is – unsurprisingly – driven more by administrative and political concerns than it is by geographical realities. In other countries it is well understood that local government boundaries are artefacts devised purely for administrative convenience, with any historical consistency in their definitions resulting as much from institutional inertia as from a respect for a clear local identity. The time is overdue for British researchers to adopt a similarly sceptical view, accepting that the aspirations raised by the 1969 Royal Commission have not been fulfilled and so local authority boundaries do not provide an adequate representation of the boundaries between genuinely distinct places.

Starting in Britain with Hall et al. (1973), almost all academic attempts to define 'multipurpose' urban-centred regions have emphasised the local labour market as the key feature which individuates one town or city, with its hinterland, from the next. Later research stressed that the local labour markets of different occupation groups can vary widely in size and configuration within the same parts of the country, mainly due to differences in average commuting distances (Coombes et al., 1988). Thus the reductionism of definitions based solely on commuting data is compounded by the blurring of major differences between the labour market areas of different social groups. At the same time, an increasing number of studies in other fields have reinforced the distinctiveness of localities by demonstrating the subregional variations in, for example, housing markets (Maclennan et al., 1990). As a result, it is timely to devise locality definitions which take into account a range of different factors such as, for example, localised patterns of use of major consumer services (Openshaw et al., 1988).

The recognition of the role of many different factors in shaping localities contrasts strongly with the relatively straightforward model of Hall et al. (1973) in which boundaries were demarcated by inspection of commuting patterns alone. This approach to boundary definition, 'privileging' evidence on commuting patterns, can be traced to

- an emphasis on patterns of flows or interaction, with commuting data being the only readily available information on peoples' movement in and around each city; and

- the origins of boundary definition methods in regional science, with its neoclassical assumptions about the primacy of economic considerations such as the labour market (and journey-to-work patterns in particular).

It is surely necessary now to move forward from this reductionist approach and instead seek to represent a diverse range of evidence on the multifaceted nature of places in Britain today. This chapter's aim thus becomes to move beyond all previous boundary definition methods, with their dependence on a single aspect of places (such as commuting patterns), so as to represent a wide spectrum of the multifaceted nature of localities. The first challenge which then arises is to impose some structure on the ideas which are associated with the term 'locality' – the term adopted here as signifying a place which is at a scale which typically embraces a single city, or sizeable town, and its adjacent rural areas.

Localities

Before embarking on the challenging task of devising new analytical tools for defining locality boundaries which take into account numerous different aspects of localities, it has to be recognised that the concept of locality is still as far from being 'pinned down' definitively as was the related concept of community when it was reviewed by Bell and Newby (1972). For present purposes, a starting point can be to consider the major aspects of local socioeconomic life which tend to be cited in the debate on what constitutes a locality. For example, a compilation by Cooke (1986) presented thirty-one proposed academic locality studies at the outset of a research initiative. More than half of the studies, explicitly or more vaguely, took local labour market patterns as the defining feature of their area of interest. Most of the others used local authority district boundaries, usually with no explicit justification for their choice. The only other community feature which was cited in relation to these proposed study area definitions was local social or economic history. This was mentioned in a fairly small minority of both the studies based on labour markets and those based on local authorities.

How can these different defining features of communities be brought together coherently? Much of the locality research of the 1980s was provoked by the insights of Massey (1984). In brief, localities were conceived as territories within which successive generations of people had shaped a distinctive society through the cumulative effects of their interaction with each other, with the landscape and its resources, and with the changing context within which that area was situated. Through time, this interaction creates the form of a local society, which is then often articulated in organisational forms. One example is a community's participation or voluntarism in a wide range of optional local activities, extending beyond the conventional voluntary sector (Rogers, 1987). If an area's residents show that they prefer to interact within localised groups, rather than to be 'small fish in a big pond' nearby, then this is evidence of one aspect of a distinct community.

Figure 3.1 sketches the major dimensions to this interpretation, taking as the three primary elements territory, people and society. Figure 3.1 suggests that six 'facets' to localities emerge from the interaction between landscape, people and the local society which they create. The local territory is shaped through time in terms of its distinctive landscape and also by the accumulation of facilities and other infrastructure. The local economy is seen here as an outcome of people responding to the opportunities in that area, whilst their demographic character is a fundamental factor shaping local society. That society is articulated in a variety of forms, with institutions and organisations seen here as expressions of territoriality (e.g. forms of local governance), whilst the 'softer' facets are categorised as forms of local culture. Figure 3.1 is offered here as a modest attempt to sketch out the range of issues raised by attempts at locality definitions. This approach leads then to identifying six facets of localities – landscape, facilities, institutions, culture, demography and economy – which provide a 'check list' against which locality definitions can be compared to assess their richness and relevance.

Taking a multifaceted approach to understanding localities leads on to rejecting mono-dimensional definitions of localities. A set of locality

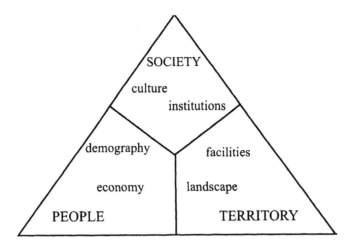

Figure 3.1   Facets of localities

definitions which is based on a single dimension – such as the familiar emphasis on labour markets – can really only be adequate for studying that one aspect of local geography. The point is that there is no clear primacy within the six aspects of localities set out here, so a set of areas defined by focusing on any one aspect alone can not be expected to be also appropriate for studies of other aspects of localities. For example, the purely institutional focus which is implied by adopting local authority boundaries as locality definitions will often be an implausible basis for the analysis of local economies or areas' cultural heritage. Thus a set of locality definitions aiming to be relevant across a range of social science research should, by the same token, be based on evidence which reflects several of the different facets of localities which are implied by a rich conceptualisation of place such as that of Massey (1995).

Boundaries

Moving towards the definition of boundaries, a key point to take from the discussion of the concept of localities is the central importance of *interaction* in various forms. The coming together of people in voluntary groups is one key form in which the importance of interaction can be seen, alongside the more familiar measures of interaction which include commuting, migration and the use of facilities. A highly distinct locality would be expected to show that this interaction is largely self-contained *within* that local area – that is, the boundary should be drawn so that there is relatively little interaction with the adjacent areas. Thus the challenge here is to define a set of locality boundaries which retains the emphasis on forms of interaction, as provided by previous research focusing exclusively on commuting, but also represents a range of different aspects of localities.

The challenge can be illustrated by the example of Sudbury – a small town which is around 100 km northeast of London (with which it is connected via a branch railway). Sudbury is in the county of Suffolk – but the border with the adjacent county of Essex lies along the river Stour that runs past the western fringes of the town. The upper Stour valley, which is thus split between the two counties, which is Sudbury's natural hinterland, is renowned for its picturesque landscape and traditional character. Pressures for development in the area are fuelled not only by this attractive character but also by its location within commuting range of the capital. In addition, the area is only about 20 km away from the substantial towns of Colchester and Ipswich (the latter being Suffolk's administrative centre). For this chapter, the principal question to be answered about Sudbury is whether there is a clearly identifiable and relatively distinct locality which comprises Sudbury and the nearby villages? If not, with which of the larger towns is Sudbury more validly identified: does its historic link with Ipswich and other parts of southern Suffolk still provide stronger ties than those towards Colchester and northeast Essex which have grown as a result of the better road and rail links in that direction? It is questions like these which are to be asked about all parts of the country, so as to discover which areas are distinctive enough to emerge as localities in their own right, and where the boundaries between them will lie.

A crucial aspect of this task is that the definitions need to be consistently applied across the whole country. The emphasis on consistency stems from the problems which arise from '…comparing apples with pears' in locality research. Comparing areas without the confidence that the areas are genuinely comparable can give rise to a variety of problems:

• in locality studies, the definition of the areas for the research was recognised to reflect a particular understanding of what 'locality' meant, and thereby also to shape the findings (see for example, Cooke, 1989); and

• in quantitative research, the importance of study area boundaries in shaping the results of analyses has been formalised as the 'modifiable areal unit problem' (Openshaw, 1984) and has been illustrated in many studies (e.g. Coombes, 1997).

As already noted, local authority areas in Britain have recently been revised but the new set of boundaries have, if anything, been defined in a way that makes them even less consistent than were the old ones because the revisions proceeded on different bases in England, Scotland and Wales, while excluding Greater London and the other Metropolitan Counties altogether.

The objective for this analysis is to provide a consistently defined set of boundaries which warrant the term 'locality' and so will be potentially of value for a wide range of different social and economic studies. To be more specific, the intention is that the definitions should be automated in a way which prevents them becoming essentially judgmental. There is no doubt that judgement plays a major role in the selection of criteria and method – for example, other researchers can be expected to critique the approach adopted here. The judgmental element which is to be avoided here is in the application of the approach: thus if Sudbury does indeed emerge as a separate locality then there should not be a lingering doubt as to whether this is the result of a consistently applied method rather than as an informal judgement. An inconsistent set of definitions is diminished in its meaningfulness and value for research, because it then becomes unclear what a statement such as 'Sudbury is a distinct locality' is actually based upon.

The methodological challenge posed by seeking consistency is greatly heightened by being linked with the aim for a multifaceted basis for the definitions. Although there are examples of consistent local boundary definition analyses – for example, the research on commuting patterns and built-up land which led to the definition of Travel-to-Work Areas and Urban Areas respectively – these have each been based on a single overriding feature. The next section of this chapter questions whether there are available 'off-the-shelf' methods which could, at least in principle, create a consistent multifaceted set of definitions.

Method

The first question at this point is whether any recent developments in regionalisation methods have provided a form of analysis which can take account of evidence on a variety of different forms of interaction. The regionalisation methodology literature is relatively slight, partly because much of the effort in technical regional science has recently shifted to the extension of Geographic Information System (GIS) techniques, and there are as yet few examples (such as Henry et al., 1995) of GIS developments reaching the regionalisation field. Three main 'traditions' can be identified from reviews such as that of Masser and Schearwater (1980):

1   the longest standing approach is rooted in manual methods and involves a multi-step procedure which typically starts by identifying central cities and moves out to assign other areas to these foci (the official Metropolitan Statistical Area definitions in the USA are the classic example);

2   more statistical approaches, derived from a numerical taxonomy approach, embrace 'black box' methods which typically revolve around a single procedure seeking to maximise a single statistical criterion; and

3   a hybrid of the above two alternatives, adopting a multi-step approach based on a traditional understanding of cities as foci for hinterlands, but using more statistical methods and criteria with successive stages of the analysis.

With regard to the first tradition, Dahmann and Fitzsimmons (1995) collated progress from on-going research into Metropolitan Statistical Area definitions: Among the contributors, Frey and Speare (1995) explicitly cite as 'state-of-the-art' the methodological developments in Britain by Coombes et al. (1986) which in fact represent an abandonment of the first tradition in favour of the third. At the same time, there has been little advance in purely statistical regionalisation methods – the second type of approach identified above – since the developments achieved by Slater (1976) in which the main progress was to be able to process larger datasets than any which had been analysed before then. It is the definition of local labour market area boundaries which has provided an application area to stimulate improved regionalisation methods. These developments have centred on the third type of approach, mainly because it provides an element of statistical optimisation in combination with an algorithm which is based on a model of the urban system. A cross-national review (Eurostat, 1992) concluded that the European Regionalisation Algorithm (ERA) – closely based on the method of Coombes et al. (1986) – provided the most flexible and reliable form of local labour market area definition.

Returning now to the question asked earlier, the conclusion here is that none of these regionalisation methods has yet shown to be able to take into account the information in several different interaction datasets simultaneously. From this perspective, even a 'best practice' method can only mitigate the limitations which are inherent to any approach which is based on a single analysis of a single dataset. The innovation which is required here is to split the whole regionalisation procedure into three phases:

- a compilation of numerous analyses from numerous datasets,

- the collation of the results from these analyses, thereby permitting

- an analysis of this collated dataset to produce a set of boundaries which is a synthesis of the information in the original datasets.

It is the second phase which is new and so requires technical innovations. As a result, the solution devised here centres on phase two of this strategy: taking as input the results of phase one and then creating 'synthetic data' which thus provides the basis for phase three of the method.

Each of the phase one analyses produces a classification of all parts of the country (for the definition of Localities here, the 'building blocks' are the 10,529 wards (sectors in Scotland) from the 1991 Census). Such a classification identifies, for each of these separate input analyses, which of the building block areas are grouped together into a single 'region' by that analysis (i.e. which wards were grouped into the same migration region, or labour market area, or whatever the classification represents). Thus the key information in each classification can be reduced to binary data by taking each pair of building block areas and identifying whether they are (=1) or are not (=0) classified into the same region. In this way, the classification list from each input analysis – which originally assigned a region number to each of the 10,529 areas – becomes re-expressed as a binary matrix of 10,529*10,529 cells (although in practice the matrix is inherently symmetrical, so only half of it is needed). For example, if area B was in the same region as area C but in a different region to area D then the cell BC would take the value 1 while cell BD would be 0 (and cell CD would also take the value 0).

The crucial benefit from re-expressing each separate classification in this binary form is that these matrices can then be cumulated to produce the final synthetic dataset which is needed. For example, if three input analyses were collated in this way, the value in each cell of the final synthetic data matrix would vary from 0 (for any pair of areas which were not in the same region according to any of those analyses) up to 3 (i.e. for any pair of areas which all three analyses had put in the same region). Viewed in GIS terms, the procedure is equivalent to layering the input sets of boundaries on top of each other and counting the number of layers in which there is no boundary between each pair of areas. It can be seen that this approach provides an assessment of the 'strength of evidence' that two areas should be grouped together. The final synthetic dataset provides, it is argued, an ideal basis for the third phase of the definitional procedure: it can also be analysed with a version of ERA which has been optimised for this purpose.

The methodological innovation of creating synthetic data removes the crucial limitation of having to rely upon a single analysis of a single dataset. By initially carrying out more than one form of analysis of the same dataset, and also analysing numerous different datasets, this approach allows that each of these patterns of linkages can then provide a separate input to the synthetic dataset. The regionalisation can then identify the recurring patterns within this range of evidence on different facets of localities, and so will define boundaries which tend to group together areas which have numerous forms of internal linkages.

Data

The substantive challenge here becomes to reap the potential benefit of the synthetic data method by being able to draw upon analyses of different datasets. Whereas previous regionalisations have been based on a single analysis of a single set of flows between areas, the synthetic data can draw upon the evidence of many different datasets. Thus the localities defined here can be based on analyses of both the 1991 Census commuting and migration datasets – as well as other datasets which have not previously been used in regionalisation analyses. In particular, the synthetic data can also draw upon:

• regionalisations based on subsets of the commuting and migration datasets – for example, the pattern of migration by older people can be considered separately so that it is neither drowning out nor dominating the rather different patterns of other age groupings; and

• a range of existing sets of boundaries – such as local authority areas – which are also indicative of which areas might be better kept together.

The sets of existing boundaries can be taken account of (alongside the analyses of interaction datasets) because they too can be reduced to the binary matrix form which, as described earlier, can then be input to the synthetic data.

In moving beyond the 'single analysis of a single dataset' regionalisation, the synthetic data approach shifts the emphasis to seeking and selecting the information on types of flow, and other forms of relevant evidence such as existing boundary sets, which will be relevant as input to the definition of localities. In the event, it proved possible to bring a large volume of relevant information together – although of course it is not possible to claim that this dataset constitutes a fully comprehensive coverage of the locality concept. Figure 3.2 lists the 39 sets of boundaries which have been compiled as phase one of the project. Several general points can summarise this very substantial task:

- the disaggregation of the census commuting and migration datasets provides a major bulwark against the analysis being dominated by, in particular, information on the behaviour of white middle class men of middle age;

- the commuting analyses provide an example of methodological flexibility, because they were produced by two different types of ERA run (termed local labour markets and commuting datasets) so as to ensure that the results are less sensitive to any specific form of analysis; and

- the banking zones were 'weighted' by being entered into the eventual synthetic dataset four times – this ensured that this rare evidence on people's 'journey-to-services' was not overwhelmed by the evidence on commuting or migration patterns (while also demonstrating another methodological option which this approach can support). It is worth stressing here that many other input regionalisations were available, but were rejected for a number of significant reasons. For example, postcode areas were included because it was thought that living in the SW area of London might well be part of a person's sense of identity, but it was not also thought that a sense of identity would often be linked to some of the other available sets of boundaries (such as telephone 'local charge' areas, whose definitions had been made available by BT). In contrast, some boundary sets from previous periods *were* included where they were thought to reflect part of people's sense of identity – most obviously, older County boundaries are reputed to be often cited by people when describing their sense of place (Coombes et al., 1992).

Another point worthy of note here is that there were many more disaggregations of the commuting data possible than were used here, but it was felt that this source should not provide more than a third of all the inputs to the synthetic dataset. Several other boundary sets were also collated but were not included in the synthetic data analysed here. For example, Standard Statistical Regions and television regions were excluded because their large average size that they would have relatively little to add to the definition of locality boundaries. At the same time, it must be recognised that some important patterns of local interaction have not been covered by the datasets compiled here. In particular, the membership and participation in local voluntary organisations proved to be impossible to measure in a consistent way.

A technical problem facing any compilation of boundaries from different sources and eras is that their original definitions are in terms of a wide range of different building block areas. Figure 3.2 shows that the input datasets selected here could each be defined in terms of one of four sets of building block areas. These were all then linkable – so to allow one set of building block areas to be a common denominator – by drawing upon 'look-up tables' created by Owen et al. (1986), who compiled the majority of the boundary sets which were accessed in terms of 1981 wards, and Atkins et al. (1993) who provided the link between 1981 wards and 1991 wards.

Results

The result of this data compilation activity in phase one of the project has been the synthetic data, generated using the method outlined earlier. Figure 3.3 illustrates the synthetic data in part of East Anglia (north east of London), with each line shown connecting a pair of adjacent wards which were found to be in the same region in more than half of the forty-two input sets of areas. It can be seen that the data has an inherent spatial 'structure' which can be clearly visualised and interpreted as localised clusters of inter-linked areas. Figure 3.3 shows, at its very centre, Sudbury and its surrounding wards as a small and rather loosely interconnected cluster (which also has some links to the large clusters centred on Ipswich to the east and Colchester to the southeast).

The ERA software can be readily applied to the synthetic data, and the algorithm's propensity to identify localised clusters in datasets such as commuting matrices here enables it to draw out this geographical structure in the synthetic data. The standard ERA criteria are a 'trade-off' of the size of an area's population and its self-containment (that is, the relative lack of linkage across the area's outer boundary). The self-containment can be here measured in terms of the synthetic data, so that the indicator provides an assessment of

Inputs' 'building block' areas	Official boundaries	Boundaries derived from prior regionalisations
Postcode sectors	Postcode districts Postcode areas	Banking zones *(NB: these were given more 'weight' than other inputs)*
Census (1981) 'small areas'	Parliamentary constituencies Enterprise Council areas Job Centre areas Local Education Authorities Districts/boroughs (as at 1971) Counties (as at 1951)	Functional regions Functional zones Local labour market areas Metropolitan regions Travel-to-work areas *(NB: these are also the current official boundaries for regional policy)*
Census (1991) 'small areas'	Districts (as at 1991) Counties/Scottish regions (as at 1991)	Migration areas of: all people women men all of pensionable age adults 45–p.a. adults 30–44 adults 16–29 children 1–15 wholly migrating households
Census (1991) Wards		Local labour markets of: all workers women men part-time workers full-time workers car commuters public transport users other mode users Commuting clusters of: all workers professionals/managers semiprofessionals non-manuals skilled manuals no/low skilled manuals

Figure 3.2 Inputs to the synthetic data for the localities definition

how far the proposed boundary is separating areas which were grouped together by a large proportion of the input sets of areas. Figure 3.4 illustrates the way that the Localities (shown here with built-up areas as a background) do appear to conform to 'common sense' expectations that most such areas should generally include a main town – with perhaps some nearby satellite towns – together with its rural hinterland.

Figure 3.4 does not in fact feature Sudbury as a Locality in its own right. An area with a relatively small population such as Sudbury would only be deemed to be a separate Locality if its synthetic data showed it to be self-contained to a substantial degree: in other words, the area would need to have relatively few links with other parts of the country. The area of the Stour Valley around the town has been grouped with it as a coherent whole, but they have then been grouped en bloc with the Ipswich area. In this way the Locality boundaries represent a compromise between following the historic County boundary – which would group the town, but only a part of the valley, with Ipswich – and following the main current road and rail links (which would keep together the town and the valley area, but would look more towards Colchester). Such a compromise suggests that the synthetic data does seem to have succeeded in finding the 'balance of advantage' out of the information available within a variety of different input datasets.

It is not coincidental that the number of Localities defined here (307) is quite similar to the widely-used 281 Local Labour Market Areas (LLMAs) of the CURDS Functional Regionalisation (Coombes et al., 1982), the 322 Travel-to-Work Areas (TTWAs) which were defined with the 1981 Census data (Coombes et al., 1986), and the number of local authorities which are emerging from the current revisions. From a statistical viewpoint, it may well be around this level of breakdown at which the advantage of greater detail, from a further subdivision of areas, would be outweighed by the disadvantage of reduced reliability and increased instability of information on areas with smaller populations. From a more geographical viewpoint, further disaggregation would tend to produce less comparable areas because some of the smaller areas would then be exclusively suburban or rural areas. Keeping together the components of each mixed urban-centred area provides more meaningful locality definitions in modern Britain where urban and rural areas are increasingly symbiotic in their linkages.

Of course, there is a vast number of different ways in which 10,529 building block areas can be combined into approximately three hundred groupings. Thus the numerical similarity between the Localities and other sets of areas is potentially misleading, because the Locality boundaries are distinct from any

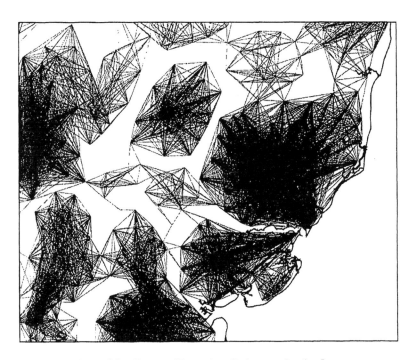

Figure 3.3   Map of Sudbury (East Anglia); synthetic data

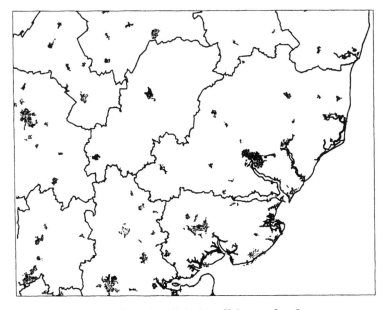

Figure 3.4   Sudbury (East Anglia); localities and urban areas

other set of areas. It is not appropriate here to dwell on a description of the Localities' boundaries, so a few key points only will be made:

• unlike TTWAs and LLMAs the Localities provide a breakdown of Greater London – a breakdown which, unlike the District boundaries, is consistent with the treatment of the other British conurbations;

• unlike TTWAs and Districts the Localities all tend to include at least one identifiable urban centre; and

• unlike all the other sets of boundaries the Localities are defined by reference to the latest Census evidence of interaction patterns, and also to a range of other evidence including the unique journey-to-service information of the banking zones.

Conclusions

This chapter has explored the question of whether statistical techniques for drawing boundaries around place-bound communities can be made relevant to a conception of places which is complex and disparate. The research reported here embraced this complexity, seeking to identify boundaries of Localities – or 'places' – in the Britain of the 1990s. The aim was no less than that these boundaries should provide an up-to-date and relevant definition of local communities across Britain for the very varied purposes of academic social scientists. This daunting task has been tackled by first recognising that a broadly-based set of boundary definitions simply cannot be achieved by applying any of the three established types of regionalisation procedure to a single dataset. The necessary innovation is to apply 'state-of-the-art' software – the European Regionalisation Algorithm – to a collation of the many strands of evidence which are relevant to Locality definitions. This collation is achieved through the development of synthetic data which codifies the critical information in any boundary set into a form which can then be combined with other similar evidence. Thus the first empirical challenge was to collect or create boundary sets which each provide a relevant strand of evidence for the Locality definitions. The chapter finally illustrates the Localities which have been defined on this basis.

The conceptualisation of localities which was adopted here stressed the clustering of a wide range of different types of interaction. To be more specific, six aspects of Localities were identified as the basis for the decisions on which datasets provide relevant information for the definition of locality boundaries. The available data for analysis inevitably left important gaps – examples include local patterns of dialect usage (Orton et al., 1978) – but did break down previously monolithic analyses of migration or commuting, so as to reflect the very different interaction patterns of distinct social groups (Simpson, 1992). This rich database was incorporated within the innovative synthetic data which, in effect, summarises the 'weight of evidence' for drawing one particular boundary rather than another. The boundaries so defined can, at best, provide no more than a 'most purpose' set of locality definitions. Whether they do meet this objective depends on a sufficiently widespread acceptance that their mapping of 'places' – made possible by an advance in regionalisation methods – has succeeded in providing a much less reductionist portrayal of localities in Britain in the 1990s than any alternative set of areas.[1]

Note

1 The boundaries of the Localities defined here are available, for academic research such as the analysis of 1991 Census data, via the Internet on the Midas national research support service (see Coombes et al. 1996).

References

Atkins, D.J.,Charlton, M.E., Dorling, D.F.L. and Wymer, C. (1993), 'Connecting the 1981 and 1991 Censuses', NERRL Research Report 93/9 CURDS, University of Newcastle upon Tyne.

Bell, C. and Newby, H. (1972), *Community Studies: An Introduction to the Sociology of the Local Community*, Allen and Unwin, London.

Cooke, P.N. (ed.) (1986), *Global Restructuring, Local Response*, ESRC, London.

Cooke, P.N. (ed.) (1989), *Localities: The Changing Face of Urban Britain*, Unwin Hyman, London.

Coombes, M.G. (1997), 'Monitoring Equal Employment Opportunity', in Kahn, V. (ed.), *Employment, Education and Housing Among the Ethnic Minorities of Britain*, The Stationery Office, London.

Coombes, M.G., Dixon, J.S., Goddard, J.B., Openshaw, S. and Taylor, P.J. (1982), 'Functional Regions for the Population Census of Britain', in Herbert, D.T. and Johnston, R.J. (eds), *Geography and the Urban Environment*, Vol. 5, Wiley, London.

Coombes, M.G., Green, A.E. and Openshaw, S. (1986), 'An Efficient Algorithm to Generate Official Statistical Reporting Areas: The Case of the 1984 Travel-to-Work Areas Revision in Britain', *Journal of the Operational Research Society*, Vol. 37, pp.943–53.

Coombes, M.G., Green, A.E. and Owen, D.W. (1988), 'Substantive Issues in the Definition of 'Localities': Evidence from Sub-Group Local Labour Market Areas in the West Midlands', *Regional Studies*, Vol. 22, pp.303–18.

Coombes, M.G., Openshaw, S., Wong, C., Hough, H. and Charlton, M. (1992), *Application of Geographic Information Systems to Community Boundary Definitions*, Department of Environment, London.

Coombes, M.G., Wymer, C., Atkins, D. and Openshaw, S. (1996), *Localities and City Regions*, (URL = gopher://cs6400.mc.ac.uk:70/00/midas/datasets/census. dir/censushelp/helpfile/ locality.txt).

Dahmann, D.C. and Fitzsimmons, J.D. (eds) (1995), 'Metropolitan and Nonmetropolitan Areas: New Approaches to Geographical Definition', Population Division Working Paper 12, US Bureau of the Census, Washington DC.

Eurostat, (1992), 'Study on Employment Zones', Eurostat Report E/LOC/20, Luxembourg.

Frey, W. and Speare, A. (1995), in Dahmann and Fitzsimmons (eds), op. cit.

Hall, P., Thomas, R., Gracey, H. and Drewett, R. (1973), *The Containment of Urban England: Urban and Metropolitan Growth Processes or Megalopolis Denied*, Allen and Unwin, London.

Henry, M., Barkley, D. and Brooks, K. (1995), 'RAS: A Regional Analysis System Integrated with ARC/INFO', *Computers, Environment and Urban Systems*, Vol. 18, pp.37–56.

Maclennan, D., Gibb, K. and More, A. (1990), *Paying for Britain's Housing*, Joseph Rowntree Foundation, York.

Masser, I. and Schearwater, J. (1980), 'Functional Regionalisation of Spatial Interaction Data: An Evaluation of Some Suggested Strategies', *Environment & Planning A*, Vol. 12, pp.1357–82.

Massey, D. (1984), *Spatial Divisions of Labour: Social Structures and the Geography of Production*, Methuen, London.

Massey, D. (1995), 'The Conceptualisation of Place', in Massey, D. and Jess, P. (eds), *A Place in the World? Places, Cultures and Globalisation*, Oxford University Press, Oxford.

Openshaw, S. (1984), *The Modifiable Areal Unit Problem*, GeoBooks, Norwich.

Openshaw, S., Wymer, C. and Coombes, M.G. (1988), 'Making Sense of Large Flow Datasets for Marketing and Other Purposes', *North East Regional Research Report*, 88/3, CURDS, University of Newcastle upon Tyne.

Orton, H., Sanderson, S. and Widdowson, J. (1978), *Linguistic Atlas of England*, Croom Helm, London.

Owen, D.W., Green, A.E. and Coombes M.G. (1986), 'Using The Social and Economic Data on the BBC Domesday Interactive Videodisc', *Transactions of the IBG*, Vol. NS11, pp.305–14.

Rogers, A.W. (1987), 'Voluntarism, Self-Help and Rural Community Development', *Journal of Rural Studies*, Vol. 3, pp.353–60.

Royal Commission on Local Government in England (1969), *Report*, Cmnd 4040, HMSO, London.

Simpson, W. (1992), *Urban Structure and the Labour Market*, Clarendon, Oxford.

Slater, P.B. (1976), 'A Hierarchical Regionalisation of Japanese Prefectures Using 1972 Inter Prefectural Migration Flows', *Regional Studies*, Vol. 10, pp.123–32.

Chapter Four

Imagined Value:
The Poetics and Politics of Place

Jean Hillier

Introduction

A feature of planning practice in the western world in the late 1980s and 1990s has been an insistence that '...room must be made for progress; the essential facilities of a growing...society must go somewhere' (Plotkin, 1987, p.2). The empirical patterns of land use which represent such 'progress', however, are often the results of the complex interplay of actors' diverse cultural perceptions, images and values underlying the activity of local planning policy-making. To divorce analysis of the output from the process amounts to divorcing analysis of action from discourse. Such a divorce misconstrues the nature of planning decision-making. As a result, we fail to understand the choices through which people become participants in processes and contribute to decisions.

In this chapter, I discuss ways in which different planners and community groups perceive themselves, their, or others' geographical places and other groups respectively, revealing cultural differences of self- and place-identity, of discourses and values; in other words, situated knowledges. I disassemble conceptions of place to understand the incorporation of identity. I explore, with relation to actant-networks, ways in which different values may come into play in influencing perceptions and politics and planning outcomes. The chapter thus resonates with that of Nigel Thrift (Chapter Two) in that it is bound up with the world of emotions, desires and imaginations of the various actants and their networks of associations.

In order for us to understand the dynamics of planning decision-making we need to explore the stories and networks of the actants involved. I tell stories from the Swan Valley in the North East Corridor of Perth, Western Australia; stories from various groups of people involved in attempting to influence a planning decision concerned with urbanisation of a semi-rural area on the metropolitan fringe. My analysis is based on a contextualised reading of the discursive and symbolic terrain generated by the urbanisation proposal. I demonstrate how individuals and groups can reinterpret and reimagine place, symbols and practices; how they can mobilise different values and logics to serve their purposes. As individuals, groups and organisations struggle to transform the social relations between them they produce new 'truths' by which to explain and understand themselves, their practices and their societies.

Values, Images, Identities

'...Identity – our sense of ourselves as individuals and as social beings – is constructed through social processes rather than being innate or pre-given' (Bondi, 1993, cited in Pred, 1997, p.124). We see the world and give identity to place through our particular self-identities and reimagine our identities as we see and interpret our relation to the world.

Identities of self and of place are intrinsically related. Moreover, identities of both are complex and dynamic; multiple identities or multiple subject positions, each of which is subject to political transformation and change. As Massey (1991, p.278) writes, '...there are indeed multiple meanings of places, held by different social groups, (and) the question of which identity is dominant will be the result of social negotiation and conflict'. There can be no one reading of place. Planners have traditionally sought to 'balance' readings, but have often brought to the very act of 'balancing', particular mind-sets which have, perhaps unconsciously, biased the scales.

Planners may also underestimate the importance of residents' attachment to their local areas and how it comprises a vital component of their social identity. A threat to their physical environment thus becomes a threat to the self.[1] Traditional forms of planning decision-making have tended to convey a message of place as identified and controlled by outsiders (the planners). Plans and policies are loaded with material, ideological and political content which may perpetuate injustices and do violence to those values, images and identities which have not been traditionally recognised. Instead of regarding places as areas with particular boundaries around, they should be imagined as '...articulated moments in networks of social relations and understandings' (Massey, 1991, p.28):

> it cannot be otherwise that identity repeatedly becomes undermined, problematic, an issue, something to be reworked, reconstructed, retrieved, or struggled over in order to reanchor (Pred, 1997, p.126).

Place becomes one of the terms of reference for the negotiation and articulation of identity. The social practices of discourse and communication are vital components of deliberation. It is therefore important to consider how the discourse of planning functions ideologically to shape attention and rationalise policy decisions; how it '...mediates among the choices made available to us, the values we collectively espouse, and our ability to act...about how we should live and invest, where and with whom' (Beauregard, 1993, pp.5–6).

In addition to the discourse of planners we need to pay attention to the ways in which other people verbalise their places in the world, their values and identities. Meanings may become more important than facts in policy deliberation. The resulting plan is '...a reworking of everyday narratives to find a potentially truer, more comprehensive one...Planning commands time by taking the narratives we have in mind and refashioning them' (Krieger, 1981, p.141).

Planning requires giving voice, ear and respect (Healey, 1992) to all participants and their values, images and identities. It means understanding the subjective nature of identity and how '...identifications emerge from the social relations we participate in and the discourses...that give them meaning' (Gibson-Graham, 1995, p.276). These social relations and discourses may serve as barriers or offer opportunities for identity building. The process of the planned transformation of place is thus both formative and disruptive of identity.

Critical Theoretical Considerations of Identity and Image

Critical theoretical approaches recognise the contingency of knowledge and understandings of self- and place-identity. Through recognition that '...norms, beliefs, identity and practices are intersubjectively constituted and historically and contextually contingent' (Leonard, 1990, p.261) we can explore different values, images and identities and how they relate in the planning process. It offers the opportunity to examine the '...knowing from within' (Shotter, 1993a) of various participants and how such knowing is placed within social, moral and political systems.

In addressing influences on the formation and expression of participants' values, images and identities, Habermas' concept of the lifeworld provides us with a helpful starting point. In brief, participants' lifeworlds comprise their perspectives of the acting subject. The lifeworld is a product of both historical traditions surrounding people and the processes of socialisation in which they are reared (Habermas, 1990, p.137).

Lifeworlds are both situation and background, both conscious and unconscious (Love, 1995, p.57).

Actors (and therefore their lifeworlds) come together at nodal points, or temporary fixations around which identities and politics are sutured in dialogic contestation of identities. A communicative participation programme can act in this manner as the nodal point or temporary fixation for the meaning and discussion of identities and values.

We should note, however, as Massey (1995) reminds us, that power is intrinsic to the constitution and reconstitution of identity. The power structures inherent in the traditional planning system, for example, have favoured elected representatives and officers of governance, who may have brought specific mind-sets and identities, both of place and local resident participants, to discussion. Fixed images lead to non-receptivity and result in participants talking past each other rather than engaging in open debate. These images and identities must be deconstructed if equivalence is to be achieved. We need to conceive of participants (or 'social agents') not as unitary subjects, but rather as '...the articulation of an ensemble of subject positions, constructed within specific discourses and always precariously and temporarily sutured at the intersection of those subject positions' (Mouffe, 1992, p.237).

The locality itself can therefore be conceptualised as comprising layers of different outcomes over time, as actors have pursued their perceived subject positions and interests, often in competition with others. Place is a meeting point where sets of social relations (i.e. actant-networks) intersect (Marsden et al., 1993).

In an actant-network, actors and actants[2] in discrete situations become bound into wider sets of relations which alter the nature of their existing worlds (Murdoch and Marsden, 1995, p.378, n.3). Commitment to such networks provides forms of identity and the basis for action. In activities such as public participation for land use planning decisions, several different actant-networks (including those of non-human actors and actants, such as aspects of nature (e.g. Callon's (1986) example of scallops in St Brieuc Bay; and Latour, 1992), and non-human intermediaries between actants and networks, (such as texts or money) will overlap and align with each other. Constructing a new network(s) by drawing upon actants and intermediaries already in established networks, (e.g. the local authority planning system, residents' associations etc), the actant-network approach allows us to begin to understand how certain actants/networks are able to impose their views over those of others.

Actant-network theory is based on the idea that as actants struggle with each other, they determine their existence, define their characteristics and attempt to exert themselves upon others through various human and non-human intermediaries. Callon (1986, 1991) terms the act of an actant exerting itself upon others as 'translation'. This process involves the four, but not necessarily sequential, nor mutually separate, stages of: incorporation – actors/actants join and are woven into networks; interessement – actants exert influence over others via persuasion that their position is the best one. Competing alliances are undermined; enrolment – actants lock others into their definitions and network so that their behaviour is channelled in the direction desired by the enrolling actant(s); and mobilisation – the actant now speaks for/acts as ventriloquist for (Haraway, 1992) represents the others who have become 'redefined' and passive. The representations of interest made by the lead actants are accepted as legitimate by those ostensibly being represented. The represented are reduced to being recipients of action.

Translation is therefore the mechanism by which society takes form. Unpacking these mechanisms enables us to begin to understand some of the power relationships in the land use planning decision process; an explanation of '...how a few obtain the right to express and to represent the many silent actors of the social and natural worlds they have mobilised' (Callon, 1986, p.224).

The notion of power is central to the actant-network approach, developing, as it does, Foucauldian ideas of power/knowledge. Action is power-full.

> Those who are powerful are not those who 'hold' power but those who are able to enrol, convince and enlist others into associations on terms which allow these initial actors to 'represent' all the others (Murdoch and Marsden, 1995, p.372).

In so doing, they displace or speak for the others whom they have deprived of a voice by imposing their definitions, images and values upon them.[3] A network is thus composed of representations of beliefs, values, images and identities, of self, others and place. Debate and conflict occur if new representations challenge ('betray') the legitimacy of the old.

Actants will utilise whatever resources/intermediaries (including scientific documents, surveys, petitions etc) are available to them in order to persuade other actors to their representation or view in the pursuit of their goals.[4] Inevitably, some actors/actants will be able to mobilise a greater amount of resources than others'. In addition, although representers claim to speak for those represented, '...a representation cannot capture all there is to be represented' (Marsden et al., 1993, p.31). The represented, or non-present, (e.g. nature, people of lower socioeconomic status who tend not to participate, those not yet moved into the area, the unborn etc) could always 'speak' differently. Translation, if left to its own devices, is seldom equitable or just.

Places are therefore 'shaped' by the representations of actant-networks. They are dynamic; constructed representations by actors/actants at a particular point in time, building upon the remains of previous rounds of representation and struggle.[5]

Actant-network theory deflects the focus of analysis away from the idea of self-contained propositional utterances '...spoken from nowhere' by planners as though in a neutral space, towards:

> textured locations where it matters who is speaking and where and why, and where such mattering bears directly upon the possibility of knowledge claims, moral pronouncements, descriptions of 'reality' achieving acknowledgement, going through (Code, 1995, p.x).

Translation becomes a struggle for discursive hegemony and a means of representing place, remaking it and altering it in the process.

Examination of networks enables us to unpack how domains of inquiry and representation are constructed so that certain representations can be made and others cannot:

> not because of any explicit prohibition or because they are clearly beside the point, but because of ossified perceptions of what the point is; because they do not fit, do not mesh with what points in the established discourse know how to respond to – and because of a reluctance to reconsider those boundaries (Code, 1995, p.4).

The identification and definition of a planning policy problem therefore cannot be taken for granted, but depends on its discursive representation. The very act of definition is itself a powerful one, restricting alternative views and constructs, and in many instances '...the choice of a definition of such a problem ... typically determines its 'solution' (Harmon and Mayer, 1986, p.9).

It is also important to note that the struggle over translation does not take place in a vacuum, but in the context of the existing institutional praxis and actor/actant-spaces (Law, 1992) of planning. This gives planners and those participants who are comfortable with the discourse of planning a distinct advantage over those who are not. The abilities to '... persuade, impress and inspire ... are distributed unevenly' (Turner, 1994, p.111), and as a result, '... any representation tends to take sides, even as it comforts itself with the illusion that it does not' (Clegg and Hardy, 1996, p.698).

Through acts of translation one or few imageries win out over others which are less acceptable to decision-makers and their target group. Clashes of imagery may include local residents' representations of their area as a place to live, home, a lifestyle, tradition, as opposed to governance's images of a space to develop, space to make profits, the future. There is conflict between interests, values and views of what the area is and what it ought to become (Massey, 1991, p.276). Development is out to work in one way or another for political ends (Sujic, 1992, p.84). In the process, local citizens may be losers, but few people care to look.

Images and Identities: the Poetics of Space and Place

In order to understand the behaviour of actants in actant-networks, it is important to comprehend their images/identities of who, where, why and how they are. As such, I now offer an exploration of these key concepts, with emphasis on citizens and agencies of governance.

The late 1980s and 1990s have witnessed the intellectual meetings of what Agnew and Duncan (1989) term the geographical and sociological 'imaginations'.[6] These meetings have re-emphasised the importance of space and place and, often, drawing on the work of Michel Foucault, their interconnections with power. Space is now rarely represented in social and cultural theory as:

> neutral, continuous, transparent...Instead...space itself [is] refigured as inhabited and heterogeneous, as a moving cluster of points of intersection for manifold axes of power which cannot be reduced to a unified plane or organised into a single narrative (Hebdige, 1990, p.vi).

It is now generally accepted that space and place are socially constructed out of human interrelations and interactions. Several authors have rejuvenated Hägerstrand's concept of space/time geography (e.g. Massey, 1993), whilst in debates around identity, space and place also figure prominently. Pred (1984, p.279), for example, identifies place as involving:

an appropriation and transformation of space and nature that is inseparable from the reproduction and transformation of society in time and space. As such, place is not only what is fleetingly observed on the landscape ... it also is what takes place ceaselessly.

That which '... takes place ceaselessly' is not simply physical creation and de-creation of landscape, but also sociocultural mediation of a '... felt sense of the quality of life (Pred, 1983, p.58).[7]

The shaping of place is the outcome of power struggles between various actant-networks' identities, images, aspirations and values within the existing social order. Harvey (1973, p.31) suggests that if we are to '...evaluate the spatial form of the city, we must, somehow or other, understand its creative meaning as well as its mere physical dimensions'. We need to go beyond identification of conflicts of interest to unpack the cultural differences in participants' lifeworlds which influence their ways of giving meaning, value and expression to tangibles and intangibles and the different aspects of meaning which are formulated through such interpretations: the poetics of place. We need to understand how the same sets of signs are read differently by different people and how people make connections between their interpretations of things and the overall ordering process of the planning system. It is this idea that meaning is a sociocultural construction which foregrounds representational processes (such as public participation strategies) as being hermeneutic and ideological that underpins my debate. (See also Derrida, 1994.)

It should not be surprising, then, that people react to proposals for urban change in a variety of ways, not all of which are comprehensible to others involved, yet which may well be patterns of action guided by deeply entrenched beliefs, norms and values from their lifeworlds. '...Social space, therefore, is made up of a complex of individual feelings and images about and reactions towards the spatial symbolism which surrounds that individual' (Harvey, 1973, p.34). It should also not be surprising that many of these different images and values conflict with and counteract each other.

Planners' traditional 'external' (Thomas, 1994, p.34) and powerful location has important implications for the understanding and discussion of claims, values and identities. It has tended to obviate a truly participatory approach in which participants have the opportunity to enter into relationships of reciprocal respect. Instead, it has hegemonically validated particular, specific forms of evidence, stressed the importance of a separation between the knower and the known, and treated personal characteristics of the knower as irrelevant. Observations are regarded as objective intellectual positions rather than as social constructs, thereby denying local contextuality and difference. Stories are irrelevant.

Planners fail to recognise that their own rational technical discourse and its professional terms and definitions are themselves social constructs. Moreover, they deny themselves, as well as other participants, the opportunity to ensure that their stories are respectfully understood. Stories provide a link between private and public realms, they provide insights into meanings, behaviours, values, images and identities. '... Communities cannot exist without stories' (Maines and Bridger, 1992, p.366).

Other important aspects influencing outcomes include structural power differences between participants and their networks which may give some people more advantage or control over others; the history of relationships between participants, including previous experiences and prior attitudes and beliefs about each other which participants bring to the discussion; and also the social environment in which participation takes place. All the above serve to influence the type of relationship participants will have with the networks and processes in which they engage with each other (Lerner and Whitehead, 1980).

I offer below some stories as illustrations of a range of different values, images and identities and their influences on actors' behaviours. The stories represent a small (and inevitably biased) sample of those told in the debate over government proposals for urbanisation of a semi-rural area in the northeast of Perth, Western Australia.[8]

Responses to Proposals for Urban Change: Stories from the North East Corridor, Perth, Western Australia

Perth is located in the south west of Western Australia on the Indian Ocean coast. Urban and regional planning began in Western Australia with white settlement of an Aboriginal-occupied country in 1829. Since that time, the Perth metropolitan region has grown from a small, isolated colonial outpost into a modern metropolis with a population forecast of some two million people by 2021. Several local authorities, in particular those at the urban fringe, such as the Shire of Swan, are experiencing increases of up to 6 per cent a year, while population densities remain notoriously low. In 1990 Perth's overall urban density was just 10.8 persons per hectare, a figure comparable with that for rural Europe. Perth thus represents a sprawling mass whose tentacles are reaching out to devour the green fringes of the built-up area. The Swan Valley represents one of these fringes in the northeast of the metropolitan area. Located in a region of overall water shortage, relying on ground water reserves, the Valley is a delicate, low lying environment, with a high water table, prone to flooding. White residents enjoying semi-rural lifestyles, engaging in viticulture, small holding farming and so on, live close to Aboriginal communities in an area of considerable Aboriginal and white settler heritage. The practice of settler communities living *on* the land, exploiting it for its natural resources and using it to grow crops and for building upon, contrasts starkly with the Aboriginal concept of living *with* the land, in sustainable harmony, a land alive with spirituality, rich with human sharing in the past and present. Yet what represents some 120,000 or so years of history and culture is in danger of disappearing under western-influenced 'civilisation' and bureaucracy.

The Western Australian state government in 1990 identified a potential population for the North-East Corridor by 2021 of 225,000 people, an increase of some 220,000 over the existing total and to be housed predominantly in 'urban villages' (see also Lloyd-Jones et al., this volume). Although planners adopted a 'participatory' approach to planning in the Corridor, in an attempt to reach consensus, tensions remained between the values, images and identities of the different participants, as indicated below.

'The Spirit of the Swan Valley'

Individuals and groups create identity for themselves and the places they represent through their stories. As the stories below indicate, actors live in '...imagined environments' (Donald, 1992) or '...communities of memory' (Bellah et al., 1985) which are regarded as being 'ours' and 'mine' rather than 'theirs' (Shotter, 1993b, p.125). Images, identities and values are socially constructed. They are complex and dynamic, reflecting the continually negotiated transactions going on between actors. Identities and images may infer perceived (il)legitimacy of behaviour and value judgements as to land use, lifestyles and so on.

Fifty-five actors in the North East Corridor public participation process were interviewed regarding their images of the Swan Valley area. Actors included officers of governance at State (Ministry for Planning, Main Roads Department, Water Corporation, Department of Environmental Protection) and at local authority levels, elected members, developers and local residents. Local resident respondents included vignerons, horsiculturalists, poultry farmers, artists, teachers, architects, craftspeople and others. An interview was also conducted with Mr Robert Bropho of the Aboriginal Nyungah Circle of Elders. Some actors strongly supported the urbanisation proposals while others just as strongly opposed them.

The stories below are those of multiple subjectivities; of actors with a variety of identities, images and values. The Swan Valley is a place which many actors call home, but it has become a place of power plays, conflict and struggle, full of difference and touched by the power brought to bear on it by the identities and networks which strove to ground themselves in its place (Honig, 1996).

In order to lend some comprehensible structure to the analysis, I have chosen to explore actors' images under broad categories of officers of governance (predominantly planning officers) and local residents,[9] using headings of several themes which were mentioned regularly; the environment, home, rural lifestyle, a working area and heritage. There also appeared to be distinct differences between the actors themselves in terms of their perceptions of their and others' self- and place-identities. For instance, there were marked differences, sometimes overlapping, sometimes conflicting, between those who were pro-urbanisation and anti-urbanisation, between long- and short-term residents (excluding Aboriginal peoples), between Euro-Australians and Aboriginal people and between what were perceived as being legitimate or illegitimate uses of land.

I am aware of the hegemonic dangers of classification and the potential trap of regarding categorised identities as fixed. I offer the classifications as temporary aids to cognition rather than cognition itself (Horkheimer and Adorno, 1991, p.219) and hold them open to scrutiny and reformulation. The categories are diverse composite identities, full of differences of opinion, values and images, offered as a temporary determination only; '…a provisional nodal point subverted, asserted, and reconstituted through (the) contingent social relations' (Natter and Jones, 1997, p.149) of the North East Corridor/Swan Valley public participation process.

Officers of Governance – Form and Function

Officers of governance tended to hold functional and professional images of the Swan Valley area, centred on issues related to their work. An officer from the Department of Environmental Protection, for example, described the Swan Valley in terms of its:

> key issues: a source of groundwater, uncleared bush (101).

Planning officers' imagery was dominated by location and topography:

> a large area divided by the river into two distinct parts (004).

> there is the railway, and the location of the vineyards. The core area is the area with the best vineyards etc. West of West Swan Road there are more sandy soils, a few vineyards...There was sand mining north of Gnangara Road, Ellenbrook and some pine plantation (113).

and land use:

> a mix of urban/rural residential and rural (001).

> a scenic route on the western side. The eastern rural area is a working area with wayside stalls (021).

> the western side is more tourists. The eastern side is a rural area – horticulture. It's working rural (004).

Space is assumed to be neutral:

> complacently understood to be fully defined by dimensional measurements ... and by trigonometric descriptions of the geometrical relationships between objects, which are thought to sit in a kind of vacuum (Shields, 1997, p.187).

Space is a 'container' of activity; of living, farming and tourism. There is little explicit recognition of the value judgements in any of these images. Where officers did give some overt impression of value, it was often negative:

> it's really not core, but grazing with weeds (004).

> viticulture/market gardeners' kids are now not wanting to stay on the property but to subdivide and move out. Current production has virtually ceased in market gardens. Swan Valley viticulture is only 23% of WA's grapes (004).

The area is not seen as an entity in itself with intrinsic value, but rather for what it can produce, extrinsic economic value. As such, from the above planner's images, it would appear to be of little value other than for subdivision for residential development. Land is regarded as a resource, to be given value through human exploitation and 'productivity'. This use value is economically measured.

Only one planning officer, despite stating planning to be a 'technical job', saw beyond functional imagery to:

a very special place, of high landscape value to the community and of high heritage value (072).

His was to be a voice, however, literally in the wilderness.

A planning officer's view of the Swan Valley and the North East Corridor tends to be Euclidean and instrumental. It regards the area in two-dimensional form on a map, geometrically divisible into discrete lots for the provision of housing and urban infrastructure, and as having no value in itself:

but rather its only value lies in its being 'put to work' as an instrument in the restless process of production: the 'being of things' is eclipsed by the 'doing of things'(Hoggett, 1992, p.107).

This is a view of 'physical space' which, Bauman (1993, p.145) suggests, is arrived at through the:

phenomenological reduction of daily experience to pure quantity, during which distance is 'depopulated' and 'extemporalised' – that is, systematically cleansed of all contingent and transitory traits ...

which may include Aboriginal history and sacred sites.

Planners' visual geography is presented as being objective; a verifiable truth. However, appearances often deceive. '... This is the duplicity of vision' (Rodaway, 1994, p.124). Sight both offers the observer a detached, so-called objective view, but yet it is that very sight which gives a selective interpretation of appearances by its choice of composition. This composition of view is subjective, determined by cultural (in this instance, professional) practice. The maps and plans which result from the planners' view suggest '... a detachment from the world and a power or control over the world in the hands of the map owner (or reader) which previously was the preserve of God. This is perhaps to speculate, but nevertheless the bird's eye view is a different style of use of the eye to everyday visual experience down on the ground in amongst the houses and streets, farms and fields of day-to-day life' (Rodaway, 1994, p.141).

Planners' representations tend to formulate '... all the problems of society into questions of space' (Lefebvre, 1996, p.99). Aesthetic and cultural values are ignored or transformed into quantities in equations of spatial residential demand and supply. The rational technical corporate narrative of planning focuses on 'growth' and 'progress', marginalising alternative stories about the meaning and value of place (Trigger, 1997). To question this narrative of space is to question planners' reality (Shields, 1997).

Local Residents – 'Strong, Capable and Creative Individuals'

A 'Peaceful, Restful and Beautiful' Environment Despite the Shire's advertising of the Swan Valley being dominated by environmental images and permeated by the colour green (Shire of Swan, 1996), few local residents mentioned the natural environment as an important theme. Of those who did so, most were impressed by:

> a peaceful, restful and beautiful area (047).

> an impression of space and open areas (106).

The founders of the Ellenbrook Environmental Group specifically mentioned the 'flora and fauna' (112) and the importance of nature:

> natural resources can't be replaced (112).

but only one resident took a more holistic view:

> this is all an environmental system which is part of the health of the river. It all contributes in an intrinsic way to the health,…an intrinsic link between what happens on the land and the health of the area and the river (045).

Others, held a less favourable image of the environment:

> a bit scrappy; urban blight (107).

> lots of renters and vacant lots (107).

> full of noxious weeds (Patterson's Curse) (049).

> a dust bowl – waste land (041).

and supported plans for urbanisation to produce what they regarded as:

> a more aesthetical [*sic*] environment (049).

Home – 'The Place of Milk and Honey' For most residents, the Swan Valley as home is an integral component of their imagery and identity of the area and its value to them. Whether this be as a working area or affording a rural lifestyle as explored below, the notion of home was frequently mentioned, with respondents often emphasising their lineage in the Valley as a badge of pride and legitimacy (of both residence and opinion):

> I've lived here all my life. My parents and grandparents lived here. It's a fifth generation business (109).

> one's childhood and having been brought up here and your father and father's fathers having worked on the land (056).

> my parents worked here. I was born here (104).

> I've lived here for 23 years. I've brought up my kids here (107).

> with my parents working a vineyard since 1960, it was a support base for myself and my family (044).

A colonial pedigree was regarded as a matter of some honour. The 120,000 years or so of Aboriginal presence in the area, however, was invisible. The Swan Valley identity is of a white settler area, the descendants of whom still live there and call the Valley 'home'.

Several residents clearly regarded their home as property; an economic investment in lieu of/in addition to their superannuation, or as an asset to leave to their children:

> I saw my own land as superannuation (107).

while others perceived it as a haven, emphasising the aesthetic value of the area:

> my image of this place is 'paradise'. It's the place of milk and honey, because one person sells milk and someone else sells honey (043).

Home, therefore, is imagined as a site of security (financial/lifestyle) and identity. It is portrayed as a place of nurturing (raising families and crops) and respect. However, as is well known, home is often in reality a site of insecurity and threat. It is these anxieties, translocated to the external environment of the Swan Valley, which spurred residents to become involved in the participation programme in order to 'protect' their romanticised image of home.

A Rural Lifestyle of 'Spacious Comfort' The location of the Swan Valley on the fringes of the Perth metropolitan area offers residents a semi-rural environment, with vistas over a green landscape, combined with reasonably good access (thirty minutes by car) to the CBD:

> the best of both worlds (063).

> there is close proximity to the city and race tracks and there is the country-type lifestyle (048).

> rural but close to the city (105).

The image of a rural lifestyle is clearly important to residents, who spoke emotively and emotionally about the area. Residents valued:

> the peace and quiet of the place (051).

> space away from noise and people (051).

> an alternative place to live. It's affordable and is spacious (044).

> freedom and space ... spacious comfort (064).

Spaciousness is a key aspect of the above. The residents value space and low density living as a good environment for both raising children and for retiring:

> animals and space. A good place to bring up a family (070).

> an ideal spot for retirement and relaxing (068).

> a good place to retire to (047).

One person even suggested that:

> neighbours get on because of the distance (070).

contrasting with planners' oft-heard claims that high residential densities are necessary for 'building community'.
      Aesthetic values are important, based in subjectivity and in intangibles such as 'freedom', 'peace and quiet' and 'space'.

'Identity to the Valley' – A Working Area For other residents, the image of the Swan Valley is as a working area. This is an economic image, based in affording residents an income. It also gives them an identity, either from viticulture:

> this area's primary industry is viticulture and dried fruit production. It also gives identity to the Valley (056).

poultry farming:

> viticulture, winery and poultry farming in a heavy way – a classical rural area (073).

or craft and tourism:

> I work from home as an artist and we make furniture. We're strong, capable and creative individuals of the land (042).

The notion of a 'Right to Farm' was mentioned on several occasions:

> I come from the Right to Farm point of view (056).

> you need things like the Right to Farm policy (104).

> we're heavily involved in the Right to Farm (073).

These statements raise ethical questions of who and what has rights; humans? nature?, whether property rights include rights over types of use? and whether that use may impact upon others (such as wind-borne pesticides, salination etc)? Should farmers have a Right to Farm if they thereby degrade and salinate their land?

Tourism – An Opportunity for 'Growth' Economic values also underlie the identity of the Swan Valley as a tourist area:

> an opportunity for tourist growth as a green area so close to the city (108).

> an impression of space and open areas associated with the wine industry, offers the passive recreation of the river and soft tourism potential (106).

There is disagreement, however, between those people who envisage tourists as being attracted to open space and green landscapes and who oppose plans for urbanisation:

if we don't protect it we're mad (041).

and those who earn their living from tourist-related industries (crafts, restaurants etc), some of whom regard urbanisation (providing it is not in their back yards) as offering the potential for increased custom:

> because we have to make money (042).

> you legislate so people will invest money and develop agricultural tourism and a style of living that will make money and give employment to quite a lot of younger people. Not just a park. Some people think with tourism, everything has to be beautiful, look nice, not smell. We are a working area (042).

Parks, which do not 'make money' are thus implied to be of little, if any, value. Aesthetic values are seen as of secondary importance to economic values (and associated odours) even though it may be the aesthetic qualities which actually attract tourists to the Valley.

Several of the vignerons were themselves ambivalent, recognising potential problems linked with an increased population in proximity to vineyards (restrictions on pesticide spraying, hours of wine-making etc), yet relishing the prospect of an increased market for their produce. They resolved their dilemma by lobbying:

> to save as much of the Swan Valley as possible, especially the most vital parts (especially the fertile soils for vines) and were prepared to give up areas like West Swan and Henley Brook which aren't really part of the Valley anyway (109).

except to those who live there perhaps?

I also question the extent to which incoming residents to the North East Corridor would be likely to purchase local handmade furniture, paintings, and boutique wines from the cellar door.

Heritage – A Piece of White History As indicated in the section on imagery/identity as 'home', many residents were proud of the perceived heritage of the Swan Valley area. This heritage was almost exclusively seen as white colonial settler heritage:

> a piece of history. The first area settled. Lots of original inhabitants' descendants (108).

I'm from a family of first settlers. I have a sense of admiration for those early immigrant settlers like the Yugoslavs and the Italians (071).

born in the Valley into a pioneering family. Full of heritage (062).

the Slav and Italian people who made the Swan Valley and showed us how to grow grapes (047).

The 120,000 years of Aboriginal heritage in the area remained invisible, unvalued.

Some people felt 'insulted' that officers of governance appeared to ignore their views:

> I feel very insulted that they take so little notice of those who have looked after the land for so many years … I don't think they realise what it means to work a piece of land and own it for part of your lifetime, and then they come in and say 'we are going to take a portion of it'. It's not fair. The bureaucracy come and take what land they say they need away. It leaves you hurt and annoyed by having something that is yours taken away. They don't understand the central importance of the pieces of land (047).

A resident of English colonial descent, whose ancestors may have engaged in 'cleansing' the land of Aboriginal people, here passionately expresses anger and loss at land being 'taken away'. She ironically has no thought for the Aboriginal peoples who themselves 'looked after the land for so many years' only to have it 'taken away' from them. She cannot recognise the 'hurt' and 'annoyance' which Aboriginal people must have felt and still feel.

Only one resident recognised the heritage of Aboriginal people in the Swan Valley:

> Aboriginals were never given special interest as the original owners of the land (112).

contrasting with the 'terra nullius' assumptions of other residents, developers and officers of governance.

Differences of Opinion

As illustrated by the above, residents' self- and place-identities, images of the area and values often varied widely with respect to the same issue. I now turn to offer some understanding of these variations, according to crude distinctions between those who were pro-urbanisation or anti-urbanisation, Euro-Australian or Aboriginal, long-term or short-term residents, and between what was regarded as 'legitimate' or 'illegitimate' use of land.

'Our Own Interests at Heart' – Pro-urbanisation and Anti-urbanisation There were residents who

> were arguing that the land was their superannuation and they'd be unable to sell it if it wasn't zoned urban (109).

and others who

> will naturally sacrifice other people's back yards for their own (109).

Several residents who supported the urbanisation proposals believed their land was bound to increase in economic value:

> We wanted a subdivision of our land to 1 to 5 acre blocks, but this proposal was knocked back...We've lost in finances by thousands of dollars (049).

Others, such as the craftspeople, largely supported urbanisation as they regarded an increased population as a source of potential custom and income:

> because we have to make money we understand that we couldn't let the development of Perth by-pass the Valley because Joe Blow and such and such didn't want it (042).

On the other hand, residents who opposed urbanisation tended to do so from a more aesthetic and lifestyle perspective. Their image of the Swan Valley was, as indicated earlier, that of

> spacious comfort (064).

and for keeping

> a horse [in] the peace and quiet of the place (051).

In the North East Corridor, however, predominantly due to effective lobbying and mobilisation of others by an actant-network comprising a number of Valley businesspeople (restaurateurs, artists, vignerons etc),[10] the image of the eastern side of the Valley as a working area of small businesses with tourism-generating potential, became accepted and influenced the Minister for Planning's decision to relocate new residential development in the west. For 'lifestylers' such as the above, '... the horse had already bolted' (108)!

'About Our Values' – Euro-Australian and Aboriginal Residents As indicated above, the image of the Swan Valley held by most residents was of an area of white settler heritage; people who 'improved' the land through industrious and courageous settlement. Aboriginal people did not

> figure (047).

in such an image.
  Aboriginal people were often perceived in the negative, with claims of sacred sites being in the way of white people and progress:

> Aboriginals got involved claiming the land was the home of the golden swamp tortoise or some such thing (043).

> the Aboriginal Bennett Brook campaign was a 'no go' area. This area was declared a special place and preserved. As far as the people who have been living in the area for generations, their values were not considered whatsoever (055).

Residents' revisionist images of local history ignore the length of Aboriginal presence in the Swan Valley and the important spiritual value of sacred sites:

> sacred sites were claimed to be in the area. If you bring in minority groups (i.e. Aboriginals), they focus on their own need, have their own agenda, alienate the institutions and the majority of the community and take over (067).

as if Euro-Australian interest groups act differently!
  This local councillor continued:

> there is a time to bring them in, when a broad set of parameters have been set. Bropho is not indigenous to the area. Involving them reduces our credibility as a group with the departments and instrumentalities (067).

Omission of Mr Bropho's honorific as a Nyungah Elder may be due to cultural ignorance. However, the speaker cannot comprehend that his claim that only indigeneity affords legitimacy of opinion would equally silence the voices of everyone else.

A suggestion that Aboriginal people were:

> the original owners of the land (112).

was not echoed by any other Euro-Australian residents.
Aboriginal images and place-identity of the Swan Valley are very different
from those of the Euro-Australians. Aboriginal people value the land for its
spiritual and mythological significance. They come from and are part of the
land. Their everyday existence, their past and their future are intrinsically
interrelated with the land, as Mr Robert Bropho, of the Nyungah Circle of
Elders indicates:

> we're the last of the river people in this area'All the dreaming stories are still
> within our minds (112).

> we've stood here hard and long. My mum stood here – she's dead – my sisters
> and brothers, my granddaughter, we sit for a cause and a purpose. The land is
> important (112).

> us people, me and my friends, my sisters and brothers, my mother and father
> that's dead, we stood in those vineyards when they was in full bloom,…but all
> that's gone, that's gone … The top of the vineyards with the Reid Highway
> cutting across and smashing out the areas where we trod once; all the springs up
> along Bennett Brook have stopped flowing, the natural springs where we drunk
> water (112).

The loss of family and of the land is heartfelt. It threatens Aboriginal
people's very existence:

> you're building your white society, your concrete jungles, your suburbias, …
> but where's ours, what was once ours? We can be forced out, dragged out of the
> land, our roots out, pushed out, moved here, moved there, assimilated, become
> nothing, become part of a movement that'll die out (112).

> these trees here won't be on the land any more. They'll be gone: sheoak, jarrah,
> woolly bush. They'll all be gone … All the natural plants will be flattened and
> under the concrete highways and byways and cities (112).

Yet the Aboriginal people have a vision. It is based in their past and in
nature, the land:

we're looking up the track, to what white man calls the future, – we call it the 'hopes of tomorrow'. We look that way with the experience of what we came through; things we've encountered while passing through, back there in the past, to where we are now, and we have got a vision (112).

the plans we've got in our minds, we need space too (112).

But these visions are threatened:

all our dreaming stories could be in and round those hills and these valleys and all of a sudden developers come and they want to start building ... Gradually all that tree line and the dreamings and things disappear. In the place of that there'll be a concrete jungle. Our visions don't look good against the concrete jungle (112).

Essentially, as Mr Bropho says:

it's about our values (112).

These stories highlight the entirely different world in which Aboriginal people live as compared to the concerns of the Euro-Australian residents and the planning system. We see the importance of spiritual values and cultural argument against economic values and technical argument, the perception as alien of paper, reports, maps and charts, and of the planning system and what it represents. Memory and tradition are keys to beginning to understand Aboriginal attachment to the land. Memory is embodied in identity. There is little objective distinction between space and time.

In the tone, as well as the content of the stories, we recognise '... issues, details, relationships and even people' (Forester, 1993b, p.31) who have been ignored and unappreciated in the past. We recognise not only claims that Aboriginal people have over the land, but the importance of their self- and place-identity and '... a history of betrayal and resulting fear, suspicion, distrust – which must be acknowledged, respected and addressed if working relationships are to be built' (Forester, 1993b, p.31).

Memory and mythology are intrinsically bound up with the construction of Aboriginal identity. In the stories above, memory and traditional knowledge are being used politically, yet the actant-network of Aboriginal actors has been completely unable to 'enrol' the planners. Despite a meeting of the two networks, Callon's stage of 'interessement' was not reached. Aboriginal people failed to persuade the planners of the importance of their representation of the area. The two sets of actants failed to recognise and understand each others' intermediaries; Aboriginal sacred sites and stories and the texts, maps and plans of the planners.

'Johnny-Come-Latelies' – Long-term and Short-term Residents

Excluding Aboriginal people, evidence of long-term residence and connections to the Swan Valley tended to be presented as a badge affording legitimacy of identity, image of the area and its land use:

> age or length of time people had been in the district did affect people's viewpoints (048).

Opinions from long-term residents were vaunted as being of greater value than those of 'transient' (062) newcomers or 'Johnny-come-latelies' (073):

> our area was familial or historically based. The other groups were less tolerant. (056).

Long-term inhabitants identified themselves as 'stable' and loyal to the area.

> Stable residents who called Swan Valley 'home' (062) …

were perceived as being more likely to oppose urbanisation than:

> other, more transient people [who] would be happy to stay until development and then take the money and run (062).

> newcomers wanted to sell (063).

> there was obviously an element of the new people on the block opposing the traditionalists. There was some resentment … by the traditionalists. New people were more prominent and interested and involved … They were probably more articulate and also knew how to work the process (106).

Shorter-term residents, who wanted to protect their spacious lifestyle, were made to feel decidedly non-valued:

> we have no history here (102) (residents for ten years).

> we feel very vulnerable (051) (residents for eight years).

These opinions may well be 'sour grapes' on the part of those who resented the Minister for Planning's urbanisation decision, influenced by the actant-network of relative 'newcomers' and:

> people who don't even live in the area (049).

'Grazing with Weeds'? – 'Legitimate' and 'Illegitimate' Uses of Land

Some uses of land were definitely regarded as being more valuable, even more legitimate, by longer-term Euro-Australian residents. Vignerons, and several other residents, perceived viticulture as the highest valued use of land. Other land uses were worthless by comparison:

> areas for vineyards, and other areas – non-viable land (055).

> not suitable for living or to make a living because it's full of noxious weeds (Patterson's Curse) and it's not a viable productive option (049).

Even preservation of the environment was valued as second-rate:

> a fertile area which should be left to agriculture, … however, DPUD wanted to protect bits that are good agricultural land (047).

Horsiculture, or hobby-farming, was not regarded as a legitimate use of land by either traditionalist residents:

> the area is steeped in tradition and importance. Lots of the good soil is wasted there (e.g. by hobby farming) … You should have to buy a licence with the land to ensure appropriate land use. Lifestylers are often silly (115).

This vigneron resident comments that the Swan Valley is 'steeped in tradition'. He does not mean Aboriginal tradition, however, but rather white colonial tradition, especially of 'serious' farming. He clearly regards hobby farming/ horsiculture as a 'waste', an 'inappropriate' use of the land, presumably as compared with vine growing, and goes as far as to suggest that land purchasers should be licensed for appropriate uses. Leaving land 'fallow' is not envisaged as an appropriate use: it is not productive.

Others would even prefer to see residential development:

> it's full of noxious weeds (Patterson's Curse) … more suitable for village zoning … More manageable, an ideal area for increasing rating lots; opportunity for

more people to enjoy Valley life, and the size of properties that could be established would help to eradicate weed, animal studs etc. The result would be a more aesthetical environment (049).

(I question whether roofs of new suburbs would be more 'aesthetical' than open vistas of grazing lands, and whether it is these vistas which people 'enjoy' as an essential part of 'Valley life'.)

or planning officers:

it's really not core but grazing with weeds (004).

the shire came and observed the area, said it wasn't being viably used and thus would be suitable to be repossessed (057).

Such sentiments were expressed vociferously and made horsiculturalists feel marginalised and unvalued:

the feeling that came out of the whole process was the pressure that we had to do something with our property; we couldn't just sit out here with our one horse and have acres of land....

you had to justify the land being left almost idle, otherwise we were warned that people will come in and build houses on it. The Shire basically gave us that impression ... They'd imply you would be better off if you had something going for the land so that you could justify the property (051).

the Shire didn't consider us much of a priority ... They used the Patterson's Curse covered land as an excuse, saying, 'well, this land is useless. We may as well build here' (051).

Land, according to the enrolling colonial narrative, is a resource which must be brought into productive use for economic gain. Land is seen as a marketable commodity with commercial value. Amenity, aesthetic and spiritual values do not count. Nonproductive uses are unjustifiable, illegitimate.

These stories indicate the range of images residents have of the Swan Valley; as an area of colonial history, of spacious environment, and offering a rural lifestyle, all of which need to be preserved as accessible to them. The identities of many are as property owners with a concern for the value of their investments. Local residents view their properties as much more than units of shelter. They are financial investments, lifestyle symbols, social settings and bases for business and leisure activities (Healey, 1997). Residents recognise the diversity of their identities, values and aspirations, and within the overall network of non-indigenous residents in the Swan Valley there nested several smaller, often overlapping actant-networks. Even within the smaller networks there were often different representations of the Valley and a lack of complete agreement as to desired outcomes. Some networks, such as the Friends of the Valley, were more successful than others in enrolling the ultimate decision-maker, the Minister for Planning, and persuading him of their values and points of view:

> general quality values (quality of life) were dismissed as irrelevant or incidental. Dollar values were given much higher value (103).

> aesthetic values don't seem to count any more (057).

Overall, actor's images and values jostled together as each actant attempted to

> define what we think the Valley should be (056).

As this respondent continued:

> in a way we were forming a Valley identity and exploring who we are (056).

Self- and place-identities are inextricably intertwined. They are complex and dynamic. Whichever image/identity and concomitant values enrolled and mobilised others at any point in time in the Swan Valley story depended, as one planning officer recognised:

> on the ongoing politics (022).

Conclusions: the Poetics and Politics of the Swan Valley

I have attempted to depict the Swan Valley in the North East Corridor of Perth, Western Australia, as a nodal point where sets of social relations and identities, representations and images of place, meanings and values temporally and temporarily intersect. State government proposals to urbanise the North East Corridor and the public participation process which followed, led to the construction of agency as actants formed into temporary networks and jostled for influence over the planning decision. Complex chains of actant-spaces aligned around alternative representations of the Swan Valley and the North East Corridor: pro-urbanisation, anti-urbanisation etc.

I have called upon actant-network theory to help unpack the processes of translation of representations. Actants' stories of images of themselves and of other groups, and of their and others' geographical places reveal complex and dynamic alliances and differences. There are many networks at play. Overlapping, contrasting and conflicting images, identities and values are evoked for substantive and political purposes.

Such images, identities and values are intrinsically related to actants' beliefs, social relations, institution structures, material practices and power relations (Harvey, 1996). Actants bring conceptions from their lifeworlds and their previous and ongoing interrelationships with other actors into a process constrained by the institutional structure and practices of the Western Australian planning system, and in which power relations are inherently unequal.

Planners are experts. The difference between experts and laypersons is essentially that laypersons' knowledge, as we have seen, embodies tradition and cultural values; it is local and de-centred. Planners' expertise, on the other hand, is disembedded, 'evacuating' (Giddens, 1994, p.85) the traditional content of local contexts, and based on impersonal principles which can be set out without regard to context; a coded knowledge which professionals are at pains to protect.

> Expert systems decontextualise as an intrinsic consequence of the impersonal and contingent character of the rules of their knowledge-acquisition ... Place is not in any sense a quality relevant to their validity; and places themselves ... take on a different significance from traditional locales' (Giddens, 1994, p.85).

Planners traditionally believe themselves to be neutral, rational, experts (see Hoch, 1994), offering objective and balanced appraisals rather than making value judgements. Yet planners must inevitably bring their own values into their work, making judgements as to the good versus the right; what is important, which interests should carry how much weight, what is possible to be achieved and so on. Planners and governance reserve the ultimate power to define, redefine, organise and reorganise space into a place of their choosing.

Planners, therefore, often seek to enrol other actors into their representations. Their goal is mobilisation; acceptance of their plans as legitimate by local residents. Public participation programmes are often utilised as the means of persuasion, but as Hoch (1994, pp.110–11) warns, '... when planners treat plans solely as weapons of political warfare, they lose faith in the power of ideas and images'. Planning should be regarded as more than a process of competitive bargaining. Such an attitude blinds planners to the legitimacy of multiple subject positions and values and robs them of opportunities to think critically and to engage in truly deliberative decision-making.

In the Swan Valley/North East Corridor story, actants attempted to enrol other participants, and especially, the decision-makers, into their representations, some far more successfully than others. As one would expect, given the statutory powers of planning officers, their rational technical images and values of the area had an important, but, in this instance, not a determining influence on the Minister for Planning's decision to urbanise the western side of the Swan Valley rather than the technically more suitable eastern side.

The decision was influenced by the astute channelling of energies by actants on the eastern side of the Swan Valley into the representation of their area as a working area, vital to the livelihoods of vignerons etc, and as an area with substantial economic potential for generation of tourism dollars, through marketing its white colonial heritage, local crafts and produce. The poetics of place are strong and appealing. As are the politics. As Callon and Latour (1981, p.292) comment: '... strength is *inter*vention, *inter*ruption, *inter*pretation and *inter*est' (emphasis in original).

Returning to the poetics rather than the politics of place for the moment, the difference between the views of the planners and local residents may be summarised as the difference between space and place. Even so, space is not merely a passive, abstract two-dimensional arena on which things can happen. Space and place are both constructs – they are surfaces of inscription and identity, offering different meanings to different people. The inauguration of the planning system enabling the division of land into privately held and precisely demarcated lots has traditionally given planners more power/ authority than local residents and therefore their interpretations of place and identity generally take precedence. Such interpretations may often threaten places and identities as understood by local residents, manipulating, recognising and reconstituting them anew.

It takes considerable physical resources (of personnel numbers and skills, of time and money) and of relational resources (personal contacts) for other actant-networks to effect successful resistance to the representations and values of the planning system as occurred in the North East Corridor.

The politics of place often involves a contest of images, identities and values. Aesthetic values and images of spaciousness and rural lifestyles, including horticulture, were eclipsed by economic values and images of returns on investment and tourism potential. Place was therefore not simply a context for the local definition of social power, identity and values, but rather '… crucial to the terms of reference of such negotiations' (Jacobs, 1994, p.770). Negotiations that appear on the surface to be about urbanisation or facility siting, are actually much more complex, and are about identities and meanings, values and power, poetics and politics.

Notes

1   See also Dalby and Mackenzie (1997).
2   Haraway (1992) explains that actors are not the same as actants. Actors operate at the level of character and actants at the level of function. Several actors may (but need not) comprise one actant. Actants are thus (collective) 'entities doing things in a structured and structuring field of action' (Haraway, 1992, p.313).
3   'To translate is also to express in one's own language what others say and want' (Callon, 1986, p.223).
4   Utilisation or manipulation of information to persuade others to a certain viewpoint provides linkages to the Habermasian concept of the systematic distortion of communication (SDC). For more detailed explanation see Hillier (1995a).
5   It is impossible to conceptualise a diagram of actant-networks over time. I offer the metaphor of an infinitely expanding Rubic cube, wherein each small segment represents an actant, interacting with the others it touches. Through time, the cube may be turned partially or entirely. The faces of some segments will remain touching in their previous 'networks', whilst others will form new networks. New patterns and relationships of networks are formed with every twist of the cube, while the traces of some old patterns (or their influence) may still be retained. See also McManus' (1996) metaphor of a Magical Infinite Cog Machine.
6   See, for example, collections edited by Agnew and Duncan, 1989; Duncan and Ley, 1993; Keith and Pile, 1993.
7   For example, as Said (1978, p.55) explains: 'the objective space of a house – its corners, corridors, cellars, rooms – is far less important than what poetically it is endowed with…so space acquires emotional and even rational sense by a kind of poetic process, whereby the vacant or anonymous reaches of distance are converted into meaning.'
8   For more detail of the debate, see Hillier, 1995b; 1995c; Healey and Hillier, 1995; 1996.
9   Interviews with developers did not furnish sufficient usable information for this analysis.
10 The Friends of the Valley group.

References

Agnew, J. and Duncan, J. (1989), 'Introduction' in Agnew, J. and Duncan, J. (eds), *The Power of Place*, Unwin Hyman, London, pp.1–8.

Bauman, Z. (1993), *Postmodern Ethics*, Blackwell, Oxford.

Beauregard, R. (1993), *Voices of Decline*, Blackwell, Cambridge, MA.

Bellah, R., Madsen, R., Sullivan, W., Swidler, A. and Tipton, S. (1985), *Habits of the Heart*, University of California Press, Berkeley, CA.

Callon, M. (1986), 'Some Elements of a Sociology of Translation', in Law, J. (ed.), *Power, Action, Belief: a New Sociology of Knowledge?*, RKP, London, pp.196–233.

Callon, M. (1991), 'Techno-Economic Networks and Irreversibility', in Law, J. (ed.), *A Sociology of Monsters*, Routledge, London.

Callon, M. and Latour, B. (1981), 'Unscrewing the Big Leviathan: How Actors Macro-Structure Reality and How Sociologists Help Them to Do So', in Knorr-Cetina, K. and Ciccurel, A. (eds), *Advances in Social Theory and Methodology*, RKP, Boston, MA.

Clegg, S. and Hardy, C. (1996), 'Conclusion: Representations', in Clegg, S., Hardy, C. and Nord, W. (eds), *Handbook of Organisation Studies*, Sage, London, pp.676–708.

Code, L. (1995), *Rhetorical Spaces*, Routledge, New York, NY.

Dalby, S. and Mackenzie, F. (1997), 'Reconceptualising Local Community: Environment, Identity and Threat', *Area*, Vol. 22 (2), pp.99–108.

Derrida, J. (1994), 'Sending: On Representation', in Fuery, P. (ed.), *Representation, Discourse and Desire*, Longman, Cheshire, Melbourne, pp.9–34.

Donald, J. (1992), 'Metropolis: The City as Text', in Bocock, R. and Thompson, K. (eds), *Social and Cultural Forms of Modernity*, Polity Press, Cambridge, pp.417–61.

Duncan, J. and Ley, D. (ed.) (1993), *Place, Culture, Representation*, Routledge, London.

Dworkin, R. (1977), *Taking Rights Seriously*, Duckworth, London.

Forester, J. (1993a), *Critical Theory, Public Policy and Planning Practice*, State University of New York Press, Albany, NY.

Forester, J. (1993b), 'Beyond Dialogue to Transformative Learning: How Deliberative Rituals Encourage Political Judgement in Community Planning Processes', Working Paper, Centre for Urban and Regional Studies, Haifa, Israel.

Gibson-Graham, K. (1995), 'Identity and Economic Plurality: Rethinking Capitalism and Capitalist Hegemony', *Environment and Planning D, Society and Space*, Vol. 13, pp.275–82.

Giddens, A. (1994), 'Living in a Post-Traditional Society', in Beck, U., Giddens, A. and Lash, S. (eds), *Reflexive Modernisation*, Polity Press, Cambridge, pp.56–109.

Habermas, J. (1990), *Moral Consciousness and Communicative Action*, MIT Press, Cambridge, MA.

Haraway, D. (1992), 'The Promises of Monsters: A Regenerative Politics for Inappropriate/D Others', in Grossberg, L., Nelson, C. and Treichler, P. (eds), *Cultural Studies*, Routledge, London, pp.295–337.

Harmon, M. and Mayer, R. (1986), *Organisation Theory for Public Administration*, Little, Brown and Co, Boston, CA.

Harvey, D. (1973), *Social Justice and the City*, Edward Arnold, London.

Harvey, D. (1996), *Justice, Nature and the Geography of Difference*, Blackwell, Oxford.

Healey, P. (1992), 'Planning Through Debate: The Communicative Turn in Planning Theory and Practice', *Town Planning Review*, Vol. 63(2), pp.143–62.

Healey, P. (1997), *Collaborative Planning*, Macmillan, Basingstoke.

Healey, P. and Hillier, J. (1995), *Community Mobilisation in Swan Valley: Claims, Discourses and Rituals in Local Planning*, University of Newcastle-upon-Tyne, Dept of Town and Country Planning, Working Paper 49, Newcastle-upon-Tyne.

Healey, P. and Hillier, J. (1996), 'Communicative Micropolitics: A Story of Claims and Discourses', *International Planning Studies*, Vol. 1(2).

Hebdige, D. (1990), 'Introduction', *New Formations*, Vol.11, pp.vi–vii.

Hillier, J. (1995a), 'SDC, or How to Manipulate the Public into a False Consensus Without Really Trying', in Dixon, G. and Aitken, D. (eds), Institute of Australian Geographers, Conference Proceedings, 1993, Monash Publications in *Geography*, No. 43, Monash University, Melbourne, pp.111–26.

Hillier, J. (1995b), 'Planning Rituals: Rites or Wrongs?', paper presented to AESOP Conference, Strathclyde University, August.

Hillier, J. (1995c), 'Discursive Democracy in Action', in Domanski, R. and Marszal, T. (eds), *Planning and Social-Economic Development*, Lodz University Press, Lodz, pp.75–100.

Hoch, C. (1994), *What Planners Do*, APA, Chicago, IL.

Hoggett, P. (1992), *Partisans in an Uncertain World: the Psychoanalysis of Engagement*, Free Association Books, London.

Honig, B. (1996), 'Difference, Dilemmas, and the Politics of Home', in Benhabib, S. (ed.), *Democracy and Difference*, Princeton University Press, Princeton, NJ.

Horkheimer, M. and Adorno, T. (1991), *Dialectic of Enlightenment*, Continuum, New York.

Jacobs, J. (1994), 'Negotiating the Heart: Heritage, Development and Identity in Postimperial London', *Environment and Planning D, Society and Space*, Vol. 12, pp.751–72.

Keith, M. and Pile, S. (eds) (1993), *Place and the Politics of Identity*, Routledge, London.

Krieger, M. (1981), *Advice and Planning*, Temple University Press, Philadelphia, PA.

Kristeva, J. (1982), *Powers of Horror: An Essay in Abjection*, Columbia University Press, New York.

Lake, R. (1994), 'Negotiating Local Economy', *Political Geography*, Vol. 13 (5), pp.423–42.

Latour, B. (1992), 'One More Turn After the Social Turn…', in McMullin, M. (ed.), *The Social Dimension of Space*, University of Notre Dame Press, Notre Dame, IN.

Law, J. (1992), 'Notes on the Theory of the Actor-Network: Ordering Strategy and Heterogeneity', *Systems Practice*, Vol. 5, pp.379–93.

Lefebvre, H. (1996), *Writings on Cities*, trans. Kofman, E. and Lebas, E., Blackwell, Oxford.

Leonard, S. (1990), *Critical Theory in Political Practice*, Princeton University Press, Princeton, NJ.

Lerner, M. and Whitehead, L. (1980), 'Procedural Justice Viewed in the Context of Justice Motive Theory', in Mikula, G. (ed.), *Justice and Social Interaction*, Springer-Verlag, New York, pp.219–58.

Love, N. (1995), 'What's left of Marx?', in White, S. (ed.), *The Cambridge Companion to Habermas*, Cambridge University Press, Cambridge, pp.46–66.

McManus P. (1996), 'An Ecological Political Economy of Sustainability: Nature, Forestry and Trade', unpublished PhD thesis, Department of Geography, University of Bristol.

Maines, D. and Bridger, J. (1992), 'Narratives, Community and Land Use Decisions', *The Social Science Journal*, Vol. 29(4), pp.363–80.

Marsden, T., Murdoch, J., Lowe, P., Munton, P. and Flynn, A. (1993), *Constructing the Countryside*, UCL Press, London.

Massey, D. (1991), 'The Political Place of Locality Studies', *Environment and Planning, A*, Vol. 23, pp.267–82.

Massey, D. (1993), 'Politics and Space/Time', in Keith, M. and Pile, S. (eds), *Place and the Politics of Identity*, Routledge, London, pp.141–61.

Massey, D. (1995), 'Thinking Radical Democracy Spatially', *Environment and Planning D, Society and Space*, pp.283–8.

Mouffe, C. (1992), *Dimensions of Radical Democracy, Pluralism. Citizenship and Community*, Verso, London.

Murdoch, J. and Marsden, T. (1995), 'The Spatialisation of Politics: Local and National Actor-Spaces in Environmental Conflict', *Transactions of the Institute of British Geographers* (NS), Vol. 20, pp.368–80.

Natter, W. and Jones III, J.P. (1997), 'Identity, Space and Other Uncertainties', in Benko, G. and Strohmayer, U. (eds), *Space and Social Theory*, Blackwell, Oxford, pp.141–61.

Plotkin, S. (1987), *Keep Out*, University of California Press, Berkeley, CA.

Pred, A. (1983), 'Structuration and Place: On the Becoming of Sense of Place and Structure of Feeling', *Journal for the Theory of Spatial Behaviour*, Vol. 13, pp.45–68.

Pred, A. (1984), 'Place as Historically Contingent Process: Structuration and the Time Geography of Becoming Places', *Annals of the Association of American Geographers*, Vol. 74, pp.279–97.

Pred, A. (1997), 'Re-presenting the Extended Present Moment of Danger: A Meditation on Hypermodernity, Identity and the Montage Form', in Benko, G. and Strohmayer, U. (eds), *Space and Social Theory*, Blackwell, Oxford, pp.117–140.

Rodaway, P. (1994), *Sensuous Geographies*, Routledge, London.

Said, E. (1978), *Orientalism*, Penguin, Harmondsworth.

Shields, R. (1997), 'Spatial Stress and Resistance: Social Meanings of Spatialisation', in Benko, G. and Strohmayer, U. (eds), *Space and Social Theory*, Blackwell, Oxford, pp.186–202.

Shire of Swan (1996), advertising folder, Shire of Swan, Midlands.

Shotter, J. (1993a), *Conversational Realities*, Sage, London.

Shotter, J. (1993b), 'Psychology and Citizenship: Identity and Belonging', in Turner, B. (ed.), *Citizenship and Social Theory*, Sage, London, pp.115–38.

Sujic, D. (1992), *The 100 Mile City*, Andre Deutsch, London.

Thomas, H. (1994), 'Introduction', in Thomas, H. (ed.), *Values and Planning*, Avebury, Aldershot, pp.1–11.

Trigger, D. (1997), 'Mining, Landscape and the Culture of Development Ideology in Australia', *Ecumene*, Vol. 4 (2), pp.161–80.

Turner, S. (1994), *The Social Theory of Practices*, Polity Press, Cambridge.

Chapter Five

The Integrated Metropolis: A Strategy for the Networked, Multi-Centred City

Tony Lloyd-Jones, Bill Erickson, Marion Roberts and Stephen Nice

Introduction

A Strategy for the Polycentric Metropolis

This chapter discusses the evolving form of urban areas and argues that the shape of cities is increasingly polycentric. This is a process that is occurring on a global scale (see, for example, Dick and Rimmer, 1998) although our focus here is the European and, more especially, the UK context. Though more fragmented, however, the metropolis continues to operate as a loosely-knit functional whole in which city centres retain a pre-eminent, if more specialised role.[1] Rather than resisting the evolution of such a form, as is suggested by, for example, both the 'urban villages' movement and the proponents of the 'compact city', the authors suggest that a multi-centred metropolis should become more integrated and made to work more effectively and efficiently. To do this, it is suggested that design, planning and managerial effort is put into the existing networks of movement and communication, paying particular attention to the nodal connections between the networks.

Such a strategy would help to meet the goals of environmental sustainability and social equity by increasing accessibility and connectivity, easing congestion and decreasing energy consumption. Greater accessibility would also allow the metropolis to become more economically sustainable, allowing it to operate more efficiently and its spatial functions to adapt to changing economic circumstances.

The final part of our argument is that through greater connectivity, a greater degree of specialisation and concentrated growth in metropolitan sub centres can occur, increasing the basis for stronger local identities to develop. This spatial strategy at the metropolitan scale provides a starting point for addressing the imaginative and associative features of 'place' which are fundamental to our experience of the city. At the local scale, urban design should seek to integrate cities and towns more thoroughly by creating identity and reinforcing the locational attributes for nodes, sub-centres and key features of the networks. In doing this, urban designers and managers need to take cognisance of the extended knowledge of place which the information revolution has provided and the extended and modified capacities for experiencing and operating in the metropolis that the new technology offers. Such a strategy has implications for a re-orienting of urban design away from its traditional focus on sites and centres towards an inclusion of networks, transport interchanges and suburban sub-centres.

Structure of the Argument

This chapter originated out of response to a European Commission call for research proposals to develop an interpretation of a human-centred city for the twenty first century through the use of new technologies (Roberts et al., 1996). The urban concepts developed by the study were to be accompanied by ideas about possible innovations and changes to the city's key elements and public meeting places, or 'agora'.

A common response to this desire for a humane city in which the local and the global are reconciled has been the promotion of 'urban villages' (Aldous, 1992), most recently incorporated in the latest revision of the UK Government's Planning Policy Guidance Note 1 (DoE, 1997). This paper offers a different approach, which has been evolved partly through doubts about the desirability and feasibility of the urban 'village', but primarily because the analysis starts from a different point in its review of contemporary urban trends. Even if it were desirable to return to the forms and practices of the pre-industrial city, which a focus on traditional mixed use communities and town centres implies, the scale and organisation of domestic life and the European economy would make this impracticable (Thompson-Fawcett, 1996; Roberts, 1997).

This chapter first reviews current trends within city spatial structure, in terms of the centralisation and decentralisation of activities and the formation of sub-centres. It then moves on to consider the way in which towns and cities evolve, the importance of movement and communication systems and shifting concepts of the public realm. Particular emphasis is laid on the notion of connectivity, between centres and sub-centres and between public and private. This section uses London as an example, as the city with which the authors are most familiar, but parallel illustrations could be made using any large metropolitan city. Here, we introduce the notion of an 'armature' as a framework built upon the primary connecting networks and a device for reinforcing the city's identity.

The importance of connections is also pertinent to the third section of the paper, which considers briefly the effect of mass communication systems on conceptions of place and argues the need for urban designers to positively enhance local identity. Finally suggestions are made about the way in which urban designers, planners and managers can play a role in promoting the development of a sustainable, human-centred city – a form which the authors term as the 'integrated metropolis'.

The Space of the Metropolis

Centralisation and Decentralisation

There has been much recent debate about the shape of the future city, in terms of centralisation and decentralisation (see, for example, Jenks et al., 1996; Graham and Marvin, 1996). Two divergent trends have been documented; the first towards a metropolitan renaissance and the second towards suburbanisation and dispersal.

The 'bullish' view of central cities[2] concentrates on their successes, particularly the successes of the 'world' cities (Sudjic, 1995). Many major metropolitan centres have enjoyed a period of economic and cultural expansion over the last decade and a half, due to the globalisation of markets and, in particular the financial sector and the growth of the information economy. Sassen (1994), in particular, has argued that these factors have led to a new hierarchy of cities, with the 'global cities' increasing in economic performance, whilst older industrial centres continue to suffer decline.

On the global economic stage, it is increasingly cities rather than nation states, that are competing for dominance. In the broader development context, economic and political change over the past two decades is bringing a paradigm shift in attitudes towards the role of cities. The World Bank, for example, sees a historic shift away from the institutions of the nation state towards a 'triumvirate' of supra-national organisations and nation states (Yusuf, 1999). Globally, the move away from centralised state control towards political decentralisation, participation and partnership means that the focus is increasingly on the towns and cities as centres of local governance and, in particular, on the role of the metropolitan cities as important administrative centres.

In the era of a telecommunications revolution, city centres have retained and often increased their importance as spaces for face-to-face interaction, transactions and creativity (Bianchini and Landry, 1995). Various city authorities have boosted their performance through cultural regeneration projects (Bianchini and Parkinson, 1993; Loftman and Nevin, 1995), but meanwhile the arts, culture and entertainment industries are becoming an increasingly important part of many city's economies (Bancroft et al., 1996).

In physical terms, the urban landscape of city centres has itself undergone a renaissance in much of the developed industrial world. Simultaneous with the construction of the high towers for new corporate finance, many inner city districts have been subject to new waves of gentrification and upgrading of older residential areas and the reclaiming of older commercial and industrial buildings for upper and middle-income housing (Raban, 1974; Zukin, 1991; Smith, 1996). Whilst there has been an overall decline in manufacturing industry within inner city areas compounding problems of industrial dereliction, the re-population of many inner city areas by immigrant groups has led, not only to a rich cultural diversity (Senett, 1991; Hayden, 1995), but also to new, more specialised opportunities for economic growth (Sassen, 1996; Porter, 1995).

Industrial cities have seen successive waves of decentralisation which have progressed from suburban residential expansion to commercial and industrial 'deconcentration'. Suburban commercial and industrial development began as small-scale ribbon development along the main routes out of the cities. The need for readily accessible buildings with large footprints in amenable surroundings prompted the suburban location or relocation of industrial estates, university and hospital campuses and the regional shopping centres, retail, science and office parks that followed (Thomas and Cousins, 1996).

These types of large single-use complexes have tended to be strung out along the main suburban arterials and orbital roads like beads on a necklace.[3] The United States provides the most extreme examples of such patterns of development in terms of its suburban hinterlands. Over the last decade and a half, however, the UK and Western Europe have experienced the growth of out-of town developments on a new scale, and of entire suburban and rural communities whose growth and continued survival are dependent on car use.

In the US, Garreau (1991) has charted the emergence of concentrated peripheral development, which he argues is associated with social aspirations, the feminisation of the workforce and the development of transport infrastructure. Garreau describes these developments as 'Edge Cities'.

Typically, they are concentrated around major highway intersections on the periphery of major cities and consist of 'centres' which are an amalgam of retail malls, offices, leisure centres and work places as well as suburban housing. Suburbia, traditionally, has been associated with a lifestyle dependent on stereotypical gender roles, with a male breadwinner commuting to the centre and dependent wife and children staying on the periphery. Garreau argues that the new lifestyles associated with dual earner families have both responded to and provoked the emergence of edge cities. In these new locations both halves of a couple can enjoy easy access to employment and leisure, whilst at the same time being able to live in a single family house with a garden.

Planning regulations and cultural differences have tended to curtail the growth of such 'Edge Cities' in Europe. Nevertheless, huge amounts of commercial development have occurred around and in corridors leading to airports (Heathrow in London, Schipol in Amsterdam) or on orbital highways, such as the North Circular in London or the Périphérique in Paris. These peripheral developments have, ironically, released floor space for a new wave of metropolitan expansion in the inner city, permitting vacant offices to be redeveloped as homes and derelict industrial buildings as 'loft' apartments or artists studios (Coupland, 1996).

Flattened Hierarchies

The dispersal of some of the urban functions traditionally associated with the central cities (city centre business and retail services, inner city manufacturing and warehousing) coupled with an intensification of those that remain, has resulted in a more spatially-specialised metropolitan layout. Developments on the edges of towns and cities and activities in the centres are beginning to assume complementary roles. Less specialised retail and commercial functions have moved out, not only to suburban locations, but also to non-metropolitan city and town centres within the commuter belts of the major cities.

Of course, any large metropolitan city or conurbation develops a hierarchy of centres and sub-centres as a normal process of physical development. However, the emerging urban structure is a more complex, polycentric form encompassing revitalised metropolitan centres and new peripheral developments alongside the stratified hierarchy of established town and suburban centres. Although this structure has not fully developed, a system of related town centres across a metropolitan area has already been observed and documented in the London Policy Advisory Committee's report on town centres in London (LPAC, 1996).

Improved transport and telecommunications networks in suburban areas have provided low density catchment areas for some of the retail and leisure functions traditionally associated with these centres. The same networks provide pools of labour for industry and commerce of a size to match those of the inner city areas. The population is more spread out, but people can travel more quickly by car to the new strategically-located workplace and service functions.

This development, with the more specialised role of the metropolitan centre as the focus of specialised ('command and control') business and administrative activities, 'producer services', education, creative and cultural industries, leisure and tourism, and other traditional inner and city centre activities dispersed to a system of sub-centres. This has echoes of a more general process of organisational change noted in 'post-industrial' society – the emergence of flattened hierarchies.[4]

This notion of a metropolitan area with traditional centre and urban sub-centres also suggests Graham and Marvin's (1996) diagram for a 'Post-Fordist Global Metropolis' (Graham and Marvin 1996, p.344). However, the argument of this chapter is that this concept could be humanised and its propensity for sustainability increased by focusing attention on its integration and imageability.

Networks and the Contemporary City

Considering the connections between the traditional urban centres and new sub-centres leads to the notion that it is the communications networks which form the essential building block for a model of the city's structure, rather than either the urban block, or the neighbourhood. This observation is at variance with the model of city development suggested by the 'urban villages' idea, which proposes the neighbourhood or quarter as a fundamental component of the town or city and transport as a second order system of linkages.

The urban system, as Christopher Alexander so aptly described it, is organised as a semi-lattice, with activities serving a variety of different sized and overlapping catchment areas (Alexander, 1965). Activity within the city is governed by what Hillier and Penn (1993) describe as a 'movement economy'. They refer to the city as a physical system consisting of two components: a continuous network of spaces and a collection of functional locations associated with particular land uses. They describe the system as a network operating on the basis of origins and destinations everywhere. This description of a network of destinations is at variance to the traditional transport model of the nineteenth-century city, which has radial arms projecting from a centre.

The loosely structured but overlapping functional specialisation of cities is what gives them their resilience and adaptability to long term economic change. It gives rise to a type of mixed use that is based not on local autonomy but, as Jane Jacobs described it, on 'organised complexity' (Jacobs, 1965). Unless people are physically restrained from travelling or transporting goods, the notion of a discrete self sufficient urban neighbourhood, a notion which is sometimes implied by the proponents of an 'urban village' approach, is unworkable. The substance of the city is underpinned by its movement systems.

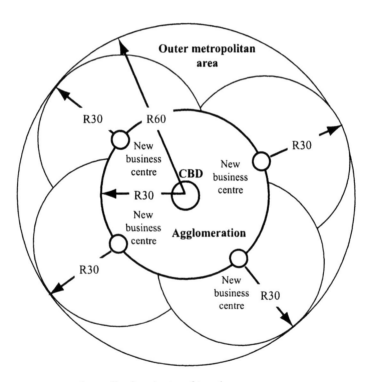

R = average commuting radius in minutes of travel

Figure 5.1   Travel time constraints and the multi-centred metropolis: how the '100-mile city' has developed

Movement Systems and the Street Network

As Rossi (1982) and other commentators have observed, it is usually the street system which is the most enduring part of the city. The street has two fundamental qualities: the first is as a route of communication and the second is as a site of local interaction. The positioning of these functions varies at different scales and in different technical forms, depending upon whether, for example, the street is a back street, or a main thoroughfare.

The street forms the primary structural network of the city. This primary network supports and enables the multitude of private communicative and cognitive networks of the citizens. Lynch (1960), for example, noted that the path was the most important organising principle of most individuals' mental maps.

Modern forms of transportation, and the planning and engineering responses to them, have changed the simple historical relationship of city block and a street network serving the dual purpose of communication and interaction. Our experience of the city is now mediated by transportation systems that are dislocated from the public life of the street. Victorian engineers attempted to speed the flow of road traffic with new urban highways to limited effect. More successful were their surface railway systems which carved great holes in the urban fabric around the new railway stations and goods yards, whilst railway embankments, cuttings and viaducts appeared in every district.

The underground railway brought a new experience of insulated travel. Car, tram and bus coexisted with the pedestrian in city streets formerly clogged with horse-drawn vehicles. However, the demands for more free-flowing traffic in the era of mass car ownership after the Second World War brought a new and more devastating wave of large scale road building. The engineering feats of the urban motorway builders often exceeded in scale and disruption the efforts of the Victorian railway builders.

These new transportation networks formed separate layers superimposed over (or under) the original street network. They have prevented congestion from freezing the economic life of the city, allowed the city to expand and for areas to become more specialised and associated with particular land-uses. This has often been at great cost to the urban experience but also, in the case of well designed railway or airport terminals, enhancing with the opportunity for creating new and uplifting public spaces.

Transport can be seen, then, as the primary element in the urban structure, with the movement system as a whole consisting of larger cross-city transport networks crossing and sometimes interacting with the local street network and one another. The movement system as a whole is articulated where these various networks interact and creates local points of intensity in the city. Other forms of technological advance, such as the skyscraper, phone systems and air conditioning have simultaneously allowed a degree of compression, permitting literally thousands of people to occupy quite small areas at particular times of day (Koolhaas, 1994).

As noted, the emergence of increased traffic movements and associated large scale road infrastructure today means that major inter- and intra-urban roads have become just as dislocated from the city's public life as rail transport corridors were in earlier decades. Interaction with the public realm is increasingly being concentrated at the junctions or nodes in these systems where changes occur between scales or mode of transport.

For example, a retail corridor has developed around the Brent Cross intersection in the northwest of London. This corridor consists not only of the original shopping centre which was built in the 1970s and has now doubled in size, but also includes a multistorey furniture and home goods shop, one of the major hotel chains, a toy retailing centre and other lesser retailing warehouse shops. This 'corridor' has a difficult relationship with the existing bus and Underground network. In many of the surrounding neighbourhoods, more than 50 per cent of households are carless and so excluded from easy access to these services. The area is covered by a system of radial public transport systems that have developed since Victorian times. However, the necessary lateral connections, interchanges and linkages with the local street system which would draw the poorer neighbourhoods into the catchment of the retail corridor are lacking. The lack of articulation of the movement system in this area means that social differentiation is reinforced, with poorer households limited to lower grade retail services.

The Importance of the 'Armature'

New technologies of movement have seemingly led to a compression of both time and space (Harvey, 1989).[5] Similarly a commuting journey from the Wiltshire town of Swindon to the terminus at Paddington in the centre of London takes as long as an Underground and bus journey from an outer suburb to the centre of London. Such apparent reductions and paradoxical relations of distances and travel times suggest that the previous hierarchies of neighbourhood, district and metropolitan scales need some reinterpretation. Furthermore the size and scale of the modern metropolis can be bewildering.

The challenge for the human-centred city is to reconcile the personal and the local with the metropolitan. With this in mind, it is useful to distinguish the most important elements of an urban pattern or framework from the general fabric or 'tissue' of a city – mainly consisting of residential districts. It seems probable that these elements will comprise the following: the most memorable and used streets, the arteries of communication, places of exchange and assembly and key buildings and complexes in the service and social infrastructures. Examples of these might be the principal streets and thoroughfares, rail and other stations, airports, stadia and public halls, shopping malls, bus depots, major concentrations of public entertainment such as Leicester Square, airports and lively public spaces, such as Camden Lock in North London. These elements could be categorised as the points of convergence of the networks and key features of the elements themselves. To give an example Oxford Circus and Oxford Street are important features both of the tourists' and Londoners' mental maps whereas New Oxford Street and Lower Regent Street are not.

This categorisation will be similar to the 'nodal structure' posited by Gosling and Maitland (1984) who suggest that such a model can act as a scaling device in the city, persist through changes in the built fabric and reconcile differences between the specialised functions and the collective use of the city. One of the earliest manifestation of this idea, and one which is close to the strategy being put forward in this chapter, is David Crane's notion of the Capital Web, a comprehensible symbolic urban structure at the metropolitan scale, incorporating Kevin Lynch's ideas of legibility which are discussed below (Crane, 1960; Buchanan, 1988). Others refer to this structure as an 'armature' (Calthorpe, 1993; MacDonald, 1986), the term that we have adopted in this text. It consists of those components which are of general public utility and amenity. The armature is not the network as a whole; rather it comprises the key features of the various urban networks which combine to form a core of movement, activity and meaning.[6]

If an integrated transport/land use and urban design approach to sustainable cities represented the hands-on aspect of this work, its guiding notion was the idea of an equitable and coherent metropolis with a strong sense of symbolic identity for its inhabitants. This approach traces its origins back to Kevin Lynch's classic work, *The Image of the City*, in 1960, and the subsequent work of Lynch, Appleyard and others at MIT.

Changing Concepts of the Public Realm

Public spaces form an important component of the 'armature'. Changes in social relations and technology have eroded the functions of public space, as traditionally understood (Sennett, 1977), but there is evidence that it has been replaced by other types of meeting places. Here distinctions of public and private can be ambiguous, but it is feasible to include privately owned but publicly accessible spaces, such as public buildings, shops and malls, with the concept of the generic street network. Similarly, historic places of assembly have their modern counterpart: the shopping centre, the multiplex cinema and the leisure centre or gymnasium.

MacCormac (1987 and 1996) has argued that in considering the changed character of the public realm, it is necessary to distinguish between the types of activities which now take place in it. In a series of articles, he has argued that a distinction may be made between 'local' transactions and 'foreign' transactions. Local transactions are such as might occur between small entrepreneurs and their customers in face-to-face interaction – for example the activities associated with a tobacconist or a small print shop. Those which he terms foreign transactions are associated with inter-regional or national exchanges of information – for example the placing of an order with a foreign bank or communications between the national headquarters of a transnational corporation.

The interesting aspect of MacCormac's argument here is the acknowledgement he gives to the changing concept of the public realm. Rather than proposing that the physical is replaced by the virtual, he suggests that the public realm simultaneously comprises both traditional physical interactions (exchanges of goods, face-to-face social interactions) and virtual interactions (exchanges of information).

Much has been written about the possibilities which will be opened up by the development of new technologies. To date the dominant users of advanced telecommunications infrastructure have been the large transnational corporations and government agencies. Greater public access is now becoming possible with the emergence of intelligent networks capable of transmitting large quantities of information at high speed to individual personal computers via a telephone link.

Access to these networks is bringing increased knowledge about and intervention in the urban systems which operate in our cities and could, ultimately, provide greater choice and efficiency in their use. Communication and information technologies are providing greater information about city

The Integrated Metropolis 113

events, activities and facilities, their locations, timing and means of access. In the provision of such increased choice and knowledge it seems probable that the number of journeys will increase, thereby extending and increasing the use of the present day meeting places (Graham and Marvin, 1996). An example of this trend can already be observed in the popularity of mutliplex cinemas, which are based both in and out of town centres, leisure centres and theme parks. Such concentrations are likely to more than compensate for the loss of those functions that are being or might be overtaken by developments in new information technologies, such as for example, home shopping and home working.

The physical effects of telematics are currently the subject of research (Jones and Cassidy, 1995). In a more qualitative fashion, the influence of other types of information on the perception and development of the city has also been recently examined. It is to this perceptual, cognitive side of the 'information explosion' that the paper will turn next.

The Metropolis as Place

Space and Subjectivity

Lynch's study of imageability emphasised the difficulties which many urban dwellers have in relating one part of a city to another. In order to make each local aspect of the 'armature' more vivid attention should be focused on the way in which each 'local' centre or element reinforce and support the other. Many studies on the cognitive images people form of cities emphasise the importance of movement (Walmsley, 1988; Lynch, 1960). It follows that to be memorable features of identity should also relate to patterns of movement and activity. This requires not only a holistic approach to the various urban systems but also one which can operate at a range of scales.

The power of Lynch's schema of the mental map, which uses paths, nodes, districts, edges and landmarks as ordering devices to understand the structure of an urban area, is that it can be applied at a range of scales, from a small brownfield site to the city as a whole. The problem that arises is that in lived experience, each individual is simultaneously operating at a range of scales. Increasingly daily experience is shared between several districts. Each of these districts becomes part of an individual's 'home range', although knowledge and sense of attachment may differ for the locus of different activities. An individual's understanding of the metropolis is expanded through direct as well as mediated experience. The notion that each individual carries a personal 'schema' or mental map of urban knowledge has been widely accepted (Appleyard, 1981). For each person, the city becomes a mosaic of places, some of which are well known, others partly, by repute or not at all together with a socio-spatial schema which links and relates them (Walmsley, 1988).

In a large metropolis, workers and residents may simultaneously know several areas in great detail and yet hold a sketchy schema of the city as a whole and a further idea of the city as part of the region. To compound this complexity, some of the images which may be held of places and districts within the city may not have been gained, as Lynch's subjects did, from direct experience, but instead may have been gleaned from magazines, the TV or other means of communication. Lynch's mapping system still has great relevance today, but some authors have argued that in order to truly comprehend the contemporary metropolis, it is important to recognise that there has been a paradigm shift and that we now exist in an age where certainty has been replaced by doubt and unity by fragmentation.

Place and Identity

Throughout twentieth century literature, art and films have dwelt on the difficulty of knowing cities, elaborating their contingency, their possibilities for disappearance and assumed identity, for chance encounters, for danger, for excitement, for despair. The vastness of contemporary cities, of which London is not an untypical example, has been a theme of cultural representations of the city since Dickens (Williams, 1985). In his famous poem *The Wasteland*, T.S. Eliot used the phrase 'unreal city' to describe London and this phrase has been taken up by cultural commentators as an appropriate metaphor for contemporary urban life (Timms and Kellay, 1985). The city, and subjective experience of it, is no longer a unity; it exists in multiple interpretations and is subject to shifts and changes through time.

The relation between place and individual partakes of these shifts and changes in meaning, of changing viewpoints and altered subjectivities (Pile, 1996; Lefebvre, 1991). Geographers have long rejected the notion that places have singular and fixed identities with clear boundaries (Massey, 1992). The perceptions of place change and as this happens, so the place itself changes.

A review of the evolution of urban form needs to take account of the process by which shifting perceptions of place alter the particularity of physical space. An attempt to comprehend and manipulate the potential form of cities at the beginning of the twenty-first century requires a sensibility towards connecting associations of place with the physical, direct experience of space. This observation is by no means original and much of the recent work of cultural geographers has been directed towards this end.[7]

Whilst place has always existed at the level of the imagination, from the tales of the first adventurers in Homer's *Iliad* onwards, it seems probable that the explosion of information associated with the information revolution is extending such knowledge at an increasingly rapid rate. Information has become more readily and widely available through films, TV and the print media as well as on the Internet. Such an expansion offers the prospect of more movement and of places becoming more specialised as people are willing and able to travel to them.[8]

The Commodification of Place

Some commentators, such as Wilson (1991) have remarked on a tension which they perceive between the potential which cities offer for disorder, transgression and rebellion; an impulse which they argue confronts the desire of planners and architects to impose a civic and social order, which is compounded by an increased desire to control and 'package' space.

Urban space is becoming increasingly commodified, in the mall, the historic tour, the tourist destination (Relph, 1976; Zukin, 1991). One of the dangers of this commodification is that, places can become a series of stereotypes and everywhere can become like everywhere else. It is a paradox that, in an age where more information is available to an ever widening group of the population and the means to exploit it in terms of movement exists, the specific character of certain popular locations are in danger of being destroyed. In this context, the importance of establishing a structure of places with a distinct identity and imageable connections between them becomes vital.

A New Structure of Metropolitan Urban Form

Diagnosis

To summarise the argument so far, it has been suggested that current trends point towards the formation of a multi-centred metropolis, in which traditional centres have assumed a new, more specialised role in parallel with the emergence of a profusion of new suburban or peripheral sub-centres. The key influence on the development of this form has been the networks of movement and communication. In order to influence the pattern of development and to make it more 'liveable' designers should concentrate on its most important generators, which are the 'nodes' or points of convergence of the movement systems and the 'armature' or most significance stretches of the key channels of movement.

Such a description is hard-edged and physical. It has also been argued that, what Raban has termed the 'soft' aspects of city life, are equally important. Perceptions of spaces and places shift and change and as they do the character and popularity of specific places alter, expand and decline. There is both a need to overlay or map this 'soft' understanding of the places of the city on to the more discrete understandings of transport, land-use and urban form in order to build up a more accurate view of the 'shape' of the contemporary metropolis.

The strategy of reinforcing the identity of the metropolis and its web of symbolic associations by identifying and strengthening an urban armature also raises a number of issues of practical concern. Three of the most critical are social exclusion, sustainability and governance.

The new workplaces and service centres emerging on the periphery of large metropolitan cities are wholly based on access by the private car and serve middle class communities. Access for poorer, inner city communities is difficult and often impossible. Garreau has pointed out that even in the United States, where the edge city phenomenon is well advanced and very many cities have a greater amount of office and retail floorspace in out-of-town locations than in the traditional downtown areas, the density of peripheral development has nowhere reached a level which would warrant the construction of effective mass transit systems.

The situation in London and other larger urban centres in the UK and elsewhere in Europe is different although similar problems result. As we have seen in the case of the Brent Cross 'corridor', the area is well served by a system of radial public transport systems which offer considerable potential for linking the new sub-centres with poorer districts but which lack the necessary lateral connections, interchanges and linkages with the local street system.

The view that a high energy, high pollution economy is not sustainable in the long term is now widely accepted. The modern metropolitan pattern of urban form and activities is clearly neither energy nor pollution efficient. Public transport systems designed to meet extreme peak one-way flows of commuters at two points in the day are wasteful at other times. Furthermore many public transport systems were designed along radial routes whereas now journeys are increasing between suburban centres and districts. Car-based transport-intensive urban forms such as suburbs in general, and out-of-town centres in particular, compound and magnify the problem many times over.

Apart from the appeal of cheaper living space and, increasingly, access to well-paid jobs in commerce and industry, the suburbs offer a refuge from the messiness of the city centres but with absence of the concentration and vitality that the traditional centres offer. Although current policies (DoE, 1997; DoE, 1996) are designed to redirect development towards a 'compact' city, the extent of suburbanisation means that this task will either take place over a highly extended time scale, or is doomed to failure. As an exclusively car-based existence is unlikely to be sustainable in the long term, urban designers and planners must address the issue of how a more urban, public-transport based lifestyle can compete with the attractiveness of suburbia. It is the contention of this paper that giving a tangible character to the concept of the network will play a vital role in this process.

Furthermore, if the city is conceived as a network of interrelated centres and sub-centres, the issue of governance becomes critical. Whilst devolving decisions down to the lowest level of accountability may be necessary from the point of view of democracy, our arguments about the interconnectedness of networks suggest that a strategic level of governance is crucial in order to ensure the most effective functioning. If, as has been suggested, the nodes or sub-centres are also important, then the implication is that administrative boundaries should not be placed to coincide with them, as frequently happens.

Conceptualising the Integrated Metropolis

The concept of an *integrated metropolis* is based on combining an integrated approach to transport and land use planning with the idea that the new urban sub-centres should be able to develop their own identity through a degree of specialisation within the urban region, dependent on parallel improvement in public transport and communications networks. Certain points within these networks, particularly the interchanges between one form or level of transport and another, form natural nodes for the development of a new style of urban sub-centres.

Increased density and the greater use of public transport are interdependent. With the continuing growth in car ownership and use, growing congestion and pollution in inner cities will sooner or later force the introduction of policies to control private car use, such as is now being discussed for Edinburgh and other cities. At the same time car-dependency is likely to persist for the foreseeable future in lower density residential areas and some form of gradualist approach is inevitable.

Rather than expecting autonomous urban villages to develop, the immediate aim should be to encourage the most efficient use of transport systems to distribute existing inefficient commuter flows among a number of centres. Urban management systems should be developed, overlaid onto existing physical structures to channel and regulate movement flows.

For example, the public transport application of passenger information and operational control systems linked to traffic control and driver information systems could increase flexibility of use and the ability to switch between transport modes based on up-to-the-minute information. In this scenario, the short term aim is for the local densification of suburban development. Achieving this would involve overcoming the historic dislocation of the transport network from the urban fabric in these areas, that is, literally attempting to retro-fit and densify suburban development around transport nodes.

This activity, rather than detracting from the city centre would rather maintain its dynamism by strengthening its connections with the periphery. The bias would be towards densifying the more central suburban centres, with the long-term aim of achieving a more compact overall metropolitan structure.

The integrated metropolis would therefore suggest a change in attitude to peripheral development which would neither, on the one hand, be the response of the *laissez-faire*, let the market rip and build wherever there is desirable or available green field space, nor on the other be opposed to any form of development but brownfield infill. The position is nearer to that taken by some Dutch authorities with their suggestion of an urban hierarchy ('the ABC Strategy')[9] and to that proposed by Friends of the Earth (1994) in their document *Planning for the Planet.*

We would suggest in addition that the design and mediation of the new sub-centres is of critical importance to the success of the concept for an *integrated metropolis*. Such sub-centres would need to incorporate the urban design lessons which have been painfully accrued in recent years about how to make cities liveable. In an intriguing paper Cervero (1995) provides evidence for importance of the design of suburban sub-centres in terms of choice of commuting by car or by public transport. He suggests that where the densities of sub-centres are higher and workers can easily walk to restaurants, banks and other services along pedestrian friendly routes, then car-sharing and use of public transport rises.

Coupled with this effort at the level of physical form, there would also be a need to intervene at the imaginative level, creating new perceptions of spaces both through cultural activities and through actively managing space to counteract trends towards privatisation and commodification. Again the role of urban management would complement that of design by actively intervening in the market to ensure that the 'symbolic economy' of the city has an element of sustainability.

Such transport and cultural management systems would also be able to offer a speedy response to the ebb and flow of city life, permitting growth in some areas whilst accommodating decline in others. If design and management attention were to be focused on to the 'armature' as defined, then change could be admitted without major disruption to the city as a whole. In this vision of a future city, the virtual networks of information and communication would be used positively to mediate the least beneficial aspects of the physical systems of movement and exchange.

Integrating the metropolis, then, would be an exercise in both physical design and urban planning and management. As such it offers an extension to the concept of the public realm and to the role of urban designers. Attention would no longer be focused on the square and on site-based problems, but would shift focus to the transport interchange, the high street and the sub-centre. Furthermore the public realm would be seen as a place of connections: between modes of transport, between public and private and between the imaginative, the virtual and the physical.

Conclusions

This chapter has argued that current trends suggest that many major metropolitan areas are experiencing an urban renaissance and a simultaneous suburban and peripheral expansion. Communications infrastructures provide a key to understanding of the city's structure in terms of its dynamic of growth, historical persistences and perceptual schema. However transport networks and urban sub-centres are becoming increasingly homogenous and divorced from the physical fabric of the city.

A humane, more sustainable and perceptually coherent city form could be assisted by the intervention of urban designers and urban managers. This concept is termed 'the integrated metropolis'. In this form of intervention, the main 'armatures' or key routes and places throughout the city structure would be made more physically legible, humanely managed and more closely integrated through the public transport system. These measures, combined with densification and the application of urban design principles to urban and suburban sub-centres, would encourage more even and intense use of public transport systems and enhance the environmental quality of the city as a whole, without recourse to an overly detailed masterplan of design guidance.

By intervening at the levels of the physical, the imaginative and the virtual, change could be accommodated. Important continuities of routes and spaces could be maintained, whilst other parts of the urban fabric could be subject to quite drastic transformations.

The concept of the 'integrated metropolis' implies an expanded concept of the public realm and a shift in focus for urban designers as well as those responsible for the operational management of cities and its longer term strategic planning. This paper was originally conceived as a vision for the shape of urban areas post-millennium. It is now offered as a practical contribution to the sustainable cities debate.

Notes

1   The argument that the metropolitan area remains the pre-eminent functional spatial unit of contemporary urban society is put forward by the US Congress, Office of Technology Assessment in their paper, *The Technological Reshaping of Metropolitan America*. An increasingly popular alternative to this view is the metropolis with a single major focal centre is being supplanted by networked systems of cities, each with its own specialised centre. However, our view is that such urban systems have been a feature of industrial society since the emergence of the first conurbations. The much-touted super city of the Pearl River Delta region between Hong Kong and Guanzhou, for example, differs from 'megalopoli' identified elsewhere in the developed world only in the extreme pace of its development.

2   We use here the term for the central administrative area of a metropolitan area as defined by the US Bureau of Statistics. In the UK, the equivalent would be the primary municipal area of a conurbation, in most instances a major provincial city or, in the case of London, the Greater London administrative area. Conceptually, if not strictly correctly in geographical terms, we use this term to denote the old urban centre comprising the 'downtown' city centre or central business district and inner city ring of higher density residential and manufacturing areas. Much of the recent new development has taken place beyond the boundaries of the central cities, as so defined, although many outer suburban areas, of course, remain within the administrative boundaries of the central cities.

3   Malone and Rockhart (1995) suggest that the growth of such developments represent a 'third order' response to transport technologies. They suggest that the first order effects were those of substitution, as when one type of transport technology replaced another, for example, when cars and trains were used instead or horse-drawn carriages. Second order effects comprised an increase in demand, as for example when there was an overall increase

in transport use. The 'third order' occurs with the emergence of 'transport intensive' urban structures.

4   Vertically organised, 'deeply-hierarchical' bureaucratic structures are being broken with flexible team-based units answerable directly, rather than through intermediaries to enhanced centres of power.

5   This means, for example, that the journey by Underground from London's Piccadilly to Heathrow takes as much time as a plane flight from Heathrow to Paris.

6   An armature is therefore not the entire road network, nor all of the public buildings, nor just the 'nodes' in a Lynchian sense of the term as centres of concentration. It might comprise elements of all of these; its essential feature is that it is composed of the most significant features of the public and semi-public realm.

7   See for example Westwood Williams (1997).

8   An obvious functional example of this would be the growth of theme parks and other leisure attractions, knowledge of which is gained through advertising. At a more cerebral level guided tours are now available through attractions as diverse as Dickens's London, Joyce's Dublin and Jack the Ripper's East End.

9   The Dutch ABC principle, or 'the Right Business in the Right Place' advocates positioning new office developments close to public transport nodes with defined plot ratios and parking standards. The proposal for the 'integrated metropolis' builds on this idea.

References

Aldous, T. (1992), *Urban Villages*, Urban Villages Group, London.

Alexander, C. (1965), 'The City is Not a Tree', in LeGates, R. and Stout, F. (eds) (1996), *The City Reader*, Routledge, London.

Appleyard, D. (1981), *Liveable Streets*, University of California Press, Berkeley, CA.

Bancroft, P., Doyle, J., Glaister, S., Kennedy, D. and Travers, T. (1996), *London's Size and Diversity: The Advantages in a Competitive World*, Corporation of London, London.

Bianchini, F. and Landry, C. (1995), *The Creative City*, Working Paper No.12, Demos, London.

Bianchini, F. and Parkinson, M. (eds) (1993), *Cultural Policy and Urban Regeneration: The West European Experience*, Manchester University Press, Manchester.

Buchanan, P. (1988), 'What City', *Architectural Review*, No. 1101, November.

Calthorpe, P. (1993), *The Next American Metropolis*, Princeton Architecture, New York.

Cervero, R. (1995), 'Changing Live-Work Spatial Relationships: Implications for Metropolitan Structure and Mobility', in Brotchie, J., Batty, M., Blakely, E., Hall, P. and Newton, P. (eds), *Cities in Competition: Productive and Sustainable Cities for the 21st Century*, Longman, Melbourne, Australia.

CM3234, Secretary of State for Transport (1996), *Transport The Way Forward: The Government's Response to the Transport Debate*, HMSO, London.

Crane, D. (1960), 'The City Symbolic', *Journal of the American Institute of Planners*.

Crossman, R.H.S., *The Diaries of a Cabinet Minister Vol. 1 Minister of Housing 1964–66*, Hamilton, London.

Coupland, A. (1996), *Reclaiming the City: Mixed Use Development*, E and FN Spon, London.

Davis, M. (1992), 'Fortress Los Angeles: The Militarization of Urban Space', in Sorkin, M. (ed.), *Variations on a Theme Park: The New American City and the End of Public Space*, Hill and Wang, New York.

Department of the Environment (1996), *Planning Policy Guidance Note 6: Town Centres and Retail Developments (PPG)*, HMSO, London.

Department of the Environment (1997), *Planning Policy Guidance Note 1: General Policy and Principles (PPG1)*, HMSO, London.

Dick, H.W. and Rimmer, P.J. (1998), 'Beyond the Third World City: The New Urban Geography of South-East Asia', *Urban Studies*, Vol. 35(12), December.

Fell, A. (1985), *Every Move You Make*, Virago, London.

Friends of the Earth (1994), *Planning for the Planet: Sustainable Development Policies for Local and Strategic Plans*, Friends of the Earth, London.

Garreau, J. (1991), *Edge City: Life on the New Frontier*, Doubleday, New York.

Gosling, D. and Maitland, R.B. (1984), *Concepts of Urban Design*, Academy Editions, London.

Graham, S. and Marvin, S. (1996), *Telecommunications and the City: Electronic Spaces, Urban Places*, Routledge, London.

Groosmith, G. and Groosmith, W. (1995), *The Diary of a Nobody*, Penguin Classics (first published 1892), Harmondsworth.

Hall, P. (1988), 'The City of Theory', in Legates, R. and Stout, F. (eds) (1996), *The City Reader*, Routledge, London.

Harvey, D. (1989), *The Condition of Postmodernity*, Basil Blackwell, Oxford.

Hayden, D. (1995), *The Power of Place: Urban Landscapes as Public History*, University of California Press, Berkeley, CA.

Hepworth, M. (1987), 'The Information City', *Cities*, No. 4, pp.253–62.

Hillier, B. and Penn, A. (1993), 'Dense Civilizations: The Shape of Cities in the 21st Century', *Applied Energy*, No. 43, pp.41–66.

Jacobs, J. (1965), *The Death and Life of Great American Cities: The Failure of Town Planning*, Jonathan Cape, London.

Jenks, M., Burton, E. and Williams, K. (eds) (1996), *The Compact City: A Sustainable Urban Form?*, E and FN Spon, London.

Jones, P. and Cassidy, S. (1995), 'The Role of Telematics in Contributing to Urban Transport Policy Objectives', *Built Environment*, Vol. 21(4), pp.223–35.

Koolhaas, R. (1994), *Delirious New York: A Retroactive Manifesto for Manhattan*, 010, Rotterdam.

Lefebvre, H. (1991), *The Production of Space*, Basil Blackwell, Oxford.

Loftman, P. and Nevin, B. (1995), 'Prestige Projects and Urban Regeneration in the 1980s and 1990s: A Review of Benefits and Limitations', *Planning Practice and Research*, Vol. 10(3/4), pp.299–315.

LPAC (London Planning Advisory Centre), *London's Town Centres; A Heath Check*, London Planning Advisory Centre, London.

Lynch, K. (1960), *The Image of the City*, MIT Press, Cambridge, MA.

MacCormac, R. (1987), 'Fitting in Offices', *Architectural Review*, Vol. 181(9), pp.50–51.

MacCormac, R. (1996), 'An Anatomy of London', *Built Environment*, Vol. 22(4), pp.306–11.

MacDonald, W. (1986), *The Architecture of the Roman Empire Vol. II: An Urban Appraisal*, Yale University Press, New York.

Malone, Rockhart, (1995), 'Computers, Networks and the Corporation, The Computer in the 21st Century', *Scientific American Special Issue*, New York.

Massey, D. (1992), 'A Place Called Home?', in Massey, D. (ed.) (1994), *Space, Place and Gender*, Polity, Cambridge.

Mitchell, B. (1995), *City of Bits*, Routledge, London.

Pile, S. (1996), *The Body and the City*, Routledge, London.

Porter, M. (1995), 'The Competitive Advantage of the Inner City', *Harvard Business Review*, May–June, pp.55–74.

Raban, J. (1974), *Soft City*, Hamilton, London.

Relph, E. (1976), *Place and Placelessness*, Pion, London.

Roberts, M. (1997), 'Future Cities, Past Lives: Gender and Nostalgia in Three Contemporary Planning Visions', *Planning Practice and Research*, Vol. 12(2), pp.109–18.

Roberts, M., Nice, S., Lloyd-Jones, T. and Erickson, B. (1996), 'The City as a Multi-Layered Complex of Simple Units New Tools for the Renaissance of the City, in Europe', European Conference, Berlin, 15–17 November 1995, Conference Proceedings, Berlin: TVFF and European Commission DGXII.

Rossi, A. (1982), *The Architecture of the City*, Oppositions Books, Cambridge University Press, Cambridge.

Sassen, S. (1994), 'Place and Production in the Global Economy', in LeGates, R. and Stout, F. (eds) (1996), *The City Reader*, Routledge, London.

Sassen, S. (1996), 'Gender, Ethnicity and Economy', in King, A. (1996), *Re-Presenting the City: Ethnicity, Capital and Culture in the Twenty-First Century Metropolis*, Macmillan, Basingstoke.

Sennett, R. (1991), *The Conscience of the Eye*, Faber and Faber, London.

Sennett, R. (1993), *The Fall of Public Man*, London, Faber (first published 1974).

Smith, N. (1996), 'Gentrification and the Revanchist City', in King, A. (ed.), *Re-Presenting the City: Ethnicity, Capital And Culture in the Twenty-First Century Metropolis*, Macmillan, Basingstoke.

Sudjic, D. (1995), 'The Slicker Cities', *The Observer*, 19 February.

Thomas, L. and Cousins, W. (1996), 'The Compact City: A Successful, Desirable and Achievable Urban Form?', in Jenks M. et al. (eds), *The Compact City: A Sustainable Urban Form?*, E and FN Spon, London.

Thompson-Fawcett, M. (1997), 'The Urbanist Revision of Development', *Urban Design International*, Vol. 1(4), pp.301–22.

Timms, E. and Kellay, D. (1985), *Unreal City: Urban Experience in Modern European Literature and Art*, Manchester University Press, Manchester.

US Congress, Office of Technology Assessment, (1995), *The Technological Reshaping of Metropolitan America*, OTA-ETI-643, US Government Printing Office, Washington, DC.

Walmsley, D.J. (1988), *Urban Living: The Individual and the City*, Longman, Essex.

Westwood, S. and Williams, J. (eds) (1997), *Imagining Cities: Scripts, Signs, Memory*, London, Routledge.

Williams, R. (1985), *The Country and the City* (first published 1973), Hogarth, London.

Wilson, E. (1991), *The Sphinx in the City*, Virago, London.

Yusuf, S. (1999), *World Development Report 1999/2000: Entering the 21st Century – Development Imperatives*, World Bank, Washington. DC.

Zukin, S. (1991), *Landscapes of Power: From Detroit to Disney World*, University of California Press, Berkeley and Los Angeles, CA.

Chapter Six

Urban Futures? Integrating Telecommunications into Urban Planning

Stephen Graham and Simon Marvin

Introduction: Urban Planning and the Technological Future of Cities

It is now widely argued that the increasingly pervasive applications of linked computer, media and telecommunications technologies constitute nothing less than a wholesale shift of our economy, society and culture. Social scientists regularly now talk of a new, emerging 'digital age', an 'information society', or a 'network society' (see Gosling, 1997; Castells, 1996). Such a transition is widely believed to be a new industrial revolution, a societal technological and economic shift across capitalist civilization of similar magnitude to the industrial revolution through which every aspect of society is transformed (Graham and Marvin, 1996).

As part of this shift, cities, and the corridors between them, are being permeated with widening arrays of telecommunications grids – conventional phone networks, wireless and radio systems, cable networks, satellite systems, Internet, data and video networks. These silently and (usually) invisibly underpin booming flows of voice, data, video and images across all walks of city life and development. Indeed, every aspect of the life of advanced industrial cities is now cross-cut with all manner of computerised and 'tele-mediated' communications exchanges, and transactions, most of which are now based on digital principles (meaning that they are based on the streams of zeros and ones used in computers). As Geoff Mulgan (1991) once put it, '... the re-definition of the city as a system for producing and switching information is highly visible'.

IT and telecommunications networks are thus becoming, in a very real sense, the very sinews of our society. For our profoundly urban societies, and for the whole gamut of actors, agencies, policy-makers, organisations, and individuals who currently depend on cities in various ways, the relationship between new media and telecommunications technologies and the future of our cities is clearly of critical importance. But what does this so-called 'digital age' really mean for our cities? What future is there for our urban areas, as more and more of the traditional roles and functions, which first generated the need for urban concentration, seem likely to be possible across distance via advanced telecommunications links?

Will our cities face some electronic requiem, some nightmarish *Blade-Runner*-style future of decay and polarisation? Or can they be powerhouses of economic, social and cultural innovation in the new electronic media? And, perhaps most importantly from the perspective of urban planning, what roles are there for urban policies, plans and strategies, and for urban design, community development and transport policies, within the shift to a so-called 'tele-mediated' urban life, based more and more on all types of on-line interactions?

The co-evolution of cities and electronic interactions is increasingly emphasised in technological debates within academia. Debates about 'cyberspace', telecommunications and the future of cities are currently proliferating within disciplines as diverse as architecture, cultural studies, communications studies, science and technology studies, and urban sociology and geography (see, for example, Mitchell, 1995; OTA, 1995; Graham and Marvin, 1996; Castells, 1996). Attention is increasingly being directed to exploring how the economic, social and cultural aspects of cities interact with the proliferation of advanced computer-based telecommunications networks in all walks of urban life (Graham, 1998). Here, the common 1980s assumption that the new communicational capabilities of new media technologies will somehow 'dissolve' the city has waned. Rather, it is now clear that most IT applications are largely metropolitan phenomena. They are developing out of the older urban regions and are associated with new degrees of complexity within cities and urban systems, as urban areas across the world become relationally combined into a globally-interconnected, planetary metropolitan systems (Graham and Marvin, 1996). Research here now centres on the degree to which city economies can be maintained in a world of on-line electronic flows; the ways in which place-based and 'virtual communities' interact; and the related interactions between urban cultures rooted in traditional public spaces, and 'cybercultures' operating within the virtual spaces accessed from computers (see Mitchell, 1995 and Graham and Marvin, 1996, for reviews).

Despite the central importance of the 'urban' in cyberspace debates, however, issues of urban policy and planning have been virtually absent within both the popular and academic sides of the discussions. New information and communications technologies are usually seen to be some disembodied, external 'wave' of change. Their urban 'impacts' are usually seen to follow inevitably from their effective '... collapse of distance' as a constraint on human life (The Economist, 1995). Such scenarios also usually imply that all cities (say, for Europe, London, Leeds, Charleroi, and Athens) will somehow all be 'impacted' in the same ways. Such so-called 'technological determinism' is attractive because it creates powerful scenarios, clear stories, and because it accords with the dominant experience in the West, where, as Stephen Hill (1988) puts it, the pervasive experience of '... technology is one of apparent inevitability'.

Questions of agency and local policy and planning therefore tend to be ignored in the simple recourse to either generalised, future-oriented debates, or to macro-level, binary models of societal transformation. In these, new technologies are seen to be somehow autonomously transforming society *en masse* into some new 'information age', 'information society' or 'cyberculture'. As the American geographer Robert Warren (1989, p.344) argues, '... benign projections [about telecommunications and the future of cities] give little indication that there are significant policy issues which should be on the public agenda'. In the emphasis on private entrepreneurship and the transcendence of place, the discourses of the 'information society' thus tend to imply that local municipalities, policy agencies and planners might even be little more than irrelevant distractions in this exciting and epoch-making transformation driven by private media, communications and property interests. Consequently, little thought is being put towards how urban policies, plans and strategies can *engage with* new technologies as policy agents to try and help shape *desired* urban futures in a purposive manner.

With utopianism and crude technological determinism often dominating popular and, in many cases, academic debates, it is not surprising that the potential roles of urban policy-makers and planners in 'socially shaping' new technologies in cities at the local level are usually overlooked (see, for example, Negroponte, 1995; Martin, 1995). This neglect, however, is problematic. It means that a fast-growing wave of urban experimentation with tele-communications, which is currently emerging across advanced industrial cities, is largely ignored within urban planning and policy debates. This is a problem, because such innovation promises to have major practical and theoretical implications for how we might consider the future of cities, urban policy and planning. It may also offer lessons on the broader question of how we might best understand the relations between cities and new communications technologies, and how we might address the crucial question of thinking about the 'local' and the 'urban', in an increasingly tele-mediated and globalised era.

This chapter attempts to address this problem by inserting urban planning into debates about new technologies and the future of cities. It has three parts. In the first, we set the context for local, planned intervention on IT and telecommunications by reviewing the evidence on the complex inter-dependence between cities, transportation and face-to-face interactions, and electronically-mediated interactions. We do this by looking in turn at transport-telecommunication relations, the broad links between urban economies and the so-called 'information economy', the relations between urban and so-called 'cyber' cultures based on IT systems, and, finally, the ways in which urban communities and 'virtual', IT-based communities are interdependently linked. In the second part of the chapter we go on to review a broad, international range of emerging policy initiatives which aim to help shape the articulation between the built form and socioeconomic development of cities, and the electronic interactions within such cities, and between them and the 'outside' world. Finally, in section three, we assess the significance of these policies and suggest ways for creatively integrating telecommunications into urban policy and planning practices and strategies.

The Metropolitan Dominance of the 'Digital Age'

To understand why cities will be central to the 'digital age', we need to explore the *complex inter-relationships* between electronic and urban interactions in the economy, culture, and society. We need, in short, to understand how our urban life stands in a state of subtle, two-way, *articulation* with electronic interactions (see Robins, 1995). We also need to understand why the level of the city and urban region might be a crucial one for exploring new policy innovations which make the most of the potential of new technologies, in a way which has meaning in relating to the urban worlds in which the vast majority of us live, work and act out our lives. To further explore the co-evolution of cities and telecommunications, which is essential as a basis for successful urban policy and planning innovation in these areas, we need to look in more detail at its four key aspects: transport-telecommunications interactions; the links between urban economies and the 'information economy'; interactions between urban cultures and cybercultures; and the subtle interactions between place-based and 'virtual' communities in cities.

Transport/Telecommunication

Conventional approaches to transporttelecommunications relations stress the environmentally beneficial role of telecommunications technology. It is often assumed that telecommunications can unproblematically substitute for physical transport flows and movement, reducing the need for travel, and so lowering levels of pollution and urban congestion. For example, BT's Environmental Manager argues that: '... telecommunications technology is likely to play an increasingly important role in offering a more environmentally sound alternative to travel ... Apart from a saving in energy the switch to telecommunication services would have other environmental benefits such as reduced noise levels, fewer new roads and lower levels of urban pollution' (Tuppen, 1992, p.81). Jonathon Porrit, one of the UK leading environmentalists, hails this fusion of communications and computing technologies as one of the 'tools for sustainability'.

Early research on the potential for trade-offs between telecommunications and transportation networks was commissioned by the US government in the mid-1970s in response to the energy crisis. This work simply compared the energy costs associated with communications through the telephone, and physical forms of communication such as personal travel by car, train and aeroplane (Nilles et al., 1976). The energy savings associated with communications by telecommunications created much excitement about the potential for trade-offs between telecommunications and transportation.

Initial interest in the role of telecom/transport trade-offs focused on the potential for the displacement of work-related commutes. In the mid-1970s, Jack Nilles invented the term 'telecommuting' to describe home or neighbourhood-based working using computers and telecommunications technology (see Nilles et al., 1976). Tele-based communication was seen as a solution to the problem of congested urban environments and long commutes to centralised offices. It was assumed that telecommunications would simply substitute electronic flows for the transportation of people and freight along more polluting road, rail and air networks. There were a number of attempts to demonstrate the potential substitution effects of teleworking on travel patterns and estimate energy savings. In the US context, these demonstrate that telecommuting has the potential to save between 1–3 per cent national energy consumption, figures which were not as great as the early proponents of teleworking might have expected (Nilles, 1988). These reports also have highlighted some of the 'rebound' implications of teleworking including extra energy consumed in home, movement out to higher-amenity areas, increasing total commute distances and the rapidly filling of road space through high latent demand (see Marvin, 1997).

The UK Department of Environment, Transport and the Regions' traffic projections show how demands for mobility and movement, both within and between cities, are unlikely to reduce, even whilst telecommunications use continues to burgeon. Overall, transport and telecommunications *actually feed off and fuel, more than simply substitute, each other.* While telecoms undoubtedly have some potential to substitute for journeys and more routine interactions there is considerable evidence that the relationship between transport and telecoms is more complex (Graham and Marvin, 1996). Rather than simply substituting, telecoms have highly *complementary* relationships with physical travel. This, we would argue, can actually result in three forms of traffic *growth*.

First, telecommunication play a central role in *improving the efficiency and effectiveness of transport networks,* so reducing the cost of travel. Complex computer ticketing, transaction systems and air-traffic control systems help reduce the costs of air travel, making it more attractive as our perceptual understanding of the world increases. Electronic information exchange also plays a major role in the organisation and management of transport networks. Such innovations help to extend the reach, reliability and usefulness of transport flows through air travel, autoroute guidance, fax, mobiles, e-mail, real-time information, and electronic data interchange-based 'Just-in-Time' logistics systems. A single flight of a 747, for example, has been estimated to generate 50,000 electronic exchanges in booking, maintenance, refuelling, airport management etc.

Second, access to cheaper telecommunications increases an individual's or organisation's 'perceptual space', creating more opportunities for physical travel. The more we get to know about the world, whether from a leisure, recreation, or business opportunities point of view, the more we demand new forms of physical travel to support flows of goods or to directly experience the quality of interaction that can only be achieved through physical contact – usually in cities. The people with the greatest demands to use phones and mobile computers are business travellers. People who telework and move far from cities may actually travel further overall because they travel further for other trips like shopping or because their fewer commutes are over longer distances.

Finally, congested roads create new demands for telecommunications. Mobile phones may actually help to sustain larger traffic jams because they allow 'dead' time to be converted to 'live' working time. It is no accident that some car manufactures now sell cars with car phones, faxes, or mobile computers – the ideal way of staying in touch with work and home, once a driver is stuck in a gridlock or slow moving traffic. In this way tele-communications helps overcome our resistance to travelling by cars on roads which are congested, as real time information overcomes many of the uncertainties and difficulties of travel. In short, what appears to be happening is a major expansion in all forms of communications. Although some substitution may undoubtedly be taking place, overall growth of electronic and physical mobility simply overwhelms the contribution of substitution.

Urban Economies/Information Economy

Current advances in telecommunications are a phenomenon which is overwhelmingly driven by the economic dynamism of cities, particularly larger, internationally-oriented, metropolitan regions. City-regions have important assets in an internationalising economy, based more and more on flows of information, services and 'symbolic' products like media, advertising, cultural services, and electronic entertainment (as well as movement of people, goods, and commodities). They support face-to-face interactions, especially for higher-level decision-making functions, in a world of fast flows and great volatility. We should not forget the sheer infrastructural advantages of cities. Cities also have the high-quality physical, service and telecommunications infrastructures to extend access efficiently to distant places and markets. Whilst remote, rural areas might still have old-fashioned and poor quality analogue telecoms infrastructure of the old monopoly (BT), our main city centres now have three or more separate, high capacity digital systems competing in price and quality (with many others selling specialised services). London's City and West End districts have at least four superimposed optic fibre grids (those of BT, Cable and Wireless, MFS and COLT) and countless other service providers who deliver over these networks. Eighty per cent of investment in telecoms in France goes to the Paris city-region.

But cities still offer unrivalled place-based, as well as electronic, contact potential. Today's uncertain and globalising economies make trust, constant innovation, and 'reciprocity' more and more important, which can only be fully-forged through on-going face-to-face contact. Stressing '... the extraordinarily social nature of modern economies', the geographers Nigel Thrift and Kris Olds (1996, p.316) write that '... it is clear that face-to-face interaction has not died out. Indeed, in some sense it has become more important as reflexivity (including an enhanced ability to see oneself as others see us) has become built into economic conduct'. Tony Fitzpatrick, (1997, p.9) the Director of Ove Arup, argues that:

cities reflect the economic realities of the 21st century. Remote working from self-sufficient farmsteads via the Internet cannot replace the powerhouses of personal interaction which drives teamwork and creativity. These are the cornerstones of how professional people add value to their work. Besides, you cannot look into someone's eyes and see that they are trustworthy over the Internet.

On the consumption side, too, the whole range of consumer services, now so important in urban economies – tourism, shopping, visiting museums and leisure attractions, eating and drinking, sport, theatre, cinema etc. – are all growing and seem likely to resist any simple, substantial substitution by 'on-line' equivalents.

Major urban places support dense webs of face-to-face links, transactional opportunities, agglomeration economies, access to wide pools of specialised labour, services, property and infrastructure, and 'soft' cultural and social advantages. Here the emphasis is increasingly on the *qualitative* aspects of urban economies and urban places, and the increasing dominance of urban economies by symbolic and representational flows and outputs, which may or may not be linked closely to commodity flows and outputs – what Lash and Urry (1994) term 'economies of signs and space'. Thus, in today's urban economies, the spiralling use of telecommunications becomes combined with the spiralling use of transport and a continuing, perhaps even growing, reliance on face-to-face contacts and meetings, largely in cities: what the father of the 'Megalopolis' concept, the geographer Jean Gottmann, used to call the '... spiralling mass of bits of information'. What many people interpret to be a post-urban shift might actually be a transition from traditional, core-dominated, monocentric cities towards complex, extended and polycentric city-regions made up of a multitude of superimposed clusters, grids and internal and external connections.

This is an important argument, which leads us to stress four points. First, growing flows of electronic information may require *more* face-to-face contact to make sense of it all as the Bristol geographer, Nigel Thrift, has shown with his work on City of London electronic traders. Second, much of the electronic exchange on networks like the Internet actually represent cities as places to visit, consume, travel to, or live within, as the many tourist and municipal and urban services sites on the Web demonstrate. In the US, the fastest-growing web sites are those that try to integrate the Internet at the level of the metropolitan region simply because this has most salience to Net users. Private operators of integrating city-level web sites in the USA have grown massively recently, attracted by the increasing maturity of the web as a diffused medium and by their calculations that '... 80% of purchases are made within a 20 mile radius of the home' (McElvogue, 1997, p.2).

Third, it is easy, given the hyperbole about globalisation, to radically underestimate the degree to which tele-mediated flows operate to sustain very local relations. The vast bulk of electronic exchanges, for example, are very local indeed: 60 per cent of all phone calls and e-mails move within single buildings (Graham and Marvin, 1996). And, finally, even when stories are apparently about decentralisation and substitution, essentially urban dynamics are usually at play. Most teleworking, for instance, is done for part of the week in the zones within and around the large cities that allow people to go to the office on one or two days a week for face-to-face meetings. When IT does support so-called 'dis-intermediation', directly linking consumers and producers across distance – as is the case with many call-centres delivering routine services on-line – their destinations tend not to be rural spaces but smaller, provincial, cities or, in sectors like on-line computer programming, far-off cities like Bangalore in India.

Urban Cultures/Cybercultures

Thirdly, the centres of many of our larger cities are experiencing renewed growth as interlinked centres of growing cultural industries (arts, theatre, dance, music, publishing, fashion, media, graphic design, photography, architecture, leisure, sport etc.). The importance of city centres has recently been re-emphasised, based on the widening assertion that such 'cultural industries' may, with appropriate policies, interlace positively within a framework of public space to support the emergence of 'creative cities' (Landry and Bianchini, 1995). The central idea driving such policies is that cities can only thrive when strategies recognise that '... the defining characteristics of cities are high density, mixed use, stimulus, transactions and above all diversity' (Montgomery, 1995). But how do urban cultures interrelate with much-vaunted 'cybercultures', at a time when *electronic* cultural interactions are exploding, fuelled by digital technologies, and the blurring of boundaries between computing, media, and telecommunications industries and technologies?

It is clear, at the level of large organisations, that large cities *already tend to dominate* the sectors that are blurring together with the emergence of multimedia: TV, publishing, art and design, film, and media and tele-communications. Such firms continue to rely on large cities for all the reasons stated above. But the prospects for creative synergies between urban and cybercultures seem extremely strong at the much more dynamic level of small and micro-firms. In an apparently paradoxical twist, the continuous innovation in the Internet, digital media, and multimedia content industries, so often hailed as supporting the 'death of distance' by media and industry pundits, is being fuelled by intensely local networks based on face-to-face interaction in selected urban districts.

In fact, as the value-added in IT industries shifts from the zones dominated by hardware production to places that can sustain innovation in software and content, so the focus of the industries may actually be shifting from Silicon-Valley-like Research and Development campuses, to central, old-city, locations. In the cultural industries, the creative small firms that dominate Internet software, digital design, and World Wide Web services, far from scattering towards rural idylls, seem, in fact, to be concentrating into (a small number of) gentrifying metropolitan 'information districts' like SoHo and Tribeca in New York, Shoreditch in London, and Temple Bar in Dublin. As well as having good (broadband) telecom connections and tailored, 'Internet-ready' office spaces, such districts are thriving through processes which, arguably, are analogous to those which spawned the first industrial districts in nineteenth century cities. In a detailed study of SoHo and Tribeca in Manhattan, for example, Dan Hill (1997) found that the raw material for such industries is the sort of informal networks, high levels of creativity and skill, tacit knowledge, and intense and continuous innovation processes that become possible in an intensely-localised culture, based on on-going, face-to-face contacts supported by rich, dense and interdependent combinations of meeting places and public spaces. Clustering in certain 'information districts' may thus support the informal and on-going innovation networks and serendipitous contacts that seem central to the success of small and micro digital arts and creative firms (Hill, 1997).

Most importantly here, the Internet, with its 'spiralling mass' of information, communication, transactions and specialised media flows, is now weaving into support every aspect of urban functioning in contemporary city-regions. Such trends are most advanced in the USA, which demonstrates the strong metropolitan bias of both the production and consumption sides of the Internet. On the *production* side, for example, down town New York's 'Silicon Alley' has emerged, along with districts in downtown San Francisco and other large cities, as a remarkable concentration of micro and small firms, based on digital art and design, Web production, and digital and multimedia services. These draw on the City's unparalleled arts, cultural industries, and literary traditions. One of the main motors of the recent economic renaissance in Manhattan, Silicon Alley encompasses over seven hundred new media firms who rely on intense, informal, local contacts to sustain continuing innovation and interaction (Hill, 1997). Interestingly, urban planning and policy is beginning to find ways of supporting this new information district, as we shall see in the next section. It must be stressed however, that currently only a relatively small number of urban districts are being redeveloped in this way. Moreover, these 'organic' spaces are very difficult to develop 'artificially' – that is, in the absence of an existing appropriate, high skill levels, contact networks, supportive services, and local entrepreneurial culture.

On the *consumption* side, it seems that the metropolitan dominance of the Internet might actually grow rather than decline, as it becomes massly diffused, accepted and gradually woven into all aspects of urban life. This is certainly the recent experience of the world's most mature Internet market, the USA (Moss and Townsend, 1997). The top fifteen metropolitan core regions in the US in Internet domains accounted for just 4.3 per cent of national population in 1996. But they contained 12.6 per cent of the US total in April 1994. By 1996 this had risen to almost 20 per cent, as the Internet became a massly-diffused and corporately-rich system. As Moss and Townsend (1997) suggest:

> the highly disproportionate share of Internet growth in these cities demonstrates that Internet growth is not weakening the role of information-intensive cities. In fact, the activities of information-producing cities have been driving the growth of the Internet in the last three years.

Manhattan now has twice the 'domain density' (i.e. concentration of Internet hosts) of the next most 'Internet-rich' US city – San Francisco – and six times the US average (Moss and Townshend, 1997).

In such a context, there are many opportunities for weaving 'access points' – Internet and service kiosks – into the fine-grained fabric of cities, to animate, enliven and inform what goes on in the public and private realms of cities and metropolitan regions. Whilst there are many problems here to do with the high costs on technologies, highly uneven social access and skill levels, and dangers of oppressive surveillance, a growing range of initiatives at the urban level are currently experimenting with new media solutions to support the improved delivery of public services, support community networking, and enhance local economic, social and cultural development.

But such public initiatives are far outweighed by the sheer *economic* logic of the Internet. Already, private Internet providers are themselves starting to develop integrating web sites at the urban level. These aim to support coherent and legible relationship between the many services on the web that fall within a particular city and the population of that city. The need for 'urban Internet guides' is especially powerful in the larger 'global' cities that dominate Internet innovation and use. New York, for example, now has over 10 dedicated 'virtual city' web sites that aim to draw together various portfolios of local Internet-based services (Graham and Aurigi, 1997).

Urban Communities/Virtual Communities

Finally, all aspects of the social use of telecommunications remain highly dominated by, and bound up with, the lives and social worlds of urban populations and communities. It is in our metropolitan regions that the most rapid diffusion of mobile phones, cable systems, and the Internet, have developed, and where the rich communicational and transactional fabric of cities is increasingly supported by complex tapestries of telecommunications networks. One only has to witness the recent explosion of the use of mobile phones on our city streets to understand this. Thus, for example, the many virtual communities on the Internet are made up of both globally-stretched Use-net groups and Multi-User Dungeons (MUDs) etc. and a growing range of community networks at the local level in towns and cities, aimed at feeding back positively onto the social dynamics of individuals cities (Graham and Aurigi, 1997).

Some writers have even suggested that local urban community networks like the Cleveland Freenet, Santa Monica Public Electronic Network and Seattle Community Network, as well as the more recent 'virtual' or 'digital city' movement, represent hope for truly interactive, democratic, media systems which might help revive, enliven and inform the public realm of their host cities (see Schuler, 1996). The hope here is that local IT systems that support interactive community debates, will help to bring together the diverse social, cultural and geographical fragments of extending city regions, adding important coherence and legibility to a city's 'electronic realm' in the process. In the long run, computer networks 'grounded' in particular local communities, might be more sustainable, effective and meaningful than those which rely purely on IT-based exchange across global distance. Wakeford (1996) argues that 'grounded' community IT networks can often support higher degrees of trust (with 'persistent' rather than 'transient' identities). They can also relate more effectively to real problem-solving, can inter-relate with training centres and face-to-face contact, supporting reciprocal, frequent and supportive interactions which relate strongly with the wider public realm. Finally, these advantages can often allow them to draw in wider cross-sections of people than global Internet newsgroups.

But such assertions and rhetoric need to be tempered by the realisation that profoundly deep social divisions in access to all communications technologies are woven deeply into the fabric of our cities (see, for example, Demos, 1997). Whilst elite groups are 'super connected' to phone and IT networks at home, school, in their cars and at work, even the humble telephone is an expensive luxury in many more marginalised urban neighbourhoods. One neighbourhood in inner Newcastle, for example, had only 27 per cent of its households connected to the telephone in the late 1980s (Graham and Marvin, 1996, ch. 5). Home access to the Internet, with its prerequisites of skills, electricity, space, hardware, software, telephone, modem, Internet account, and cash for on-line and phone charges, is unlikely to be a priority for the large proportion of socioeconomic groups facing poverty, debt, and problems paying for essential bills. This places a premium on supporting access to community IT networks and Internet-based systems into the public spaces of cities.

One of the key policy issues for the tele-mediated city, therefore, is how to address deep social segmentations based on access to, and exclusion from, the new communications media, and the growing ranges of information, resources, and transactional and working opportunities offered over them (see Schön et al., 1998). As more and more IT-based systems become the norm – for example with growing reliance on home and mobile telephones, home IT systems, and electronic cash – so it becomes more and more disadvantageous to experience 'network poverty' beyond the reach of such systems. But this is not to assert that systems like the Internet can act as some 'silver bullet' to complex problems of social exclusion, in the manner of the US Speaker, Newt Gingrich's absurd, utopian, and patronising 'laptops to the ghettos' rallying cry in 1995. Rather, it is to stress that new community-based electronic networks are required which, as a matter of course, work to enrol the broadest possible range of users and voices. Such experiments must be seen as attempts to explore the fullest potential of the new media, as realms for social communications at the most meaningful geographical level to most people – that of the metropolitan region.

Emerging Telecommunications-Oriented Urban Planning Strategies

Clearly, it is no longer adequate to consider policies for cities and those for telecommunications and new media entirely separately. The above imperatives suggest that only through addressing the complex interactions between cities and telecommunications will the potential of the technology be realised. This realisation is currently leading to a wide range of policy experiments which aim to positively shape how the new media relate to specific cities or parts of cities. Early examples can be drawn from a 'bricollage' of evidence, drawn from cities in the US, Canada, Malaysia, Europe, the UK and elsewhere around the world. These examples have not yet coalesced around a coherent new paradigm of urban policy. Many can be criticised as technologically determinist, environmentally problematic, or socially exclusionary.

But we would argue that, together, they point to a new style of planning and urban policy. Such urban strategies try to shape face-to-face interactions in place (and the transport flows that sustain these) in parallel with electronically mediated ones across distance. Currently, we can identify three emerging styles of such 'urban telecommunications planning': integrated transport and telecommunications strategies, city-level new media strategies, and so-called 'information districts' and 'urban televillages'.

Integrated Transport and Telecommunications Strategies

The first set of initiatives attempt to shape and manage the relations between physical movement and mobility through the application of new media, combined within particular forms of urban physical development. Each embodies a particular conception of the relations between different forms of communication and their role in the development of the city.

Urban and Regional Teleworking Initiatives First, there are Urban and Regional Teleworking Initiatives. There are a growing set of initiatives, especially in the USA, that are attempting to grapple with the problems of developing a metropolitan-region approach to teleworking to make a positive contribution to environmental improvement – particular reducing vehicle emissions. For example, Telecommunications for Clean Air is a two year programme funded by the Californian South Coast Air Quality Management District to use telecommunications to meet rigorous air quality standards. The main aims of the programme are to identify cost-effective solutions to air quality and congestion, to contribute to economic growth, and to develop a regional approach to problem solving.

The Telework Facilities Exchange is designed to expand telecommuting participation in local government by providing low-cost, flexibly-located facilities and marketing these practices to other organisation joining the exchange (Telecommunications for Clean Air, 1994). A public sector employee would normally commute thirty-five miles each way to their office. Instead, they commuted to a vacant office a few miles from their home to use a workstation connected to their office. Those workers participating in the Programme reduced their normal vehicle miles travelled by 88 per cent. As a result, if 30 per cent of the region's 484,000 local government employees each worked one day a week at the exchange, nearly 500,000,000 vehicle miles travelled could be saved each year (Telecommunications for Clean Air, 1994).

These findings have to be treated with caution because studies indicate that teleworking can generate 'rebound effects'. Although commute trips and time can be saved, additional recreational and shopping trips may be generated. Telecommuters may also decide to live further from the city, so increasing the length of remaining commutes. And the space freed on highways is quickly filled with new commuters (see Mokhtarian, 1990; Department of Energy, 1994). But these tensions could be managed at a metropolitan level, as teleworking is coordinated within the context of wider transport and land-use strategies. The US initiatives are particularly interesting because of the high degree of organisational innovation in the delivery mechanisms for teleworking, and the much stronger links to more mainstream transport, air quality and landuse planning policies than tends to exist in Europe.

Assessments of the environmental potential of teleworking in the UK have largely remained at the level of national aggregate assessments (British Telecom, 1992; CEED, 1992). Overall, the conclusions are that the beneficial impact of telecommunications may be limited. Even assuming that teleworking continued to grow at a fast rate, the Royal Commission on Environmental Pollution concluded that it would only have a small role to play in the reduction of emissions. But, although the national environmental benefits may be small, there could be potential in large conurbations in the UK to develop initiatives within a wider environmental policy framework. A recent study by a Cambridge-based consultant, for example, argued that 1.25 million miles per year could be saved by 2,000 office-based staff at Cambridge council telecommuting (Environment, 1997). Further development work is necessary, perhaps drawing critically on the US experience. For instance, BT provides limited guidance for local authorities attempting to integrate telecommunications into Local Agenda 21 Strategies. And the Association of County Councils has started to consider how IT and telecommunications could be linked with the green agenda (BT, 1997; Association of County Councils, 1996). The key issue is the need to carefully integrate teleworking within the context of wider transportation and landuse plans.

Communication Corridors Second, there are new forms of communication corridor strategies which attempt to shape how telecommunications, transport and land use interplay within broader urban commuting corridors. Those based on existing rail/transit networks attempt to manage travel demand both on the road and rail network through the provision of teleworking centres and incentives to travel off-peak. The Metro Net initiative in Los Angeles, for example, involves retrofitting a high capacity fibre optic network along side the 300 mile regional Metro Rail and Link network (Siembab, 1992). The proposals are designed to achieve three objectives: to generate revenue through leasing capacity, to develop services to enhance ridership of the system, and to improve regional mobility through developing station-based employment and service centres. The mobility strategy has been designed to fit in with the objectives of a series of wider regional communications and landuse strategies. More specially, it is hoped that the strategy will contribute towards the implementation of the Air Quality Management Plan, the Development Plan, the Regional Congestion Management Program, and the promotion of regional economic growth. The proposals would develop telecommunications facilities at or near stations for conferences, education, and job-training, to make the Metro system a destination itself.

Further development would link both the metro and telecoms networks to targeted parcels of adjacent land, in order to attract new employers whilst maximising public transport usage. These ideas mirror proposals in the UK to set up telecommuting offices along the Folkestone to Waterloo rail line, in order to reduce the number of rush hour commuters and enable a channel tunnel link to run on existing tracks (Roarke Associates, 1994). A more recent proposal suggested building a ring of teleworking centres around the M25 to deal with predicted car traffic growth. The architects, Roarke Associates, argued that the teleworking centres would cost £450 million whereas road widening would cost £1,450 billion – a saving of £1 billion (*The Times*, 1997). Both these initiatives are at the proposal stage and have not been implemented. However, they illustrate some interesting ideas about how communications planning could integrate telecoms and transport, and start to make wider links to landuse strategies. Yet, at an institutional level, there is still considerable uncertainty as to which organisations could take the lead with such complex initiatives involving so many different dimensions of planning.

Road Transport Informatics (RTI) The third type of initiative focuses on the development of Road Transport Informatics (RTI). City-wide initiatives are rapidly emerging here, concerned with the use of RTI systems to more effectively manage transport networks. There are major initiatives in Europe, the US, and Japan and the National Economic Development Council estimate that the global IT and traffic management market will be worth £29 billion in 2010. However, objectives of RTI are often poorly defined and are not often closely linked with landuse and work patterns. These initiatives are more often characterised by a form of 'technical fix', dominated by strong producer-led interests. RTI strategies have assumed importance in the context of EU funding programmes where the technologies are seen as making a major contribution to sustainable development (CEC, 1995).

There have been a large number of feasibility schemes evaluating the potential of various forms of RTI and electronic tolling in the UK. But, again, there has been a failure to link such debates within the context of wider urban management, regeneration, and landuse strategies. These issues are being considered more widely in North America. The Highway 407, which is currently being built in Toronto, is billing itself as 'Tolls but No Jams' (*Toronto Star*, 29 July 1996, pp.A6–A7). Located in one of the most congested highway corridors in North America, a $1 billion 36 km highway will eventually connect the airport to downtown Toronto. The scheme is being developed by Canadian Highways International Corporation – a private consortium of four companies who will be funded by the receipts from electronic tolls. In return for the higher charges, users will benefit from higher road speeds than the current limit, and no traffic jams. If demand increases, the highway can be expanded to ten lanes and tolls can be raised to reduce peak travel volumes. The scheme is being marketed at those firms operating just-in-time production methods who require high degrees of certainty in travel times for the movement of goods and services. There is now major development interest in highway land involving commercial, retail, leisure and recreation and housing adjacent to the new road. This initiative is an interesting example of the combined planning of electronic, transport and landuse infrastructure, designed to develop a congestion-free, higher-speed and lower travel-time corridor through the congested region. But this new development trajectory is extremely socially exclusionary. It is very much designed to meet the needs of large international corporations and elite users prepared to pay the premium for increased certainty.

Other RTI initiatives focus on the development of local and regional initiatives in driver information and control systems. These initiatives are based on proposals to carry more traffic by making better use of the existing road network, through pre-trip planning, route guidance, traffic management and control, and network management applications. It is hoped that the provision of information to drivers on road conditions can increase the efficiency of the network to minimise delays, unreliability and environmental damage. For instance, it is estimated that driver information could increase the capacity of the road network by 1 per cent provide a 10 per cent saving in journey times and a 6 per cent reduction in mileage. The Scottish consultative document argues that the region is well placed to use these technologies because 80 per cent of the population live within a relatively self-contained belt across the country (The Scottish Office, 1993).

There are a number of problems with the emerging set of urban communications strategies in the UK. They tend to remain largely disconnected from mainstream urban strategies and have poorly developed links with landuse planning. They also tend to narrowly represent a limited and technologically-determinist view of urban futures based around notions of a producer-led 'technical fix' to the problems of urban mobility. Nevertheless, taken as a package, they do begin to illustrate some of the ways in which integrated urban planning for physical and electronic mobility.

City-Level New Media and IT Strategies

The second broad emerging policy area is City-wide new media strategies. IT strategies for community networking, local economic development, and public service delivery have been under way in many UK, European, and American cities for a decade or more. Following American experience, community networks like Free-nets, the Manchester, Kirklees, and Nottingham Hosts, and the Newcastle NewNet system, based on the Internet, have emerged which try to use computer communications to support grassroots, local economic development, and voluntary activities (see Graham and Marvin, 1996). Many local authorities are also experimenting with videotex systems, electronic kiosks and smart cards systems to deliver information on public services, and aim to improve the services themselves. Nationally in the UK, the new government report, *The New Library: The People's Network*, proposes to wire up both schools and libraries as places where IT networks can be made widely available for local communities.

Local services have developed patchily on the new urban cable networks developing across the UK. And virtually all major UK cities now have a presence on the Internet, where so-called 'virtual cities' range from simple tourist promotion and local databases, to sophisticated spaces which attempt to add coherence to all local activities on the Internet, to widen local access and skills, to open up interactive services for local debates, and to develop information and communications services which feed back positively onto the development of the home city (Graham and Aurigi, 1997). Interestingly, the most innovative virtual cities use the analogies of city 'spaces', 'squares' and 'districts', so that the many services they offer relate directly to their counterparts in physical urban space. The most sophisticated of these in the UK currently is Virtual Bristol, supported by a partnership of the City Council, Universities, and Hewlett Packard, launched in April 1997. Not to be left out, BT is exploring the concept of 'urban intranets' – Internet services that are only accessible to specified local communities.

This disparate range of local new media initiatives has two problems, however. First, they have tended to be fragmented local 'IT islands', largely ignoring each other. And second, they have usually been developed with little or no respect for how they relate to the physical urban realm or to the broader development dynamics and geographies of their subject cities. Thus, the challenge for UK cities is to shape coherent partnership-based strategies aimed at harnessing all types of new media applications – Internet, cable, kiosks, telephone, infrastructure – to their economic, social and cultural development needs. Such issues need to begin with social, geographical and institutional issues and policy needs and move onto how new technologies might meet these needs – rather than the other way round. Institutional solutions need to be found that harness the entrepreneurial energies of the new media industries, and their growing interest in market-based local initiatives (like the booming commercial metropolitan Internet sites in the US), whilst linking creatively and positively to the fragmented sets of agencies involved, in the broadest sense, in the governance of UK cities (local authorities, development agencies, health, education and information institutions, firms, schools, the community and voluntary sector etc.). Clearly, urban media 'Master plans' will be impossible: what is needed are strategic frameworks so that the innumerable local media investments and initiatives emerge to be more than the sum of their parts.

Finally, and most importantly, from the point of view of this chapter, there needs to be a much more thoroughgoing attempt to link urban media strategies to the development of cities themselves, so ensuring that, wherever possible, synergies can be developed between media and place-based exchanges. Progress is being made here, however, at both the urban and regional levels. At the city level, strategic planners in cities like Amsterdam and Lille have already attempted to integrate new media into the future urban visions. In dozens of cities across the world, 'teleports' and 'telezones' have been designated in particular urban districts blending advanced office and business space and sophisticated telecommunications facilities. In the US, ambitious 'Smart City' new media strategies are tentatively starting to consider land-use planning and urban policy issues – as our discussions of strategic urban corridors and information districts demonstrate. Already, in some such (highly affluent) communities like Palo Alto and Blacksburg Virginia, very high levels of Internet and e-mail access and use have begun to transform the communicational fabric of urban areas as these new media become woven into the fabric of urban life (see Graham and Marvin, 1996). Predictably, in a private-sector-led planning process, the consultancies engaged in 'Smart Community' planning argue that '...cities unprepared for these [new media-based] changes risk being consigned to geopolitical obsolescence before they even know what hit them' (International Center for Communications, 1997).

In the UK, the packaging of IT infrastructure with individual land-use developments – business parks, 'telecottages', 'wired villages' etc. – is increasingly common. But efforts are also starting to link broader urban media strategies with urban-wide development strategies. After a period when grant, training and technological support was 'pepper-potted' through the city, Manchester is increasingly gearing its broad telecoms and IT initiatives to specific urban redevelopment and re-use projects, and to strategic discussions about combating social exclusion in the City. A widening range of new physical, IT-oriented projects have emerged linked into the network services on offer: the Electronic Village Halls (linked to community centres and initiatives through the City), existing managed workspaces in New Mount Street, and proposed ones in the 'Northern Media Quarter', and a centre for Multimedia development and applications in Hulme (Carter, 1996). A similarly broadly-based IT and new media strategy, known as the GEMESIS project, is underway in adjacent Salford, backed by a broad partnership between the cable company, IT firms, local universities and training providers. In partnership with its university sector, Manchester/Salford, like German cities such as Berlin and Bochum, is also building a new broadband Metropolitan

Area Network ('MAN') infrastructure ring in the City that will spur efforts to regenerate the inner city through research and development and scientific innovation.

Europe-wide, cities at the vanguard of new media strategies are cooperating through the 'Telecities' network to exchange experience, develop lessons for best practice, support pilot initiatives, and lobby the EU for further support. Telecities also links into Europe's efforts to support the emergence of what it terms a 'Regional Information Society' through its broadly based Inter-Regional Information Society Initiative (IRISI). This supports integrated packages of ICT based pilot projects in designated regions in sectors as diverse as education, health, social services, transport and logistics, media and public services. But, again, there exist few links between the way the EU is considering ICT applications, services, and infrastructure, and its broader considerations about its spatial development in the future (CEC, 1997).

'Information Districts' and 'Urban Televillages'

The final area where new media policy is becoming directly linked with policies for particular urban spaces is the emergence of 'information districts' and urban 'televillages'. Building on the debates about 'urban villages' in Europe, and the 'new urbanism' movement in the US, interest is growing rapidly in how media infrastructure and services can be designed and managed, geared to sustaining and feeding back on particular urban districts. In California, the concept of the 'TeleVillage' – an integrated urban place supported by a whole suite of ICT infrastructures and services – is gaining support. The Blue Line TeleVillage, a two square mile area on one of the new public transit corridors in LA, is based on a holistic strategy to manage land use, transport trips and electronic communications so that synergies emerge between the three, creating a 'liveable' community with reduced automobile use, higher community-based activities, and higher urban densities than in the usual LA suburbs (Siembab, 1995).

Physical places for supporting IT training and services – community centres, computer centres, telework centres, IT links in schools, hospitals, transport facilities and libraries, and electronic kiosks in public and semi-public spaces – are integral to the plan which is backed up by a broad, public-private-community partnership, and an extensive array of on-line public services. In partnership with the public transport operators in the LA region, a new fibre network is being developed to link together whole constellations of

TeleVillages across the region. Different packages of IT and telecoms infrastructure and services are being offered for different land uses; 'distributed' organisations are being encouraged; and attempts are being made to include more marginalised social groups. The philosophy is that IT-based retrofitting in existing US urban areas will mean that many urban problems might be addressed '...with very little new physical construction and no dramatic changes in density' (Siembab, 1995).

The other emerging example of combining new media and urban regeneration at district level is the concept of the 'information district'. Here, the emphasis is on creating urban 'milieux' that sustain economic growth in new cultural and 'symbolic' industries, where informal face-to-face contact is essential, whilst also providing high capacity on-line linkages to the wider world. Such strategies are inspired by the emergence of 'information districts' described above. Most often, information district strategies emerge organically, as in the cases considered above – New York's Silicon Alley, Dublin's Temple Bar, and Manchester's Northern Quarter – where clusters of such industries emerge spontaneously in inner urban districts. Then, the challenge is to intervene to further support the growth of small and micro firms in the relevant sectors, whilst also ensuring appropriate property is available and that broader efforts are made to improve the broader urban realm and the contribution of the industries to the economic and social revitalisation of the city as a whole (Hill, 1997). Thus, both New York and LA have offered grant schemes and tax exemptions to small and micro firms in the new media sectors. Backed by the powerful New York New Media Association (NYNMA), specialised multimedia centres, offering managed workspaces and high-level telecoms bandwidth, have also started to emerge in Silicon Alley, as have dedicated venture capital funds and orchestrated events and programmes designed to encourage local face-to-face networking. Elsewhere in the USA, the city of Spokane, in Washington State, has wired up much of its downtown to attract multimedia firms.

In Europe, strategies at the neighbourhood and district level have begun to look to coherent interventions in the urban realm, new media, and, at the institutional level, to try and either sustain, develop or encourage, local clusters of multimedia firms. Manchester has explicitly adopted the Silicon Alley model to support its Northern Media Quarter, on the edge of the city centre. Sheffield's well known Cultural Industries Quarter (CIQ) strategy, aimed at clustering the broadest possible range of media, design, music, film and cultural-related industries firms in one part of the City centre, is now backed-up by a widening range of on-line services financed by a public private partnership called NEO

(Hill, 1997). Dublin's Temple Bar district is backing up its physical regeneration efforts, weaving a parallel infrastructure for electronic, multimedia exchange.

In London's Soho media core, mean while, a specialised telecommunications network was recently constructed by a consortium of film companies called 'Sohonet'. This system links the tight concentration of film and media headquarters in the district directly to Hollywood film studios, allowing on-line film transmission and editing over intercontinental scales, via highly-capable, digital, broadband connections. The network is seen as a critical boost to the broader global ambitions of the UK film and cultural industries.

Conclusions: Integrating Telecommunications into Urban Planning

In this chapter we have attempted to demonstrate that new information technologies actually resonate with, and are bound up within, the active construction of urban places, rather than making them somehow redundant. Urban places and electronic spaces are increasingly being produced together. The power to function economically and link socially increasingly relies of constructed, material places which are intimately woven into complex media infrastructures which link them to other places and spaces. '... Today's institutions', argues William Mitchell (1995; p.126), '... are supported not only by buildings but by telecommunications and computer software'. Thus the articulation between widely-stretched media and telecommunications systems, and produced material places, becomes the norm. It is, indeed, a defining feature of contemporary urbanism. '... Constructed spaces', continues Mitchell:

> will increasingly be seen as electronically-serviced sites where bits meet the body – where digital information is translated into visual, auditory, tactile or otherwise sensorily perceptible form, and vice versa. Displays and sensors for presenting and capturing information will be as essential as doors (Mitchell, 1994).

As cities extend into polycentric metropolitan regions, the spaces of the city are being constructed within broader, and more complex, urban fields, networked together by more sophisticated, integrative technological networks.

With the above examples, we have started to map the emergence of a potentially significant shift in urban strategies based around the idea of trying to shape how built spaces and electronically-mediated interactions work in parallel. Reviewing a set of innovative initiatives, it is apparent that planning initiatives are proliferating, which try to actively shape the articulations between the development and use of new media and communications technologies and urban places. Such initiatives are supported by widening efforts by planners, urban development agencies, transport bodies and media firms to understand the complexities through which electronically-mediated communications interact with land use, the urban realm, transport and face-to-face contact. Moreover, it is clear that the initiatives reviewed above are only the start. Virtually every western city worth its salt now seems to use 'cyber' and 'silicon' as obligatory prefixes in its urban marketing campaigns. Many beyond those discussed above are also exploring how they can address places and IT networks in parallel.

We would argue that the current growth of explicitly urban telecoms strategies and initiatives are broadly to be welcomed. This is for three broad reasons. First, they are acknowledgements that city-telecoms interactions are intrinsically bound up with contemporary metropolitan life. Second, these policies are based on much more sophisticated understandings of the complex and subtle relations between new media and urban life than those 'Death of Distance' or 'End of Cities' ideas generally implied by dominant 'information society' debates. And third, these proliferating policies suggest that the articulations between urban spaces and new media technologies are open to innovative, local, and planned interventions which can bring benefits which neither untrammelled market forces nor distant central state hierarchies can deliver.

But what might these nascent policies mean for urban planning and urban development more broadly? Obviously, speculation is difficult in such an embryonic policy arena. In these conclusions we would therefore like only to address two key questions. First, are urban telecommunications initiatives likely to be able to succeed in shaping positive synergies between place-based interactions and development and electronically-mediated interactions and development? Or are they merely stylistic and symbolic, aimed at adding value and high-tech kudos to prestigious real estate developments? Second, what might these initiatives mean for broader notions of the 'city' and for ideas of integrated metropolitan-wide planning? More particularly, are these initiatives likely to reinforce and recreate new forms of socioeconomic exclusion and environmental damage, or might they genuinely emerge as useful attempts to develop more inclusionary and sustainable urban futures?

Turning to the first question, we must first sound some notes of caution. For, despite the widening range of initiatives, we remain highly cautious of their current usefulness, in terms of both their magnitude and direction. In terms of their magnitude, we must raise serious warnings against *overstating* the potential role of telecommunications and information technology in urban strategies. Whilst most approaches to urban strategies are still grappling with new ways of planning for transportation grids and urban places in parallel, it is still the case that electronic interconnections and networks are most often still hidden and taken-for-granted.

In terms of direction, it is clear that even when land use, transport and telecoms are considered in parallel, real progress will only come when two further problems are addressed. Firstly, policy-makers will need to actively fight against prevailing assumptions (which are actually deeply embedded within western culture as a whole) that new technologies can somehow be rolled out as technical 'quick fix' solutions to complex urban problems. In a context where most urban policy-makers and planners lack knowledge and experience of the telecommunications sector, there is the danger that urban strategies could uncritically embrace the transformational rhetoric that characterises contemporary notions of technology 'impacts' upon the city that we touched on at the start of this paper. New telecommunications initiatives are still often intimately connected with utopian and deterministic ideas of technology's beneficial and linear impacts upon the social, environmental and spatial development of cities. Developing more nuanced and sophisticated concepts of the potential roles of telecommunications in urban strategy will require policy-makers to look more critically at the role of technology in contemporary urban strategies.

Achieving this, however, is difficult for another reason. Powerful media and technology firms are exploiting the hyperbolic rhetoric of 'cyberspace', the 'information superhighway' and the 'global information society' to enrol poorly-informed urban public policy-makers into making local 'partnerships' to develop new information districts, communications corridors, and 'high tech' economic development zones of various sorts. Growing inter-urban competition, and the tendency for urban policy-makers to jump on the latest policy band wagon, is being exploited by a wide range of consultants and media conglomerates. Such organisations are keen to add value and symbolic kudos to their own efforts to build up demand for new configurations of real estate and developed spaces, and all the associated technological hardware and services embedded in them. Public subsidies, discounted land deals, infrastructural assistance, credibility and the sheer marketing weight of public policy-makers can do much to raise the profile of new, planned 'high-tech' spaces (and, therefore, developer profits). But the real benefits of such initiatives to localities may be dubious or massively over blown because they remain inappropriate to real local needs. Thus, planners and local policy-makers need to educate themselves as quickly as possible about the burgeoning worlds of new media technologies. They need to be wary of being seduced into expensive partnerships of dubious real local benefit by the lustrous promises of information age hyperbole. It is here that critical local debate about the real communicational needs of urban places, and the policy models that derive from these, is necessary.

Above all, planners must be sensitive to the important *symbolic* power of information and new media technologies, as signifiers of 'high tech' modernity. They must also be attentive as to whose interests this symbolic power serves and how. Arguably, this symbolic power (which, by its very nature is very visible), is as significant, perhaps more significant in some cases, that real new applications or telecommunications infrastructures (which often remain unknown or hidden). Labelling a place 'cyber' this, 'silicon' that, or 'tele' something else, is an affirmation that it is switched in to global circuits of economic, cultural or social exchange via electronic networks. It is a potent, symbolic, attempt to lure in mobile capital, people and investment, which adds value to fixed infrastructure, land, and real estate even when they are clearly in tension with highly dynamic and mobile flows of services, media, information and money over telecommunications grids.

Such symbolism can take extreme forms. At one stage, for example, Edinburgh city council considered building an artificial satellite dish on its Maybury business park because BT argued that there was no technological need for one in the City (which still has 'world-class' satellite facilities accessible from other places) (Graham, 1999). Of course, if local policy-makers willingly embrace this symbolic power and use it creatively to their own advantage, through place marketing strategies and the like, all well and good. But they must be careful not to be duped by it, and not to uncritically believe all the promises of corporate and media firms that this new (publicly subsidised) media or IT network will miraculously solve all local problems of traffic congestion, social polarisation, economic development, environmental sustainability, and so on.

Which brings us on to our second question: what might these initiatives mean for broader notions of the 'city' and for ideas of integrated metropolitan-wide planning? Here, too, there is a need for concern. In the light of the above discussion, we clearly need to unpack the social assumptions and biases built into current urban telecommunications initiatives. We need to ask how urban telecommunications initiatives might link to wider urban debates around social equity, the public realm and culture, economic development, and environmental improvement. With such a strong supply push from powerful media and real estate interests, there are clearly dangers that urban telecommunications strategies are being configured in highly biased ways that might perpetuate and reinforce widespread existing trends towards social and spatial polarisation in urban areas.

The danger is that the foci of initiatives will centre overwhelmingly on configuring new media technologies according to the needs and geographies of affluent, privileged nodes, spaces and corridors in metropolitan regions whilst ignoring and excluding marginalised zones. The former, of course, are already at the vanguard of IT applications and are the 'hot spots' of demand for all forms of telecommunications and media applications and services (Graham and Marvin, 1996). In the context of liberalising telecommunications regimes, the risk is that market forces will encourage both corporate and media interests and urban policy-makers to invest their efforts in communications corridors for the highly mobile, information districts for the information elites, and media consumption spaces for affluent professionals with high disposable incomes. In short, urban telecommunications strategies may simply work to extend the existing relational privileges of powerful zones, spaces and interests in the city.

Such fragmented policy 'packages', superimposed as patchworks across the urban landscape, reflects wider trends within urban governance towards the collapse of the notion of coordinated, metropolitan-wide planning (Graham and Marvin, 1999). Complex patchworks of special interest zones and public-private governance initiatives are tending to replace systematic, metropolitan-wide public planning (Boyer, 1996). As Bosma and Hellinga (1998, p.16) argue, in contemporary planning practices, '…the primary matter of importance is no longer an integral approach, but the cheerful acceptance of regions as an archipelago of enclaves'.

Urban telecommunications initiatives are clearly contributing to such an 'archipelago of enclaves' The worrying thing about the urban tele-communications initiatives reviewed above may work to both reflect and sustain wider social polarisation trends. Thus, within cities, smart transport corridors and 'wired' enclaves might support forms of 'telematics super-inclusion' (Thrift, 1996) for elite groups, allowing them to live in cocooned (often sometimes walled) enclosures, whilst still accessing personal and corporate transport and telematics networks. Meanwhile, however, a short distance away, in the interstitial urban zones, there are likely to be 'off-line' spaces (Graham and Aurigi, 1997), or 'lag-time places' (Boyer, 1996, p.20). In these, often-forgotten places, access to the new technologies will remain highly problematic. Time and space will remain profoundly real, perhaps increasing, constraints on social life, because of welfare and labour market restructuring and the withdrawal of banking and public transport services.

But perhaps we are being too negative here. For we must also stress the positive potential of urban telecommunications initiatives as well as the need to be wary of their symbolic power and cautious of the possibilities that such initiatives may reinforce urban social and spatial polarisation. Progressive, inclusionary telecommunications and IT policies, integrated into particular urban strategies and designed to tie cities together rather than split them apart, might have important, positive roles in shaping the articulation between place-based and electronically-mediated realms. They might help, quite literally, to 'ground' the globally-integrating world of new media interactions, making them more meaningful in real places, real communities, real lives. Such initiatives may help to 'embed' new technological innovations in particular places, rather than just supporting an evermore momentous de-localisation through market-driven forces of globalisation in the economy, society and culture. And, given enough stress on the needs of low income communities, such initiatives might actively counter wider urban polarisation trends (see Schön et al., 1997).

Indeed, one might even argue that *without* active, progressive resistance to untrammelled globalisation and the colonisation of local spaces by global media markets, mobilised through the rubric of creative, place-based, IT strategies, social need, the particularities of place, freedom of expression and local cultural diversity may tend to be squeezed out of the corporate, commodifying logic of globalisation. As Grossman (1995) puts it, '...media conglomerates will not fill the vital educational, civic, and cultural needs' of real places and real cities. Strategies like the one in Manchester show that, just because privately-inspired urban IT initiatives have followed a particular trajectory, this does not mean that these cannot be challenged by incorporating wider social and environmental concerns into policy development.

References

Association of County Councils (1996), *Green Communications: Planning for Telematics, Teleworking and Telecounties*, Environment Committee.

Bosma, K. and Hellinga, H. (1997), 'Mastering the City', in Bosma, K. and Hellinga, H. (eds), *Mastering the City*, NAI Publishers, Rotterdam.

Boyer, C. (1996), *Cybercities: Visual Perception in an Age of Electronic Communication*, Princeton University Press, New York.

British Telecom (1992), *A Study of the Environmental Impact of Teleworking*, A Report by BT Research Laboratories.

British Telecom (1997), *Telecommunications Technologies and Sustainable Development – A Guide For Local Authorities*, British Telecom.

Carter, D. (1996), '"Digital Democracy" or "Information Aristocracy"? Economic Regeneration and The Information Economy', in Loader, B. (ed), *The Governance of Cyberspace*, Routledge, London, pp.136–54.

Castells, M. (1997), *The Rise of the Networked Society*, Blackwell, Oxford.

CEC (1995), 'Contributions of the Information Society to Sustainable Development', in ECOTEC (1996), *Information and Communication Technologies for Sustainable Technical Development, Final Report*, CEC, Brussels.

CEC (1997), *European Spatial Development Perspective*, CEC, Brussels.

CEED (1992), 'The Environmental Impact of Teleworking', *UK CEED Bulletin No 38*, March–April, pp.10–11.

Demos Collection (1997), *The Wealth and Poverty of Networks*, Demos, London.

Department of Energy (1994), *Energy, Emissions and the Social Consequences of Telecommuting, Energy Efficiency in the US Economy*, Technical Report One, DOE/PO–0026.

The Economist (1995), 'The Death of Distance, Telecommunications Survey, 30th September–October 6', *The Economist*.

Environment (13/11/1997), 'Flexible Working Could Reduce Traffic', *Environment*.

Fitzpatrick, T. (1997), 'A Tale of Tall Cities', *The Guardian On-Line*, Thursday 6 February, p.9.

Gosling, P. (1997), *Government in the Digital Age*, Bowerdean Press, London.

Graham, S. (1998), 'The End of Geography or the Explosion of Space? Conceptualising Space, Place and Information Technology, Progress', *Human Geography*, Vol. 22 (2), pp.65–185.

Graham, S. (1999), 'Satellite Dishes', in Pile, S. and Thrift, N. (eds), *City A–Z*, Wiley, London.

Graham, S. and Aurigi, A. (1997), 'Virtual Cities, Social Polarisation and the Crisis in Urban Public Space', *Journal of Urban Technology*, Vol. 4 (1), pp.19–52.

Graham, S. and Healey, P. (1999), 'Relational Theories of Time and Space: Issues for Planning Theory and Practice', *European Planning Studies*.

Graham, S. and Marvin, S. (1996), *Telecommunications and the City: Electronic Spaces, Urban Places*, Routledge, London.

Graham, S. and Marvin, S. (1999), *Splintering Networks/Fragmenting Cities: Urban Infrastructure in a Global-Local Age*, Routledge, London.

Grossman, L. (1995), 'Maintaining Diversity in the Electronic Republic', *Technology Review*, November/December, pp.23–6.

Hill, D. (1997), 'Cultural Industries in the Digital City', unpublished MA dissertation, Manchester Metropolitan University.

Hill, S. (1988), *The Tragedy of Technology*, Pluto, London.

International Center for Communications (1997), *Building Smart Communities*, Guidebook January, International Center for Communications.

Landry, C. and Bianchini, F. (1995), *Creative Cities*, Demos, London.

Lash, S. and Urry, J. (1994), *Economies of Signs and Space*, Sage, London.

McElvogue, L. (1997), 'Bright Sites, Big City', *Guardian On-Line*, Thursday 20 February, pp.2–3.

Martin, W. (1995), *The Global Information Society*, ASLIB, Aldershot.

Marvin, S. (1997), 'Environmental Flows: Telecommunications and the Dematerialisation of Cities', *Futures*, Vol. 29 (1).

Mitchell, W. (1994), 'Building the Bitsphere, or The Kneebone's Connected to The I-Bahn', *I.D. Magazine*, November.

Mitchell, W. (1995), *City of Bits: Space, Place and the Infobahn*, MIT Press, Cambridge, MA.

Mokhtarian, P. (1990), 'Relationships Between Telecommunications and Transportation', *Transportation Research*, Vol. 24A (3) pp.231–42.

Montgomery, J. (1995), 'Urban Vitality and the Culture of Cities', *Planning Practice and Research*, Vol. 10 (2) pp.101–9.

Moss, M. and Townshend, A. (1997), 'Manhattan Leads the Net Nation', available at http://www.nyu.edu/urban/ny_affairs/telecom.html.

Mulgan, P. (1991), 'The Changing Shape of the City', in Hall, S. and Jacques, M. (eds), *New Times*, Lawrence and Wishart, London.

Negroponte, N. (1995), *Being Digital*, Hodder and Stoughton, London.

Nilles, J.M. (1998), 'Traffic Reduction by Telecommuting: A Status Review and Selected Bibliography', *Transportation Research A*, Vol. 22a (4), pp.301–17.

Nilles, J.M., Carlson, F., Gray, P. and Hanneman, G. (1976), *The Telecommunications-Transport Trade Off*, Wiley, Chichester.

Office of Technology Assessment (1995), *The Technological Reshaping of Metropolitan America*, Congress of the United States, Washington, DC.

Roarke Associates, (1994), *Telecommuting Offices – A Proposal for Congestion Relief on London and S E England Rail Services*, Roarke Associates.

Robins, K. (1995), 'Cyberspace and the World We Live In', in Featherstone, M. and Burrows R. (eds), *Cyberspace/Cyberbodies/Cyberpunk*, Sage, London, pp.135–56.

Schön, D., Sanyal, B. and Mitchell, W. (eds) (1997), *High Technology and Low Income Communities*, MIT Press, Cambridge, MA.

Schuler, D. (1996), *New Community Networks: Wired for Change*, Addison Wesley, New York.

Scottish Office (1993), *A National Driver Information and Control Strategy for Scotland*, a consultation document.

Siembab, W. (1992), *Metro Net, Fibre Optics and Metro Rail: Strategies for Development*.

Telecommunications for Clean Air (1994), *South Coast Air Basin*, Institute for Local Self Government.

Thrift, N. (1996), 'New Urban Eras and Old Technological Fears: Reconfiguring The Goodwill of Electronic Things', *Urban Studies*, Vol. 33 (8), pp.1463–93.

Thrift, N. and Olds, K. (1996), 'Refiguring the Economic in Economic Geography, Progress', *Human Geography*, Vol. 20 (3), pp.311–37.

The Times (1997), 'Teleworking Could Save a Billion', 9 July.

Tuppen, C.G. (1992), 'Energy and Telecommunications – An Environmental Impact Analysis', *Energy and Environment*, Vol. 3 (2), pp. 70–81.

Wakeford, N. (1996), *Developing Community Intranets: Key Social Issues and Solutions*, Paper for BT.

Warren, R. (1989), 'Telematics and Urban Life', *Journal of Urban Affairs*, Vol. 11 (4), pp. 339–346.

Chapter Seven

Multiple Meanings of Space and the Need for a Dynamic Perspective

Ali Madanipour

This chapter aims at exploring a way of understanding space and place that can be used in spatial planning. It argues that space is often understood from limited, at times dichotomous perspectives, and that to overcome these limitations, space and place should be approached at the intersection of these traditional dichotomies. It starts by discussing the rising significance of space in managing cities, followed by emphasising the multilayered meaning of space. It then outlines some of these perspectives and argues for the need for a broader, more dynamic perspective in understanding space and place. The paper argues that understanding and managing places is only possible through negotiation between agencies involved at the intersection of these potentially conflicting interpretations.

The Multi-Dimensional Significance of 'Place'

The significance of place is emphasised from a variety of perspectives and for a variety of reasons. There is an increasing interest in the qualities of places, particularly on the part of the policy makers. For too long, it has been argued, most recently by the New Labour government in Britain, departmental and sectoral separation has prevented effective attention to be paid to the mounting social problems. What is asked for is 'joined up' working, crossing the barriers between various government agencies and between the public and private sectors. A renegotiation of the division of labour may lead to some blurring of the functional boundaries of the departments and agencies, boundaries which could have a negative impact on the delivery of service. Bringing these forces together, therefore, requires a new focus, which has increasingly been the 'place'. To create this spatial, rather than functional, focus, a number of area-based initiatives, therefore, have been introduced.

The New Deal for Communities, with a budget of £800m over three years, deals with intensive regeneration of small neighbourhoods, starting with seventeen pilot schemes. Another programme is Sure Start, to support young children in deprived neighbourhoods, providing for childcare, primary health care, play, and support for families. Single Regeneration Budget, a programme already in its sixth year, is being revamped and transferred to Regional Development Agencies, targeting areas on average with 25,000 people, i.e., larger than the New Deal for Communities. Health Zones, Education Zones and Employment Zones are also being introduced, targeting areas of intense social exclusion (Social Exclusion Unit, 1998).

The idea of using place as a means of management is of course not new. This is particularly evident in the tradition of developing new neighbourhoods, from the neighbourhood units of the British New Towns to the current urban villages. Some times the idea of 'inventing' a new place has been manifest in new administrative boundaries, which may or may not relate to the existing sense of place among the people of an area. Creating a new place, or redefining an old one, has therefore been among the tools of city management, as part of the efforts to give order to cities. At its worst, this management led to social engineering, which was engaged in creation of places with particular aims for a simplified order.

Another reason for the interest in place has been the increased despatialisation of activities. The new technologies of communication have increasingly made it possible for news and information, as well as money, goods and services, to be exchanged without close contact. From the printed word, which had rivalled the word of mouth as a method of communication among large numbers of people, to the satellite technology and the Internet, which facilitate a constant flow of global communication, many new vehicles are now at work towards despatialisation of social activities. These new technologies have made it possible to earn a living, consume products, and even engage in the political process without necessarily leaving the front door, which could have a direct impact on the shape of social relationships and their spatial manifestations. In this sense, attention to places finds a particular significance. Places are more and more expected to work as a medium of overcoming the degree of functional dispersion and disintegration in cities and human societies.

The place is also a major constituent of the sense of identity. The intensified globalisation has brought with it the need for a clearer sense of identity, as historically rooted in particular places. Rootedness in places plays a considerable role in the sense of wellbeing of people, who may feel exposed to the global forces beyond their control. This may have some potentially negative effects on the ability of different groups to live together peacefully, as each makes a claim to the place they call their home. Heated nationalism, racism and xenophobia are among these negative dimensions. Nevertheless, the role of place in the construction of social identity cannot be denied, an issue that has been at the forefront of concerns in a globalising world.

Also the place has been used as a signifier to establish new identities, in a culture which strives towards appreciating the multiplicity of identities and of tolerably accommodating difference. The celebration of difference and multiculturalism are among the hallmarks of the new forms of urbanism. The metropolitan areas, in particular, are places where an amazing variety of ethnic and cultural groups as well a range of social and economic groups live. Rather than promoting melting pots, where all differences fade away, the current trend has been to celebrate these differences. One of vehicles of constructing, or coming to terms with, a diversified society has been the qualities of places, where different groups have colonised different parts of the city. To these groups, the qualities of these places are closely related to their sense of group and individual identity (Zukin, 1995).

In addition to this cultural role, places have found a new social significance. Throughout the nineteenth and twentieth centuries, cities have spread into the countryside and suburbanisation has coincided with socio-spatial segregation, where different social and ethnic groups are separated from each other. For long, this social fragmentation has caused concern among the political and cultural elite. If social segregation and exclusion find spatial manifestation in space, then overcoming them would require an awareness of spatial dynamics. The place has, therefore, been increasingly seen as one of the vehicles of combating segregation and fragmentation.

Qualities of places have, on the one hand, a direct relation with the concerns for the assertion of identity and overcoming of socio-spatial segregation and exclusion. On the other hand, the concern for the quality of place is embedded in economic and social change in cities. As manufacturing industry has been replaced by the service sector as the main base of the economy, cities are transformed to accommodate the change. Rather than concentrations of industrial workers, cities are now housing new groups with different needs. Cities need to compete in the global space to attract the highly mobile capital and the lesser mobile skilled labour. The regeneration and gentrification of the urban areas are among the means with which places are promoted in the global marketplace, to attract visitors, investment and jobs. Cities are being reshaped and re-imaged to address the needs of the new economy. In Britain, this has included, among others, the attention to urban design, promotion of a European style café society, twenty-four-hour cities and use of cultural industries in urban regeneration (Ashworth and Voogd, 1990). Attention to these qualities of places finds major importance in managing the transition to a new economic base.

Yet another development, which has led to an interest in place, has been the concerns about environmental sustainability. To confront environmental degradation, both at global and local levels, much attention is being paid to the way new environments are being developed and managed. Many questions about density and mobility, for example, are being raised in connection to searching for alternative models of development. The interest in the qualities of places, therefore, has come to the fore with a new strength, and from a perspective that had never been articulated as such in the past.

The spatial dynamics of cities and the qualities of places in the new global space, therefore, are increasingly important. Place is increasingly used as a means to integrate activities and groups, to assert identities, to support economic development, to combat rootlessness, and to cross the bureaucratic barriers (Madanipour, forthcoming). This may pose a danger in concentrating on the container and not its contents, a new environmental determinism or an ecological fallacy. It may also be used to help improving the actual conditions of life for large numbers of citizens.

This attention to place is often focusing on the most visible places of a city, the derelict eyesores of industrial decline or the showpieces of the city centre. The deprived neighbourhoods may find themselves marginalised in the rising significance of place, as their offerings in the marketplace are not valued highly. Also what is considered marketable is discussed, promoted and even invented, such as Chinatowns, which are associated with successful businesses and a possible connection with powerful Asian economies. Far less (or no) attention, however, has been paid to the promotion of Africatowns or Indiatowns, even though they may actually exist in cities.

This diverse set of meanings reflects the multiplicity of agencies that are engaged in development, exchange and use of places. Acknowledging this multiplicity leads us to the notion that the meanings of place and space are socially constructed. As these agencies have diverse role and interests, places can have multiple, and at time conflicting, meanings, even for single agencies, meanings that are assigned to places through social processes.

Multilayered Meaning of Space

The spaces around us everywhere, from the spaces in which we take shelter to those that we cut across and travel through, are part of our everyday social reality. How can social life be imagined without being involved in going from one place to another, without thinking about this and other places, without communicating with each other across space? Our spatial behaviour, which is defined by and defines the spaces around us, is an integral part of our social existence. As such we understand space and spatial relations in the same way that we understand the other component parts of our social life.

The facts about the world, John Searle (1995) argues, can be divided into two categories. The first category is what he calls 'institutional facts', facts that only exist by human agreement, because we believe them to exist. Another category is that of brute facts, those that exist independently of human institutions. Most elements of the social world belong to the first category, from money to marriage, property and government. The fact that a piece of paper has a value of, for example, five pounds is a social fact. Without our institutionalised agreement, it is no more than just a piece of paper. The brute fact about the space of our cities, therefore, is that it is a collection of objects and people (and other life forms) on the surface of the earth. The social fact about the cities, however, is that these objects and their relationships have been created by human agreement and bear particular significance and meaning for people. The sheer physical presence of roads, schools, and houses does not render them meaningful. It is the collective intentionality, the capacity of humans to assign functions, to symbolise these objects beyond their basic presence that makes them part of the social reality.

This process of symbolisation, in which physical objects are assigned with meaning, is what separates space from place. Whereas space is open and is seen as an abstract expanse, place is a particular part of that expanse which is endowed with meaning by people. Place, therefore, is embedded in social processes and its meaning is derived from the social practices of a particular society. The significance of symbolism in the construction of social reality, however, shows how there can be more than one interpretation for the social facts. As one of the most important dimensions of our social world, space finds different interpretations and meanings. As different groups give different meanings to space, it becomes a multilayered place, reflecting the way places are socially constructed (Knox, 1995).

Beyond Limited Perspectives

Recognising that space has multiple meanings is just the first step in searching for an answer for the problem of approaching the subject matter. If we review the current and historical approaches to space, we see many dichotomies; as one approach has been established, another has emerged to challenge it. Yet often the meaning can be found beyond these narrow dichotomies.

One of the major differences of perspective into understanding space has been the debate on absolute versus relational space. One view holds that space is a real thing, and exists independently of the objects within it. It is an entity with unlimited extent, which frames and contains all material objects. This notion of space, called 'absolute space' was developed by Newton and has been used ever since in many branches of science. Another notion of space, called relational space, holds that space is no more than the relations between other things. This notion was first developed by Leibniz as a reaction to absolute space. According to this view, space and time are only relations between objects and events and have no existence of their own. Relational space, therefore, was seen as the '...positional quality of the world of material objects', as opposed to the absolute space as the '...container of all material objects' (Einstein, 1954, p.xiii). In a sense, both these concepts of space are, as Albert Einstein put it, '...free creations of the human imagination, means devised for easier comprehension of our sense experiences' (ibid.). The debates about them, however, have had a direct influence on understanding, and shaping, the built environments of the twentieth century.

Even a brief search in the fields of urban geography, urban sociology, urban planning, and architecture shows the diversity of perspectives and understandings of space. As places which bring together human beings, parts of the natural environment, and material objects, urban areas are nodes of human societies. These complex socio-spatial agglomerations are often studied from different perspectives. Our reading of urban form will be different, depending on what element we are interested in and how we choose to study it. There are clear trends, however, that can be traced in a study of these approaches to the understanding of urban space. At least three different perspectives can be identified in the study of urban spaces. Due to the limits of discussion here, my sketches or the example mentioned should not be taken to be intending to oversimplify complex discussions or offering an exhaustive review of the literature. What is argued here is that none of these perspectives can be sufficient in reaching a better understanding of place without the insights of the others.

The first perspective sees the city as a collection of artefacts: buildings, roads, trees, and other material objects. Most of architectural and some urban geographical writings fall within this perspective. The way this urban space is structured is therefore understood to be a matter of classifying these material objects into meaningful groups and exploring people's relationships with them. One way of studying urban space is to explore its relationship with nature. Urban space can, for example, be seen as 'created', as distinctive from natural, space. The relationship between the created and natural, therefore, becomes essential to understand, how natural processes inside the urban area and outside it have an impact on the city (Hough, 1984). Another way of understanding the city is to concentrate on its relationship with time. Some concentrate on the city as the built environment, attempting to classify building forms and street patterns according to their period of development and styles (e.g. Whitehand, 1987; 1992). This is a temporal classification of urban space, which develops a sense of the historical evolution of urban space and the impact of such evolution on its current character. Yet another form of classification is to focus on the urban space's relationship with human activities. The urban space of material objects, therefore, can be classified in accordance with the way it is being used. This is a spatial classification, which aims at understanding the land use patterns, analysing it in terms of its particular mix of use and density (e.g. Bourne, 1971; 1982). This can concentrate on the centre-periphery relations, in how city centres and suburbs correlate, as contrasting entities or component parts of urban regions. The relationship between these various areas, as physically exemplified by transport networks is studied to analyse the urban structure, where streets and squares, as spines and nodes in the movement patterns, are primary elements in the constitution of urban space.

This perspective, therefore, is interested in describing and explaining how material objects and artefacts came into being and are being transformed and used. Its main shortcoming is that the study of people and processes are brought into play in a secondary capacity. In a very broad sense (and at its extreme, with some simplification), the approach, in all its different varieties, is more interested in environment than in people. While understanding space is essential in understanding people who make it and use it, it is by no means a substitute for understanding people's patterns of thought and behaviour, which has a causal impact on the study of place-making.

The second perspective, on the other hand, sees the city as an agglomeration of people. The two traditions of urban ecology and political economy are the main trends in social sciences, particularly in human geography and urban sociology, that correspond to this perspective. It often criticises the first perspective as being descriptive, or that it does not address what really matters in the city, i.e., its social relations. If it does address social relations, the second perspective stresses, it fails to go deep enough. So this perspective offers a geometry of social relations.

Some of the different directions that this approach takes can serve as examples. One strand looks for what brought people together in the city and the general patterns of this process. The study of the process of industrialisation and its impact on urbanisation, therefore, becomes an area of study for explaining the city's features through how industrial production processes attracted workers and created large urban agglomerations (Scott, 1990). What finds particular importance is to study the rise and agglomeration of units of production, the development and change of capital and labour markets, as well as the dynamics of organisation and reorganisation of production. Others are concerned to study these relationships in the wider context of the world economy and the role an urban area plays in the world system, and how the movement of capital and labour, and the goods and services they produce, across the world can structure cities in new ways (Sassen, 1994).

Yet others look at the patterns of consumption in the city space. We can look at urban space to see how socially and spatially it is stratified: how rich and poor are segregated in different places and neighbourhoods, and the contribution of the land and property markets and regulatory frameworks of land use planning to this process. The organisation of housing areas, for example, and their relationship with each other and with the city as a whole offers one such pattern. It is possible to study how the cities are structured along all sorts of differentiation, including life style, ethnicity, gender and age, and how some appreciate and identify so strongly with this diversity while others have no other choice but to be segregated in this way. Another way to understand urban space is in terms of the public-private relationships, which structures urban space by allowing some people to have access to some places and activities while constraining the access to others (Madanipour, forthcoming).

This perspective, therefore, concentrates on people and on the general processes at work in the cities, which determine their livelihood. When talking of urban form, however, it often stops at general, abstract levels, uninterested, or unable, to explain it any further. The social geometries it unpacks are often large scale, and do not pay enough attention to its environmental context. A reverse of the first perspective, this perspective is more interested in people than places. One way that some have tried to overcome the shortcomings of these two perspectives is by looking at how cities are developed. They look at how urban space was produced by the construction industry in urban development processes, elaborating an understanding of the way urban space is structured through the patterns of its production, as well as consumption and exchange, a perspective that can offer a dynamic understanding of space in the context of how people assign meaning through its production and use.

The third perspective criticises the two others as views from above. It argues for a phenomenological viewpoint, taking into account the way first person perspective develops and how this is central to the way we understand and experience places. An example of this view from above is looking at city streets from the top of any high rise building, or from the any flying aircraft, where the rich diversity of life seems reduced to abstract lines and no story can be revealed to us from such a distance (de Certeu, 1993). The way social sciences and humanities tend to understand urban environment, this perspective argues, is seeking structural patterns, to find out how society and space are structured. This leads to viewing the city in some abstraction, emptying it from its colour and emotions. In the same way, following the social scientists, urban planners and designers search for new ways of giving order to places, turning them into manageable and orderly component parts of a larger unit. Those who seek structural patterns and those who strive to impose an order onto the diversity of the city, they argue, are neglecting the rich density of life as it unfolds in the city, with its range of sights and sounds and life experiences. Both in our understanding of the city and in our prescriptions for it, we aspire to see order and to give order to the complex array of objects and events that we come across in the city. It is therefore considered an alternative approach to leave these rationalist, abstract positions and embrace daily life, where spontaneity, difference, and disorder, rather than order and clarity are the norm.

This perspective refreshes our understanding of urban space and offers us new insights, challenging the notions of objectivity, geometry, structure, and order used by the first two perspectives. But we find one major problem with this emphasis on subjectivity and spontaneity of everyday life. We can be trapped in our first person narrative, in our perceptions of difference, unable to communicate with each other, as our increasingly pluralistic circumstances might entail.

There is no doubt that each of these perspectives offers some insight into understanding the city. None, however, seem to be convincing enough to stand as the only plausible approach. The emphasis on space needs to be complemented with that on society, to arrive at a socio-spatial understanding. The view from above, the third person view of experts and of abstract thinking, needs to be combined with that of the first person to offer a convincing account of the socio-spatial phenomena. In other words, the political and economic considerations of city processes need to be coupled with the cultural and aesthetic viewpoints.

The Need for a Dynamic Approach

There has been a number of historically established tensions around how to understand and interpret cities. As we saw, those with an interest in the city as a collection of artefacts have concentrated on the material objects in the city and the meaning these have for people. On the other hand, those with an interest in how people interact and live their lives have tended to see the material objects and spaces these occupy as epiphenomenal (Colquhoun, 1989). This dichotomy is one reflection of a more ancient dichotomy between the material and the mental, and the debate between empiricism and rationalism (Madanipour, 1996). One way of escaping this dichotomy has been the use of the concept of intentionality, the 'aboutness' or directedness of most conscious states. Beliefs, thoughts, wishes, dreams and desires, as well as the words we use to express them are about things. This concentrates the attention on the materiality of the city, through concentrating on human bodies or on the material objects in the city, partly as a critique of the rationalism of modernist thought. This may be a welcome invitation to realism extended to those, such as structuralists and post-structuralists, who were largely engaged with representation, rather than a material reality beyond representation (Eagleton, 1983; Lefebvre, 1991). Emphasis on materiality, however, could cause new limitations if only approached pre-linguistically. Materiality can only make sense if representation and substance are interconnected and understood through social practices which produce them. The material city and its representations are both produced through social practices which create social reality, giving one ontological objectivity and the other epistemic objectivity (Searle, 1995). The socio-spatial configuration of the material city, the world of people and objects, therefore, becomes a medium of representation and action, which can only be understood when these different dimensions are overlaid onto one another.

The interplay of rationalism and empiricism, i.e., of reason and senses, has played a central role in the modern consciousness. A number of observers (including Taylor, 1989), have noted that the modern sense of identity is shaped by the tense relationship between reason and emotions, as historically played out in the relationship between romanticism and the Enlightenment. The modern version of this tense relationship is that between modernists and postmodernists, which dominated the intellectual debates for over a generation. As rationalism, associated with modernism, came to prevail, the celebration of subjectivity became a critical weapon and a banner of resistance in the hands of the postmodernists. As we have witnessed, during the last three decades, the two sides have tended to exaggerate each other's position in their battle. As the postmodernists have come to prevail as the new orthodoxy in the academic debates, a revived wave of 'reflective' rationalism has emerged as a response in the 1990s. Understanding space and the actions of spatial planning should be understood in this context.

In understanding the places around us, we are all too often in danger of simple generalisations. It may be the way human brain works, i.e., to simplify the diversity and complexity in order to understand it, and then to generalise this simplification to other situations. But this form of formulation can also cause constant confusion and misapprehension, as can be seen in many interpretations of cities. Another aspect of this way of misunderstanding is creating caricatures of existing stories and approaches, in order to criticise them heavily and offer alternative narratives.

It is important to note that, as human beings, our actions and thought processes include both pre-linguistic and linguistic contents. It is not the case, as many modernists claim, that our approach to cities should be entirely 'rational' and hence merely linguistic. Much of our life processes are based on bodily and emotional processes that are entirely pre-linguistic. At the same time, we cannot concentrate, as some postmodernists want us to believe, on the pre-linguistic parts of our life processes. Language, and 'rational' thinking are human features that cannot be simply ignored. Whatever we do and whoever we are, we perform a combination of rational and emotional, of pre-linguistic and linguistic functions.

It may be appealing to the romantic individual, or the anarchist or libertarian activist, to ask for a demise of order in the city. For the practical purposes of life, however, all human societies have had to establish institutions, to arrange routines, roles and regulations to organise themselves, and to run their affairs. Dealing with spaces around us is one of these affairs, which need collective action, rather than saying that all the citizens need is merely wishing to be left alone, to hide in the city crowds or to be indulged in the forbidden pleasures of the city with some excitement. Many social maladies will not be solved on their own and a disordered place can only play into the hands of the powerful, or in the extreme the tyrant.

This, however, does not mean to dismiss the need for a critical approach to order, nor that the notions of order that the modernists held were useful in this way. These notions, it must be argued, were often too simplistic and paternalistic. The society was indeed much more complex than the modernists represented or wished for. At the same time, it should be emphasised, that criticising these notions and appreciating complexity and diversity should not lead us to some inevitable inactivity, or the denial of possibility of purposeful, collective action.

One way of classifying the various perspectives into space can be dividing them into those looking from inside, i.e., the subjective views from the first person's point of view, and those looking from outside, i.e., the third person's external view. What is a home for one person, becomes a mere object for another. What is for one person a refreshing experience of feeling in touch with nature becomes for another party just a person walking past in the park. What is a rich web of emotions and attachments to places of a town for one person becomes a set of statistics on pedestrian behaviour for another. The diversity of views that can be found in the everyday experiences is also traceable in the academic studies of, and professional approaches to, space. The question always is how to approach this multiplicity. Is there a single correct interpretation of space and place? Or does this multiplicity of views mean that we should give in to a kind of relativism, where all interpretations are correct as they each represent a particular, equally valid perspective?

A place can have multiple representations, each constructed by a person or a group, each with a different meaning, each with a different claim or direction. Each person or group may have a claim to truth, that theirs is the only valid perspective through which social space can be understood. What emerges in theory and practice, however, is the need to go beyond these single-view perspectives and elaborate a dynamic, multi-view perspective into what is a multidimensional part of social reality.

An example of this multiplicity can be observed in looking at Walker, an urban neighbourhood in Newcastle.[1] The statistical representation of the neighbourhood is based on data for a census ward, seeing it as a place of disadvantage and deprivation, with all the associated symptoms. These indicators show that the neighbourhood is suffering from severe social problems, losing population, poor education and health, high rates of housing vacancy, high crime rates, high unemployment and inadequate services. This picture, which is assembled by 'experts' from pieces of information, however, appears to treat the whole neighbourhood as one homogeneous place and to give it a label. Looking from the perspective of others in the city and in the neighbourhood, plus using a different level of statistical data, a more complex picture emerges.

There is a range of different forms of differentiation in Walker. The historical pattern of differentiation, which it shares with the rest of Newcastle, follows topography. The riverbank, which is the lowest point in the neighbourhood, is known as the poorest part. By moving uphill, away from the river towards the north, the social composition changes to higher income levels. This overlap of social and physical configuration is in line with the historical development of the city, which has moved away from the riverbanks to the northern heights. Although recent regeneration efforts have revitalised parts of the river front close to the city centre, other parts of the city still follow this historical pattern.

This topographical pattern is a very crude representation of the conditions in the neighbourhood, but one that seems to have made a long lasting impression in collective memory. A multi-variable combination of statistical data, when overlaid on the map of the area, shows a different picture, one with a more complex pattern of differentiation, where some parts that are near the river are better off than those further up the bank. It shows how the social geography of the neighbourhood is more complex than is generally held to be represented by proximity to the river or by topography.

A third pattern of differentiation, which shows further complexity, is the way some parts of the neighbourhood are stigmatised, particularly by the residents themselves but also through any policy initiatives that are introduced against poverty. The residential areas in the neighbourhood are mostly public housing, and as such should have a consistent reputation. It is clear, however, that some parts and some estates are marked as unpopular by the residents, to the extent that the list of vacant dwellings in these areas are long. Again the poorest census district on the riverside has the strongest stigma. But there are areas that are stigmatised but are not detected by the district-level census data or the topographical-historical pattern. Some parts within census districts with average statistics can become unpopular with residents as areas to be avoided due to the presence of some households or particular features.

A fourth pattern is the experience of individuals from their own place in the neighbourhood, which varies widely depending on location, their length of residence, relation with others and their position in social networks. Those who have lived here all their lives often have a more positive view of the neighbourhood and fight against the stigma they see attached to their neighbourhood. Others are at pains to point out that there is only '...some bad elements in certain streets' that are the cause of all trouble. While some of the young residents wish to stay on and be connected to their social world, others see the only way forward as leaving the neighbourhood. Some residents came here with a fear of its bad reputation but their experience of living here was so positive that they disagree with any negative representation of the area. Other newcomers were so badly treated by their neighbours that they want to get out as soon as they can.

These patterns of differentiation, the topographical-historical, the statistical, and the subjective image, cannot be used only on their own to understand a place, as their validity can be limited. There are many ways of understanding a place, both depending on the position of the subject and on the scale and scope of the place they are looking at. A complex understanding of a place may contest the various forms of representation but would have to offer a multilayered representation of the area. It needs to take into account the views from outside, as well as the experiences of people who have lived in different parts of the place and the understanding they have from their physical and social environment. Statistical indicators, however, are unable to show how the situation has emerged and how it is being experienced by people. With a combination of multiple layers of representation, we can find a deeper insight into the life of a place and find ways of responding to its challenges.

Conclusions

This chapter has shown the various ways in which space is finding a rising significance in managing cities. It has argued that space finds multiple meanings through the social processes of development, exchange and use. It is therefore limiting to approach a complex and multilayered phenomenon through a single, static viewpoint.

Those who deal with place in spatial planning need to go beyond these single perspectives and beyond a perspectivist approach. It is not a possibility for spatial planning to accept relativism, to agree simply that because there are many points of view, each has an equal (or no) claim to truth. As the remit of spatial planning is to engage in regulating and transforming space, the necessity of making decisions and conducting action is prevalent. The main challenge is to act at the intersection of these perspectives and considerations. The picture that emerges at the intersection of statistical data and phenomenological accounts of life is far richer than either of these sources can offer. The understanding of place that is generated at the intersection of political and economic considerations is more comprehensive than either can show us. The picture that we can see at the intersection of political-economic and aesthetic-cultural considerations will be even more enriched with details and sensibilities that would make any understanding of place more sophisticated and responsive.

Note

1   This section draws on an EC-funded research into socially-excluded neighbourhoods in Europe.

References

Ashworth, G. and Voogd, H. (1990), *Selling the City: Marketing Approaches in Public Sector Urban Planning*, Belhaven, London.

Bourne, L.S. (1971), 'Patterns: Descriptions of Structure and Growth', in L.S.Bourne (ed.), *Internal Structure of the City*, Oxford University Press, New York. pp.69–74.

Bourne, L.S. (1982), 'Urban Spatial Structure: an Introductory Essay on Concepts and Criteria', in Bourne, L.S. (ed.), *Internal Structure of the City*, Oxford University Press, New York, pp.28–45.

Colquhoun, A. (1989), *Modernity and the Classical Tradition: Architectural Essays 1980–1987*, MIT Press, Cambridge, MA.

De Certeu, M. (1993), 'Walking in the City', in During, S. (ed.), *The Cultural Studies Reader*, Routledge, London, pp.151–60.

Eagleton, T. (1983), *Literary Theory*, Blackwell, Oxford.

Einstein, A. (1954), 'Foreword', in Max Jammer, *Concepts of Space: The History of Theories of Space in Physics*, Harvard University Press, Cambridge, MA, pp.xi–xvi.

Hough, M. (1984), *City Form and Natural Processes*, Croom Helm, London.

Knox, P. (1995), *Urban Social Geography: An Introduction*, Longman, Harlow.

Lefebvre, H. (1991), *The Production of Space*, Blackwell, Oxford.

Madanipour, A. (1996), *Design of Urban Space: An Inquiry into a Socio-Spatial Process*, Wiley, Chichester.

Madanipour, A. (forthcoming), 'Why Are the Design and Development of Public Spaces Significant for Cities?', *Environment and Planning B: Planning and Design*, Vol. 26.

Sassen, S. (1994), *Cities in a World Economy*, Pine Forge Press, Thousand Oaks, CA.

Scott, A. (1990), *Metropolis: From the Division of Labour to Urban Form*, University of California Press, Berkeley, CA.

Searle, J. (1995), *The Construction of Social Reality*, Penguin, London.

Social Exclusion Unit (1998), *Bringing Britain Together: A National Strategy for Neighbourhood Renewal*, Cabinet Office, London.

Taylor, C. (1989), *Sources of the Self: The Making of the Modern Identity*, Cambridge University Press, Cambridge.

Whitehand, J.W.R. (1987), *The Changing Face of Cities*, Blackwell, Oxford;

Whitehand, J.W.R. (1992), *The Making of the Urban Landscape*, Blackwell, Oxford.

Zukin, S. (1995), *Cultures of Cities*, Blackwell, London.

PART II
CHANGING GOVERNANCE
PROCESSES

Changing Governance Processes

Angela Hull

Part One has shown the diverse ways people from different disciplines, backgrounds and life experiences conceptualise about space, place and territory. Changing mobility patterns over recent years mean that we experience space in different ways: the same geographical area can be the slow space of our 'home' and our lived-in neighbourhood, a fast space we move through as we travel to work, the regimented environment of work, or a relaxation space. The same place therefore has different meanings to different people. Social scientists have been trying to understand the complexity of time-space relationships in terms of the interaction of cultures and global resource flows. These new ideas supersede the notion of space as 'fixed', as a container for our lifecycle experiences and relationships which can be modelled, controlled, and predicted.

Spatial planning systems born out of the welfare contract at the end of World War Two reflect a reality where the nation state was dominant, when the central institutions of government were expected to take the lead in producing strategies with the help of their expert advisors. The 'top down' and 'bottom-up' metaphors of public policy analysis sought to describe these rigid relationships of government. These metaphors encapsulated the flows of political energy in a tent-like structure held taut by the tension between central direction and local agency. The deliberations of elected politicians and their executives at national and local levels within this structure of representative democracy could only ever seek to represent a narrow band of interests and values in society. Yet the authority and the democratic legitimisation of these traditional government processes has given the representatives considerable power over spatial, economic and social questions.

Increasingly the negotiated outcomes of the debates to resolve 'social problems' within these existing authoritative arenas are being questioned. There are disagreements over what is problematic, how to define the parameters of a problem and how it has been caused, what measures to take to reduce the problem, and who should address problem reduction. Spatial planning systems have at times failed to understand both the finegrain of neighbourhood concerns about the distinctive qualities of places and been unable to anticipate the outcome of public sector intervention on market behaviour (Healey and Barrett,

1990; Lefebvre, 1991). The growing realisation of the inability of existing 'experts' to comprehend the complexity of societal system dynamics and, in particular, the impact of one action on another, has led to the search for new expertise in problem definition and solution.

The chapters in Part One argue for a multifaceted analysis of the experiences of place, seeking out the different images and representations and the connections between places. New arenas for discursive exchange on societal futures are emerging in civil society in response to transnational debates on global environmental concerns. People are reflecting on how their daily lifestyles impact on their environment and searching for ways to protect the spaces around them from the negative impacts of others. There is a new opportunity to refresh the process of decision-making with new conceptions of place and territory. This raises the question of whether the established institutions involved in spatial planning can 'zoom out' to incorporate these concerns for places. There is the danger that the formal spatial planning systems will be increasingly by-passed if they ignore this challenge (Vigar et al., 2000).

The chapters in Part Two look at the response of the existing governance and spatial planning systems to the challenge of new social movements, with their often 'radically' different ways of conceiving space and place and cultures of decision-making. The case studies from the Netherlands, England, France and the United States show how old spatial planning practices are being adapted to intersect with some of the new voices and debates on strategic planning. In this respect the case studies in Part Two provide innovatory benchmarks in our search for new processes and new forms of spatial planning in response to a changing governance context. They show the potential of the existing vertically articulated spatial planning systems to promote the local articulation of place qualities and capacities. In the past, strategic spatial plans have been criticised for their neglect of place and the distinctiveness of local spaces, serving instead to attract major investment flows to specific sites (Castells, 1989; Adams, 1994; Healey, 1998). If the processes of spatial planning can be refreshed with the 'cacophony of voices' Maarten Hajer refers to, how will the incorporation of different norms and criteria influence the tools and instruments of spatial management in the twenty-first century?

The chapters by Hajer, Hull and Vigar, and Motte look at what sort of changes are happening now. These chapters show how the established corporatist structures of governance are responding to multiple voices on how to plan for spatial quality. The emphasis in the first two chapters is on the processes of decision-making and how this could have more equitable and effective outcomes. Motte illustrates how different processes of strategic plan-making can produce quite different outputs in terms of the instruments of spatial management and the representation of local concerns. However, the meshing of spatial planning systems with political structures, to respond to ethical and political questions about the impact of spatial decisions, is proving a much more difficult and complex issue to address. The last three chapters assess the potential of new processes, practices and technologies to make this happen. They highlight the dangers if we fail to acknowledge diversity and difference, to set up adaptive spatial planning systems and to address the quality of spatial planning outcomes.

In Chapter Eight, Maarten Hajer looks at the challenge of institutional redesign facing Dutch strategic planning at the start of the twenty-first century. Calls by the Dutch government in the 1990s to reinvigorate democracy and widen governance have led to the planning system being bombarded by a multiplicity of interventions on how best to achieve 'spatial quality'. He uses discourse analysis to understand the value orientations, knowledge sources and institutional preferences of the three strongest storylines in the Dutch debate.

Several policy issues are raised by the case study. How to deal with the tensions created by the forceful exposition of sectoral proposals without undermining already agreed spatial visions? Yet how to ensure also that new ideas are explored and inform evolving strategies to build up a culture of innovation? New institutional structures need to evolve to handle conflict and diversity of opinion. The message here is to 'zoom out' to take on board the diversity of culture and ways of acting.

Hull and Vigar, in Chapter Nine, look at the interaction of key actors in the centralised and highly sectoralised UK planning system. They take three case studies of strategic spatial planning in the 1990s to investigate how national policy criteria are translated vertically down through the structures of regional and local government decision making. They argue that institutional structures and the language used in policy debates structure reality, facilitate some perspectives and conceptions of space and society, and hinder other conceptions. The 'plan-led' system and the move to district-wide development plans have created an institutional structure able to handle 'end-of-pipe' conflict but with little success in engaging with civil society.

They suggest that the New Labour government's agenda of 'modernising' local government and encouraging greater local accountability provides an opportunity for the planning system to recognise and appreciate the diversity of perspectives on place and space. They propose a redesign of the structures and procedures of governance which will ensure that the choice of spatial futures is conducted as close as possible to those who will have to live with the impacts of the decision choice.

Alain Motte, in Chapter Ten, takes two case studies from Lyon and Nîmes in France to demonstrate how the different processes and tools of strategic plan-making can produce quite different outputs. He compares both the process of elaboration and the style of a traditional detailed, spatial plan (Lyon) with a quickly produced, iterative, flexible strategic plan (Nîmes). Some decentralisation of planning powers in the French planning system in the late 1980s paved the way for local actors to elaborate new conceptions of place. Both cities took the opportunity to use the plan-making process to create a local shared vision which would integrate and commit key actors to the city. The Nîmes plan is seen as innovatory because it '…abandons the distinction between deliberation and implementation. It has become an iterative, heuristic ever-moving process, relying on the integration of a growing number of urban [public art] projects'.

The key role here was played by the small, single purpose urban planning agency which managed the process of reaching agreement on the implementation of the spatial vision between a wide range of organisations. The Chapter raises several questions about how to mesh at the local level single issue public agencies which work through vertical governance networks, and local government agencies interacting horizontally to achieve a vision (contract or plan) which represents the political, social and spatial coherence of a place. How do you reconcile the central government concerns to manage space in an abstract way with the local concerns to produce places in their specific historical settings? Both the plans described in these case studies have been drawn up by an urban elite of professionals and developers. How have they then addressed the concerns of local people?

In Chapter Eleven, Innes and Booher look at this issue of how to incorporate the diversity of concerns about the way we use space and place where power in society is diffused and intelligence distributed. They present a portent of management complexity in a society (the United States) characterised by a maze of independent decision-making institutions leading to fragmented systems of power and information diffusion. To resolve the political conflict over what are complex issues of economics, public finance, and environment they recommend an adaptive approach to building up shared understandings and operational agreement on the strategic spatial issues. Rather than managing space through the traditional, top-down and formal plan-making approaches, the authors draw on complexity theory to suggest how to create adaptive and innovative governance systems relying on distributed intelligence and the parallel processing of information.

Businesses in the United States are now beginning to realise that a quality environment is necessary to their own success and that wasteful city growth patterns have reduced economic competitiveness. The authors propose three principal strategies to galvanise these concerns which involve the development and use of indicators and performance measures in new ways, the use of collaborative consensus building, and the creation of new forms of leadership. This approach is tested in a case study of California, where governance and interests are particularly fragmented and complex, and where past attempts to control outcomes have been counterproductive and unsustainable.

Patsy Healey, in Chapter Twelve, reviews the role that spatial plans have played in Britain as vehicles to generate 'integrative conceptions of place'. She identifies two main purposes: managing conflict over the use and development of land, and promoting the particular qualities of places. Since the 1940s, these have sometimes meshed together in formal spatial planning processes and at other times drifted apart. Healey argues that there is now strong evidence of a reassertion of place-focused concerns. This can be found in interpretations of what is required to facilitate the competitiveness of companies, in how local agencies can realise environmental sustainability, and in the role of place in defining people's sense of identity.

These concerns are leading to collaborative institution-building and policy development between those who have a 'stake' in a place. She discusses how the tensions between these horizontal, fluid relationships and planning systems driven by neo-liberal performance criteria can be resolved. How can you transform a planning system which has come to emphasise specific policies and projects, and which fragments the overall consideration of how to manage spatial change in a geographical area? She concludes by setting the parameters for a planning system which will facilitate more collaborative, multiparty, place-making practices.

In the last chapter, Ted Kitchen takes these ideas as his starting point for exploring how a future British planning system could foster policy processes which are more inclusionary and responsive to multiple needs. He looks at the first half of this new century and speculates about the transformation of ideas, systems and practices that will be required to address the pollution, transport and equity issues in achieving sustainable development. He draws on his experience of planning in the City of Manchester to look at the likely trajectories of both the process and the substance of government intervention in the way localities are shaped by different interests. He looks forward to an interactive form of spatial management which will change bureaucratic relationships between central and local government and between technical officer and elected councillors. Looking to the future we have to contemplate change that we cannot even imagine today. To help us adapt, we need to rethink the analytical techniques we use to manage spatial change and transform the way we consult on spatial options through the use of new forms of interactive and virtual reality technologies.

The emphasis in this collection of papers in Part Two is on the process issues necessary to distil a common view on place qualities and capacities. Several of the authors argue that the key to this lies in building up a local policy culture which is well integrated, well connected and well informed, and which can readily mobilise to capture opportunities and enhance local conditions. Innes and Booher suggest a role here for innovatory leaders who would be charged with the task of creating consensus on how to address problematic aspects of the system. Important to the emergence of urban municipal administrations with powerful mayors will be the development of appropriate performance measures which will hold these administrations accountable and which capture the attention of ordinary people.

One of Hajer's fears is that in trying to reach consensus through a more pluralistic democratic process we may create new problems. Without some understanding of desired outcomes and without a recipe for how to get there we will become bogged down in short term utilitarian arguments and policy incoherence. This will fail to maximise participation and deliberation over cross-cutting policy issues. He highlights the fundamental tension between maximising participation, and maximising consent and support.

The contributions to Part Two agree that spatial planning systems of governance in this new century must adapt in order to:

- acknowledge the diversity of situations, learn to recognise local specificities and work with the grain of the dynamic complexity identified in Part One. These refer to institutional as well as material conditions;

- develop adaptive capabilities, rather than searching for 'optimising' ones;

- develop strategies collaboratively, in the form of visions, or enduring orientations which are widely shared to create a 'shared myth'. Visions will be more robust and enduring if they are not imposed;

- open up new possibilities and serve to aid coordination and mobilisation

structures and formal tools are less important than processes of interaction and learning;

- develop new planning instruments (indicators etc.) which can identify 'problems' and monitor the effectiveness of chosen policies.

References

Adams, D. (1994), *Urban Planning and the Development Process*, UCL Press, London.
Castells, M. (1989), *The Informational City: Information Technology, Economic Restructuring and the Urban-Region Process*, Blackwell, Oxford.
Healey P. (1998), 'Collaborative Planning in a Stakeholder Society', *Town Planning Review*, Vol. 69 (1), pp.1–21.
Healey, P. and Barrett, S.M. (1990), 'Structure and Agency in Land and Property Development Processes: Some Ideas for Research', *Urban Studies*, Vol. 27 (1), pp.89–104.
Lefebvre, H., (1991), *The Production of Space*, Blackwell, Oxford.
Vigar, G., Healey, P., Hull, A. and Davoudi, S. (2000), *Planning, Governance and Spatial Strategy-Making in Britain*, Macmillan, London.

Chapter Eight

The Need to Zoom Out: Understanding Planning Processes in a Post-Corporatist Society

Maarten Hajer

The Societal Context of Planning

The analysis of planning as an 'argumentative' process has established itself as one of the more innovative perspectives on planning and policy analysis over the last decade (Fischer and Forester, 1993; Majone, 1989; Throgmorton, 1992; Healey, 1997). The analysis of 'frames', 'practice stories', 'story lines', 'metaphors', 'doctrines', 'paradigms' or 'rhetorics', has effectively shown how language fulfils a key role in shaping (policy-) realities and functions as a important vehicle of power (Forester, 1993; Healey and Hillier, 1996; Hajer, 1995; Rein and Schön, 1994; Faludi and Van der Valk, 1994). Planners have been followed around and partly for this reason we now share much more knowledge as to how practical planning processes actually work, how power is exercised and how analytical, political and designer discourses intermingle in planning debates. The argumentative turn was in this sense an essential step in liberating the planning scene from its often 'scientist' or positivist overtones (Fischer, 1990).

The argumentative approach has come to play a prominent role among the critical perspectives in planning studies. But how much has this perspective to say about the challenges that face planning in the late 1990s and early 2000s? This chapter argues that the argumentative turn has produced a set of essential insights in the functioning of planning processes and has contributed to the wealth of ideas on new practices that could make planning, above all, more democratic. Nevertheless, for critical planning studies it is time to 'zoom out' and (re)examine the social context in which argumentation and planning take place and what role the new 'discursive institutions' play and should play. This chapter focuses on one element of the new context of planning: the new social relationships between state and society. Using a case study on strategic planning in the Netherlands it is shown that the established institutional practices of planning are increasingly bypassed. New 'discourse-coalitions' have emerged that have effectively reconstructed the relationship between state and society even though these institutions legally remain in place as the official sites of decision-making. By zooming out and seeking to understand the social dynamics in what might be called our 'post-corporatist society' the chapter endeavours to get the challenge of institutional (re-)design back into focus.

Post-Corporatist Society

What is meant by the phrase 'post-corporatist society'? The label relates to the fact that many European polities are currently experimenting with extended democratic rights (e.g. referenda or citizen initiatives). In a parallel track, critical journals in policy analysis and planning are full of debates on discursive designs, participatory planning, collaborative planning, or interactive decision-making. All these suggestions indicate that the capacity of the existing institutional arrangements falls short of accommodating the demand for discursive exchange with societal actors. The German sociologist Klaus Eder (1995b) described our predicament as that of a 'post-corporatist' society: we still have traditional arrangements in place but have become aware that the state is often talking to the wrong actors and in the wrong sort of context. Similar to authors like Francois Ewald or Ulrich Beck (1993) he explains the emergence of new democratic practices from the fact that society needs new consensus producing practices to replace the double arrangement of parliamentary democracy supported by corporatist practices. For all their differences, these authors argue a case that suggests that the '... social pact of industrial society' no longer functions because both the players and the problems have changed: the demise of the old class structure has undercut the effectiveness of the prevailing corporatist practices of negotiation that, next to the representative democratic practices, used to produce consensus and a shared sense of direction. Similarly, the shift from conflicts over the distribution of welfare (Beck's 'Goods') to conflicts over environmental threats (Beck's 'Bads', e.g. technological or ecological risk but also amenity) has so far not produced institutional arrangements that have a similar level of sophistication as the corporatist arrangements of the post war welfare state (Eder, 1995a; 1995b; Ewald, 1986; Beck, 1986; 1993). Whereas in the days of industrial society, state society relationships could predominantly take the character of exchanges between organised labour and organised capital, these corporatist arrangements are now no longer seen as the legitimate representatives of societal interests and ideas. This chapter seeks to examine to what extent and how Dutch strategic planning is effected by this phenomenon and how it has responded to the new societal developments.[1] The overall goal of the chapter is to provide some material for a discussion on what sort of institutional practices we should be thinking of if we want to facilitate strategic planning in a post-corporatist society.

It is therefore important to make an analytical distinction between arguments for institutional renewal that are primarily *normative* and those that are *functional*. Drawing on Eder (1995) we can distinguish at least two sorts of arguments in the discussion on new democratic practices: *normative* and *functionalist* arguments. The familiar call for 'deliberative democracy' (Habermas, 1992) or 'strong democracy' (Barber, 1984) are first and foremost normative. Here democratic practice is seen as a goal in itself. The typical argument is that the representative democratic institutions (or the institutions of strategic planning for that matter) cannot be seen as truly democratic since they do not produce a sufficient level of public deliberation and in actual fact keep a gross inequality in political decision-making in place (interest groups dominating the discourse on problem perception and the thinking about solutions). A second line of argument is functionalist in nature. In those cases it is typically argued *that new social circumstances* call for a renewal of democratic practices as e.g. with 'discursive designs' (Dryzek, 1993), 'social maps' (Schwarz and Thompson, 1990) or 'reflexive institutions' (Eder, 1995). Hence Dryzek relates his ideas for discursive designs to the inability of instrumental rationality to deal with newly emerging complex social problems, just as Schwarz and Thompson approach new participants as sources of previously institutionally suppressed knowledge (hence: 'divided we stand').

This sort of sociological take on institutional change illuminates an important problem with the discussion on new democratic practices. Those who argue in favour of renewal for *normative* reasons seek to achieve a different set of goals and thus may have different institutional preferences than those that argue for renewal for *functional* reasons. However, this problem is rarely a topic for discussion. Instead it is often argued (or simply assumed) that the normative ideal of new democratic practices and the functionalist ideal of new democratic practices are mutually supportive, and can be seen as a positive sum game. Hence democracy is argued to be the medicine to the illness of an 'institutionalised irresponsibility' (Beck, 1989) causing environmental degradation. Likewise, deliberation (which is a normative argument for democratic practice) is argued to be a useful tool to gather new ideas that can, at a later stage, become the basis of policy making. This *might* be true but is by no means the necessary outcome of new democratic practice. What is more, Eder's analytical discussion on democratic practice shows that both normative and functionalist argumentative perspectives are *in themselves* contradictory. The two primary normative criteria for democracy are equality and deliberation. Yet maximising equality tendentially reduces the depth of deliberation and vice versa. Similarly, the functionalist criteria effectiveness and efficiency tend to bite one another: maximising efficiency – defined as finding the optimal allocation of resources under conditions of scarcity – runs against the effectiveness criteria of democratic practice – measured in its capacity to generate acceptance of particular decisions.

The new democratic practices thus seem far from the ideal positive sum game solution, facilitating both sound strategic planning and rejuvenating democracy. The new democratic practices that are so dear to critical academics, stand in the crossfire of normative and functional criteria, both of which are internally contradictory. It also suggests that new democratic practices will by no means automatically support the case for a form of planning that would help to bring about a more ecologically benign social-spatial relations. They are necessarily the product of a trade off between some of the criteria mentioned above.

Argumentative Analysis as Critical Perspective on Planning

Under this difficult sign, how can we define what the issues for strategic planning in a post-corporatist society should be? What should be done? Now, there are at least two familiar definitions of what a critical science is about (Latour, 1997). There is, first of all, the *Kantian* perspective of a critical science that seeks to determine the limits to knowledge. This form of critical science would especially try to resist all too blunt suggestions regarding the possibility to know future developments and would also be reluctant to develop grand theories regarding the 'true' nature of change of society. A second possible definition may be called a *Brechtian* critical science. Here the critical refers to the constant attempt to lift the veils that hide the 'real' powers in society. Latour positions himself more or less in contradistinction to these two familiar traditions. He suggest that they assume far too much trust in the – social – sciences and argues for a perspective of examination, a perspective comparable to that of the art critic, that examines, is curious, and stands in the sign of the 'humour of truth' rather than in the biting tradition of what he calls an 'irony of critique'.[2] Given his role in the social sciences at this moment in time, this Latourian take should be considered more seriously than some people might be inclined to. In actual fact his distinction might help appreciate the way in which older categories of thought may hinder us in thinking about our reality in new terms. It is not difficult to construct present developments in the world of planning in terms of general 'loss' of qualities, of 'froth' and of irresponsibility. But perhaps one should go one step further and really engage in the various perspectives and examine them in their 'positivity' as Foucault argued. Latour even uses the word 'love' to distinguish his attitude from that of the old 'critical' tradition. For Latour to love does not mean to *fall in love* but to remain committed even when things seem to go wrong. He thus criticises the tendency to tell apocalyptic stories about reality. The perspective of the *art critic* implies that one remains committed to art, examines all the objects and variations and through commentary seeks to contribute to the debate on form.

The recent wave of discursive or argumentative studies in policy analysis and planning seems to comprise elements of all three – dare I say – critical perspectives. The Kantian element also comes out in the now widespread recognition that the societal role of the planner for a long time depended on the suggestion that the planner was a scientific expert on space and, being the expert, produced a superior sort of knowledge regarding the ideal spatial organisation of society. Roughly after the belated reception of Thomas Kuhn's work on paradigms it has become problematic to rely on expertise in such a one dimensional way. The Kantian element features in the insistence, on the part of the argumentators, on a 'post-positivist' epistemological base for analysis: they would for instance argue that the study of language is important since the way in which we talk about the world is more than just a matter of description: it actually changes that reality and orders our perception of it (Fischer and Forester, 1993). Just as it can show to be extremely important to consider where things are said. Because of this, the discursive analysis tends to focus on in-depth case study work. They generate knowledge on the question how language is drawn upon in a particular context and how meaning is allocated in that process. What comes back is the suggestion that the concepts we use and the problems we see are not as innocent as they may seem but do actually structure our thinking about reality. What is more, where the discursive or argumentative analysis is comparative, it would typically show how the same words, concepts or phrases do actually mean quite different things at distinct places (Hajer, 1995).

The discursive turn also carries Brechtian elements. After all, its goal is not simply to show the way in which language influences social reality. Characteristically this is combined with an analysis of how power is exercised through discourse and discursive exchanges. Hence under the influence of the argumentative turn we see a twist in one of the key points of orientation in the debate on the future of strategic planning: the debate on 'globalisation'. Here the argumentative perspective shows itself to be wary of a 'realistic' interpretation according to which globalisation would be taken as a 'fact' to which planning has to respond. Authors like Thrift (1994, 1996) or Hirst and Thompson (1996) approach globalisation as a functional 'myth' instead and would see the emergence of the term 'globalisation' as a figure head of a tendency to underplay the potential for state intervention in more general terms. In this sense the argumentative approach always had a fairly clear commitment to show how the languages in planning debates fulfil a role in structuring reality, hindering some perspectives in the development while facilitating others. Their question therefore is much more oriented to finding out *how globalisation is produced locally*. The point of this extension of the argumentative approach is that it would resist conforming to seeing yet another typology (for some examples, see Newman and Thornley, 1996, p.14) as its ideal product but orient itself on understanding the way in which specific cities, regions or countries position themselves in the context of a changing order. Conceptualisations such as the 'blue banana' fail to address the role that is there to play for active 'world making', whether this is through the classical practices of 'policy making' or otherwise. In this context Newman and Thornley quite rightly observe that:

> cities are not just passive places in which international capital or prestigious functions locate but, in the new global competition for growth, have themselves become important actors in creating opportunities for economic development and influencing the new urban hierarchy (1996, p.16).

Precisely the idea of planning discourses as – active or passive – moments of 'world making' carries a critical potential.

Interestingly, the emergence of the argumentative perspective as a form of critical planning studies from the mid-1980s onwards is also a matter of self-reflection. After all, the planner's interest in the role of language emerged at a point in time at which planners were themselves confronted with the devaluation of their own professional discourse. With the coming to power of the Thatcher and Reagan governments 'comprehensive city planning was rejected as a hangover from the modernist, statist, technocratic post-war period' (Healey and Williams, 1993, p.702) and the language of 'planning' – with its barely hidden conviction that the state is needed to correct the market and help sustain the 'weaker' and vulnerable sections of society – was discredited as a legitimate way of expressing oneself. The state was no longer the solution but had become part of the problem. Consequently, planning was put in the dock as an anachronism. It was seen as the cornerstone of the political project of the welfare state to which neoliberals wanted to develop an anti-programme.

However, it is in this thinking about the influence of Thatcherite discourses that the third type of critical thought seems important. After all, for a long time the biting critique of Thatcherism as a reactionary societal project seems to have blurred the complex nature of the crisis of planning and state – society relationships. Historically, they more or less coincided with the coming to power of Thatcher and Reagan. The *Latourian* critical perspective would examine Thatcherism in all its facets but would also appreciate the fact that the past does not necessarily give us the most useful criteria by which to judge its significance. In other words, the analysis should not be reduced to the examination of the 'perverse' effects and the aberrations from the existing structures. The past is no 'blueprint' for how to go forward. Today we are working on the reinvention of strategic planning but without a recipe. That seems a good reason to *zoom out*. A modest agenda is to analyse how society is reconstituted through the use of concepts, technologies and coalitions also within the domain of strategic planning (also Callon and Latour, 1981). We can show the consequences of the various projects and we might be able to come up with some suggestions as to how certain unwanted effects might be avoided. That seems the rather modest, primarily procedural agenda for an argumentative analysis of planning.

In this chapter argumentative analysis stands for an approach to the reality of strategic planning that looks, first of all, for the rival metaphors and storylines that define the challenges, that bind actors together and determine the focal points of controversies. Secondly, one would seek to make out a 'language' or 'discourse' from which these storylines derive their meaning. Thirdly, one would seek to reconstruct the existing coalitions that shape up around these discourses cum storylines. Fourthly, one would look for the institutional practices through which the utterance of the respective storylines takes place. Institutional practices are here understood as comprising a wide variety of practices through which the process of argumentation and persuasion takes place (including specific journals, the activities of a professional association or activist NGO, a particular division of a department or ministry, an opinion page in a daily newspaper, a judicial provision for public participation, as well as the publication of White Papers, statements by ministers of the cabinet, etc.). Fifthly, it would look at the technologies that are 'enlisted' in the project of planning and the way in which discourse and technologies interrelate (Latour, 1991).

How can such an analytical perspective be made operational? In an earlier project this approach was used to analyse environmental politics. In *The Politics of Environmental Discourse* I claimed that the reality of environmental politics should be understood not simply as a fight over whether or not to become active in fighting environmental degradation but much more as a fight over the definition of what the problem 'really' was. In that social-constructivist vein a new dimension became visible in environmental politics. Environmental politics could be seen as the confrontation of an established way of framing issues of pollution and degradation with a new perspective (or 'policy discourse') on environmental problems, that I labelled 'ecological modernisation'. One of the defining characteristics of ecological modernisation was the idea that environmental politics should be conceived of as a 'positive sum game': the discovery of pollution or degradation should no longer be seen as something that endangered the fruits of modern production and development, and that would endanger profit margins and business prospects. On the contrary, ecological modernisation suggested that one should seek to make a profit out of environmental problems. This way of framing the environmental issue obviously had major implications for the way in which 'emblematic' environmental issues such as acid rain at the time were approached. A comparative analysis could be used to trace how this new policy discourse influenced the controversies over acid rain in Great Britain and the Netherlands.

Ecological modernisation was an example of a discursive structure, a way of conceiving the challenges inherent in the environmental issues as much as a way of talking about emblematic environmental problems like acid rain. A discourse was defined as '... a specific ensemble of ideas, concepts, and categorisations that are produced, reproduced, and transformed in a particular set of practices and through which meaning is given to physical and social realities' (Hajer, 1995, p.44), while storylines were defined as '... narratives on social reality through which elements from many different domains are combined and that provide actors with a set of symbolic references that suggest a common understanding' (ibid., p.62). I always thought of discourses a bit akin to Foucault's notion of epistème: something that derives its power from the implicit, from the fact that people would not always necessarily be aware of the fact that they are thinking in terms of a particular discursive format. On the other hand I have tried to keep a distance to this structuralist notion of epistème (Foucault, 1973). Firstly by explicitly focusing on the words and concepts that people actually uttered (thus allowing for a much more detailed empirical analysis). Secondly by insisting on the importance of strategic behaviour: actors can do things with words and words do not simply do things to people. At the time the idea of a new policy discourse might have seem heroic, especially if one looked at it from a British perspective. After all, it can hardly be maintained that this eco-modernist way of talking about the environment was dominant in the mid-1980s. Since then, however, it is hardly possible to get a policy measure through without conforming to the 'win-win' format that is a corner stone of the eco-modernist perspective on environmental problems (and, as we will see below, this format exercises its influence in the sphere of strategic planning as well). What is more, what was discernible at the time was the fact that there was a very significant difference between what I called *discourse structuration* and *discourse institutionalisation.* Discourse structuration would take place where actors would start to frame their policy realities in terms of a particular discourse. Discourse institutionalisation, on the other hand, would require that institutional ways of handling problems, organisational routines and legal arrangements would be changed accordingly. This differentiation also indicates that an argumentative analysis is not blind to the institutional dimension of planning processes. However powerful language utterances might sometimes be, in the end they require an institutional response in order to make an impact. Admittedly, the terms discourse structuration and discourse institutionalisation are somewhat primitive yet the point of this differentiation was that one should keep an eye open for the fact that a policy domain can be characterised by a discrepancy between the realities of public debates and the realities of institutional practice. A few years later this seems to have been a valid point. Ecological modernisation now seems to have established itself as the prime language in which environmental problems are to be framed while at the same time the 'translation' of this discourse into new institutional practices has got stuck (Fischer and Hajer, 1998).

In this chapter I want to draw on the argumentative analysis to understand the challenge for Dutch strategic planning in the coming years. For that purpose I loosely draw on the methodology described above.

The Political Context: Strategic Planning and 'The Polder Model'

Today the concept of the 'Dutch model' or 'polder model' is one of the best known Dutch export products apart from flowers, cheese and RTL quizmasters and entertainers. Over the last year the Netherlands has gained a worldwide reputation for its economic success. Within ten years the storyline on the economic performance of the Netherlands changed from 'Dutch disease' to 'Dutch miracle'. This newly gained reputation seems to be supported by 'the facts': as one of the few European countries the Netherlands seems to have succeeded in reorganising its social security system without causing major social disruptions. Indeed, one of the main worries nowadays is a possible *shortage* of labour power in the middle long term. The 'Dutch model' distinguishes itself first and foremost from other approaches in what is undoubtedly is core characteristic: stable labour relationship and a shared perspective on future development of work.

Now, it is interesting to see how this 'Dutch miracle' is currently narratively reconstructed. Here two storylines can be distinguished. The prevailing story narrates the Dutch model as having its base in a historical consensus culture of *shared public space* (which was well analysed by Hemerijck, 1993). It suggests the success of the Dutch economy is based in the Agreement of Wassenaar of 1982. At that time the Dutch employers organisations and trade unions (in the Netherlands known as 'the social partners') agreed to keep wages down in exchange for a collective effort to create jobs, partly by reducing the normal week's work from forty to thirty-six hours. The state committed itself to reduce government spending and alleviate the – tax – burden on business and industry. A second story sounds altogether different. It suggests that the Agreement of Wassenaar was not the start of the Dutch miracle but precisely the last eruption of the old 'corporatist' economic institutions. It suggests that the origin of the Dutch model is in the reconceptualisation of the labour problem that occurred in the late 1980s. It suggests that the government was focused on reducing 'unemployment' and tried every possible trick to achieve this (including the manipulation of statistics – for instance by re-labelling part of the unemployed as 'disabled workers'). Around 1990 this focus on the reduction of unemployment made way for a strategy of employment creation and reducing 'inactivity'. Interestingly, in this narrative the old 'corporatist' institutions far from being the solution were seen as part of the problem (after all, the trick of re-labelling the unemployed was something that came with the active consent of the 'social partners').

It is interesting to see how the Dutch miracle relates to strategic planning. In actual fact we can discern a very similar institutional fight. In the wake of the economic recession of the late 1970s the Netherlands was forced to rethink the role of government in economic affairs. The discovery of 'new' international economic relationships and new neo-liberal ideas about the role of the state in economic affairs also led to a reorientation in the thinking about strategic planning. By the mid 1980s it was trying to make a fresh start. Various research projects were initiated to re-examine the context in which strategic planning was to take place. Most important document was the 1986 report *Ruimtelijke Perspectieven* (*Spatial Perspectives*). This provided the analytical basis for a new White Paper on spatial planning that appeared in March 1988 (locally known by the acronym *VINO* for fourth White Paper). First and foremost, spatial planning was discovered as a potential instrument of economic policy. It was the first White Paper on spatial planning that focused on the definition of the main economic infrastructure. In this context it, secondly, emphasised the international dimension to Dutch strategic planning. It introduced the concept of 'mainport' and 'transport axes' (connecting the mainports to the – German – *Hinterland*). The task for strategic planning became one of developing the Netherlands as a region in an international economy. A third important innovation was the emphasis on the need to develop 'public private partnerships' as instrument of spatial planning. The state had to become 'market-oriented' which meant a break with the classical concern of planning as guardian of the 'weak and the vulnerable'. The break with the past can further be shown by looking at what was *not* included in the White Paper. It meant the de facto split up of the long lasting marriage of Dutch spatial planning with public housing. In an era in which economic growth could no longer be assumed, the economy recaptured centre stage. Furthermore no special attention was given to the issue of spatial segregation or to the provision of a guarantee that the 'market-orientated' planning would not lead to land speculation on part of the private partners (all Priemus, 1988; Faludi and Van der Valk, 1994, ch. 12).

Hence to a certain extent it seems fair to suggest that the developments in Dutch strategic planning at least might have supported the recovery of the Dutch economy. The turn away from the traditional focus on using planning for the extension of the welfare state (by providing high quality public housing and by keeping market forces in check) and the new attention for the role of planning in building the spatial base for a economic recovery indicate that it at least *might* have contributed its share. Since that time some elements have made a reluctant come back in the *VINEX*, the 1992 supplement to the *VINO* that was presented as a social-democrat held the post of Minister for Housing, Spatial Planning and the Environment in the succeeding coalition cabinet. Yet for the purpose of this chapter it is more important to see to what extent the institutional practices of Dutch planning actually changed over the last decade. Here strategic planning had elements that make it different from the way in which the first narrative constructed the 'Dutch model'. In that story very traditional 'corporatist' practices were identified as key to the success of the Dutch economy. In this sense the first story of the 'Dutch model' seems to run against the sociological wisdom. After all, the days of corporatism and class culture are supposedly behind us. We now live in a post-industrial, post-corporatist or even a risk society in which the old institutional practices are out of touch, focus on the wrong issues and can no longer provide the necessary legitimisation (Eder, 1995; Beck, 1993). The agreement of Wassenaar, pivotal in the first narrative, suggests that the well known channels of communication that were institutionalised directly after the second world war are still energetically in charge.[3]

Although we have to be careful, the changing reality of strategic planning seems to be more in line with the second story line. Over the last decade the Dutch indeed experienced the erosion and evasion of the traditional planning practices. Here new 'public-private partnerships' had to bring the market actors into the decision-making and implementation. What is more, planners were much more self-conscious about their role and their allegedly troublesome record. Obviously, the *VINO/VINEX* were 'mere' White Papers and to be able to compare the reality of the world of labour relations to the world of strategic planning one would have to look at the *institutional* practices that emerged since then. What sort of institutional developments can be discerned in the field of strategic planning and how do these developments relate to a social theory that suggests that the old practices can no longer be assumed to be able to play the binding and legitimising role they used to play?

In order to answer this question we will first zoom in on the changing discourses in strategic planning. We will then show how each of these perspectives actually relates to particular institutional preferences. In a third step we then evaluate the prospects for Dutch strategic planning in a post-corporatist society.

The Discursive Space of Dutch Strategic Planning

One of the most striking features of Dutch planning discourse in the 1990s is the incredible cumulation of plans, concepts and proposals. Obviously the number of actors involved in the debate has increased accordingly. In the fair of ideas and proposals the national planning agency RPD has become one player amongst many. First, there is a range of initiatives by sectoral departments that all present their own spatial strategy. Partly these studies are not official policy documents and have an exploratory status which does not inhibit that some of these plans and sketches actually structure the thinking on particular problems. This is for instance clearly the case with a study by the Department of Agriculture for what it calls *urban landscapes* (*Stads- landschappen*). This study comprises a typology of settlements that each soften the hard distinction of city and country that subsequently was taken over by local governments and project developers. Other studies, however, are formal policy documents and have a direct policy effect. A study by the Ministry of Economic Affairs, *Space for Regions* (*Ruimte voor Regio's*) takes up the commitment to develop the Netherlands as 'Gateway' to the European continent and show that the RPD is a player in a much broader coalition of actors. Apart from the activity of sectoral departments, this range of ideas further comprises initiatives from unusual coalitions of actors, such as the Dutch automobile club, environmental NGOs and Chambers of Trade and Commerce. They either present plans for a doubling of the acreage for nature and recreation or they come with complete alternative proposals for the route of the high speed rail link to Paris. Professional organisations also make themselves heard. In March 1997 a 'new map of the Netherlands' was published, showing the effects of the realisation of all the existing plans for construction and nature development until 2005. The development of this map was supervised by the Dutch urban designers association (BNS). Interestingly, they took a route via civil society and published their map in a theatrical event with a big media appeal. These professional organisations were dissatisfied with the communication via the established national planning agency RPD (although they happily received the subsidy from the national planning agency). This in fact was not the only corrective to the established RPD route. Parallel to the New Map, Dutch academics in planning and urban design initiated a *Metropolitan Debate* with which they hope to raise the standard of debate on the future of planning. At the same time at least three well-read journals constantly engage in the debate on strategic planning (*Stedebouw & Volkshuisvesting, Blauwe Kamer/Profiel, Rooilijn*, with *Archis* and *De Architect* taking up the issue on a more occasional basis). A third important element of the new discursive space on Dutch strategic planning is the new interdepartmental initiative to improve the economic infrastructure.

This so called 'ICES initiative' (for Interdepartmental Commission for the Strengthening of the Economic Structure) obviously touches on the path of strategic planning at every turn.

The sheer density of initiatives might obviously be seen as a great success. Indeed, this is by and large how the idea of effective strategic planning was launched at the time of its new start in the mid 1980s. The then Minister of the Environment, Pieter Winsemius, was a firm believer in the idea of management by speech and thought that 'internalisation' of the goals of the spatial planner in other sectors of government (as well as in society) was the best guarantee to success (for an explicit treatment of this philosophy, Hajer, 1995, pp.186–236.) What is more, this is very much how the RPD approaches the phenomenon: it is pleased with the increased attention for what it had just defined to be its central goal: the increase of 'spatial quality'. There can be no doubt that the internalisation of active thinking about how one can best achieve 'spatial quality' is an improvement if one would compare this reality with a reality of sectoral departments that can think of their respective sectoral interest only and leave the planner with the impossible task to find a superior solution that satisfies all those involved. Yet others do not take so favourable a view. They look at the conglomerate of initiatives as a cacophony of voices and opinions.

According to some commentators, the very density of opinions and initiatives has become a problem in its own right (Boelens, 1996; Van der Cammen, 1996). As the number of plans and proposals increases it becomes increasingly difficult to see on which assumptions and theories the various contributions actually rest, and – as clear criteria for choice are not available – it is either power or pragmatism that decides which route is followed in the further development of space. Furthermore, the proliferation of initiatives potentially undercuts the legitimacy and support for what are the actual, parliamentary agreed-upon plans that are being implemented. In this respect planning has always had – and will always have – a problem with the fact that it builds according to insights of a few years back while in the mean time the discussion proceeds. This was clear at the presentation of the afore mentioned New Map. Here one of the leading strategic planners of the country, Hans Leeflang, basically showed himself not surprised by the New Map that had just been revealed. According to him, this was basically what had been agreed a few years earlier. His cool statement contrasted with the emotional reactions of various public figures that were unpleasantly surprised by the new volume of real estate that was going to be built.[4] Hence, whether the density of initiatives actually is a sign of success is questionable. This doubt is further extended if one analyses the structures in the Dutch debate on strategic planning issues.

Figure 8.1 represents an attempt to generate three distinct orientations in the discursive space of contemporary Dutch strategic planning (obviously in a much stylised and simplified form). The point of the diagram is to get a better idea of the different preoccupations and orientations in the Dutch debate. It identifies three distinct orientations: welfare planning, cultural planning and economic entrepreneurialism. These orientations are primarily discursive orientations and one should resist the temptation to immediately attribute these positions to specific actors. In actual fact one will often find that actors might sometimes 'borrow' an idea from one perspective although they predominantly draw on another perspective. The point of the diagram is rather to show that one can, in principle, distil distinct, more or less coherent orientations in the debate. This can be shown looking at the structuring storylines (marked with an asterisk – '*'), the varying policy targets (PT), the planning concepts (PC) that actors adhere to and the key technologies (KT) that are identified to make planning work.

Figure 8.2 then seeks to take this analysis one step further by showing how each of the three perspectives comes with its own institutional preference. Here I loosely draw on the cultural theory as we know it from the work of Mary Douglas, Michael Thompson or Michiel Schwarz (e.g. Schwarz and Thompson, 1990). It distinguishes between a general value orientation (V) in the sense of the cultural theory. We can further examine between the institutional Preference (IP), the *sort* of expertise that is seen as most important (Es), the *role* of expertise in the planning process (Er) and the ideas about the role strategic planning has to play *in society* (Rp).

The two diagrams show two prime discourses, called 'Compact, Urban, Green' and 'Economic Entrepreneurialism', respectively. The third discourse, cultural planning, is far less prominent but reflects a perspective on planning that might, in some respects, be important to recognise when we come to discuss the future of strategic planning.

Compact, Urban, Green

The first discourse stands for the predominant orientation in strategic planning. Here we see an attempt to combine a positive, broadly social-democratic agenda for planning, in which social goals (such as integration and the creation of employment) figure prominently together with the overall idea of sustainable development. The city remains the prime unit: it is where most of the policy

Legend

*   *Storylines*
PT Policy targets
PC Planning concepts
KT Key technologies

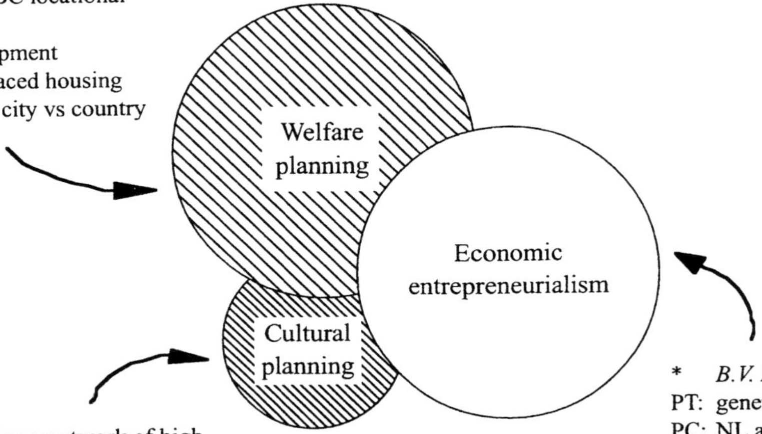

* *Compact, urban, green*
PT: social integration
PT: generate work for the urban unemployed
PT: sustainable development
PC: 'Vinex localities', ABC locational strategy
KT: EHS – nature development
KT: public transport, terraced housing
Paradigmatic dichotomy: city vs country

* *Quality of place*
PT: Netherlands to develop a network of high quality 'places'
PC: metropolitan region, urban landscapes
KT: emphasis on potential telecommunications and new transport technologies (esp. light rail)
KT: nature as 'slow space'
Paradigmatic concept: polycentric networks

* *B.V. Nederland (Netherlands Inc.)*
PT: generate growth, attract foreign investment
PC: NL as 'mainport', corridor development
PC: 'new Wassenaars', first rate cultural infrastructure
KT: EHS – nature development
KT: physical transport, infrastructure/nature as infrastructure
KT: new land reclamation for recreation and new airport
Paradigmatic concept: spatial-economic main infrastructure

Figure 8.1   The Dutch discursive space

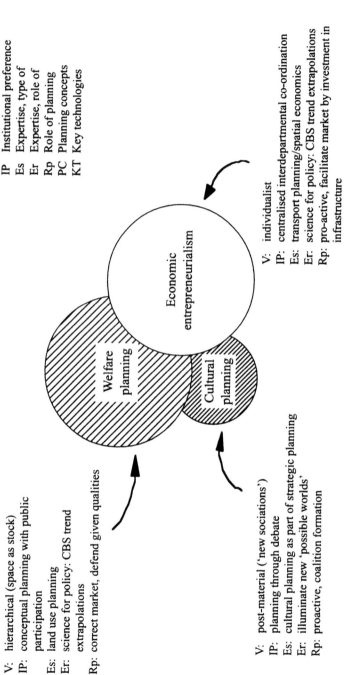

Legend

V   Valuation orientation
IP Institutional preference
Es Expertise, type of
Er Expertise, role of
Rp Role of planning
PC Planning concepts
KT Key technologies

Economic entrepreneurialism

V: individualist
IP: centralised interdepartmental co-ordination
Es: transport planning/spatial economics
Er: science for policy: CBS trend extrapolations
Rp: pro-active, facilitate market by investment in infrastructure

Welfare planning

V: hierarchical (space as stock)
IP: conceptual planning with public participation
Es: land use planning
Er: science for policy: CBS trend extrapolations
Rp: correct market, defend given qualities

Cultural planning

V: post-material ('new sociations')
IP: planning through debate
Es: cultural planning as part of strategic planning
Er: illuminate new 'possible worlds'
Rp: proactive, coalition formation

Figure 8.2   Institutional preferences

targets have to be realised. In the countryside it argues for the active nature development with the implementation of the *ecological main infrastructure (EHS)*. This would bring back – part of – the authentic landscapes as they existed before the countryside became industrialised. The High Speed Rail link (which is perceived as a necessary ecologically – more – sound alternative to the aircraft) is seen as a threat to the countryside with its characteristic openness and should therefore be routed through a tunnel, even if this is horrendously expensive. This perspective of welfare planning is seen as having a hierarchical orientation, something that was recently confirmed as the RPD and the Minister suggested that spatial planning could be usefully constructed around the metaphor of space as stock (*ruimte als voorraad*). This hierarchical predilection was the core theme in the monograph on Dutch strategic planning by Faludi and Van der Valk. They wrote that the principle underlying Dutch strategic planning is:

> the predilection for 'rule and order'. The edges of most Dutch towns being marked by canals, rows of trees, open space and the like, bear witness to the determination to keep order. Order is the rule, and rules are called upon to maintain order. This is a key to Dutch planning. Planners try to cater to their predilection, and they constantly appeal to the government of the day to live up to its responsibility (Faludi and Van der Valk, 1994, p.7).

Furthermore, this perspective emphasises the importance of public participation as a goal in itself and would see the overall task of planner-experts as bringing in the best available knowledge on future trends and organise a process in which society can democratically decide how we deal with the tasks that can be discerned from their preparatory work. Strategic planning, then, is to correct the market where necessary and facilitate it where this is desirable.[5]

Economic Entrepreneurialism

Since the mid-1980s a second position has become prominent. In this discourse of economic entrepreneurialism strategic planning concerns much more than merely land use. Where the traditional planners discourse has come to emphasise selectiveness, the goal of strategic planning in this second perspective is more inclusive. It puts the organisation of the country as its political top priority: to generate growth and to create work. In planning terms this has taken the form of a reconceptualisation of the Netherlands as a gateway to the mainland Europe. The Netherlands is to develop 'mainports' and possibly corridors if that is what would attract (foreign) investment. Yet, distribution is not all there is. It would be more attractive to generate high quality jobs in the service sector, for instance by attracting regional and European headquarters of global firms. Yet if this is what we want, we also need the sort of housing and sort of environment that this sort of highly skilled/highly paid workers value. This means, for instance, that we will need 'New Wassenaars' – after the posh residential neighbourhood north of The Hague – as well as enough nature reserves, cultural events and amenity. Urban sprawl would most certainly kill this option. To further strengthen the card of the Netherlands as economically viable region we should consider reclaiming land, this time from the North Sea. It would solve the problems with the existing airport Schiphol and would allow for the creation of new, unique recreational space. Strategic planning should not conceive of the country as made up of spatial units and social needs but as potential and as the spatial-economic infrastructure of the Netherlands Inc. (including the ecological infrastructure and the cultural infrastructure).

This entrepreneurial perspective is by nature market oriented and individualist in orientation. Yet in its present form, it definitely sees a role for the state. Strategic planning should be pro-active and should facilitate market initiative by investment in the economic infrastructure. It suggests that strategic planning is too important to be organised through the traditional channels of the Spatial Planning Act. A further strengthening of the interdepartmental coordination is required.

This second perspective is not merely a matter of a different emphasis but also comes with a rethinking of which sort of expertise is key to strategic planning. In this regard the discourse of economic entrepreneurialism implies a much more important role for spatial economists and transport planners. What it shares with the discourse of welfare planning is the reliance on trend extrapolations to determine future needs.[6]

Cultural Planning

A second rival discourse to the well known perspective of welfare planning is that of cultural planning. This discourse is much less powerful and in the diagram this is represented by a much smaller circle that is also partly hidden under its two rivals. The cultural planning discourse comprises several voices that do make statements that can be usefully subsumed under this heading. Here the emphasis is on the analysis of the quality of particular places. It suggests that society can be seen as organised around various places and that given the increasing diversity of those living in the Netherlands, planning should be about the creation of the country as a region of variety. Hence it would not necessarily argue for agricultural conservation but rather for the development of the countryside according to new wishes and insights. It would be against nature development but resist the allegedly technocratic mode of restructuring the countryside with the EHS scheme. It wants to rethink what are the qualities that need protection and brings in ideas about 'slow' and 'fast' landscapes, about urban landscapes that blur the city/country differentiation. It does not see the high speed rail link as a threat to the countryside but as an existing chance to add a new element to it. Likewise, telecommunications and innovative transport technologies are seen as potential carriers of its preferred spatial structure: the polynuclear network in which all citizens personally construct their ideal life. It is not interested in formal structures of 'public participation' and slightly wary of the power of representative institutions but beliefs in the power of creative debates between various groups. It recognises the importance of what Lash and Urry (1994) call the 'new sociations': a mixed bag of arrangements, occasional alliances and events in which actors from a diverse background take part. It focuses on the *cultural task* of planning and is not so much oriented towards the trend extrapolations that are conducted by the Central Planning Office (CPO) in their long term explorations (LTVs). The planner is much more seen as an expert that can help design. Indeed the designer has a role to play in showing society new 'possible worlds' (Van der Cammen, 1996). Not needs but wishes are central to this perspective and public involvement is not a matter of duty (as in the welfare planning) or of organising legitimacy ('draagvlak' – in the entrepreneurial perspective) but of figuring out how a coalition can be constructed to actually keep a particular vision upright.[7]

This is of course only a rough sketch of three distinct orientations in the Dutch debate on strategic planning. Yet it shows that the Dutch discursive space includes markedly distinct approaches to strategic planning. If one would connect these discursive positions to actors, it seems as if the economic entrepreneurial position gains ground. This is not at all surprising since this position suggests the possibility of a 'positive sum game' or as it is called nowadays, a 'win-win solution'. Hence it suggests that we can actually develop the country as a successful economic region *and* double the acreage of nature. Indeed, the development of nature is required for a successful economic region. Furthermore this perspective is actually promoted by what should be seen as one of the most interesting developments in Dutch strategic planning since the VINO/VINEX: the interdepartmental coordinating Commission on the Economic Structure (ICES) is a practice that now effectively fulfils part of the role that used to be fulfilled by the official practices of the Spatial Planning Act, such as the National Planning Commission (RPC). What is more, the ICES prepares the decision-making on the way in which the funds from the gas exploration are to be divided. In an official Act it was determined that this should be used for infrastructure development only. Because of the typical win-win discourse on economic entrepreneurialism, it can also be used for the development of the EHS and the soil cleaning programme. This obviously creates a whole new situation for strategic planning. In the Dutch context the spatial planner was nearly always dependent on other departments since it did not have any budget to spend (apart from a tiny sum for green belt maintenance). In the ICES structure the debate on strategic planning is not conceptual in nature but takes place in terms of active investment.

This institutional power behind the entrepreneurial perspective should be compared with the RPD initiative *Nederland 2030* as a typical expression of welfare planning. *Nederland 2030* is the lead up to a new White Paper by the minister of VROM on long term spatial policy. It should also prepare the ground for a possible fifth White Paper on spatial planning. It takes 2030 as its time horizon and should help formulate a spatial policy for the period 2010 to 2030 (after all, the period up to 2010 is officially already covered in the addition to the Vinex that appeared in 1996). In the period March 1996 to summer 1997 the RPD mobilised a grandiose number of actors to participate in discussions. First on five key questions, then on thirteen scenarios and, finally, on four perspectives. Broadly the format was that of *interactive decision-making* in which the process of discussion is used for correction and is an attempt to distil a common view on a particular problem, here strategic planning. It is interesting to note that the whole exercise was not meant to maximise participation but to maximise consent and support. Hence the typical participant was most likely to be a professional in the field of planning or was otherwise involved in the politics of planning. The attempt was made to respect everything that was said as much as possible and develop scientifically sound material as well. Hence apart from the public sessions the perspectives drew on support by the CBS long term studies mentioned above and organised the support of several consultants to develop a coherent idea on which instruments would be needed to achieve particular targets. In this respect the team did a great job. Nevertheless the value of the overall results of the exercise are doubtful. The perspectives do not seem to be all that different and it seems unlikely that they will be able to do what they should be able to do: focus the discussion on the key themes for strategic planning and break out of the cacophony of voices that can now be heard in the Dutch debate.

Conclusions

The chapter suggests that the Netherlands is indeed reluctantly changing its corporatist institutional arrangements for something new. Yet it is as yet unclear what the new is going to be. A few characteristics emerge. If we consider the Dutch reality in terms of Klaus Eder's distinction of functional and normative criteria for renewal, we see that all renewal is actually motivated by functionalist arguments. In the welfare perspective the experiment with interactive decision-making is above all motivated by a wish to create a broad legitimacy for the proposals. The entrepreneurial perspective is focused on utilitarian arguments and the cultural perspective wishes for a new participatory sort of planning because this might revive the role of the planner as designer of 'possible worlds', this time *with* the people and not merely *for* them. This absence of a priority for rethinking democracy as a goal in itself seems a dubious state of affairs. Precisely in the context of strategic planning this is something that should be put on the agenda. Currently the experiments with totally outdated concepts of democratic renewal such as referenda make that politicians do not successfully accommodate the societal wish to have a serious say in the (re)design of their environments. Here the third, cultural perspective comprises a few suggestions that deserve further exploration. Indeed, there are several Dutch examples of incidental practices that showed that the idea of planning through active coalition-building can work, in particular on the regional level.

The second – related – inference from this analysis is that conflictual debate is out. Win-win is in. Indeed, it seems as if this is an epistemic notion in the Foucaultian sense: all contributions to the debate on strategic planning seem to have to conform to this format in order to be taken seriously. Obviously, this influences what can be said meaningfully. The suggestion that strategic planning has above all a role to play in the context of a successful economic model in this respect seems to inhibit the appreciation of the more fundamental challenge that is inherent in the social-cultural developments.

Thirdly, a proactive role for the planner can rejoice in widespread support in the Netherlands. The idea to look at nature as something that can be developed is not met with a public outcry and the investment in new infrastructure has so far not lead to protests of the sort we know from Britain or Germany. What is more, this time strategic planning takes place in a context in which the government is actually in the position to invest large sums of money in innovation. This also implies that the planning tends to orient itself to those that govern the infrastructure money. This seems to have unfortunate institutional consequences. The entrepreneurial perspective is not very innovative in terms of its organisation of the planning process. It conceives of planning as effective coordination between sectoral departments. Central government knows what the goals are, just as it knows what the instruments are. Due procedure is what is needed. Here the third perspective seems in many respects more entrepreneurial in style. In the cultural perspective planning is seen as coalition building and argumentation. It shifts strategic planning much more in the direction of civil society. Here the task of strategic planning might be to facilitate coalition building and the provision of the institutional arrangements that would prevent powerful interests and vested science/experts from dominating the creative debate. In Dutch planning practice the established corporatist institutions no longer fulfil the central role they used to play. Yet the trend in institutional renewal seems to largely deny the sociological wisdom concerning the nature and needs of a post-corporatist society.

Notes

1   In this chapter I use the label 'post-corporatist society' simply to focus on *a specific element* of social change. Hence I do not necessarily see the label 'post-corporatist society' as the label that best describes society as a whole.

2   His *Aramis – The Love of Technology* can be read as an expression of this perspective (Latour, 1996).

3   This suggested discrepancy between sociological wisdom and the events in terms of the first story on the 'Dutch model' should be corrected slightly if one would take the content of the acclaimed agreement of Wassenaar into account. After all, the basis of that agreement was the trade in of *money* for *time*. In that respect the basis of the Dutch model indeed seems to lie in an increased appreciation of the post-material values, in this case time and time-sovereignty.

4   In the mean time another member of the panel, the Secretary General of the Ministry of Transport and Water Management and one of the leading figures in the afore mentioned ICES, had dozed away, but that is another matter.

5   Sources: Structuurschema Groene Ruimte, Ruimte als Voorraad, VINO/Vinex, Nota EHS, speeches Minister de Boer, Ruimtelijke Verkenningen 1990, 1994, 1995, 1996, Nederland 2030, Groene Hart nota.

6   *Ruimte voor regio's*, ICES brief 17 September 1996 (Second Chamber 1996–1997 25 017).

7   Manifest BNS, Blauwe Kamer/Profiel, Keijenbergdebat, burgerzaallezing M. de Boer, papers RoRo team, various academic contributions.

References

Barber, B. (1984), *Strong Democracy – Participatory Politics for a New Age*, University of California Press, Berkeley, CA.

Beck, U. (1986), *Risikogesellschaft – auf dem Weg in eine andere Moderne*, Suhrkamp, Frankfurt/M.

Beck, U. (1989), *Gegengifte*, Suhrkamp, Frankfurt/M.

Beck, U. (1993), *Die Erfindung des Politischen*, Suhrkamp, Frankfurt/M.

Boelens, L. (1996), 'Randstad Holland – Haar Meerdimensionale Onoverzichtelijkheid en Haar Nieuwe Opgave', *Archis*, (1996), No. 1, pp.66–80.

Callon, M. and Latour, B. (1981), 'Unscrewing the Big Leviathan: How Actors Macro-Structure Reality and How Sociologists Help Them to Do So', in Knorr-Cetina, K. and Cicourel, A.V. (eds), *Advances in Social Theory and Methodology*, Routledge and Kegan Paul, Boston, MA, pp.279–303.

Cammen, H. van der (1996), *Mogelijke Werelden: De Wereld van de Ruimtelijke Planning*, TNO, Delft.

Dryzek, J. (1993), *Discursive Democracy*, Cambridge University Press, Cambridge.

Eder, K. (1995a), *The Spirit of Environmentalism*, Sage, London.

Eder, K. (1995b), 'Die Dynamik Demokratischer Institutionenbildung', in Nedelmann, B. (ed), *Politische Institutionen im Wandel*, Westdeutscher Verlag, Opladen, pp.327–45.

Ewald, F. (1986), *L'Etat Providence*, Paris.

Faludi, A. and Van der Valk, A. (1994), *Rule and Order – Dutch Planning Doctrine in the Twentieth Century*, Kluwer, Dordrecht.

Fischer, F. (1990), *Technocracy and the Politics of Expertise*, Sage, London.

Fischer, F. and Forester, J. (eds) (1993), *The Argumentative Turn in Policy Analysis and Planning*, Duke University Press, Durham.

Fischer, F. and Hajer, M. (eds) (1999), *Living with Nature-Environmental Politics as Cultural Discourse*, Oxford University Press, Oxford.

Forester, J. (1993), 'Learning from Practice Stories', in Fischer, F. and Forester, J. (eds), *The Argumentative Turn in Policy Analysis and Planning*, Duke University Press, Durham, pp.186–212.

Foucault, M. (1973), *The Order of Things*, Vintage Books, New York.

Habermas, J. (1992), 'Drei Normative Modelle der Demokratie: Zum Begriff Deliberativer Politik', in Münkler, Herfried (ed.), *Die Chancen der Freiheit – Grundprobleme der Demokratie*, Piper, München, pp.11–24.

Hajer, M.A. (1995), *The Politics of Environmental Discourse – Ecological Modernization and the Policy Process*, Oxford University Press, Oxford.

Hajer, M.A. (1996), 'Politics on the Move – The Democratic Control of the Design of Sustainable Technologies', *Knowledge and Policy*, Vol. 8 (4), pp.28–39.

Healey, P. (1994), 'Development Plans: New Approaches to Making Frameworks for Land Use Regulation', *European Planning Studies*, Vol. 2 (1), pp.39–57.

Healey, P. (1996), 'The Communicative Turn in Planning Theory and its Implications for Spatial Strategy Formation', *Environment and Planning B*, Vol. 23, pp.217–34.

Healey, P. (1997), *Collaborative Planning – Shaping Places in Fragmented Societies*, Macmillan, London.

Healey, P. and Hillier, J. (1996), 'Communicative Micropolitics: A Story of Claims and Discourses,' *International Planning Studies*, Vol. 1 (2), pp.165–84.

Healey, P. and Shaw, T. (1994), 'Changing Meanings of "Environment" in the Bristish Planning System', *Trans. Inst. Br. Geographers*, Vol. 19, pp.425–38.

Healey, P. and Williams, R. (1993), 'European Urban Planning Systems: Diversity and Convergence', *Urban Studies*, Vol. 30 (4/5), pp.701–20.

Hemerijck, A.C. (1993), *The Historical Contingencies of Dutch Corporatism*, unpublished DPhil thesis, University of Oxford.

Hirst, P. and Thompson, G. (1996), *Globalisation in Question*, Polity Press, Cambridge.

Latour, B. (1991), 'Technology is Society Made Durable', in Law, J. (ed.), *A Sociology of Monsters: Essays on Power, Technology and Domination*, Routledge, London, pp.103–31.

Latour, B. (1997), 'Ein Neuer Empirismus, ein Neuer Realismus' (interview), *Mittelweg 36*, Vol. 6 (1), pp.40–52.

Majone, G. (1989), *Evidence, Argument and Persuasion in the Policy Process*, Yale University Press, New Haven, CT.

Newman, P. and Thornley, A. (1996), *Urban Planning in Europe – International Competition, National Systems and Planning Projects*, Routledge, London.

Priemus, H. (1988), 'Trek op sterk', *Rooilijn*, Vol. 21 (special issue), pp.21–6.

Rein, M. and Schön, D. (1994), *Frame Reflection: toward the Resolution of Intractable Policy Controversies*, Basic Books, New York.

Schwarz, M. and Thompson, M. (1990), *Divided We Stand – Redefining Politics, Technology and Social Choice*, Harvester Wheatsheaf, London.

Thrift, N. (1996), *Spatial Formations*, Sage, London.

Throgmorton, J.A. (1992), 'Planning as Persuasive Storytelling about the Future', *Journal of Planning Eduaction and Research*, Vol. 12, pp.17–31.

Chapter Nine

Structures and Processes in Strategic Spatial Plan Preparation: The Participatory Agenda

Angela Hull and Geoff Vigar

Introduction

Britain elected a Labour government in 1997 on a manifesto to modernise the welfare state and strengthen citizen participation. The previous Conservative government had introduced the concept of 'active citizens' as the leitmotif of sustainable communities. New management paradigms came to take a hold on the public sector, with calls for 'citizen's choice' and responsiveness to users and local communities, and support for a broader system of local governance involving multi-stakeholders in partnership. The Labour government is building on this with an agenda to 'modernise' local government, which encourages greater local accountability, better service performance and a more strategic focus between partner organisations. These promptings potentially herald a new participatory democracy at local government level, where independent and active citizens would be keen to take the initiative to improve the quality of life of their communities (DoE/MAFF, 1995).

This chapter provides a snapshot of the dynamics of English strategic spatial planning in the 1990s prior to the election of New Labour and assesses the extent of change required if British planning is going to acknowledge the diverse meanings and values local people attach to the places they live in. We look at how the actors within the planning system are 'making places' within our case study areas and how their distinct conceptualisations are used and assimilated. Our analyses are primarily drawn from detailed case studies of Lancashire, West Midlands and Kent, carried out for research sponsored by the ESRC in the 1990s which given an account of how central government tries to structure decision-making (Vigar et al., 2000). We revisit the same material in this chapter but focus on how, in those extensive pieces of research, we looked at the local response to central direction, the clarity of the message received, and the local interpretation of who have a stake in the outcomes of development control come to interact in the decision-making arenas. The chapter first sets the context to strategic spatial planning in England at the beginning of the 1990s and then discusses the thematic structure to the chapter. The three case study areas are then introduced and the way in which multiple meanings attached to place come to be incorporated in the strategic spatial planning process are discussed. The last section lays down recommendations for a more inclusionary process of decision-making which seeks to acknowledge the diversity of spatial cultures expressed in Part One of the book.

Development Plans: A New Agenda?

Both of John Major's administrations (1990–92, 1992–97) pushed for comprehensive, up-to-date, plan coverage to provide a clear framework for the determination of planning applications. Two Acts of Parliament, at the start of the 1990s, encapsulated these changes. The first of these, the 1990 Town and Country Planning Act, increased the legal status of spatial plans in stating that development control decisions should be taken 'in accordance with the plan unless other material considerations indicate otherwise' The environment minister in charge said:

> [the] major shape of development in a district will therefore be determined earlier in the process – as the plan is prepared. This underlines the importance of public participation (Herbert-Young, 1995, p.299).

The second statute, the Planning and Compensation Act 1991, consolidated moves to streamline the form and procedures for plan-making. Strategic spatial plans – structure plans and unitary plans were to be prepared by the remaining County Councils and the Unitary Councils in metropolitan districts. The more detailed spatial plans – district-wide local plans, the minerals local plans, and the waste local plans were primarily the responsibility of the lower tier of district authorities (Cullingworth and Nadin, 1997). These plans can now be amended without recourse to the previous lengthy procedures to gain government approval.

These Acts have therefore increased the importance of plan consultation arenas as the main mechanism for stakeholders to express their preferences for spatial change. Central to this is the capacity of stakeholders to make representations at pre-consultation, deposit and inquiry stages, to prompt intervention by the Environment minister, and to seek court orders quashing modifications. These levers have been used particularly by the development industry to more effectively influence and inform the local authority of their land market and commercial needs. The inherent tensions between shorter plan preparation timescales, wider participation and the enhanced legal status of the local plan has led to unintended policy outcomes:

> Greater involvement, together with greater reliance on experts, will almost certainly mean greater delay in plan production, which is contrary to the requirement set out by both the Government and the courts that plans be up-to-date, specific and relevant (Macgregor and Ross, 1995, p.55).

The two Acts and their embodiment of a plan-led system were driven by a number of factors not least of which was an attempt by central government to avoid making decisions about new settlement proposals in Southern England in the late 1980s (Newman and Thornley, 1996). The power to choose at local level is heavily circumscribed by criteria specified in national guidance and by the '... competitive economic environment which often determines local political priorities' (Thornley, 1996, p.7). Despite the intent to streamline the process, there has been serious slippage in plan preparation. The government responded by urging local authorities to remove much of the detail from spatial plans, to use the six weeks consultation period on the 'deposit' plan more effectively and strategically, to prepare early for the public inquiry, to negotiate agreements with objectors prior to such inquiries, and to set a firm agenda for the inquiry. Recently, the New Labour government has suggested that local authorities should set realistic targets for the management of the process, and omit one of the formal consultation stages in an effort to improve the '...economy, efficiency and effectiveness' of plan preparation (DETR, 1998). Thus despite the increased status of development plans there appeared to be a danger that local plans would become toothless, visionary statements lacking any real detail and driven by decisions made outside the strategic plan-making process. How far development plans have proved to be 'real' expressions of local choice able to express the desires of local voice in the face of potentially conflicting messages from central government is discussed below.

Research Themes

The research project covered a twenty-four month period through 1995–97, examining five issue 'windows' onto spatial strategy-making processes in three case study areas. We focused specifically on the function of the strategic spatial plan looking at the policy direction from central government, the process of preparation, and the views of participants on the process involved. Our research looked for evidence of local agency in using plan procedures and in formulating the strategic spatial plan. The capacity local actors have to further their own specific interests at the expense of central government intentions has been well discussed in the policy literature (Barrett and Fudge, 1981; Hjern and Porter, 1981; Rhodes and Marsh, 1992; Hanf, 1993; Ham and Hill, 1993). We examined the stores of knowledge judged important in defining policies, and identified the arenas in which issues are debated and the impact on local stakeholders. From this we gained a feel for who gets involved and who is excluded. The specific questions we asked of our data are discussed below.

Central Government Intervention in Plan Preparation

We looked at the way central government sought to influence plan policy through the advice given on particular spatial issues and through the use of governmental powers to direct or stall policy choice in our case studies. Of key interest in the central direction versus local agency debate, is the action taken by central government ministers and civil servants to ensure the intention of national policy is carried out.

Local authorities must consult with the government through their regional offices about the timing of the plan review and plan preparation arrangements. The government is a statutory consultee during the preparatory stages, and when the plan is put 'on deposit' for wider consultation and later 'modified', the government has the right to submit objections. The working relationship with the government's regional officers is therefore important for plan progression. Previous research has shown a lack of consistency in approach by the government's regional officers (Hull et al., 1994). On some policy issues, ambiguous advice has led to confusion; on other issues, the regional officers have used their powers to meticulously reword or delete local plan policies which were 'too detailed' or 'negative' (Rosen, 1993; Hull et al., 1995; Long, 1996; Jones, 1996).

Influence can of course translate from local to central government. The abolition of one stage of the development plan process referred to earlier was an innovation by two Kent local authorities which was initially looked on sceptically by regional civil servants. Thus, the cases below explain to what extent and how specific local interests have taken primacy over, or given a lead to the government's own policies.

Stakeholder Interaction in Plan-Making Arenas

We examined the interaction between the different participants in the processes of spatial strategy preparation as they negotiate the 'qualities to be promoted' in places, and the values and norms they brought to this exercise. Whilst it is difficult to determine the level of influence an actor may have had in 'behind the scenes' negotiation with the local planning authority, the level of participation in the formal consultation arenas can at least be identified (Webster and Lavers, 1991). Despite these methodological difficulties, the most active 'set' of participants in plan preparation arenas are clearly those within the development industry (Barlow, 1995), and particularly the larger companies (Adams, 1994; Webster and Lavers, 1991). Business interests have become increasingly involved in a variety of initiatives associated with spatial strategy making in recent years, but little of this was in the statutory processes of development plan-making. This could lend support to the idea that development plans have been sidelined and the real business of governance is occurring elsewhere.

The Citizen's Voice in Policy Formulation

The framing of policy making processes influences the level and form of participation from the public. In the United Kingdom, in the 1990s, a more streamlined plan preparation process increased interaction at the public inquiry stage. However, this was a quasi-legal arena with a technocratic style of argumentation, which was unsuited to dealing with large numbers of objectors who wish to appear and cross-examine officers, unless they are relatively expert in cross-examination (Webster and Lavers, 1991).

Commentators have argued that both the procedures and the decision-making rules serve to shield the active participants from the full impact of local politics (Barlow, 1995). Conflict on detailed site-specific issues is reduced by the absence of statutory rights for third parties to object to development control decisions. In fact, developers have argued that these corporatist, exclusionary decision processes should become the norm for the regional governance arrangements, with specific targets and compliance monitoring for minerals and housing production being stated in regional policy guidance. Developers often prefer to short-circuit local planning arenas and '...to have a discussion at a central level' (Albrechts, 1995), rather than subject their proposals to a wider range of concerns and criticism.

Government sponsored environmental and regeneration programmes in the 1990s (Local Agenda 21, Going for Green, the Single Regeneration Budget Challenge Fund) have emphasised local involvement and community capacity building. These programmes, along with the planning system, are creating expectations for greater openness, and that citizens and local communities have a role to play as custodians of the quality of their environment. The Labour government in a series of consultation papers in 1998 entitled 'Modernising Local Government' explored ways in which local authorities could be more respecting of the worries, desires and aspirations of their electorates than previous attempts to involve the public. Local authorities are being encouraged to demonstrate their commitment to individuals as citizens through improved public accountability and openness and through the involvement of user groups to advise and influence decision-making.

We have sought to examine, therefore, how development plan consultation exercises were framed. Did such a framing exercise pay particular attention to the specific place concerns of local residents or were development plans framed in a technical way that emphasised speed and efficiency criteria? We have looked for evidence that the plan represents the preferences of a wide section of its constituent population.

Kent, Lancashire and the West Midlands: The Influence of Localities

We use our research data from three areas to assess the influence of local stakeholders on policy formulation and implementation. The case studies present discourses about urban region spatial organisation, which identify the underlying power relations and the institutional capacity to interlink economic, environmental and social factors and different stakeholder groups.

Kent, Lancashire and the West Midlands provide differing contexts in terms of institutional arrangements, economic history, division of labour, cultural traditions, political alignments, and spatial and physical form. Yet recently they have all looked to the European mainland when organising ideas for their spatial strategies and inward investment. To overcome their perceived peripherality, Lancashire has chosen a strategy which emphasises the connections to the European Union, with routes and nodes where the mainland flows to Lancashire and vice versa. Kent's conception as being part of a Euroregion but fearful that people and investment could flow through a corridor across the county, has led to a strategy designed to capture investment from this corridor. In the West Midlands a continuity of direction for spatial strategy, focused around 'urban regeneration,' is apparent from the 1970s onward. Birmingham, which has been our main focus of study here, pursued a business-oriented, economic growth strategy through the 1980s which attracted a lot of attendant criticism (Loftman and Nevin, 1997). At the regional level, both the West Midlands Forum of local authorities and the North West Regional Association of local authorities have become increasingly important in developing strategic approaches to, for example, the provision of large sites for inward investments. Kent has been pursuing such supra-county matters through the Euroregion arrangement with Nord Pas de Calais, and the regions of Belgium. Coordination within the South East of England is poorly developed when compared to the North West and West Midlands regions. So at first glance there appears to be considerable local diversity and possible opportunities for local voice despite increasing centralisation (Newman and Thornley, 1996). How far this diversity exists and who are its promoters and beneficiaries is explored below.

Kent

The third Kent Structure Plan was adopted in 1997 and provides a planning framework to 2011. The plan updated the 1990 plan. The main difference between these two plans was the dominance of an environmental discourse in the latter. Indeed the speed with which the third review was instigated may reflect the rise to prominence of such issues in the county.

For spatial strategy-making purposes, the county was loosely divided into two areas, one where the protection of the countryside was the overriding principle and the other where the creation of employment opportunities was paramount, within certain environmental and planning constraints. This reflected socioeconomic conditions in the two areas. However the issues facing Kent were also strategic in nature in that the opportunities and threats associated with the building of the Channel Tunnel were central to all concerned. To this end a key factor behind the County Council's and others agencies' work were the 'Impact' reports carried out on behalf of the county by PA Consulting in the late 1980s.

The confluence of the pressures to create jobs and the existence of brownfield sites in the north and east, and the pressure not to develop in the

South were thought to make the planners role somewhat easier with a broad consensus existing over strategic direction for the county. Kent County Council, however, recognised that the differentiated nature of the demand for housing and employment land in Kent implied that it was not this simple. The sort of high quality users Kent wanted to attract would only be interested in areas beyond those which Kent might wish to see development going to in ideal circumstances. This was recognised by the County Council and a portfolio of sites throughout the county sought to take advantage of this differentiated demand pattern.

Policy Contestation Issues of housing and infrastructure were two key areas for centre-local interaction in Kent. Central government stalled the adoption of the structure plan to force Kent to provide for the housing numbers indicated in regional planning guidance. The county, on its part, was working to ensure that its structure plan figures were translated into local plans by appearing at public local inquiries to make sure districts conformed. However, the development industry remained concerned that some districts, and the structure plan to some extent, were allocating land in areas that were unlikely to be attractive to the market. The housebuilders, in particular, considered the local authorities to be failing in their duty to translate central government household projections in a reasonable way to local level.

Similarly major decisions over East Thames Corridor and the Channel Tunnel Rail Link stations meant that the structure plan and local plans were waiting on decisions from central government. The whole strategy of areas was hinging on government decisions over major infrastructure schemes.

Stakeholder Interaction We focus on the Thames Gateway area which was, and is, a major strategic development opportunity on the eastern boundary of Greater London. The Kent Thameside initiative was an attempt to capture the benefits of this for northwest Kent. The partnership embraced the government's thinking on public-private partnerships: a collaboration between the main landowner (Blue Circle Properties), the three local authorities (Dartford Borough Council, Gravesham Borough Council, Kent County Council), and a higher education establishment (University of Greenwich); the initiative sought to take a 30 year view of the area. Land use planning in the area was guided by a regional planning guidance note (DoE, 1994b), which had clearly been influenced by some partner organisations in Thameside, not least the landowner Blue Circle Properties.

Blue Circle Industries, as the main landowner in the area, took on the strategic leadership role in setting up the Kent Thameside initiative in April 1993 and producing a strategic infrastructure and land-use vision for the area, *Looking to the Future* in 1995. Although the Kent Structure Plan effectively gave approval in principle to two development proposals in the vision, they were introduced late in the plan preparation stages and therefore subject to little debate. Similarly other development proposals were introduced in the two district wide local plans in this part of north Kent.

Market thinking had embraced the public sector organisations, who strove to be seen to be working with the 'movers and shakers' in the area. To some extent the initiative operated outside the frameworks being developed in the strategic spatial plans, which was seen by some partners as allowing freedom to devise a vision for the area unconstrained by established planning policy. Others argued that an exercise on this scale would effectively steamroller the statutory planning framework when attempts were made to incorporate it in such a frame. The county argued that partnership work in the non-statutory arenas bolstered the statutory planning work, helping the process of legitimisation, through explanation and maintenance of dialogue, especially crucial with big landowners. It remained however that each partner in Thameside '... trusts each other as far as they can throw them' (interview), possibly reflecting the negotiations yet to be undertaken to extract maximum gain from the partnership and a history of difficult relations between many of the partner organisations, not least the county and the districts. There was a sense that the power of the commercial pressures for development in this area had thrown the plan-making process into disuse and planners were unsure how to deal with such power:

> We all want development, but what sort, what controls do we need. Are we saying change is so rapid we need any investment, more hotels ... or should we be saying the market is different – we have appropriate planning policies and we should aim for the following types of development over the next ten year period not two? (planning officer).

Blue Circle Industries also took the leadership role in gaining commitment to the spatial vision contained in *Looking to the Future*. The vision document was sent to each of the 80,000 household in the area. *Looking to the Future* was a statement of ambitions and opportunities to improve the quality of life of residents. Fourteen thousand new homes were promised by 2020, some four hundred hectares of newly created open space and water features, more than 180,000 square metres of retail floorspace, and up to 1.5 million square metres of employment uses. Like a commercial, this vision was 'sold', to different audiences. First of all, a team of community liaison facilitators were employed to organise seminars and gather feedback from the community. Secondly, they took their vision out to the main statutory holders of community interest – the health and education services, and the churches. This was all part of a search for wider ownership of the strategy to demonstrate that local backing for their vision existed. In terms of public opinion it was virtually split down the middle as to whether the vision was a 'good thing'.

Lancashire

The Lancashire structure plan, *Greening the Red Rose County*, was also adopted in 1997. It updated the plan adopted in 1990, but was intended to provide guidance only until 2006. The deposit structure plan had eight aims. The first of these was '...to make significant steps towards sustainable development and growth'. It was however clear from our interviews that despite a great commitment toward sustainability issues the key issue of concern to the County Council was job promotion particularly in the east of the county.

Policy Contestation Lancashire was a key player in the North West region's collaborative attempts at producing a broad spatial strategy to lever in investment and jobs, and to demonstrate a coordinated approach to European Union funders and investors alike. In many ways the structure plan reflected this strategy, with an emphasis on transport corridors linked to policies for strategic development locations to attract investment. Throughout the plan's broad, strategic focus the 'environment' was conceived as a backdrop for investment and place marketing. A significant role though was played by the county planners to drive forward the importance of environmental considerations, through specifying robust policies on pollution and landscape conservation. In each case their efforts were diluted by the combined action of the Government Office for the North West and other interests within the County Council itself.

Shifts centrally in transport policy and funding had undermined the strategies of some local plans. Dependent on road schemes for either strategic direction or for housing allocations, Lancaster and Chorley local authorities found themselves in the difficult position of being unable to progress their district-wide local plans due to road schemes having fallen through on which they depended. Lancaster City Council had been pressing for a western bypass for some time and in this they were supported by the County Council. The western bypass was part of a land-use strategy to open up the west side of the city to development and, to some extent, stem the flow of commuting from the north of the River Lune where most people lived to the south of the Lune where most of the jobs were. The western bypass was clearly a central component of the City Council's emerging local plan and without it finding housing land in the District would be considerably more difficult. The Lancaster western bypass proposal was however defeated by shifting policy beyond the control or indeed influence of local players. Cutbacks in funding for both trunk roads and for local road schemes meant that the western bypass simply was not acceptable.

In some senses the complexity of Lancaster City Council's arguments were not taken on board by the Inspector at the structure plan inquiry. The issues of finding sufficient land for household growth and the new transport link were inextricably linked. The road would have opened up whole tracts of land for housing. There has however been no subsequent reduction in the housing allocation for the district. Lancaster City Council argued that their allocation of 8,300 new dwellings was inconsistent with the structure plan strategy of shifting development eastwards. The high unemployment rate in Lancaster and the lack of emerging job opportunities in the district coupled with the poor take-up of industrial land also called into question the ability of Lancaster to provide jobs for these people. The end result, they argued, would be commuting out of the District to the main employment centres in the east and south of the county. Continual negotiations over housing and transport issues between the District, the County Council and central government have continually forestalled the production of the district wide local plan.

Stakeholder Interaction The Examination in Public of the structure plan provided a discursive arena to progress policy on a number of issues. Our interviews showed that it was seen as a reasonable method for getting consensus between those actors with a statutory responsibility. Developers, on the other hand, felt that there was a paucity of central direction in this process, with the Government Office allowing local authorities to adopt their local plans unhindered. They, therefore, had to get involved in the build up to plan production, because this was the only way to change plan policy direction.

The ruling Labour group on Lancaster City Council had argued that their support for the western bypass in part reflected the attitudes of the majority of residents in the District. In general terms there was thought to be a 50:50 split amongst Lancaster residents over the western bypass. The local Chamber of

Trade, and the Port of Heysham were vocal supporters of the western bypass and they visited the previous transport minister to press for the scheme. Lancaster University also favoured the scheme and would have benefited from improved access had it gone ahead.

The transport situation in Lancaster has had a high profile in the local media and most groups, including the environmental and business communities, have had their say in elements of it. The media can rarely if ever be categorised as being neutral however. Most interviewees perceived the main paper in Lancaster to be pro-roads but the media generally has been a major arena for the discussion of transport issues in the District. The stance of the paper was thought to reflect its networks to advertisers and the views of the Chamber of Commerce, largely one of the same.

In Lancaster a very active green network of environmental organisations exists which seeks to have influence over a number of policy areas, transport being perhaps the prime example. Transport proposals in the District would appear to have been a major 'call to action' for environmentalists in the area. In Lancaster groups such as Friends of the Earth, Dynamo, Critical Mass, the Lancaster Green Action Network, the local Green Party, and individuals and groups at the University, meet if not formally then certainly at a social level which facilitates coordination, mobilisation and debate. Some of these groupings, particularly the deeper green organisations were viewed somewhat sceptically by some officers of the County Council:

> Certainly there has been a very vocal group centred in the university...local people have become involved ... you seem to get a more rational discussion from local residents than from the more hysterical types which say don't build roads at any price', I've got more sympathy with them than the professional protest lobby (highways engineer).

Despite this lively local debate in Lancaster on the environmental and growth issues faced by the city, the local authority were unable to nurture the debate sufficiently to provide support for their infrastructure funding bid and the 'balanced' growth policy. This can partly be explained by professional and institutional practices which create barriers to involvement with 'laypeople'. The outcome also reflected their peripheral geographic status on the western limb of the county and their peripherality to spatial strategy debates which favoured economic development to the east of the county.

West Midlands

The public sector in the West Midlands has a strong tradition of working together at conurbation and regional levels. This has provided a store of ideas and intellectual and relational capital to draw on when dealing with strategic issues. Perhaps as a result, a great deal of continuity in policy exists. Unitary Development Plans in the conurbation set the context of an urban regeneration focus for new housing and employment use which was supported in the region as a whole.

Policy Contestation The recession in the regional economy in the 1980s which led to the rationalisation and closure of large companies focused the attention of policy-makers on attracting inward investment. This new approach had the potential to dilute and destroy previous policies of urban regeneration and lead to competition between the conurbation and the shires to offer attractive development sites. The creation of two urban development corporations in the West Midlands by the government during this period also was thought to undermine some of the technical inputs to local plan production particularly when land zoned for employment in the conurbation was released for retail use. A key split in the regional consensus was the continuing development of an out-of-town retail complex at Merry Hill, which arose outside the development plans frame, and which has had a major impact on districts and their subsequent plans. This reflected a conflict in issue agendas which might have taken from the power of the development plan had not renewed consensus formation at the regional level been successful.

There was thus some disquiet in the 1990s over the processes for allocating large employment sites for inward investors, not least because the process was felt to be taking place outside the planning system. It was felt that after sites were chosen by a group of selected interests, including the Government Office for the West Midlands, they would enter the planning system for debate but with considerable advocacy and weight. This provided the impetus for collaboration at the regional level and the district level to select a 'portfolio' of freestanding premium sites which would be reserved for inward investment.

Stakeholder Interaction Of our case study areas, the West Midlands metropolitan districts were the first to prepare their Unitary Development Plans with five out of the seven districts adopting a plan prior to 1993. This speed of preparation was achieved largely by rolling forward existing plans which were primarily oriented toward urban regeneration issues, but was critically dependent on the institutional capacity developed at regional level prior to this. This essentially consisted of a history of working together, and a consensus over the general direction of policy (an urban regeneration focus), despite tensions between the districts over some issues.

The process of revising the planning guidance for the region raised issues about the phasing of the premium sites and investment in transport infrastructure. Developers argued that fighting for sites on a site-by-site basis through the appeal system was too time-consuming. Both the Government Office and the regional forum of local authorities appear to have mobilised for widening consensus and more explicit criteria for site selection. A certain level of agreement over the criteria in the regional guidance for the release of premium sites was eventually reached between local authorities, business interests and the regional office. This 'success' can be attributed to the long-established political and officer networks in the region which helped build up the capacity to come to a common view and to deal with the difficult issues such as the balance between urban regeneration and peripheral development.

Public participation appears to have been carefully managed in the West Midlands. The main strategic issues of finding sites for employment and housing were resolved by a relatively small group of 'experts' in each policy community. Only if strategic level agreements could not be reached, did the negotiation shift downwards to the local plan level, where the decision process encountered a wider range of values and concerns. The task of political management was much harder at this level.

In Solihull, the debates about housing growth raised specific spatial concerns. Residents put great store by protecting the amenity and environmental qualities of their lived-in environments. The local authority and the regional association could not ignore the strength of local feeling where it was well-articulated. Solihull had absorbed substantial housing growth in the past and further deletion of the Green Belt were taken as a non-negotiable given by local residents. They helped to broker a compromise which traded employment site development for housing growth.

Case Study Discussion

Policy Direction

The degree of central control over the strategic plan-making process increased during the 1990s through the further use of non-statutory guidance notes, and through the more detailed specification of plan-making procedures. In many ways this reduced the diversity of plan approach and expression. Such local discretion that could be exercised in the early stages of plan-making had largely been removed or diluted in intent by the conclusion of the public inquiry in our case studies. This was not necessarily central capture of local debate and local variations, but through the requirement that the plan-making process must involve key stakeholders in policy deliberation. The furtherance of local consensus also required developer interests to 'test' their (major) development proposals through the development plan process. Local policy debates nested within regional strategic debates and national policy concerns. At each stage of the negotiation on place-making, it was advantageous to have a knowledge and understanding of previous debates on the issue.

The emergence of the plan-led system was seen by the developers we interviewed as leaving key strategic spatial decisions to the uncertainties of local political action. This group of respondents also felt that the move to plan self-adoption gave a local authority carte blanche to do what it wished, in particular to ignore the Inspector's report. They argued that the overriding importance of the plan-led system, which was likely to reduce the chances of planning permission by appeal, appeared to swing the pendulum back towards local political discretion. They recognised that developer interests do not necessarily coincide and whatever the plan policy some will be disadvantaged but some clearly felt that highly organised not-in-my-back-yard (NIMBY) groups were distorting otherwise open technical processes of land allocation. These feelings may be given added currency because of the diminishing influence of some of these powerful groups at the centre. Business interests are being told to '...get in the inquiry with every one else' (civil servant). This represents a clear shift from the insider status some groups had in the 1980s (Holiday, 1993).

In some issue areas, plan policy is a land use translation of a centralised process. This is particularly so in transport and minerals, and to a lesser extent in housing land allocation. Transport policy due to the fiscal and regulatory dependence of the local on the centre, has to read and conform to current Department of Transport thinking to get things done, otherwise the plan's legitimacy in undermined. Cuts in expenditure at central level, for say roads, have upset land allocations and indeed the entire planning strategy in parts of our case study areas where plans hinged on road schemes which five years ago looked highly likely to get funded. One problem we encountered in both Lancashire and Kent was that the 'new' importance ascribed to the development plan meant that local authorities tended to hide behind it and felt unable to operate beyond it. Thus, landowners and developers who wished to take a long-term view of their landbanks were continually thwarted by the failure of local authorities to consider anything beyond the lifetime of the plan and what it contained. Plan visions are being seen as too short-term by larger landowners, who are trying to take a more longer-term view of their land holdings.

Stakeholder Interaction

Partnership working was firmly on the planners' agendas in all our case studies. This followed the central government agenda of getting local authorities involved with an increasing number of stakeholders to lever in resources for mutually beneficial objectives. Most of this partnership work is going on outside the planning system however and there are fears that such corporatist arrangements could enter the planning system merely to legitimise decisions and with great advocacy.

The key players in strategic spatial planning arenas do not appear to have changed in recent times. Business interests are unhappy about many aspects of the planning system and about individual proposals. The plan-led system has put subsequent pressure on the planning system in terms of resource and management costs, notably in the inquiry process. In addition the cost to the legitimacy of the plan when it takes six or more years to get to adoption is potentially substantial.

The concerns of ordinary members of the public were influential in the strategic plan-making agendas in our case studies. However, public representations were unlikely to play a significant role in the key plan-making arenas. There were proactive approaches to consensus building in all areas. Only in Lancashire, did the concerns of local politics make a direct impact on the inspector at the Examination-in-Public of the structure plan. The role of local groups in mobilising environmental arguments against the Lancaster Western Bypass had an important impact on the final outcome. Here the district authority had a regeneration and growth strategy which depended on one vital element, a new road. There was a well-aired debate on the plan strategy in the local media, but the local authority seems not to have used this opportunity to build up network capacity and knowledge resources which they could have utilised at some later date, such as in the arena of the development plan's Examination-in-Public. However that is not to say that public opinion is not reflected. Local officers and politicians anticipated conflict over particular site allocations and acted accordingly.

We were able to identify that to some extent the more active participants were short-circuiting local planning arenas by lobbying at broader spatial scales. Developers were becoming impatient and adverse to local political discretion. This reflects both the uncertainty of managing local NIMBY attitudes and the time resources necessary to consult effectively with the wider public interest. We gathered evidence of both developers and local authorities foreclosing participation from some members of the public. This is compounded by the structure and processes of plan-making with its narrow land use agenda laid down in government guidance notes and by the dominance of technocratic values in argumentation.

The role of the local authority in spatial change is one of resolving competing claims over land use. The active players in policy making arenas were those of the local authorities, developers, local businesses and national environmental groups. The district-wide development plan that emerged in the United Kingdom in the early 1990s does not help in engaging other players. The old system of area-specific (gives people a local focus more attuned to them), subject-specific (easier to identify stakeholders), and action area plans (combination of the two), had this better wrapped up. There appears to be a noticeable negative correlation between settlement size and the level of interest shown by the public in spatial plan-making consultation exercises. In our case study areas, planners looking to review their plans were clearly trying to steer the consultation to avoid getting lots of objections. This meant altering only what was necessary, not what should be altered.

Conclusions

Institutional structures, as we have seen in our case studies, make a difference to the ability of different interest groups to be heard, to act and influence the process of policy formation. The design of the structures and procedures preference interest groups conversant with administrative protocol, and with abundant techno-rational skills of argumentation and negotiation. The procedures could easily be redesigned to ensure that the choice of spatial futures is conducted as close as possible to those who will have to live with the impacts of the decision choice, and in a discursive style which is comprehensible to local people.

Real choice could be exercised more effectively by local communities if the plan-making process was able to consider the economic and social issues at the same time as the land use considerations. Moreover, if this 'community plan' was linked to the spending plans and policies of the local authority, in toto, and other public agencies, this would create much stronger links between the public and those with a governance role. Maybe, this is what the Labour government is contemplating in the proposal that all local authorities will prepare a *Community Plan* which will act as a coordinating framework for the provision of local services, innovative partnership initiatives, and provide the strategy for bids for central government top-up funding (DETR, 1998b). To be really meaningful, they would also need to be linked to the mainstream budgets of public sector agencies including the newly created Regional Development Agencies.

In conclusion we can suggest several recommendations for the design of a more people-oriented planning system:

- central government needs to provide a clear broad framework of national spatial policy objectives which can be consistently applied across all policy sectors. Some of these goals must address the procedural issues of ensuring that a representative socioeconomic cross-section of society is involved. This should include either formal rights to participate, or requirements that all sections of society should be canvassed on the policy decisions which may directly affect them;

- local authorities and other institutions should use every opportunity to increase the understanding at local level of the range of concerns held by different groups about the place qualities and capacities of specific local areas;

- local authorities should promote new ways of working which build up local neighbourhood capacity to survey the place qualities and capacities of their area, produce outcome measures and action programmes and monitor the achievement. Different neighbourhoods will require additional support to reach an acceptable level of participation in local governance;

- it is important that all levels of governance – the centre, regional and local levels – join in this process of exploring the diversity of ideas on problem definition, are informed by a range of 'data' and 'knowledge', and support a diversity of solutions;

- planners will have to learn new skills in listening, negotiation and capacity building to support the effective involvement of more groups in planning.

This will require the use of new innovative approaches to joint working with different interest groups using interactive techniques as well as face-to-face consultation.

References

Adams, D. (1994), *Urban Planning and the Development Process*, UCL Press Ltd, London.
Albrechts, L. (1995), *Innovation in Plan Making in Belgium*, paper to Innovation in Development Plan-Making workshop, Leuven, 26–28 January.
Barlow, J. (1995), 'The Politics of Urban Growth: "Boosterism" and "Nimbyism" in European Boom Regions', *Journal of Urban and Regional Research*, Vol. 19 (1).
Barrett, S. and Fudge, C. (eds) (1981), *Policy and Action*, Methuen, London.
Cullingworth, J.B. and Nadin, V. (1997), *Town and Country Planning in the United Kingdom*, 12th edn, London, Routledge.
Department of the Environment (1994), *RPG9; Regional Planning Guidance for the South East*, HMSO, London.
Department of the Environment and Ministry of Agriculture, Food and Fisheries (1995), *Rural England: A Nation Committed to a Living Countryside*, HMSO, London.
Department of the Environment, Transport and the Regions (1998a), *Modernising Local Government: Improving Local Services Through Best Value*, DETR, London.
Department of the Environment, Transport and the Regions (1998b), *Modern Local Government: In Touch with the People*, Cm 4014, The Statistical Office, London.
Ham, C. and Hill. M. (1993), *The Policy Process in the Modern Capitalist State*, 2nd edn, Harvester Wheatsheaf, Hemel Hempstead.
Hanf, K. (1993), 'Enforcing Environmental Laws: The Social Regulation of Co-Production', in Hill, M. (ed.) (1993), *The Policy Process: A Reader*, Harvester Wheatsheaf, London, pp.88–109.
Healey, P. (1983), *Local Plans in British Land Use Planning*, Oxford, Pergamon.
Herbert-Young, N. (1995), 'Reflections on Section 54A and 'Plan-led' Decision-making', *Journal of Planning and Environmental Law*, B33–B44, Sweet and Maxwell, pp.292–305.
Hjern, B. and Porter, D.O. (1981), 'Implementation Structures. A New Unit of Administrative Analysis', in Hill, M. (ed.) (1993), *The Policy Process: A Reader*, Harvester Wheatsheaf, London, pp.248–65.
Holliday, I. (1993), 'Organised Interests after Thatcher', in Dunleavy, P. et al. (eds), *Developments in British Politics*, Macmillan, Basingstoke.
Hull, A.D., Healey, P. and Davoudi, S. (1995), *Greening The Red Rose County: Working Towards An Integrated Sub-Regional Strategy*, Department of Town and Country Planning WP No. 58, University of Newcastle, Newcastle.
Hull, A.D., Marvin, S. and de Cani, R. (1994), *Renewable Energy Policies and Development Plans: A Review of 457 Local Planning Authorities in England and Wales*, Energy Technology Support Unit, Didcot.
Jacobs, B. (1993), 'Birmingham: Political Restructuring, Economic Change, and the Civic Gospel', in Clarke, S.E. and Goetz, E.G. (eds), *The New Localism: Comparative Urban Politics in a Global Era*, Sage, Newbury Park, CA, pp.65–82.

Jones, A. (1996), 'Local Planning Policy – The Newbury Approach', in Tewdwr-Jones, M. (ed.), *British Planning Policy in Transition*, UCL, London, pp.61–77.

Kent Thames-side Partnership (1995), *Kent Thames-side: Looking to the Future*, Kent Thames-side, Dartford, Kent.

Loftman, P. and Nevin, B. (1994), 'Prestige Projects Development: Economic Renaissance or Economic Myth? A Case Study of Birmingham', *Local Economy*, Vol. 8 (4) pp.307–25.

Long, J. (1995), 'Unaccountable Delay on Route to Plan Adoption', *Planning*, 1127, p.10.

Macgregor, B. and Ross, A. (1995), 'Master or Servant? The Changing Role of the Development Plan in the British Planning System,' *Town Planning Review*, Vol. 66 (1), pp.41–59.

Newman, P. and Thornley, A. (1996), *Urban Planning in Europe*, Routledge, London.

Peck, J. and Tickell, A. (1994), 'Local Modes of Social Regulation? Regulation Theory, Thatcherism and Uneven Development', *Geoforum*, Vol. 23 (2), pp.347–65.

Rhodes, R.A.W. and Marsh, D. (1992), 'New Directions in the Study of Policy Networks', *European Journal of Political Research*, Vol. 21, pp.181–205.

Rosen, B. (1993), 'Department Gets Pedantic about Presumptions', *Planning*, 3/9/93, pp.20–21.

Thornley, A. (1996), *Is Thatcherism Dead? Planning and Urban Policy in Britain in the 1990s with a Particular Look at London*, paper presented to the ACSP/AESOP Conference in Toronto, July.

Vigar, G., Healey, P., Hull, A.D. and Davoudi, S. (2000), *Planning, Governance and Spatial Strategy-Making in Britain: An Institutionalist Analysis*, Macmillan, London.

Webster B. and Lavers, A. (1991), 'The Effectiveness of Public Local Inquiries as a Vehicle for Public Participation in the Plan Making Process: A Case Study of the Barnet Unitary Development Plan Inquiry', *Journal of Planning and Environmental Law*, Sweet and Maxwell, pp.803–13.

Chapter Ten

The Influence of New Institutional Processes in Shaping Places: The Cases of Lyon and Nîmes (France 1981–95)

Alain Motte

Introduction

The institutional reform of decentralisation in France in the early 1980s endowed the *Communes* with large autonomy in matters of the elaboration and revision of strategic spatial plans.[1] In fact, it was not necessary for the *Communes* to revisit (or to elaborate new) strategic plans in spite of the serious problems they might raise in terms urban development.[2] Moreover the *Communes* had used this instrument in the 1970s under the strong pressure of the central state, but had never really made it their own (D'Arcy, Jobert, 1975).

When strategic spatial plans were reviewed during the 1980s and 1990s they were initiated locally by local authorities willing to state politically and explicitly a strategy of development. The aim was to solve the problems (mainly economic problems) the urban region was confronted with. These plans were elaborated locally. If the state was still playing a part in them, its role had shifted from that of the 1970s, as the state was no longer dominating, specially in the use of legal instruments.

In the study of these new forms of strategic planning,[3] two cases are particularly interesting in the French context, Lyon and Nîmes, which were given wide national recognition during the 1980s and the early 1990s. These cities produced plans which are very different in nature and their comparison makes it possible to define the characteristics of the renewal of the forms and role of plans.

The experience in Lyon (1983–92), under the influence of the *Agence d'Urbanisme de la Communauté Urbaine de Lyon*,[4] the planning agency, renewed the old (1978) *Schéma Directeur d'Aménagement et d'Urbanisme*. The Lyon innovation in revising the *Schéma Directeur* was to produce a shared strategic 'vision' of the development of the agglomeration. The elaboration of this *Projet d'Agglomération*, which was not a legal procedure, was a way to concentrate public actions into common and priority themes and to avoid conflicts between *Communes* about the potential use of land.

The Nîmes case shows also one of the effects of the decentralisation reform in France in that the renewal of strategic planning involved the move away from the more traditional form of *Schéma Directeur*. The *Plan d'Ordonnancement*[5] is not a strategic spatialised plan in the traditional sense of the term but a group of 'urban projects' which are progressively linked together in space and time. It is both a media oriented operation (with images of, for example, '... a city without suburbs'[6]) and a mode of production of urban space. It was elaborated by the mayor of Nîmes and a small *Agence d'Urbanisme* and negotiated toughly with public and private actors of the city. Therefore, this is more an institutional approach than a classic plan and it includes a strong strategic vision of the city and agglomeration development.

The hypothesis on which we are going to work is that plans consist of elaborating a local shared 'vision' which is capable of integrating the locale with the global pressure for change, and which will re-embed key stakeholders (and their interests) in the locality.

The notion of locale '... refers to the physical settings of social activity as situated geographically' (Giddens, 1990, p.18). In pre-modern societies space and place coincide as social activities take place in the spatial dimensions where the presence of agents is prevailing. With the development of modernity space is progressively distinct from place, with the insertion of the self in globalisation processes in which more abstract relations prevail. Modernity creates then a discrepancy between space and place, in which abstract spaces, 'non-spaces' are dominant. The 'radicalisation of modernity' is an integration of the local and global levels, with the re-embedding of institutional relations in places.

To examine this hypothesis we will first describe the process of plan elaboration in the two case studies, to set the context before we reflect on the forms and roles of plans.

The Lyon and Nîmes Case Studies

The 1978 *Schéma Directeur d'Aménagement et d'Urbanisme* (SDAU) for Lyon, hindered the development of the urban area in the early eighties and was unable to adapt to the evolution of the urban area of Lyon (Motte, 1997).

The revision of the *Schéma Directeur* was seen increasingly as a necessity between 1983 and 1985. A main question emerged as fundamental: what is the future of Lyon? The procedure of the *Schéma Directeur* initiated in 1983–85 was based on a prevailing perception of the demographic and economic challenges with which the actors of the urban area were confronted and the requirement for economic development. However the *SDAU* raised also serious legal problems: the discrepancy between the *POSs* and the *SDAU* was making appeal proceedings possible.

The process consisted, for the main actors, in distancing themselves from the formal legal procedure of elaboration of a *Schéma Directeur* by giving priority to the debates between the communes on the challenges of the urban area. The urban area of the *Schéma Directeur* is composed of 71 *communes* (55 of which belong to the *Communauté Urbaine* of Lyon (COURLY)); each one endowed with important powers in terms of urban planning.

The elaboration of the *Schéma Directeur* (including the *Projet d'Agglomération*) was placed under the direct and immediate responsibility of the locally elected representatives through the appointment of a specific body, the *SEPAL*. At the same time they used their own technical body, the *Agence d'Urbanisme de la Communauté Urbaine de Lyon*. Economic institutions were also active in the policy process, in particular the Chamber of Commerce and Industry, together with the state services (*DDE, DDA*).

The initial stage of the *Projet d'Agglomération* involved the reflective analysis of the strengths and weaknesses of the urban area, as opposed to prediction or forecasts. The first document produced was the *Lyon 2010: Un Projet d'Agglomération pour une Métropole Européenne* which aimed to define the strategic orientations of development of the urban area as a whole, covering economic, social, transportation and environmental matters. The *Schéma Directeur* was then elaborated following the legal procedure, which allowed it to 'translate' spatially the operative strategic choices. The *Schéma Directeur* was approved in 1990 by the SEPAL but was the successful subject of appeal by a 'green' representative of the COURLY which invalidated the document. After much hesitation about the procedure to be adopted a new *Schéma Directeur* was produced, then approved in 1992.

The Nîmes case study illustrates the experimental development of urban intervention, starting from an attempt to integrate art into the city (1983–88) to a coherent urban planning policy, integrating urban projects within a planning perspective (1992–95) (Motte, 1996).

Decentralisation was adopted by the municipality in 1983 very soon after the municipal elections. The *commune* renewed the *POS* and granted building permits. The dominant conception of urban action was focused on 'Art in the City' (1983–86). The municipality accelerated the realisation of architectural objects by international personalities (Stark, Boltanski, Raysse). At the same time the idea of acting on larger urban spaces was developed in a study of the southern part of the town.

That idea was expanded in the second period (1986–90), with development of specific parts of the town, through the transformation of public spaces and the implementation of the 'Ville active' economic development project. At that stage the *Zone d'Aménagement Concerté* procedure was generalised and a public-private company, the SENIM was created, enabling the municipality to control urbanisation processes. The mayor seized the opportunity of the disastrous floods of 1988 to unite the population around the municipality and to dominate the *Préfecture* and the state services.

The third period started in 1990 with the creation of the planning agency, the *Agence d'Urbanisme et de Développement de la Région Nîmoise*, which allowed the elaboration of the *Plan d'Ordonnancement*. This urban region plan was widely reported by the media (with an exhibition at the Centre Pompidou in Paris for example) and it achieved the integration of the different parts of the town. It was invented to answer one main question: how can we 'make' the city today?

The fourth period (1993–95) could be described as the period of the implementation of the principles of the *Plan d'Ordonnancement*, whose challenges were the explicit break between the urban conception and the daily implementation of urban production processes.

We will start our study of the forms and role plans by analysing the vision of the future of places.

Plans Are a 'Vision' of the Future of Places

Plans can be identified materially: maps, documents and images. This material form varies from one context to another: maps of present and future land use, general documents presenting coherent policies, images consisting in visual or conceptual pictures. The Lyon plan is firstly a traditional map of land use which has been superseded by the image of strategic planning orientations (Figure 10.1). The latter includes two central axes: the rivers and the east-west axes. The diagram blooms into five petals representing the territorial development of the urban area. The immediate interpretation of this diagram shows a flower opening to the east, showing a vision of the future. This rich

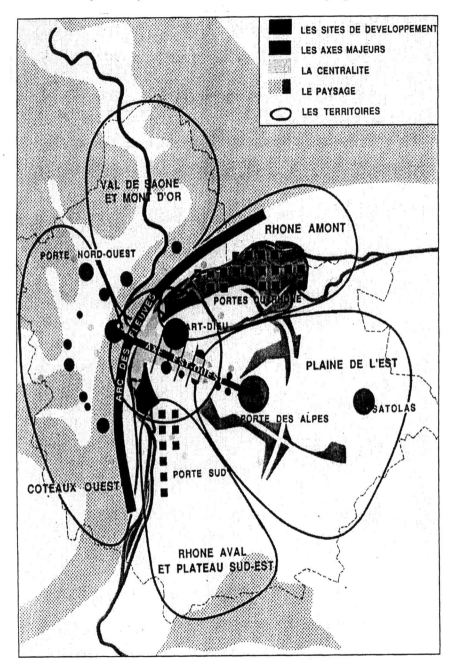

Figure 10.1 Lyon general plan

multicoloured document is an attractive and direct illustration of the will of modernity on the urban area. The written document itself (193 pages) devotes a large place to cartography and colour charts. The policies are systematically illustrated by maps.

The Nîmes Plan d'Ordonnancement is an image, changing and evolving in design and colours. The background keeps nevertheless a constant shape from one picture to another: the North-South links (Foster axis) and East-West (Donato project). The use of the green colour, more or less bright, is also one of the characteristics of these pictures.

Through this material form and these main ideas these plans are building a 'vision' of the city which is a conception of the future and the identity of the city, not only in itself but in its links with other parts of France or Europe.

In the case of Lyon the principal idea giving a structure to this vision is Lyon European Metropolis. The notion of a European Metropolis was a real 'consensual myth' (Davezies and Prud'homme, 1989a; Lavigne, 1989) which permitted a move from the traditional orientation turned towards Paris to a new relation with the other European metropolises, Frankfurt, Milan or Barcelona. More profoundly, the myths of Lyon[7] were underlying the *Schéma Directeur* document: autonomy from Paris, openness to the international context, cooperation of the elites and particularly of the public actors.

The Nîmes *Plan d'Ordonnancement* gives a global image of the city, aiming to give a general meaning to public action. This image integrates the main municipal policies. It wants to attract through the notion of an urban future. This image shows strong principles: axes replace zones. The key elements are the notions of links (spatial and historical), identity (of place but also place in a global context), order (spatial, aesthetic, political).

Plans Define Place Planning Orientations and Principles

Plans help to reduce future uncertainties. They give principles of action for economic development and space organisation. They make decision criteria explicit. But they organise the development of the city within more general forces, considering the reinforcement of the characteristics of the places.

A significant feature of the renewal in the Lyon experiment was the development of a 'strategic' document aiming to 'position' the city from the point of view of its development. The main challenge of the 1960s and the 1970s was to organise spatially economic and urban growth. The new challenge was to attract innovating activities in an economic background that had become international. In the document *Lyon 2010* emerges a new conception of the making of the city: there were challenges to take up, policies to carry out, with an obsessive focus on the notion of an European metropolis or Eurocity. Three policies were at the centre of the *Agglomération* project and the *Schéma Directeur*: to turn Lyon into an European metropolis, to implement a policy which gives priority to development, to focus planning on specific spaces and favoured axes.

The distinction between key policies, principles of planning, territories and sites was fundamental as it provided the missing and necessary links between major strategic actions and transformations of specific spaces. The key policies (11 in *Lyon 2010*, 13 in the *Schéma Directeur,* 1992) were dealt with by underlining the main challenges and the suggested options. The principles of planning were localised priorities. The territories were represented by the five petals of the flower (5) plus the centre (Figure 10.1). They were different from the territories of the POSs of the urban area and from the traditional spatialised divisions. They were spaces of specific treatment (City centre, East plain, West plateaux, hillsides, upstream and downstream Rhône, South East plateau, Saône valley). The definition of these territories was an attempt at finding a balance between the different spaces of the urban area. The analysis of their situation and vocation resulted in the suggestion of planning themes and schemes. The strategic sites identified in the *Schéma Directeur* 1990 were defined as those sites which benefited from an interesting situation, a potential of development and important land resources. Therefore an action controlling urbanisation could be carried out together with a strategic project and elements of implementation. High-stake spaces endowed with a specific image, the sites were at the heart of the planning strategy (i.e. Part Dieu, Satolas).

The project of the Satolas airport two kilometres from the centre of the urban area is typically representative of the choices that have been made. The aim was to set up a multi-transport centre combining the plane, the TGV and the motorway, relying on the Eastern bypass of the urban area. This challenge was taken up by all the actors of the urban area and financed by all the 'partners'.

In the Nîmes case, the *Plan d'Ordonnancement* raises first of all a fundamental question: how can we 'make' the city today? It provides a new approach to that inherited from the *SDAU* of the 1970s: hierarchy between strong and weak elements of the town, no detailed plan for the whole urban region, use of historical symbols, integration of parts of the town by interconnecting them.

The *Plan d'Ordonnancement*, published in December 1991 is a combination of urban projects which are dynamically linked together in spatial and time terms. It deals simultaneously with a selected number of urban dimensions, in organising hierarchically the strong and the weak elements. It was produced through the close partnership of the mayor and the Urban Agency. The urban projects (Figure 10.2) have been externally designed by architects and planners of international reputation (Foster, Donato for example). They have enabled the mayor to structure both the 'vision' of the city as well as to set up local forums which create a link with the local agents.

Innovation in the processes of plan-making can be observed in both the Nîmes case study, where it is considerable, and in the more 'traditional' Lyon case study. What is fundamentally new is that the plan becomes in fact a continuous process, abandoning the distinction between elaboration and implementation. It has become an iterative, heuristic ever-moving approach, relying on the integration of a growing number of urban projects. We must also underline the shortening of the 'elaboration' of the Lyon plan: there were only two years between the installation in February 1990 of the Urban Agency and the publication of the plan in 1992.

The Nîmes and Lyon plans show that both strategic orientations and principles of action are emerging at town and urban region level. They converge toward a renewed meaning about the place as such: historical symbols of the place are part of the plan and give sense to the whole process. It is not only spatial aspects of the town which are regulated by the plan but also the identity of the locales.

Places Are Constructed Through Planning Mediation Processes

Plans are the outcome of local and national mediation processes. One of the characteristics of modernity is the relocation of institutional relations, which can therefore be enacted further and further away from the site. The Lyon and Nîmes plans show how local and national mediation can be exerted at the same time, but also how it becomes progressively meaningful in the specific context of the place.

In the elaboration of the *Schéma Directeur* in Lyon there was a shift from the state (*Ministère de l'Equipement, DDE*) to the *Agence d'Urbanisme*. The technical officers of this agency played a structuring part throughout the process and the procedure. They took on several responsibilities. First they provided a direct service to the local representatives, who through a specifically appointed body (*SEPAL*) took all the decisions. Secondly, they brought a

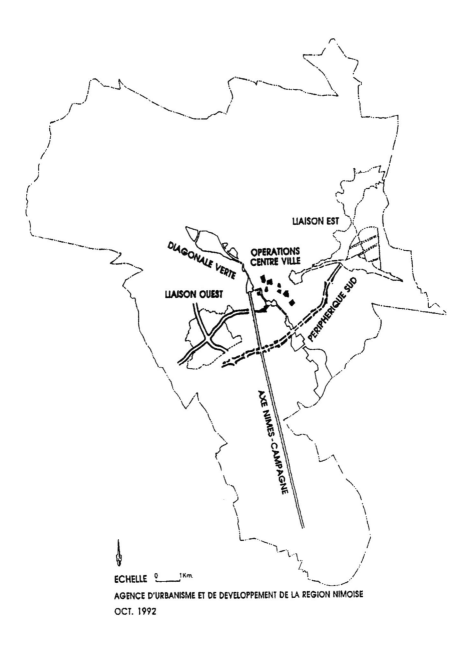

Figure 10.2 Urban Projects of the Plan d'Ordonnancement de Nîmes

Source: Agence d'Urbanisme et de Developpment de la Region Nimoise, October 1992.

technical vision of urban planning (for instance through a real awareness of demography) together with the development of scientific and technical know-how. Finally, they promoted for the local representatives in particular the notion of *agglomération*, with its general logics in the European context. The notion of intercommunal *agglomération* does not correspond to the logics of operations at the level of the *commune* and the *canton*.[8] The technical officers were trying permanently to enlarge the scope of the local representatives beyond the limits of their administrative and political areas of competence. The role of the technical officers was fundamental in this context as it permitted their intervention where necessary, on the one hand to push the politicians to take up the challenges, on the other hand to find satisfactory solutions to these challenges. The technical officers were also permanently looking for the right geographic scale to deal with the problems of the urban area.

We must mention the control of this experiment by the head of *the Agence d'Urbanisme*, a highways engineer (*Ponts et Chaussées*), who besides his personal qualities as a mediator, supported the emergence of new rational tools, with important help from the State. This emergence was made all the more difficult by the institutional complexity of public powers in the *Communauté Urbaine*. The institutions were often in conflict, but dialogue between the politicians was possible, independently of their ideological positions. The SEPAL, which was established to elaborate the procedure of the *Schéma Directeur* was respectful of the fundamental political balance first between political tendencies, then between the *communes* members of the COURLY, and finally between the *communes* outside the COURLY. This 'balance', this 'dialogue', this 'common work' have indeed created a myth which was often quoted in the political and technician discourse about the experiment.[9]

From a local point of view, at communal or urban area level, the approach of the *Schéma Directeur* brought about a renewal of the concept of the 'logics of *agglomération*'. In Lyon, this concept was embodied in an institution, the *Communauté Urbaine*, but the notion of inter-communality had to be re-initiated permanently, as one of the most common features of the French local public system is to confine its scope to the communal frame. Therefore the political debate insists on the very conception of what was to be the territory of the *Schéma Directeur*: should it be the whole urban area of the *Schéma Directeur* or a method of coordinating the POS into a communal vision? The choice of a scale considering first the whole urban area and its coherent development logics, with the integration of the *Communes* logics, has given a useful tool in the implementation of the urban policies. Since 1992, all the flexibilities of the planning document have been used fully by the *Communauté Urbaine* in ordering development.

One of the questions which emerges from the Lyon case deals with the relationship between the elected representatives and the technical officers, but the relation was much more complex than a situation dominated by the representatives can suggest. The technical officers and in particular the director of the *Agence d'Urbanisme*, had in fact redefined the nature of their relations with the politicians. They were one of the main actors, rarely appearing under the spotlights, but contributing strongly to the structuration of the whole process and exerting also the political and technical arbitrations which were necessary to conduct a process resulting in concrete action.

The Nîmes *Plan d'Ordonnancement* is intimately linked to the *Agence d'Urbanisme de la Région Nîmoise*: both were designed and implemented quite simultaneously from 1989–90, and were tightly integrated. Trying to link urban planning and urban action is one of the most important aspect of the plan, which, like the *Agence d'Urbanisme,* is a mediation tool.

It is necessary at this stage to note the role of the Equipment Ministry (Architecture and Urbanism Direction) in the creation of the *Agence d'Urbanisme*: the mayor of Nîmes was helped, even incited, in his urban approach by the Ministry.[10] The cross political legitimisation was very important and gratifying for the two public agents.

Considered locally this link created by common action was to a certain extent more important than the plan itself: the main objective was to develop progressively, forums for public debates in which the city could be seen differently. The *Agence d'Urbanisme* officially set up in February 1990 is a very small organisation: eight to ten persons including the secretariat. It is unable to carry out studies on its own. It is an agency which is responsible for managing studies made by public or private agents, its role consisting in defining their common points and integrating these studies. This Plan Agency Process relies on the daily integrative role of the Planning Agency. The plan is a flexible frame allowing interpretations and dialogues with public and private agents at local level:

Each investor, developer, each institutional actor often develops an intervention, which, initially, is in contradiction with the Plan d'Ordonnancement. It is necessary to fight so that intervention regains the 'sense' of the city (Agence d'Urbanisme, 1994 Bilan d'étapes, p.22).

Mediation is set up with agents of the public and private sphere, not with the whole population of the town or the urban region. The mayor's objectives behind this was to establish, in parallel with the lively associative networks, a municipal associative network. The importance given to the urban projects reinforces the authority of the local authorities to deal with any dissenting voices in the town or the urban region. To complete this broad outlook of the type of mediation exerted by planning agencies, we must consider the political dimension of the plans.

Places are Shaped by Political Planning Processes

Plans are the result of legal procedures and institutional processes. Abstract legal procedures often require pre-established forms imposed by the state, while institutional processes are specific to each place. In the Lyon case we have illustrated the scale of the political and administrative endeavour to sustain the political building of the place. In the Nîmes case it is a means for the mayor and the Urban Agency to impose the idea of a possible change in the nature of the city development.

In the Lyon case, the *Schéma Directeur* was used as an electoral platform for the municipal representatives. Whilst the first conference in December 1984 was held 18 months after the 1983 municipal election, the official closing conference of the plan process '*Lyon 2010*' in December 1988 took place three months before the 1989 municipal elections. The *Projet d'Agglomération* was a powerful act of political communication used in particular by the mayor Francisque Collomb to improve a somehow dull and obsolete image. However this strategy fell short: the mayor was severely beaten in the 1989 election by Michel Noir who embodied for the voters of Lyon the modernity of the *Projet d'Agglomération*.

Urban planning became a prominent element on the Lyon political scene aimed at imposing the idea of the modernity of a development project. This project therefore included a promotional dimension aimed at improving the image of the citizens and of their city, erasing the negative aspects of the latter or dealing with them in terms of solutions to be found in the future.

Both the 1983 election and the process of decentralisation made it necessary for the local representatives to position themselves differently both in their relations with Paris and with the citizens. Decentralisation required their symbolical acceptance of local responsibilities. The *Schéma Directeur*, centred on the notion of Eurocity, was one of the instruments they chose in Lyon to legitimate their new position.

The target of the document was more the Lyon elite than the general public. It was fabricated to make them dream '... blurred objectives, abundance of illustrations, concealment of the difficulties, elegance of the logo' (Davezies, Prud'homme, 1989a). The locally elected representatives prepared their re-election in a communal frame (Davezies, Prud'homme, 1989b) which entailed four constraints: they must give a satisfactory image of the present situation, they must project a promotional image of the future. The *Schéma Directeur* must reduce in a minimum way their local margin of liberty. It must also promise something positive to each local representative. The level of urban reality was comprehended in the least conflictual way, which gave a vision often comprising of geographism or landscapism and underestimating the difficult and controversial questions such as unemployment and social problems. Reaching consensus was fundamental. The projects included in the *Schéma Directeur* were so numerous that obviously they could not all be realised. There was therefore the necessity to make a choice while respecting the local aspirations. When a consensus could not be reached in the Lyon context, the solution was found in the local political forces at work. One of the most severe criticisms occurred in the 1989 debate and was taken up by the Press. It was suggested that the urban organisation in Lyon was informal, even permissive, and also that the *Schéma Directeur* was too flexible and open with few precise references to specific sites. The gravity of the situation in the Lyon urban area in the early 1980s therefore accounts for the action taken by the public authorities and for the progressive emergence of a political and administrative consensus aiming to define policies for the urban area.

In the Nîmes case study, we must underline the dominating and authoritarian attitude of the mayor in the elaboration and the implementation of the plan, as the whole process was organised around him and ensued from his personal choices. Moreover his personal bearing on these policies was considerable. The pattern of institutional relations which was established can be compared to a designer creating new fashions. The city was decorated with works of art, then public spaces were adorned with an international perspective. The perspective shows the explicit connection which was built to link the locale with globalisation. The mayor's comprehension of his city was focused on its architectural and aesthetic dimension, but this conception influenced his policies much beyond these dimensions. Behind the images, principles of urban organisation did exist. This integrating perspective of municipal action also had institutional consequences, particularly in the mode of structuring the Nîmes public sphere. The mayor and the Urban Agency defined an affirmative point of view, promulgating rules around which negotiation must take place. In this way, the Nîmes plan acted as a political instrument to give shape to the city.

Conclusions

We have tried to show how plans constitute a local shared 'vision' integrating the city in the 'radicalisation of modernity'. They attempt to relocate key stakeholders in a locale.

The study of the Lyon and Nîmes case studies open up new perspectives on the mode of reshaping urban planning and plans in the 1980s and 1990s. The nature of urban planning has changed in both cases, through new perspectives to manage physical settings and institutional relations. New instruments, specific to those places have been invented and used to set up new urban development principles. There has been a reconstruction of the public sphere and of the relation between the public sphere and the local society, with a new 'vision' of the future of the city. The *Projet d'Agglomération Lyonnais* and the *Plan d'Ordonnancement Nîmois* aim to create a sense which transforms the very comprehension of the development of the city and of its relations with the agents who constitute it.

In the Nîmes case study the reshaping of the planning process around the integration of urban projects which have their own dynamics solve the classical problems of traditional planning: time and implementation. The time taken to carry out the plan is one of the dimensions which plans traditionally try to dissociate: to separate out through different approaches of forecasts, projections, prospective. The dissociation of time is one of the characteristics of modernity (Giddens, 1990, p.17). The Nîmes radical modernity perspective consists in reincorporating time into the spatial dimension of each urban project, giving an answer to the question of time in general, by a pragmatic answer founded on specific principles which have their own temporal dynamics.

In the spatial policies a restructuring of the places occurs. The hypothesis was that in the French context the central state managed 'space', which is abstract, and local actors were producing places, i.e. locales in specific historical settings. Therefore the very nature of the action of local agents has changed. This change is 'global'. The duality of the public intervention is also evident: it is both symbolical and physical, conceptual and material. It includes ways of understanding situations, building compromises, organising and mobilising agents so as to generate actions which give sense to places.

These processes constructed places through the specificities of the locales, in their institutional dimensions.

Notes

1   Strategic Spatial Plans (*Schémas Directeurs*) coordinate the long term intervention of public powers at the urban area level. The *Plans d'Ocupation des Sols* are sorts of Local Plans which regulate land use in details. They must me conform to the *Schéma Directeur*. See Punter, 1989.

2   Strategic plans had been elaborated in a context of the overestimation of both economic and demographic growth.

3   New ideas about public management emerged during the 1980s. The main points are the following: to consider the urban region, to select the main policies for the public sphere, to set up processes of change.

4   In the French context, the *Agence d'Urbanisme* is a mainly technical planning agency which is closely linked to local political power, particularly at the level of the commune. The mayor of the commune at the centre of the agglomeration generally exerts a strong influence.

5   'Ordnance' (plan). The word '*ordonnancement*' is not used in the French planning system, except in Nîmes (1989–95).

6   Suburbs have a negative meaning in French.

7   *Le Monde des Débats*, October 1994, pp.14–17.

8   *Département* = electoral area.

9   *Le Monde des Débats*, October 1994, which questions the myth.

10 The Director of the *Direction de l'Architecture et de l'Urbanisme* was Jean Frébault, previously Director of the *Agence d'Urbanisme de Lyon*.

References

Arcy, F. (d') and Jobert, B. (1975) 'Urban Planning in France', in Hayward, J. and Watson, M. *Planning, Politics and Public Policy: The British, French And Italian Experience*, Cambridge University Press, Cambridge, pp.295–315.

Davezies, L. and Prudhomme, R. (1989a), *Le Contenu du SDAU de la Région Lyonnaise*, Créteil: Institut d'Urbanisme de Paris/L'OEIL (MEL – Plan Urbain – Avril 1989).

Davezies, L. and Prudhomme, R. (1989b), *Le Elaboration du SDAU de la Région Lyonnaise*, Créteil: Institut d'Urbanisme de Paris / L'OEIL (MEL – Plan Urbain – Avril 1989).

Giddens, A. (1990), *The Consequences of Modernity*, Polity Press, Cambridge.

Lavigne, J.C. (1988), 'Prospective et Planification Urbaine: La Révision du SDAU de la Région Lyonnaise', *Économie et Humanisme* (MEL – DRI opération 8603024 – collaboration de DOST, F.) Lyon.

Motte, A. (ed.) (1995), Schéma Directeur et Project d'Agglomération, Juris-Service editions, Paris.

238 *The Governance of Place*

Motte, A. (ed.) (1996), *Nîmes: Emergence Locale d'une Pensée Globale de l'Urbain et Pratiques D'aménagement. Aix-en-Provence: I.A.R. – C.I.R.T.A.* (Recherche Plan Urbain – Appel d'Offres Production Urbaine).

Punter, J.V. (1989), 'France', in Davies H.W.E. et al., *Planning Control in Western Europe,* HMSO, London.

SEPAL, Agence d'Urbanisme de la Communauté Urbaine de Lyon (1988), *Lyon 2010 Un Projet d'Agglomération pour une Métropole Européene,* Agence d'Urbanisme de la Communauté Urbaine de Lyon, Lyon.

SEPAL, Agence d'Urbanisme de la Communauté Urbaine de Lyon (1992), *Schéma Directeur de l'Agglomération Lyonnaise. Rapport,* Agence d'Urbanisme de la Communauté Urbaine de Lyon, Lyon.

Chapter Eleven

Metropolitan Development as a Complex System: A New Approach to Sustainability

Judith Innes and David Booher

Buyers, sellers, administrations, streets, bridges, and building are always changing, so that a city's coherence is somehow imposed on a perpetual flux of people and structures. Like the standing wave in front of a rock in a fast-moving stream, a city is a pattern in time (John Holland, 1995).

Efficient firms cannot function for very long in inefficiently configured metropolitan regions (R.H. Mattoon, Federal Reserve Bank of Chicago, 1995).

Introduction

Debates over metropolitan development in the United States typically are grounded in the assumption that we must trade off between economic development and environment. They assume that economic growth causes environmental degradation and that environmental protection only cuts into the economy. The view that environment and economy are dichotomous is grounded in a concept of a zero-sum world. This way of thinking has led to bitter divisions among interests and scholars and has also made it virtually impossible to imagine a sustainable society in any realistic way. Either rich countries will have to drastically reduce consumption and poor ones be held back from wealth, or the environment will be destroyed. Cities will have to choose between clean environments and prosperity. They will either be developed according to the dictates of developers and the free market or according to the heavy-handed rule of regulators. But neither scenario is sustainable. In the first case, the metropolitan environment will become so undesirable that business will wither and people will move away. In the second, regulation will stifle entrepreneurship and reduce profits, destroying jobs and business. Increasingly in the United States, the more sophisticated businesses

' recognise that a quality environment is necessary to their own success (Mattoon, 1995; Myers Richter, forthcoming), and some environmentalists have concluded that a thriving economy offers resources to restore and protect the environment. But neither business nor environmental interests are unanimous or comfortable with such views; they go against too much that these players have assumed for too long.

New understandings of complex adaptive systems, however, provide an alternative view, in which environment and economy are no longer dichotomous. Complex systems thinking helps to dissolve this paradox while offering a workable approach to sustainability. This kind of thinking also provides planners with ways to understand the interrelationships of economics, public finance, and the environment in the metropolitan development system and to avoid the simplistic thinking that results in policies with counterintuitive and unanticipated negative consequences. Part of this new thinking involves accepting the surprising idea that control is neither possible nor desirable, but that giving up the goal of control does not mean giving up. Certain strategies can make complex systems more adaptive and innovative, and thus sustainable, but these are neither the top-down regulation nor the formal plan-making and implementation that the current California legal system envisions. Conservative economists who argue for the wisdom of the distributed intelligence and parallel processing of information that markets represent are closer to the mark in understanding how to work within complex systems than are regulators who argue for tight control and attempt to enforce carefully crafted rules. On the other hand, such economists fail to take into account that economic motivations are only part of the many forces simultaneously at work.

In this article, we will build on insights emerging from the study of complex adaptive systems to reflect on how a multiplicity of institutions, practices, and motivations jointly interact to shape metropolitan development. We will rely on the example of California, where governance and interests are particularly fragmented and complex, and where the failure to recognise the dynamics of complex systems has produced policies and laws with increasingly counterproductive and unsustainable results. We lay out some key ideas from complexity theory, illustrating their application in the California case, and then develop an alternative way to understand sustainability within a complex system framework. Finally, we suggest strategies to guide metropolitan development so that it can be more sustainable.

Development Decision-making in California

California is an excellent example for reflecting on the complex systems nature of metropolitan development. It is in constant change and evolution. With the exception of a few brief downturns, the state has been growing steadily – so that it now is, based upon its gross state product, the seventh largest economy in the world. Over the next decade, California's population is expected to grow by almost 20 per cent, its job force by over 17 per cent, and its economy to over a trillion dollars (Center for the Continuing Study of the California Economy, 1997). At the same time, it is renowned for a beautiful and diverse natural environment, which is at risk today as its limited water resources absorb the impacts of development, as its habitat for endangered species disappears, and as its air quality deteriorates. Though the state has long prospered, the path it is now on appears to be unsustainable. The state's governance mechanisms and incentive structures affecting the shaping of places are fragmented and confusing. How to intervene and effectively change the course of the state is not obvious to anyone. We will lay out here some of the factors that make California such a complex and challenging decision-making environment, but that, paradoxically, also offer the opportunity to build a sustainable system – because of that very complexity and uncertainty.

In California, the state has land use control authority, but it has elected to transfer much but not all – of this responsibility to local governments. Hence, cities and counties prepare general plans, enact zoning and other land use regulations, impose development and impact fees, evaluate environmental impacts, and issue development permits. Simultaneously, a myriad of other special-purpose local governments carry out specific governmental functions, ranging from provision of water or transportation to education. A special-purpose local government may even do mosquito abatement. Hence, there are over 7,000 units of local government (with 15,000 elected officials)[1] in California, many of which have independent decision-making authority that influences development. This maze of institutions makes public understanding of fiscal and governance responsibilities difficult. Moreover, each unit of government has challenges to operating effectively in such a fragmented context and little knowledge of what others are doing. There have been many reform efforts (e.g. California Constitution Revision Commission, 1996), but so far little success. Finally, land use decisions are also indirectly influenced by fiscal and regulatory decisions of federal agencies, such as the Environmental Protection Agency or the Department of Transportation.

The state itself has no statewide general plan or strategy, but it does require every city and county government to prepare a general plan. The state sets the required content areas of local general plans and specifies processes for adoption, amendment, and adjudication. The general plan must be long-range (20 years or more), comprehensive, and internally consistent. Land use planning and regulation is directed by city councils and county boards of supervisors, elected in nonpartisan elections, but much of the day-to-day decision making is carried out by appointed citizen planning commissions with the assistance of professional planners. There is little state oversight of the compliance of local governments with state planning law. Instead, the state relies on litigation by affected parties, such as developers, environmentalists, or neighbourhood groups. The law requires that land use regulations be consistent with the general plan, for example, and this is often the subject of litigation among competing local interests. Another common subject for litigation is application of the California Environmental Quality Act, which permits challenges to environmental impact assessments of development projects when they are thought to be inadequate. General-purpose metropolitan or regional authorities do not exist; nor does the state review the content of plans for coordination purposes or for assessing the cumulative or interactive consequences of decisions.

California local jurisdictions as well as state agencies are subject to a wide range of competing pressures from organised interests, reflecting the diverse nature of the state. Particularly active groups represent agriculture, high technology, business, builders and real estate, non-profit and affordable housing, labour unions, environmentalists, taxpayers, and neighbourhoods. These interest groups make land use planning and development even more complex, as well as highly controversial. Dealing with them can make the process for development lengthy, so that there is a disjuncture between the development action and the economic conditions that triggered the request. Approvals for a modest housing development routinely require hundreds of hours of meetings and four years of processing, whereas large-scale or complex developments can take much longer.

Overlaying this complex and fragmented institutional and political context is an even more complex and fragmented fiscal system that, in many cases, is the most important single influence on local land use decisions. State and local tax and revenue structures and program responsibilities are interwoven so thoroughly that most people have little understanding of which tax goes where and which government is responsible for which service. The three most important tax sources are the income tax (mostly going to the state), the local real property tax (the majority of which funds school districts, thereby relieving the state of some of this responsibility), and the sales tax (divided between the state and the city and county governments where it was raised). A mix of other tax sources is important too, including local utility and business license taxes, vehicle license taxes, state alcohol and tobacco taxes, and state gasoline taxes. Finally, fees on new development fund much local infrastructure. Other public facilities, both new and existing, are funded by benefit assessments on people within a special assessment district. This is a proportional tax, based on providing a service to those people and businesses that will benefit (California Planning Roundtable, 1997).

The most important factor in the state's complicated fiscal structure is a series of constitutional amendments, written and placed on the ballot by citizens and passed by voters.[2] Proposition 13 started this trend in 1977 by capping property taxes at 1 per cent of value and allowing only up to 2 per cent per annum adjustment. It immediately resulted in an $8 billion loss in local revenues. It allowed property reassessment to reflect increased value only after sale. Hence, property taxes remain low for homes or businesses that do not turn over, regardless of property appreciation or increases in the costs of providing services. They also remain low for jurisdictions with stable populations. On the other hand, new owners pay a disproportionate level of taxes in a state where housing prices have risen dramatically. They also may pay development fees, which often run as much as $20,000 per housing unit. Despite these high taxes, many local governments find that new developments do not provide enough additional revenues to fund the requisite public services; accordingly, they shy away from permitting *any* new housing (Dresch and Sheffrin, 1997).

Since Proposition 13, state and local governments have adjusted and created new devices to fill the revenue holes. These reactions have in turn caused citizens to put forward additional ballot initiatives, which do such things as place revenue and expenditure limits on all units of government, constitutionally protect a proportion of revenues for schools, require voter approval of all new or increased local taxes, and place stringent restrictions on benefit assessments. In 1991, the state legislature shifted an additional $3 billion in property tax revenues away from cities and counties to school districts to deal with a state revenue shortfall stemming from Proposition 13. The result is a fiscal system that not only challenges voter and legislator understanding and generates public frustration, but makes it difficult for any jurisdiction, including the state, to provide infrastructure or undertake other growth-related programs for environmental or economic improvement (Schrag, 1998).

With all these restrictions, the situ-based sales tax has become the most important local revenue source. As a result, cities and counties have been increasing their competition for land uses that generate sales tax revenues, decreasing their willingness to approve land uses that generate low property tax (such as affordable housing), and increasing their reliance on development fees to finance community facilities. Even employee-intensive manufacturing land uses are fiscally unattractive because income taxes go to state government and most property taxes go to school districts. As a result, communities are far more likely to approve large-scale shopping centres than to approve clean, high-profit industry. The large-scale discount shopping mall and 'big box' retail[3] are massive land users, which typically drain the commercial energy from the town centres and existing malls – to the regret of the local residents. These facilities are usually scattered around fringes of metropolitan regions in whichever towns happen to need revenues, rather than in any efficient way (Fulton, 1997).

The consequences of this pattern are, first, high costs to the region for such infrastructure as roads and sewers, as well as automobile traffic and congestion and air-quality problems. Second, large-scale shopping facilities may provide revenues for one town, but they undermine the economies of neighbouring towns; as their revenues shrink, their schools and services may also decline in quality. These areas then become less attractive as locations for business or middle-income residents, and the second- or third-order effect is to reduce the revenues further and increase neighbouring towns' incentive to approve regionally inefficient land uses (California Planning Roundtable, 1997). Funds for infrastructure projects have grown increasingly inadequate as a result of both the sprawling patterns and the fiscal constraints, so that by 1997 there was a projected $29 billion deficit in such funds (California Planning Roundtable, 1997). This deficit has in turn further increased housing costs, produced overcrowded schools, and closed or curtailed use of parks and libraries. Moreover, the sprawling pattern of development has increased dependence on the car, which in turn requires massive parking, causes air pollution, and reduces the potential for land use dense enough to support alternative transportation (Fulton, 1997). Other second-order effects include disturbing trends to the creation of high-priced, typically White, gated communities, protected from the costs associated with the poor or with crime (Blakely and Snyder, 1997). These trends, although damaging to the metropolitan system as a whole, increase the relative attractiveness of suburban low-density development to families with the resources to make the choice (Downs, 1994).

The overall unsustainable pattern in California is not one that can be blamed simply on popular explanations, such as Californians' love affair with the car, nor their preferences for large yards and detached housing. Nor can it be blamed on economic growth itself. Rather, it is a product of a set of interacting factors that are locked into a complex, vicious circle pattern. Efforts to intervene have been made by one or another set of interests – each grasping the elephant by only one of its parts and misunderstanding the whole. The effects of each new law and mandate have been not only to make the system more complex and less transparent, but also to produce outcomes not intended by the proponents of the change. The system has by now become too complex for anyone to solve these problems with a simple reorganisation or new law. The ramifications of any proposal are too many and too uncertain.[4]

Growing Awareness of the Costs of Sprawl

As the consequences of this complex array of conditions emerge, recognition is increasing in many quarters, including the business community, that compact development patterns are supportive of a state's or region's economy rather than harmful to it. Business has often regarded development regulation as a cost and a hindrance to competitiveness. A number of recent studies have shown, however, that business functions as part of a complex system of linked factors in the physical environment and the governmental context, as well as in the economy. For example, Mattoon (1995) has shown that efficient metropolitan land use patterns have been closely linked to competitiveness and productivity in regions across the United States. Compact patterns also have been shown to save significant fiscal resources.[5,6] The Bank of America, along with the California Resources Agency, challenged conventional wisdom in the development industry when they released a report early in 1995, arguing that '... unchecked sprawl has shifted from an engine of California's growth to a force that now threatens to inhibit growth and degrade the quality of our life' (p. 1). Another study, commissioned by the American Farmland Trust (1995), found that urban sprawl in the Central Valley of California, for example, would consume much more farmland, cause greater reduction in agricultural commodity sales, and dramatically increase the costs of public services than would compact growth. The state's Little Hoover Commission, whose mission is to investigate government and make recommendations to promote efficiency, economy, and improved service, concluded that the current processes of decision making in land use are resulting in conflicts that are costly to the state because they are preventing the achievement of more efficient growth patterns '... essential to the State's economic and environmental health' (Little Hoover Commission, 1995, p.1). A US Federal Reserve Bank report (Mattoon, 1995), documented the importance to the Midwestern economy of achieving alternatives to the existing growth patterns currently '... leading to urban sprawl and the inefficient delivery of public goods and services, that will ultimately undermine the economic prospects of entire metropolitan regions' (p.20).

Complexity Theory as a Framework

We can tackle the understanding of the shaping of places if we start with a conception of the social, political, and economic world as a complex, self-organising adaptive system, parallel to those that are being identified in the physical and biological sciences, and if we regard metropolitan development itself as a comparable complex adaptive system.[7] Complexity theory has particular application today because we are in an unstable time, where much is unpredictable and change is constant. Existing structures and patterns of relationships and organisation are in flux (Castells, 1996). Under such conditions, the predominant western world view since the Enlightenment is no longer as useful as it once was. This view has been dominated by a Newtonian, mechanistic model (Capra, 1982), which, as a model of reality, is quite alien – not only to contemporary conditions, but more generally to the way urbanists and planners understand what shapes urban patterns. The dominant, though tacit, metaphor was that natural and social systems are like machines: composed of separable parts that can be analysed and understood individually.[8] Their ensemble is nothing more than the sum of these parts. Yet nothing could be less like urban place-making, which is constantly evolving and results from perpetual and complex interaction among many parts. In mechanical systems, the parts are interchangeable. The natural tendency is for their dynamics to move them toward an equilibrium state. Having been set in motion, this machine-like universe is driven by laws that, if we could uncover them, we could use to predict its behaviour. Over time, this universe and the systems within it gradually lose whatever energy has been applied to them. The mechanistic perspective contends that, with an adequate theory, accurate observations, and appropriate inputs, we could control how a given system behaves (Hwang, 1996) and predict the results of an intervention. Yet decades of trying to change the direction of change in urban places, using this sort of carefully developed intervention, have produced little to suggest that a mechanistic approach makes sense when applied to natural or social systems.

Over the past decade, however, a new view of how systems work has begun to emerge in the thinking of many scientists and mathematicians – a view that provides a far better analogy for understanding metropolitan development and how it works than does the mechanical conception. This model is based on the study of complex adaptive systems in a state '...at the edge of chaos'. It first emerged in the physical sciences (Kauffman, 1995; Lewin, 1992; Nicolis and Prigogine, 1989; Prigogine and Stengers, 1984; Waldrop, 1992). Some have argued that this model is also powerful in understanding the functioning of social systems (Hwang, 1996; Kauffman, 1995; Kiel, 1991; Wheatley, 1992).[9] Although understanding of this model is still in its infancy and we cannot in any case explain here the theory of complex adaptive systems, we can highlight basic features that are important for our purposes to distinguish it from the mechanistic view.[10]

The dominant metaphor for this new world view is, rather than the world as machine, *the world as organism*, with all the consequent implications of growth, feedback, and evolution. Complex adaptive systems involve networks of relationships among many components, which interact in both competitive and collaborative ways, so that they co-evolve and mutually adapt. It is perhaps easiest to see this by noting how, in a complex ecological system, plants and animal species evolve in their activities in response to changes in the patterns of those species on which they depend – and in response to changes in the environment or in the introduction of new species. This adaptation occurs without the agents in the system, such as individual animals or plants, necessarily having any conscious recognition – much less deliberate intent. Indeed, these complex adaptive systems are found in physics and computer science, as well as in biological and ecological systems (Nicolis and Prigogine, 1989). They seem to be mimicking cognition in this adaptation process – to such a degree that Capra entitles his book on the subject *The Web of Life* (1996). This cognition is, however, less visible when we look at the individual agent than when we examine the ensemble, just as an ant colony has a level of intelligence that is far more than the sum of its parts.

This collectively intelligent, adaptive process is most likely to occur when the environmental conditions and influences on the systems can be characterised as being at the edge of chaos, rather than involving either substantial continuity and equilibrium or fully chaotic conditions. Equilibrium occurs in either a closed system or in systems in a stable environment. In equilibrium conditions, a system adapts to external or internal change with modest adjustments, allowing it to maintain its comparative stasis. Such a system, however, has little capacity to respond to change or chaotic inputs with significant changes of its own that would allow it to adapt to the new conditions effectively. Chaos, on the other hand, is a set of relationships so turbulent that no meaningful order exists in them, and no adaptation or response is of value. The less turbulent phase just at the edge of chaos, however, is one where there is opportunity for experimentation and development of new and more productive patterns and activities – though often only after many failures. Functioning in a state at the edge of chaos, the participants or elements in the system can coordinate complex activities and are better able to evolve than those in chaos or equilibrium conditions (Kauffman, 1995).

In this view, the interactions in the network itself lead to the system's evolving to higher states of adaptability. Essentially through a process of tinkering or randomly experimenting and making further adaptations after feedback, the system as a whole 'learns', rejecting ineffective pathways or actions and building on those that provide more desirable results. Thus, the IBM computer playing chess against Garry Kasparov 'learns' from the play itself and develops continuously improved strategies the more it plays. In the process of play or interaction in a complex system at the edge of chaos, each participant or component influences the transformation of the others. Although the general pattern of these relationships may be predictable, the details of how the system will behave cannot be predicted for any specific case or time. For example, in the case of malaria and a host immune system, one cannot predict how an individual will respond to infection – or even that a specific host will successfully adapt. There is both structure and agency at work, in that the pattern or structure can have a strong influence on action by any component, but random or intentional acts by individuals can alter the structure.

A complex system is thus, in a basic sense, out of control (Kelly, 1994). It cannot be managed by any single mind or even by a complicated set of formal policies; there is too much going on at once, too many linked components, and too much feedback and adaptation. Research has shown that distributed rather than top-down intelligence works to deal with such situations and permits creative coordinated action when many independent players are involved. Many agents, following simple rules for adjusting their actions, without seeing or understanding the dynamics of the larger system, can effectively coordinate for joint action. For example, flocking behaviour of birds can be mimicked on the computer much better by applying to each simulated bird a few simple rules, like 'do not bump into another bird' and 'keep up with neighbours but not too close', than by trying to design the pattern a priori. The application of this distributed-intelligence concept results in patterns similar to the graceful and aerodynamically efficient patterns of flocking birds (Kelly, 1994).

Top-down regulation and control strategy are far less effective than this kind of self-organising approach, based on knowledgeable agents acting individually when systems are complex and operating in a fast-moving and unpredictable environment.[11] For example, Hutchins (1995, pp.1–5) tells the story of a huge US Navy ship that suddenly loses power in a narrow channel and, as a result, also loses use of the usual indicators and gauges. This sets in motion a series of activities and communications among people with different responsibilities around the ship, as they endeavour to find a way to handle the problem without going aground or running over other boats. They make mistakes and have a number of partially missed communications. They come up with strategies to operate without reliable tools and gauges. The steering overcompensates wildly. They discover they have no whistle to warn an oncoming boat. But they manage to slow the ship and drop anchor without mishap. In this case, participants faced a situation that they had not faced before and for which there were no instructions. They had to invent quickly what to do. They could not consult or strategise and lay out the best approach. They had to use their experience and act, even without knowledge of all the other consequences on the ship of the loss of steam power or of all the other activities that were going on simultaneously. Sometimes, one person's judgment was wrong, but others compensated in what they did. They experimented and reacted collectively, and that collective response worked, albeit clumsily.

Complexity as a Perspective on the Metropolitan System

We contend that the metropolitan development system in California is now like a ship without gauges and without clear communication among the participants.[12] Each can see only a part of the problem, and each can act only individually – or at best, shout across the deck to someone else who is busily working on his or her crisis-management responsibility. Successful self-organisation and adaptation do not necessarily occur in complex systems or may only be done inadequately. If no communication, feedback, or common purpose exists among the participants, or if one agency or individual tries to make rules and intervene in a deterministic controlling way, the results are likely not only to be inefficient, but also to quite possibly fail entirely to address the problem – or even aggravate it.

Four ideas from complexity theory that will help us think in new ways about how to improve the metropolitan development system:

• simplification results in fundamentally wrong answers, and focus on individual sectors separately will be counterproductive;

• effects cannot be directly linked to causes because an intervention reverberates through the system in ways that can be only partially traced;

• even small changes introduced into the system may produce discontinuous, unpredicted effects;

• adaptive changes within a system can grow from learning generated by the individual interactions in the networks of system participants.

Metropolitan development in California demonstrates these principles. Attempts at policy interventions have not produced a smooth pattern of change; rather, they have made radical transformations that intervenors did not anticipate. The simple effort of apartment developers to control property taxes with Proposition 13 produced more fiscal uncertainty, increases in other taxes and fees, more restrictions on development, rent controls, and more state control over local governments. The effort of local government to focus on the fiscal sector alone produces land use patterns that undermine their own revenues over time and put heavy costs onto metropolitan infrastructure – which in turn means there are fewer resources to go around. We cannot pinpoint the causes of migration to suburbs because social changes, quality of public services, racial attitudes, lifestyle choices, transportation technology, and even economic prosperity may all be implicated, along with other factors (Fulton, 1997). Capital improvements in highways reduce congestion and improve air quality in the short run, just as improved gas mileage saves on non-renewable resources. But both have second- and third-order effects, producing an expansion in automobile use far exceeding population growth, which ultimately increases congestion as well as adding to the attractiveness of low-density suburban housing and vast auto-oriented shopping malls. On the other hand, in a rare case of adaptive learning, automobile commuters in the San Francisco metropolitan area have developed practices of casual car-pooling (some would call it hitchhiking) among the white-collar workers commuting to the city, so they can take advantage of special highway lanes for multi-occupant vehicles. During a recent transit strike, public officials finally recognised the value of this effort and took steps to make such a self-organising solution work better by creating special spots in San Francisco where cars can legally and conveniently stop to pick up riders.

The use of complexity theory in understanding the functioning of the metropolitan system tracks with new insights into the nature of changes in the social and political system, which have emerged over the past few decades. Charles Handy (1990) has argued that the changes society must cope with are different today because of the rapidity of economic and technological changes. Change is discontinuous, rather than part of a pattern, and even apparently minor changes can have profound implications for our lives. Handy suggests that discontinuous change requires discontinuous thinking to manage it. We can no longer think in incremental, evolutionary terms but must instead be willing to think in terms of completely different options if we are to respond to change effectively. He also observes that the model of rational control with top-down, centralised direction will not be effective in this radically different world.

> We have tried to plan and control world trade and world finance and to make a greener world. There should be a rational response to everything, we thought; it should be possible to make a better world. It hasn't worked. Management and control are breaking down everywhere. The new world order looks very likely to end in disorder (Handy, 1994, p.11).

Anthony Giddens (1994) says these changes have produced 'manufactured uncertainty', because the effort to use advances in human knowledge and controlled intervention has actually resulted in more unpredictability. This phenomenon is demonstrated by the example of California, summarised above. Giddens attributes this seeming paradox to three interlinked developments: globalisation (by which he means action at a distance that affects each individual), emergence of post-traditional society (where traditions are subject to justifications instead of accepted on the basis of faith or ritual), and expansion of social reflexivity (individuals filtering information and acting on the basis of the filtering), which is both condition and outcome of the other two.

Giddens explains social reflexivity by saying, '... Decisions have to be taken on the basis of a more or less continuous reflection on the conditions of one's actions'. 'Reflexivity' here refers to '... the use of information about the conditions of activity as a means of regularly reordering and redefining what the activity is' (1994, p.84). Hence, individuals rely less on traditions or rituals in making decisions and more on information about their conditions of everyday life, the results of their activities in that life, their most important concerns, and expert information relevant to these. They also develop the habit of tuning into or out of specific issues, based upon this filtering of information. As a result, bottom-up decision-making, autonomy, and decentralisation increasingly replace centralised regulation and hierarchical organisation. Indicators may become very important in influencing the activities of individuals. Social reflexivity also generates the extension of what Giddens calls dialogic democratisation – autonomous communications among participants forming a dialogue in which all points of view can be heard in order to shape policies and actions, rather than as an exercise in search of the 'correct' answer (1994). This presumably creates an important role for processes such as consensus-building, which facilitate such dialogue.

In trying to manage metropolitan development systems to achieve sustainability in an era of uncertainty and discontinuous change, we are going to have to develop strategies that recognise and adapt to these conditions of complexity (Courtney, Kirkland, and Viguerie, 1997). These strategies will need to be based upon a new understanding of sustainability; on the use of indicators to help guide actions and dialogue; on consensus-building to enable dialogic democracy, joint learning, trust, and innovation; and on leadership to build common meaning and purpose.

Complexity and Sustainability

Complexity theory provides new insight into the elusive goal of sustainability and suggests that many popular ways of thinking about this have been moving in the wrong direction – a direction that would make sense if the world were like a machine rather than like a growing, evolving organism. Essentially, a sustainable complex system is one that is adaptive and self-organising, with its components free to co-evolve in response to changes in each other and, as a whole, changing in response to external conditions. It learns from the feedback it gets, as it randomly or deliberately experiments with new actions. It develops the actions and pathways in its network of agents that work most effectively. In doing so, the system grows and evolves. The character and quality of its results may change, and its productivity could eventually increase, even when the external change is one that at first appears damaging. There is unlikely to be any endpoint for an adaptive system nor any ideal form; its adaptations are not predetermined but are the product of distributed intelligence and of experiments or even random events that open up new ways of doing things. The sustainable complex system not only survives, but continuously undergoes transformation.

The implication of this concept is that *sustainability is about process, not about a particular vision, pattern, set of rules, or criterion.* We cannot know just what a sustainable world will look like or even whether the one we have is sustainable. If we unduly constrain our choices as we move forward, however (as California has done), or impose a particular vision on those who come after us, we will not allow the system to be adaptive and experimental as it encounters the future. Natural and man-made disasters will occur, technology will change, and these will have impacts and reactions that we cannot even imagine. Such disasters could be transformed into the impetus for the creativity that will be needed to develop a truly sustainable society.

Mechanical and dichotomous notions, like making trade-offs between the economy and the environment, moreover, are not likely to be part of a sustainable path. A metropolitan economy needs an adequate environment, and the environment needs an adequate economy to ensure that it can be protected and improved. Increasingly, cutting-edge businesses recognise that this is a symbiotic relation (Myers Richter, forthcoming). A sustainable world is also unlikely to be one where people consume less. Not only is reduction of worldwide consumption unlikely, but consumption reduction may not be the only approach to sustainability. Fossil fuels may or may not be important in a future sustainable development path. Under the right conditions, societies can develop alternative valued outcomes and different ways of meeting human needs. This can happen because of new technologies, but it also may result from societies organising themselves in new ways, so that new and currently unanticipated values may emerge, and form dialogues that produce innovative responses.

The objection that many would surely make at this point is that it is simply too risky to let the system take its course. We can see disaster ahead, and we need to develop new rules and new forms of governance that will avert the disaster. Maybe people will wake up to this disaster, critics say, and change their values someday, but it is likely to be too little, too late. By the time they react, the resources will be depleted. People and species will disappear while we are waiting for societies to learn.

Our response is that the rules and mandates we create today will not avert disaster, though they may seem to help for a time. If we have too much hubris today and imagine that, from our limited perspective, we can solve this complex problem, we will end up having the same fragmented, counterproductive development system worldwide that we now have in California. We have no choice but to trust the intelligence and inventiveness of people everywhere to learn and to transform the system. Instead of trying to define a vision of sustainability – how to get from here to this ideal world – we need to find

ways to make the complex system we have into one that will allow the players
themselves to turn the metropolitan system into a collective intelligence that
can sustain itself indefinitely.

What Can Actually Be Done?

Policies fail to turn out as those crafting them desire – not only because of
emergent technologies, unanticipated major events, or changes in the structure
of the economy that are beyond their ability to predict or control, but also because
there are so many players who make the city what it is. Businesspeople, residents,
commuters, elected officials, and many others make millions of decisions on
a daily basis that add up to the evolving form, structure, and character of the
cities, and that shape their economies, their vitality, and the direction of change.
Yet these decisions are largely beyond the reach of any formal urban policy
or plan, much less any top-down regulatory strategy. The best planners can
do is to help the players in these places to influence the direction of change.

We therefore propose three principal strategies for improving metropolitan
system performance, each of which targets a different level or type of
metropolitan decision maker. These include development and use of indicators
and performance measures in new ways, the use of collaborative consensus
building among stakeholders who best understand the different aspects of the
metropolitan system, and finally, the creation of new forms of leadership.
Each of these strategies represents a way to make the whole system more
informed, responsive, and transformative. Together, these strategies can help
make the metropolitan development system more of a genuine learning system.
The goal is to achieve not only what is known as single-loop learning, where
information can be used to keep the system on track in response to variations
and external changes, but also double-loop learning (Argyris and Schön, 1974,
p.50). Double-loop learning involves not just maintaining equilibrium but
reassessing goals, purposes, and processes. This kind of learning results in
fundamental transformations in agents and in the system.

In this context, actions that will make a difference are related to the
improvement of *system* performance, rather than simply to the performance
of one aspect for a short time. Sustainability is a characteristic of a whole
system, and we can only work toward it by thinking in system terms, which
are unfamiliar to most people. A well-performing, sustainable metropolitan
system, for example, may be one that shows a high degree of adaptability to
global and technological change, and in which the economy moves to higher

levels of productivity rather than stagnating or collapsing into chaos. It is one where the various jurisdictions work together to meet regional needs for water, transportation, housing, economic development, and revenues over the long term, and where they have the capability both to look collectively at the interactions and relationships among these subsystems and to act at a system level, rather than for their own parochial interests.[13]

Indicators

To create a sustainable system and enhance the reflexivity of its participants, feedback and conversation are essential. The agents in the system must have knowledge so they can learn, repair, and redesign their own system. They also must explore and discuss among themselves the meanings and implications of the knowledge, as well as attempt to anticipate the consequences of various responses to it. For this purpose, we believe three types of indicators will be needed[14] – indicators that are the product of the collective intelligence of many agents, closely linked in content and design to the values and meaning systems of those agents, and directly relevant to the choices and opportunities that face them. These are not proposed to be all-purpose databanks, but rather focused ways to extend the conversation and the knowledge of participants. These are indicators to provide feedback not only to planners and policy makers, but also to residents, migrants, businesses, community groups, and public agencies, so they can make simultaneous adjustments in their own tasks and move the system more in a desired direction. Getting the selection and design of these indicators exactly right (even the imperfect information and faulty gauges on the ship were useful as a starting place) is less important than engaging the players in the design of the measures, in the understanding of their meanings and limits, and in the development of responses to them. These measures and their implications must become second nature to the people who have to internalise them, so they can respond appropriately and quickly. They will learn, through their own 'praxis' as homeowners, planners, or elected officials, to react to what the indicators seem to show. They will learn by working together and communicating about what they think is happening and what they think is working. In trying to resolve their differences, these conversations have the potential for double-loop learning, rather than simply reactive, single-loop approaches.

First, system indicators are needed – a few key measures that reflect the central values of concern to metropolitan players and serve as bellwethers for the health of the overall system. The design and use of these over time will help to form a common sense of direction and mission. The effort to develop two or three measures that really express the health and nature of the system will educate the participants about how the system works and what they collectively need it to accomplish. Preparing these is the closest to central guidance for a complex system, and they are likely to measure a broad mission, like 'dock the boat without mishap' or 'provide for the well-being of all urban residents'. The effort will require developing some agreement among a wide range of participants on the kind of city they want and perhaps on what they mean by sustainability.[15,16] An example might be a measure comparing economic performance with a pollution or environmental cleanup measure.[17] Alternatively, a measure of the annual growth of sprawl might be developed.

Second, a set of performance measures reflecting specific outcomes of various aspects of the system -such as the street or park system, the state of the water resources, or the provision of social services – will allow policy makers, businesses, or others to assess whether they should adjust specific policies. Performance measures help the experienced policy maker or planner to make sense of many interlinked activities and ongoing events in order to figure out how to act. Performance measures, which have received international recognition in *Reinventing Government* (Osborne and Gaebler, 1992) are being widely promoted in the United States under White House and Vice President Gore's leadership,[18] as a crucial element in the reorientation of government to give attention '… to customer satisfaction' and to ongoing monitoring of actions by bureaucrats, planners, and local, state, or regional elected officials. They are designed to provide feedback and accountability, but they are not evaluative measures for rewarding or punishing participants. Instead, they are collectively interpreted by experienced participants, who bring an understanding of specific events and unique conditions that affect the measure.[19] In the context of the California metropolitan system, for example, performance measures might include the number of acres of inner-city land vacant or abandoned, the acres of agricultural land used for housing, or travel times on key highway segments.

Rapid feedback indicators are the third type. These are designed to help individuals and businesses on a daily basis to get what they need in the most efficient or cost-effective way – to help them make choices and daily decisions in a real-time context. In the final analysis, a community is what the individuals, businesses, and agencies in that place do – and have done in the past. It is a product of the things they create, produce, and reproduce over time, whether buildings, practices, or institutions. It is in dynamic relation with the geographic, physical, political, and economic context in which it sits. Each of these agents reacts not only to others but also to perceptions of changes in the context and feedback on the results of their own actions. Today, the homeowners and renters, commuters, entrepreneurs, shopkeepers, clerks, labourers, service providers, and regulators have poor or limited information to guide their daily actions. They do not typically know much about the immediate consequences of their own actions – for example, how long it will take them to travel to a neighbouring town for shopping if they take their intended route, or how much money it costs to water their lawns. Yet these are forms of information that we now have the technology to provide on a real-time basis, so that these people could make choices that would be efficient both for them and for the system.

Consensus-building

A second strategy for helping create a more adaptable and sustainable metropolitan system is to establish multi-stakeholder and inter-agency or even interjurisdictional consensus-building processes designed to address problematic aspects of the system, such as air or water quality, downtown redevelopment, or metropolitan management of growth.[20] These can even be used to develop new strategies for statewide legislation that are not heavy-handed regulation but introduce changes to the incentive structures and opportunities for self-organisation.[21] The type of consensus building to which we refer involves stakeholders on different sides of an issue, each with knowledge and experience. Typically, it involves facilitated, face-to-face, long-term discussions organised around a task, such as developing a transportation plan or an agreement on water usage. It is a form of what Anthony Giddens calls dialogic democracy and results in the spread of social reflexivity as a condition of both the day-to-day activities of the participants and their collective actions as part of the consensus group. It also has the capability to create active trust among the participants (Giddens, 1994). This type of process is grounded in interest-based bargaining (Fisher and Ury, 1981) and the techniques of mediation. The method ensures that all feel comfortable and all are heard, that assumptions and boundaries are all legitimate for challenge, that technical information is provided to and tested by the group, and that consensus is sought on any actions taken. This model has been instituted for such controversial regional issues in California as growth management, habitat conservation, water supply management, and transportation.[22]

Experience has shown that many consensus-building processes have properties similar to complex systems – self-organisation, decentralisation, and inventiveness (e.g., Innes, Gruber, Neuman and Thompson 1994, p.45). Because consensus building maps so effectively onto these complex systems, it can be a particularly powerful planning method (Skaburskis, 1995). Indeed, there is no coincidence that California is a state where these processes are being created; they are a logical, pragmatic response to fragmentation and controversy, and they bring together those who know most about how the processes work 'on the ground' and who are most in a position to change the system. These processes involve continuing dialogues to work out how to act, at what point in the system to intervene, and how to monitor and adapt in response to feedback. Typically, these groups become acutely aware of the need for flexibility in the future. They make proposals full of contingent strategies and establish new collaborative group processes to oversee implementation. As a result of their learning, they become sensitised to the nature of the complex system. As a result of their communication and, in some cases, of transformative learning, they can improve on the otherwise clumsy and imperfect self-organising responses of the system. Like dialogic democracy generally, the learning, active trust, and future cooperation contribute to mutual tolerance and adaptability of the system, even if a final consensus product is not achieved.

Leadership

A new type of leadership is required to operate innovatively and appropriately in this complex, dynamic metropolitan system. We need to think of leadership in some of the new ways that are being identified in the literature of business and public management.[23] Leaders in a world of complex uncertainty have vision and focus; they are able to translate this into meaning and are capable of communicating this meaning; they are able to build trust through commitment, passion, and integrity; and they emphasise learning and risk taking in themselves and in others.

We believe Peter Senge, in his important book *The Fifth Discipline* (1990), has provided a good beginning to understanding the nature of leadership in this world of complexity and discontinuous change. The first of his five learning disciplines is systems thinking. Systems thinking is a discipline for seeing wholes and interrelationships rather than things. It is first because each of the other four disciplines is also concerned with seeing wholes instead of parts and with seeing people as active participants in shaping reality instead of as passive reactors. The other learning disciplines emphasise personal growth and learning, creating and learning to work with shared mental models, building shared visions, and team learning. Team learning has three critical dimensions. It requires insightful thought about the complex issues, innovative and coordinated action, and cross-participation of members in many teams. Instead of the leader's identifying the answers and pushing through his agenda and program unilaterally or in combination with a few advisors, these leaders must be able to help the many participants develop a common sense of values and purpose, instill a sense of mastery and empowerment among all the players, and encourage and support them in organising themselves, learning from one another, and innovating. These leaders must be able to draw on many disciplines and skills, to create and manage group learning processes, and to listen. They must help to identify the tasks to be done and the players to be brought together. They must themselves be self-reflective, like Schön's reflective practitioner (1983) or Soros's (1997) reflexive entrepreneur. Nothing can be assumed in the complex uncertain world we face. Those who help manage it best are those who can bring out the creativity in themselves and others.

Conclusions

The experience of California offers an example of the ineffectiveness of approaches to metropolitan development when based upon centralisation and control. In the face of rapid and often discontinuous change, globalisation, the emergence of post-traditional society, and expansion of social reflexivity, we need to develop new concepts for metropolitan development and sustainability. Big governmental schemes, based upon extensive rules and centralised direction that ignore the multiplicity and diversity of actors in the metropolitan system, simply do not work (Scott, 1998). We believe the emerging field of complex adaptive systems offers one model that may be useful in evolving more adaptive strategies for metropolitan development, resulting in more sustainable economies and environments. This model suggests to us that metropolitan development strategies require three elements to be successful: consensus building and other similar collaborative processes, use of a system of indicators to provide the various actors with feedback, and a new style of leadership that emphasises collaborative learning, commitment, integrity, and passion. Indeed, our experience, although only partially documented at this point, suggests that these elements are already beginning to emerge in a self-organising way in response to the discontinuous change in California. This gives us a sense of optimism about the future, despite the apparent turmoil of the present.

Notes

1   These are elected in nonpartisan local elections, often by district. Thus, these elected officials are highly independent and certainly are not governed by party discipline.

2   The California constitution allows voters to circulate and place on the ballot proposals for constitutional amendments or statutory laws without the participation of the legislature. This power has become an important source of new fiscal policy with the result of an increasingly complex and piecemeal revenue system, with some funds earmarked for specific purposes and arbitrary caps placed on other revenue sources. To raise many specific taxes now requires a two-thirds vote of the public statewide or in a particular jurisdiction. This is often not obtainable.

3   These are large-scale discounted retail outlets for things such as hardware or home items, housed in massive warehouse-like buildings surrounded typically by acres of parking. Examples are Wal-mart, Home Depot and Orchard Supply Hardware.

4   One exception to this is a creative process taking place at the state level, where representatives of the major stakeholder interests, from business and education to labour and poor and ethnic minority groups, are gradually developing a much more complex proposal involving a transformation of fiscal structures and accountability structures across the state. This proposal may be placed on the ballot for a vote in 1999. This would be, rather than a quick fix of one element of the problem, an adjustment simultaneously of a number of factors and incentive structures, in the hope that the system will become more responsive and adaptive (Booher, 1997).

5   The impact assessment of New Jersey's State Development and Redevelopment Plan estimated that, if this form of growth management were implemented, it would save the state $400 million per year (New Jersey Office of State Planning, 1992).

6   We note that we are in disagreement with virtually every claim of Gordon and Richardson (1997), who argue that sprawl is not costly. We find the premises, evidence, and arguments deeply flawed, and we believe that Ewing (1997) makes a convincing case of denying their claims.

7   We might even think of it as a fractal – a smaller version of the complex self-organising world, designed to function in that world.

8   Like human-made machines, the cosmic machine was thought to consist of elementary parts. Consequently, it was believed that complex phenomena could always be understood by reducing them to their basic building blocks and by looking for mechanisms through which these interacted. This view has become deeply ingrained in our culture and identified with the scientific method. The other sciences accepted the mechanistic and reductionistic views of the classical physics as the correct description of reality and modelled their own theories accordingly. Whenever psychologists, sociologists, or economists wanted to be scientific, they naturally turned toward the basic concepts of Newtonian physics (Capra, 1982, p.47).

9   Interestingly, the Jesuit philosopher and palaeontologist Pierre Teilhard de Chardin (1959) anticipated this connection a half century ago in his concepts of convergence and complexification.

10   Although the term 'system' has many meanings, in this context it refers to dynamical systems as first conceived by Henri Poincaré (Devaney, 1989).

11 Many kinds of research converge on this point, from studies of parallel processing in computer science to brain research, which suggests that the brain operates across neural networks to pull together widely distributed information to understand and act.

12 Although we have focused on the California case in this chapter, there is ample evidence that similar trends are at work in other regions of the United States. For example, see Kirp, Dwyer, and Rosenthal (1995) regarding New Jersey.

13 A recent book by Dodge (1996), remarkably sponsored by the National League of Cities, focuses on a similar theme. He contends that a self-organising set of linkages among cities to create new forms of governance and regional excellence is necessary because we are in a complex, constantly changing world.

14 Innes (1996) describes this set of concepts more fully.

15 In cases Innes and coauthors studied, for example (1994), they found that some collaborative groups trying to manage a regional resource were able to come up with one or two indicators that really measured overall system performance.

16 Although the step of determining mission and overall system indicator in a consensual way may be difficult, it is far from impossible, particularly with professional help at facilitating and managing the discourse. Places tend to have their own cultures and unique qualities as well as problems, and such strategic visioning can often be done consensually. But this must be an intensely collaborative effort, where groups of leaders and stakeholders decide on the problems of the city and the direction they want to go.

17 Examples of such system measures that groups have developed in other cases include, for example, the unemployment rate as a measure of the US economic performance (de Neufville, 1975) or the level and location of a salinity threshold value in the San Francisco Bay Delta Estuary system (Innes et al., 1994).

18 This is known as the National Performance Review and thus far involves a number of demonstration projects, including the Oregon Option.

19 Of course, they may at times be used in this more mechanistic way. Learning and adaptiveness are, however, the intent.

20 Examples of these are described in Godschalk (1992), Innes (1992), and Innes et al. (1994).

21 One example is the California Governance Consensus Project, which includes 35 of the most powerful interest group representatives, who have been working together for the last 2 years to craft a complex piece of legislation to change the fiscal incentives and accountability in the state in a way that will make sense from many perspectives simultaneously.

22 See Innes et al. (1994) for an account of several of these processes.

23 Leading examples of this work are insightful and useful books by Bennis (1989), Bryson and Crosby (1992), Farson (1996), O'Toole (1995), and Senge (1990), but many other examples abound in the organisational development literature.

References

American Farmland Trust (1995), *Alternatives for Future Urban Growth in California's Central Valley: The Bottom Line for Agriculture and Taxpayers*, American Farmland Trust, Washington, DC.

Argyris, C. and Schön, D.A. (1974), *Theory in Practice: Increasing Professional Effectiveness*, Jossey Bass, San Francisco, CA.

Bank of America (1995), *Beyond Sprawl: New Patterns of Growth to Fit the New California*, Bank of America San Francisco, CA.

Bennis, W. (1989), *On Becoming a Leader*, Addison-Wesley, Reading, MA.

Blakely, E. and Snyder, M.G. (1997), *Fortress America: The Rise of Gated Communities*, Sage, Thousand Oaks, CA.

Booher, D. (1997). 'Reforming California's Governance for the Next Millennium', *Western City*, Vol. 73 (10), pp.4–8.

Bryson, J.M. and Crosby, B.C. (1992), *Leadership for the Common Good: Tackling Public Problems in a Shared Power World*, Jossey Bass, San Francisco, CA.

California Constitution Revision Commission (1996), *Final Report and Recommendations to the Governor and Legislature*, California Constitution Revision Commission, Sacramento, CA.

California Planning Roundtable (1997), *Restoring the Balance: Managing Fiscal Issues and Land Use Planning Decisions in California*, The Roundtable, San Diego, CA.

Capra, F. (1982), *The Turning Point*, Simon and Schuster, New York.

Capra, F. (1996), *The Web of Life: A New Scientific Understanding of Living Systems*, Anchor Books, New York.

Castells, M. (1996), *The Information Age: Economy, Society and Culture. Vol. I: The Rise of the Network Society*, Blackwell, Cambridge, MA.

Center for the Continuing Study of the California Economy (1997), *California Economic Growth 1997*, Center for the Continuing Study of the California Economy, Palo Alto, CA.

Courtney, H., Kirkland, J. and Viguerie, P. (1997), 'Strategy Under Uncertainty', *Harvard Business Review*, Vol. 75 (6), pp.67–79.

Devaney, R. (1989), *An Introduction to Chaotic Dynamical Systems*, Addison-Wesley, Reading, MA.

Dodge, W.R. (1996), *Regional Excellence: Governing Together to Compete Globally and Flourish Locally*, National League of Cities, Washington, DC.

Downs, A. (1994), *New Visions for Metropolitan America*, Brookings, Washington, DC.

Dresch, M. and Sheffrin, S. (1997), *Who Pays for Development Fees and Exactions?* Public Policy Institute of California, San Francisco, CA.

Ewing, R. (1997), Is Los Angeles Style Sprawl Desirable?, *Journal of the American Planning Association*, Vol. 63 (1), pp.107–26.

Farson, R. (1996), *Management of the Absurd: Paradoxes in Leadership*, Simon and Schuster, New York.

Fisher, R. and Ury, W. (1981), *Getting to Yes: Negotiating Agreement Without Giving In*, Houghton Mifflin, Boston, MA.

Fulton, W. (1997), *The Reluctant Metropolis: The Politics of Urban Growth in Los Angeles*, Solano Press Books, Point Arena, CA.

Giddens, A. (1994), *Beyond Left and Right: The Future of Radical Politics*, Stanford University Press, Stanford, CA.

Godschalk, D. (1992), 'Negotiating Intergovernmental Development Policy Conflicts: Practice Based Guidelines', *Journal of the American Planning Association*, Vol. 58 (3), pp.368–78.

Gordon, P. and Richardson, H. (1997), Are Compact Cities a Desirable Goal? *Journal of the American Planning Association*, Vol. 63 (1), pp.95–106.

Handy, C. (1990), *The Age of Unreason*, Harvard Business School Press, Boston, MA.

Handy, C. (1994), *The Age of Paradox*, Harvard Business School Press, Boston, MA.

Holland, J. (1995), *Hidden Order: How Adaptation Builds Complexity*, Addison-Wesley, Reading, MA.

Hutchins, E. (1995), *Cognition in the Wild*, Cambridge, MIT Press, MA.

Hwang, S.W. (1996), 'The Implications of the Nonlinear Paradigm for Integrated Environmental Design and Planning', *Journal of Planning Literature*, Vol. 11, pp.167–80.

Innes, J.E. (1992), 'Group Processes and the Social Construction of Growth Management: Florida, Vermont and New Jersey', *Journal of the American Planning Association*, Vol. 58 (4), pp.440–53.

Innes, J.E. (1996), *Indicators for Collective Learning: Rethinking Planning for Complex Systems*, paper prepared for Presentation at the 50th Anniversary Conference, Department of Town and Country Planning, University of Newcastle, UK, October.

Innes, J.E., Gruber, J., Neuman, M. and Thompson, R. (1994), *Coordinating Growth and Environmental Management Through Consensus Building*, CPS Report: A Policy Research Program Report, University of California, Berkeley: California Policy Seminar, pp.270.

Kauffman, S. (1995), *At Home in the Universe: The Search for the Laws of Complexity*, Viking, London.

Kelly, K. (1994), *Out of Control: The Rise of The Neobiological Civilization*, Addison-Wesley, Reading, MA.

Kiel, D. (1991), 'Lessons From the Nonlinear Paradigm: Applications of the Theory of Dissipative Structures in the Social Sciences', *Social Science Quarterly*, Vol. 72, pp.431–42.

Kirp, D.L., Dwyer, J.P. and Rosenthal, L.A. (1995), *Our Town: Race, Housing, And The Soul Of Suburbia*, Rutgers University Press, New Brunswick, NJ.

Lewin, R. (1992), *Complexity: Life at the Edge Of Chaos*, MacMillan, New York.

Little Hoover Commission (1995), *Making Land Use Work: Rules to Reach Our Goals*, Little Hoover Commission, Sacramento, CA.

Mattoon, R.H. (1995), 'Can Alternative Forms of Governance Help Metropolitan Areas?', *Economic Perspectives (Federal Reserve Bank of Chicago)*, Vol.19 (6), pp.20-32.

Myers Richter, A. (forthcoming), *From Compliance to Competitive Advantage: The Effect of Corporate Culture and Profitability on Environmental Performance*, unpublished dissertation, University of California, Berkeley, CA.

Neufville de, J.I. (1975), *Social Indicators and Public Policy: Interactive Processes of Design and Application*, Elsevier Publishing, Amsterdam.

New Jersey Office of State Planning (1992), *Impact Assessment of New Jersey Interim State Development and Redevelopment Plan*, State of New Jersey, Trenton, NJ.

Nicolis, G. and Prigogine, I. (1989), *Exploring Complexity*, Freeman, New York.

Osborne, D. and Gaebler, T. (1992), *Reinventing Government: How the Entrepreneurial Spirit is Transforming the Public Sector*, Addison-Wesley, Reading, MA.

O'Toole, J. (1995), *Leading Change: The Argument for Values Based Leadership*, Jossey-Bass, San Francisco, CA.

Prigogine, I. and Stengers, I. (1984), *Order Out of Chaos*, Bantam, New York.

Schön, D.A. (1983), *The Reflective Practitioner: How Professionals Think in Action*, Basic Books, New York.

Schrag, P. (1998), *Paradise Lost: California's Experience, America's Future*, Free Press, New York.

Scott, J.C. (1998), *Seeing Like a State: How Certain Schemes to Improve the Human Condition Have Failed*, Yale University Press, New Haven, CT.

Senge, P.M. (1990), *The Fifth Discipline: The Art and Practice of the Learning Organization*, Doubleday, New York.

Skaburskis, A. (1995), 'The Consequences of Taxing Land Value', *Journal of Planning Literature*, Vol. 10 (1), pp.3–21.

Soros, G. (1997), 'The Capitalist Threat', *The Atlantic Monthly*, Vol. 279 (2), pp.45–58.
Teilhard de Chardin, P. (1959), *The Phenomenon of Man*, Harper and Row, New York.
Waldrop, M.M. (1992), *Complexity: The Emerging Science at the Edge of Chaos*, Simon and Schuster, New York.
Wheatley, M. (1992), *Leadership and the New Science*, Berrett-Koehler, San Francisco, CA.

Chapter Twelve

Towards a More Place-focused Planning System in Britain

Patsy Healey

Making Places or Regulating Sites: Choices for Spatial Planning Systems

The activity and philosophy of spatial planning asserts the ideal of improving quality of life through promoting, managing and regulating 'place-making'. The qualities of places and the qualities of place-making processes are long-established preoccupations in planning thought. There has also been an enduring emphasis on the role of spatial organising frameworks, the 'development plan', to manage spatial change, at the region, settlement and neighbourhood level. Such frameworks articulate views about how places may change over the long-term. They aim to address the quality of life in places in an integrated way, attempting to weave together economic, social, environmental and physical dimensions of what makes up a place. They present images of what places in their 'settings' could be like, both in their spatial and institutional dimensions.

But spatial planning systems and practices have often found themselves sitting uncomfortably in governance environments and policy cultures. The late twentieth century, in Britain at least, has been such a period. It has been dominated by the concerns of policy 'sectors' constructed from economic and social policy objectives. Functions have been privileged over the interconnection of activities in territories. Public policy is typically framed as if place and space were irrelevant. There are many arguments in the contemporary period to support the neglect of place and space. The dynamics of our economies these days seem to have floated free of locations and borders. Strategies to de-regulate markets pay little attention to spatial consequences. New forms of regulation, even of environmental externalities, focus on the site or the firm, not the site and firm in their local settings. In social life, it is often argued that it is people who have problems, not places (Petersen, 1985). Policy should be targeted at them directly, not at where they live. Planners are criticised for reifying place and for attempting to acquire too much control over place-making activities.

In Britain, the development of spatial planning systems and practices has been constrained by such arguments (Thornley, 1991). At the same time, the continuing support for the planning system reflects a politics which embraces a vigorous defence of place. On the one hand, care for the quality of the environment, and especially for the 'countryside', is deeply embedded in British culture and politically well-defended (Williams, 1975; Lowe and Goyder, 1983; Marsden et al., 1993). On the other hand, spatial planning has had great difficulty flourishing as a practice in a centralist state with a highly sectoralised approach to public policy (Healey, 1988). The policy response to this contradictory situation has been a progressive narrowing down of the remit of the planning system from a major role in building the New Jerusalem of the immediate post-war era to a regulatory function focusing on 'land use change'. Though often escaping from this definition, spatial planning as a system and its practices have tended to become just another functional sector of government, with its 'industry' to regulate and its client groups to work with. In the 1980s, the shape of this regulatory form was difficult to discern (Healey et al., 1988; Brindley et al., 1989; Thornley, 1991). By the 1990s, its outline has become clearer. It depends on the translation of nationally-articulated policy criteria into norms and tests to be applied to specific projects as they are 'fitted onto' their sites. Any wider concerns about places and their qualities have then to be translated into equivalent and compatible performance criteria.

Much contemporary policy discourse and academic critique of planning as an idea and a practice supports such a development. Neo-liberal political philosophy and rational choice theory dismiss a concern with place-making as largely irrelevant to current preoccupations with economic competitiveness and environmental sustainability. The post-modern turn in urban and regional analysis at one time also suggested that, in the flexible and dynamic relations of contemporary societies, spatial planning served as a bureaucratic remnant of the modernising urge, seeking to impose a regulatory order on creative processes of innovatory adjustment to new conditions (Dear, 1995).

Yet in Britain in the 1990s, we have seen the reassertion of 'plan-led planning' by central government (Rydin, 1998; Purdue, 1994). Is this a sign of the reassertion of place-focused concerns, signalling the renewal of a strategic place-focused approach? Or is it a consolidation of the performance criteria approach, with the development plan as merely a convenient way to assemble the norms and criteria, grouped together so that they can be legitimated in a big-bang conflict mediation process, rather than in a case-by-case mediation?

There has been a reassertion of place-focused concerns in public policy in Britain in recent years, focusing on both the territory and the neighbourhood (DETR, 1997; 1998b; 1999a; Urban Task Force, 1999). This reflects the tendencies discussed elsewhere in this book. If the qualities of place and territory are important, and if public policy has to acknowledge that 'geography matters', then the challenge for public policy, and specifically for the planning system, is to develop the institutional capability to respond to concerns about place-making in the contemporary period. For spatial planning practice in turn-of-century Britain, this means developing practices which break out of a sectoralised and centralised government tradition, to enable connections to be made to other areas of policy activity. In these other policy areas, such as transport, education and health, similar attempts are being made to make new, cross-sectoral links, encouraged by the New Labour government rhetoric of 'joined-up' thinking. New forms of horizontal articulation are being built up around spatial alliances to complement or replace vertical, sectoral linkages to the central state. This is leading to all kinds of efforts in place-making and in building the institutions for place-making, as is evident in, for example, regional business alliances, Local Agenda 21 initiatives, local Health Alliances, partnerships in area regeneration, and approaches to catchment area management by the new Environment Agency (Davoudi et al., 1996; Freeman et al., 1996, Bailey et al., 1995; Oatley, 1999; Wilkinson and Appelbee, 1999).

A key characteristic of many of these initiatives in horizontal linkages is their interactive quality. People and agencies are being drawn into new activities in new ways. Place-making work involves a wide universe of those with a 'stake' in a place (Bryson and Crosby, 1992). Reflecting the multiplicity of stakeholders, collaborative ways of developing and implementing policy, focusing on building new relationships through which to manage and mobilise for change, are appearing around the procedures and practices of the planning system (Freeman et al., 1996; Davoudi et al., 1996; Vigar, Healey, Hull and Davoudi, 2000). This echoes broad movements in British governance, which seek to break out of hierarchical centralism and to widen the involvement and influence of citizens and business in public policy and its implementation. In a society of multiple stakeholders, with diverse concerns, hierarchical forms of articulating public policies and firm boundaries between public and private action are being displaced by more fluid and horizontal relationships. By the late 1990s, central government was giving strong encouragement to these tendencies (DETR, 1998b; 1999a). In this context, the development plan-making provisions of the planning system potentially provide an established arena where people can come together to work out strategic ideas and build sufficient consensus to be able to take new initiatives in place-making and place-maintaining.

But this new, collaborative, multiparty form of 'regulating' the relations between stakeholders in urban regions sits uncomfortably with the regulatory form driven by performance criteria advocated by neo-liberal principles. The practice of the planning system, still in the grip of a performance criteria approach despite the reassertion of the importance of plans, collides with these new dynamics of place-making, rather than becoming an active force and a core arena within which these new collaborative forms can develop. The reassertion of plan-led planning thus has the potential to lead in two quite different directions. It could go down the narrow path of the regulation of particular sorts of externality, and jostle for power with the new Environmental Agency over who has the duty to regulate which bit of an externality effect. Or it could evolve into an active role in place-making in an interactive and facilitative way, involving many stakeholders, in processes of collaborative planning. This tension is unresolved in the New Labour initiatives with respect to the planning system (DETR, 1998a).

Why the Qualities of Places are Important

The assertion of the importance of place is widespread in European debates on regional economic development, on achieving environmental sustainability objectives, and on social change and social exclusion (see, for example, CEC, 1994; CSP, 1999). There is a frequent regression in these debates to traditional notions of place as a set of integrated socioeconomic and ecological relationships where propinquity implies a relationship. This is encapsulated in the *gemeinschaft* notion of community and the image of *Isardian* space in regional economics. However, the contemporary arguments for the importance of the qualities of places are not solely grounded in a nostalgic memory of such conditions. They arise from the experience of the disembedding from established places of many economic and social relationships, the recognition of the openness of regional and national economies and the realisation that local actions have global effects on the sustainability of the biosphere (Lipietz, 1992; Storper and Scott, 1992; Amin and Thrift, 1995; Amin and Thrift, 1995; Amin and Hausner, 1996; Healey et al., 1995).

It is just because of this disembedding, the fragmentation of many established relationships, and the way in which the networks of people and firms cut across particular spaces, seemingly disconnected from each other though adjacent, that questions are being raised about the qualities of places. People want to know whether they will be comfortable with their neighbours, whether their living environments will make it possible to accomplish the complex challenges of daily life, and what kinds of social worlds their children will encounter. As lifestyles differentiate, people seek out places which provide supports for particular lifestyles and come to symbolise particular qualities. In social terms, the place of urban regions seems increasingly differentiated into distinctive locales and niches (Healey, 1997). These then become the basis for a politics of the promotion and defence of place which expresses itself through and around the practices of spatial planning systems.

Firms, too, are place-conscious, though the dimensions of place which concern them vary. Large inward investing firms, of such symbolic concern for regional development in Britain in the 1990s, will look to the quality of regional labour markets, transport services, subcontracting networks and local institutional capacity to deliver a supportive governance context. Small and medium sized enterprises are likely to draw upon the particular qualities of the local business 'culture', for knowledge about market opportunities and regulatory constraints. Some places have specific assets, institutional capacity and business cultures which support the economic health of companies, while encouraging a flow of benefits from that activity to a broad array of local concerns. Others are unable to achieve this virtuous circle, or only at the expense of social and environmental considerations (Amin and Thrift, 1995; Healey, 1997). Just as with economic relations and social life, environmental relationships are diverse and operate at disparate scales. Any place is an intricate composite of many habitats, coexisting in a geological, hydrological and climatological framework. The significance of the relationships within the composite, and the impacts of human action upon it, encourages a place-based focus. Through this observation point, the threats to the sustainability of natural environments become visible, and the relations between local action and global consequences take on concrete meaning (Blowers, 1993).

All these tendencies mean that the qualities of place are being asserted with increasing strength in politics and policy-making these days. But the meaning of 'place' is not straightforward. It varies according to the relationships within which it has significance (Graham and Healey, 1999). Conceptions of 'place' are social constructs, interweaving the social experience of being in a place, the symbolic meaning of qualities of a place and the physicalness of the forms and flows which go on in it. In an open society, with multiple relationships crisscrossing across geographical space, any location is likely to carry significance for a wide variety of people, the different stakeholders in what happens there. The stakeholders will give a particular meaning to a location, each in their own social context. Any location may thus have multiple meanings of place layered over it. It is a complex task of collective social construction, often over a long time period, to create an enduring and widely-shared meaning of place. Yet, in the context of the *long duree* of European cultures and histories, such meanings have often developed, to be reinterpreted with new significances in different epochs. It is these meanings which are being reworked in the new policy focus on the qualities of place.

But the reassertion of concern for the qualities of places raises difficult challenges for governance processes. Conflicts may arise not only between what one person wants to do and how this impacts on neighbours. They may arise over the meaning of place which one person wants to express and the different meanings which other stakeholders seek to maintain, promote or develop. In this context, spatial planning systems are being drawn into more than just conflict management and place promotion. They have a role in place-making, in generating enduring meanings for places which can help to focus and coordinate the activities of different stakeholders and reduce levels of conflict. This is a well-established role for planning systems. The challenge in the present period is to develop the capability for place-making in full recognition of the complexity and openness of the relationships which flow across the space of a place, and the consequent diversity and multiplicity of stakeholders who actively do, or potentially could, assert a concern about a place. This requires planning systems and practices to face the hard challenge of re-orienting their conceptions of place and redesigning the processes through which stakeholders' concerns are taken into account.

Planning in a Stakeholder Society

As a social phenomenon, spatial planning presents itself in several forms. Foley (1960) noted this in his observations of British planning nearly forty years ago. He identified three forms in which spatial planning was expressed, as a government activity, that is, a policy system and its practices; as a profession or occupational group; and as a social movement, or set of beliefs and theories around which people mobilised and campaigned. There were tensions between them then, and tensions are clearly evident today. Planning systems and practices are a major institutional manifestation of spatial planning ideas, as reworked in the context of particular governance environments and policy cultures. Observing their evolution provides a revealing window on the regulatory relationships surrounding the physical/spatial dimensions of place-making.

There are many arguments which explain why complex urbanised societies generate policy systems to manage land use and development (Sutcliffe, 1981; Healey, 1983; Klosterman, 1985). Despite occasional outbursts from extreme free market theorists, debates about the purposes of planning systems tend to emphasise one or another, rather than seeking to remove spatial planning as an activity altogether from the policy lexicon. As Brindley et al. (1989) and Thornley (1991) chart so well, the 1980s in Britain was a period of confused debates about the evolution of the system and the emergence of multiple practices, as different ways of addressing spatial and land use issues were explored. Generally, the debates in Europe over the purposes of planning systems can be seen as pivoting around two kinds of purpose:

1   managing conflicts over the use and development of land;

2   promoting and producing particular qualities of places.

These two purposes are potentially interrelated. But a continual theme in the analysis of planning systems and practices as they evolve is their separation. The first purpose gets taken over by legal and administrative practices focused around disputes about the legitimacy of state restriction of property rights. The second takes place within professional and pressure group debate about place-making ideas. The first centres on maintaining established parameters; the second centres on the transformation of policies and practices. The real advances in the development of practice and in the real effects of spatial planning occur when the two are linked together. So what do the two involve?

The function of *managing conflicts* has traditionally centred around that between the individual property owner with a development project and the 'wider public interest'. This public interest was defined as the state's interest, and embraced the concern to safeguard state policies for infrastructure investment and to address adverse externality effects on other property owners and stakeholders. Affected property interests (in the British case, only aggrieved applicants) were granted redress to semi-judicial and legal arenas to challenge state decisions. Development plans and zoning ordinances provided a 'store' of legitimised warrants for these decisions, to be activated in a process of project-by-project regulation. This function, often lost sight of in British professional discourse of the 1950s and 1960s, became the dominant purpose of the planning system in the 1980s. This recognised that the development process was no longer driven by public sector investment designed to promote and produce new and 'transformed places', but by a myriad of private land owners and developers.

But the practices of the system were clearly more than this, as development interests and pressure groups struggled over policy directions and spatial organisation principles. By the 1980s, the purpose of the planning system was commonly described as a mechanism for mediating among competing interests. This recognised the increasing complexity of the mix of parties involved. More and more people, firms, pressure groups and agencies were coming to realise that they had a 'stake' in a place and were seeking a way to demand recognition of their stake (Grove-White, 1991). The 'externality effects' came alive in an active politics. In this context, plan-making processes were used as arenas within which mediation could be played out, supplementing the conflict around individual projects. They could also take on a role as a form of 'contract', recording agreements reached. As increasing emphasis was put on development plans, they came to act as a baseline framing the negotiations over specific projects (Healey, 1986; Healey et al., 1988). But this evolution, which to a large extent underpins the re-emphasis on the importance of the development plan in British spatial planning in the late 1980s, connects the debates about legitimate state restraint on property rights back to conceptions of the qualities of places.

The planning system and ideas about planning settlements emerged in Britain in the nineteenth century out of concerns about public health, social order and housing questions raised by rapid urban growth in a highly unequal society. Constraining property rights in the public interest was interlinked with ideas about new communities among many nineteenth century thinkers and promoters of new settlement forms. Throughout the twentieth century in Britain, the two strands have repeatedly drawn apart and reconnected (Figure 12.1). For most of this period, debates about the qualities of places have been dominated by the discourses of architects and engineers, informed by modernist arguments for building new cities and settlements for industrial, car-based societies. Their master plans and comprehensive urban plans articulated principles of traffic organisation, neighbourhood quality, central places and the separation of polluting industry from residential areas. In retrospect, contemporary planners criticise our predecessors for their conceptions of social life around the male-centred family and the homogeneous society, the ideas of building form which dominated the discourse, the lack of understanding of economic dynamics, and their conceptions of environment as a landscape

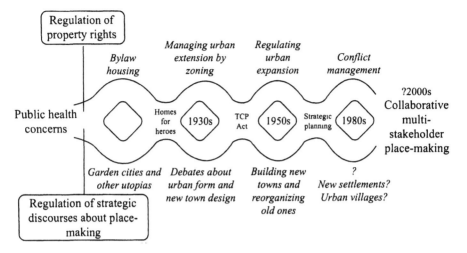

Figure 12.1 The evolution of regulatory purposes in the British planning system and its practices

backcloth and amenity for the working man and his family (see Ravetz, 1980; Hall, 1995; Healey and Shaw, 1994). Yet there was considerable attention at this time to the quality of everyday life and how the design of living places could promote improved quality of life.

Such ideas were translated across Europe into master plans and comprehensive urban plans which provided well-specified images of what places could be like, in literally concrete terms. They gave precise blueprints for how to build new bits of the city. In many instances, these principles were translated into public sector investment projects and into the zoning ordinances (and, in Britain, the development control principles), which were used to regulate private development. But this approach headed into the same problem as the administrative approach to managing conflicts. The professional conception of places and their qualities was not widely shared by an increasingly vociferous polity of active stakeholders, who challenged plans politically and in the arenas of plan preparation. Further, the assumption that the state had the power and resources to build the planners' imagined places proved increasingly unrealistic.

This 'command and control' conception of how urban planning should be done was fundamentally challenged in the later part of this century in Britain by the general critique of the power of experts and technicians, by the shortages of funds for continued building, by the change in the policy emphasis from new building to reorganising and improving the existing built fabric, and by the political power of particular sectoral interests. Development plans, apart from a few generalised assertions about district strategy, had typically become, by the 1990s, collections of policy statements for different sectors, sometimes supplemented by statements for different parts of a district. The processes of their preparation were bogged down in a mountain of objections, as the potential conflicts generated by multiple stakeholders focused on the arbitration end of the process, rather than the initial framing of ideas. This lead people to question the possibility of a collective project of place-making in a situation where there are multiple stakeholders. These may all have different conceptions of place and different things they want from it and in it, and many who are prepared to assert their stake in plan-making arenas and around specific project proposals. Is the solution to draw back from planning as promoting and producing particular qualities of places and accept the limitation to managing conflicts? Should place-making be left to the individual stakeholders to work out for themselves?

Regulating Development in a Stakeholder Society

To summarise the argument so far, the conflict management purpose of planning in Britain has moved from a zoning form to an interactive, mediatory form, to reflect the multiplicity of stakeholders and the potential for conflict among them. Both forms are grounded in an administrative/legal discourse, which has developed uneasily to accommodate negotiation and agreements over conflict resolution 'deals'. In parallel, the technical discourse of place-making realised through master planning which developed in the 1950s and 1960s has been dislodged. As a result, the purpose of planning as promoting qualities of places has tended to decay into the conflict mediation approach. It is in this context that both a more systematic form of the performance criteria approach and more collaborative approaches to strategic, multiparty place-making, were beginning to emerge in the 1990s (Healey, 1994).

Both approaches assume that planning processes should be interactive and that they will involve many of those with a stake in changes in locations. Where they differ is in the nature of the *regulatory relationship*. Surprisingly, given the considerable debate about forms of regulation in many fields of activity in British society in the 1980s and 1990s, there has been little consideration of the regulatory relationships surrounding land and property development and place-making. This is partly because of the lack of attention to place and space in public policy. But it is also because of the enormous complexity of the relationship. On the one hand, the 'industry' to be regulated is extremely diverse, encompassing all those who seek to change what is happening 'in, on, over or under' their property. The property rights involved are highly variable. On the other hand, the purposes of regulation range from making the land and property development process in itself more efficient and effective, to safeguarding valued environments and sites from land and property development operations and promoting particular qualities of places.

The Performance Criteria Form

Figure 12.2 summarises the regulatory relationship of the two approaches to the planning system which were emerging in the 1990s. The performance criteria approach takes as its regulatory object the property relationship with respect to a development site and the project proposed for it. The implicit purpose of regulation is to require those with property rights to observe certain constraints imposed to safeguard public interest objectives. These have been

	Conflict management (performance criteria)	**Place-making (collaborative planning)**
Regulatory object	rights to use and develop land	the way of thinking policy discourses frames of reference
Context	efficient land and property development markets conflicts between development and environmental interests	multiple stakeholders complex political claims for attention markets prone to failure
Discourses	norms, standards and criteria political legitimacy and legal interpretation public interest versus private rights	qualities of places spatial organising ideas strategic projects co-ordination and collaboration
Function of plans	*product*: store of norms, policy statements, etc	*product*: store of 'framing' principles about qualities of places and supporting arguments
	process: arena for conflict mediation	*process*: collective social construction of strategic organising ideas, images etc.

Figure 12.2 Emerging regulatory forms for planning systems compared

primarily environmental in Britain in recent years, though social objectives are creeping back in (DETR, 1998a). It assumes that land and property development markets work reasonably well over time, and that the regulatory process should aim to be clear and quick, delivering certainty about regulatory requirements to the 'industry'. This is to be achieved by having well-specified statements of norms and criteria, which could include targets and levels, as well as areas and sites. These express the various public interest constraints. These norms and criteria could emanate from any level of government, from the EU to the locality. To increase certainty and the efficiency of the regulatory process, the norms and criteria are expressed in policy statements, and sometimes in maps indicating specific sites. It is such policy statements and maps which together may become grouped into the vehicle of a development plan (Figure 12.3). The development plan is both a product and a process. As a product, it brings together the statements about regulatory constraints into a single place. As a process, it provides a vehicle to legitimate the exercise of each constraint. It is rather as if each plan was a product of some local Office of Development regulation, OFDEV, defining the rules of the regulatory game. But because the industry distrusts the regulators, (and central government distrusts local interpretations of the regulations), there are special mechanisms (appeals, discretionary negotiation, inquiry processes) to ensure the rights of property owners to object to over-regulation. There are much more elaborate mechanisms for objection and public consultation surrounding the planning system than in most other areas of regulation, where it is left to the 'industry'

	Conflict management	**Place-making**
From:	Zoning (regulation of land rights) Discourse: legal/administrative	Master planning (command and control) Discourse: technical/architectural
To:	Conflict mediation (planning by contract) Discourse: negotiation and agreements	Rationalist policy making Discourse: policy analysis rational argumentation technical evaluation
To:	Conflict mediation by performance criteria Discourse: norms, standards, conformance	Collaborative strategy-making Discourse: collective visioning multiple points of view consensus building

Figure 12.3 Forms of planning as developed in Britain

itself to build up its relations with its 'consumers'. This recognises the diversity of stakeholders in the qualities of places. The discourse of this regulatory process is grounded in procedural and legal argument about the legitimacy of various constraints.

It is this approach which permeated the planning system in the 1990s. It has a number of advantages, notably formal clarity about the criteria which will be applied. This gives it the appearance of accountability, as did the traditional zoning approach. It cultivates the assessment of development proposals in terms of clear arguments grounded in the criteria. Policy statements and plans act as collections of arguments to be activated in statements and plans act as collections of arguments to be activated in conflict situations. But it encounters major problems. These arise from the inherent tendencies to failure in land and property markets (Evans, 1988), the extreme diversity of the regulatory object, and the multiplicity and diversity of stakeholders. Whether the process of legitimising the regulatory principles takes place at the level of the project, or the apparently more efficient level of the plan, large numbers come forward to 'object', or just to make points. Because the stakeholders are varied, they have different views about how a project will affect their strategies and interests, and their values about a place. The focus on specific policies and projects fragments consideration of overall qualities of places and the cumulative impacts of specific actions. The emphasis on 'hearing objections' in the regulatory process pushes conflict mediation to the end of the process and encourages people to construct their concerns in adversarial terms and to take entrenched positions. Thus the process has a tendency to create 'NIMBY's, that is, defensive opposition to any change (Bryson et al., 1991; Wolsink, 1994). The way forward from this situation seems either to progress further down the path of legalised conflict resolution processes, following the tendencies already strongly evident in US planning practice (Cullingworth, 1993; Wakeford, 1990), or to find ways of developing strategic agreements about what places could be like and the opportunities and limits of transforming them. This is where the second approach comes in.

The Collaborative Place-making Form

The pressure for an approach to spatial planning as strategic collaborative place-making arises in part from the search for more efficient ways of conflict management. It is also promoted by the concern for the significance of the 'qualities of places' discussed above. There is much evidence to support this argument, especially from the US, where local government is strong relative to higher levels, the public sector fragmented and where planning argument is dominated by legal discourse. When power is diffused and intelligence distributed, conflicts will crop up in a wide variety of forms across a political community unless efforts are made to build up shared understandings and operational agreements on strategic issues (Innes and Booher, 1999). In Europe, the pressure for strategic collaborative place-making has come from the concern with place quality (Healey et al., 1997; Salet and Faludi, 1999).

In the collaborative approach to place-making, the regulatory object is the way people think about place and the meanings they give to it (see Figure 12.2 above). It is in effect the public discourse about place-making and its insertion into the thoughtworlds of stakeholders (see Innes and Booher in this book). Exercises in collaborative planning seek to maintain and transform mindsets about the meaning of places and the priorities for action. If effective, they generate strategic conviction (Habermas, 1993). Stakeholders who think differently, it is anticipated, will act differently. The concerns about social and environmental costs and about the shaping of market processes will in this way be taken into account as stakeholders imagine their strategies and projects, rather than at the formal point, much later in the process, when a project is 'taken through' the regulatory process. The approach assumes that land and property markets are prone to failure, and that, in polities with diffused power, this will be compounded with uncertainty about regulatory frameworks, unless collective efforts are made at shared strategy development. Spatial planning is thus needed to provide a framework for the efficient functioning of markets through reducing both investment uncertainty and regulatory transaction costs, the costs of conflict resolution. It is also needed to promote particular qualities of places, to achieve broader economic development, environmental quality and social development objectives.

An important task of such exercises is to translate policy principles into criteria to be used in regulating land and property development rights. The performance criteria approach which has developed in Britain provides a helpful groundwork upon which to build this translation as it emphasises argumentation around policy principles. But these principles cannot merely be articulated into abstract norms and criteria. Because of the variety of manifestations of spatial change, their social meaning and relevance have to be constructed and interpreted in the context of concrete places and the lives of real people and companies. They have then to be translated not merely into legal-administrative terms but into the way stakeholders are thinking. Strategic place-making undertaken in a collaborative way helps to articulate a shared language which can relate the concrete realities of lived experience to general principles and organising ideas and then translate them back into arguments to be used in framing investment and regulatory decisions. Such a style of place-making develops into a framework, which serves to shape and coordinate the actions and attitudes of many stakeholders (Schon and Rein, 1994; Faludi, 1996; Healey et al., 1997).

The process of strategy development is a critical activity in this approach. Often undertaken through informal or specially-created fora, it is through processes of interactive strategic imagining and consensus-building that such a language can be created, with its storylines and metaphors. The vehicle of a formal spatial planning process may provide such fora, or it may be used to translate the strategy into a form of contract among the parties. If the strategic work of collective, imaginative place-making has been undertaken well, it should have generated integrative conceptions of place. It should have shared a degree of mutual understanding and even ownership among the stakeholders. A formal development plan becomes an expression of this. Such an approach to planning generates a discourse of debate about concepts of place and their meaning, combining images and symbols to express these qualities with arguments about social, economic and environmental dynamics and their expression in the lives and meanings of people and firms in particular places. These meanings will then structure the debates about specific investment and regulatory decisions.

The collaborative approach to strategic place-making presents a demanding challenge to political communities. As a regulatory relationship, it is likely to take different forms, depending on the range of stakeholders who get involved and the institutional context of their involvement. It also requires the exercise of complex skills in managing processes of multiparty strategic imagining, consensus building and argumentation (Innes et al., 1994; Innes, 1996; Innes and Booher, 1999). Some political cultures provide much more fertile ground for such approaches than others, because their institutional histories have allowed a store of *institutional capital* to build up which encourages horizontal consensus-seeking and fosters awareness of spatial issues (Healey et al., 1997; Putnam, 1993). Nevertheless, in Britain in the late 1990s, efforts were being made at more collaborative strategic spatial planning.

Shifting Emphases and Changing Rules: Re-Inserting People and Place into Planning

The planning system in Britain at the end of the century, although it keeps much of the overall dimensions established 50 years ago, was profoundly shaped by the Tory administrations. Neo-liberal thinking, with its celebration of market processes, its failure to see the role of land use planning in underpinning land and property markets and its focus on autonomous individuals rather than people in social relations in places, accelerated the tendency towards a limited role for land use planning, governed by performance criteria. With the advent of New Labour, an opportunity has arisen for rethinking the design and practices of the planning system. This opportunity began to be taken up in 1998 (DETR, 1998), along with the wider agenda of 'inventing' regional governance and 'modernising' local government which the new administration set in train. In the rhetoric, the New Labour government embraces consultation and collaborative practices enthusiastically. Development plans should:

> encourage local people to participate actively in the preparation of plans from the earliest stages so that they can be fully involved in decisions about the pattern of development in their area (DETR, 1999b, para. 2.10).

> It is essential that the production of draft (Regional Planning Guidance) should involve the participation of regional stakeholders ... As RPG develops, providing a more holistic spatial strategy, the range of interested stakeholders will increase further (DETR, 1999a, para. 2.8).

In relation to the new Regional Development Agencies (DETR, 1997) and local government (DETR, 1998b), government advice advocates the involvement of citizens and business in policy development and delivery. It has also emphasised the importance of strategy and initiated an array of plan-making (e.g.: community plans, local transport plans). There has been much use of concepts of 'integrated' or 'holistic' thinking and action, symbolised in the 'joined-up government' metaphor (Wilkinson and Appelbee, 1999). There has also been firm support for planning. However, as in other areas of policy relevant to the qualities of places (transport, housing development), there is little parliamentary time to change the formal rules, the 'hard infrastructure' of the system. Instead, the rhetorical strategy is to change ideas and practices within the existing framework. The discretionary nature of the British planning system gives considerable scope to achieve this.

However, rhetoric, though influential, permeates policy practices in uneven ways in time and space. It is too early to see what difference it will make in the long-term. Nevertheless, some tendencies can be discerned. On the one hand, the new climate is encouraging experimentation. Collaborative processes and policy agendas are emerging in developing Joint Structure Plans and in some instances of Regional Planning Guidance. Some local authorities seeking to obtain 'Beacon' status under the 'Modern Local Government' agenda are using their planning functions as a key arena for the development of community strategies and local empowerment. On the other hand, however, the operationalisation of the rhetoric is exposing some real tensions. Within the planning system, the most obvious is between speed of decision-making and participation. Here, government advice suggest the performance criteria approach should be supplemented by collaborative practices. There is by now a barrage of criticism which argues that the focus on speed inhibits both an emphasis on participatory processes and makes it difficult to give adequate attention to the quality of decisions made. Nevertheless, the continued dominance is being slowly reduced by increasing emphasis in recent influential reports on the importance of the 'quality of places' (for example, the Urban Task Force report, 1999). The significance of 'place' is also given impetus by the promotion of the 'joined-up government' agenda, which has spawned an array of area regeneration initiatives, supplementing those inherited from the previous government. But there are considerable tensions within and between these initiatives in terms of the focus of attention and what precisely needs to be joined up with what. This revives an old tension in social policy between a focus on people (the 'client') and a focus on place (the 'area' or 'neighbourhood'). However, these days the gemeinschaft community cannot be revived to link the two.

The difficulties of sorting out how to make use of the new policy ideas is made more complex by a continuing high degree of centralism in New Labour government, and a limited ability to 'join-up' policy development and delivery at the centre. Central direction still tends to crowd out and clutter up local invention. As many have pointed out, there is a major difficulty in advocating participation and empowerment in localities while at the same time promoting a specific substantive agenda. Yet these specific agendas are being vigorously pursued, whether it be to do with reducing mobility, limiting brownfield development, promoting clusters of economic activity or making cities more compact. This tends to 'fix' policy agendas in localities. Locality stakeholders then have to respond to how to develop them. Not surprisingly, many of the new stakeholders who get involved in policy development at the regional and local level find such pre-set mental frameworks rather limiting. In this situation, there are strong tendencies for the 'partnerships' established in the 1990s, which tended to privilege the business community rather than a broader array of stakeholders, to provide the social and intellectual capital which gets rolled forward into the consultation processes and agenda setting of the new regional and local government initiatives in strategy development. This encourages the reinforcing of local 'corporatist' arrangements rather than wide-ranging stakeholder involvement. This supplements the foundations of representative democracy with 'partnership oligopoly' rather opening up to the evolution of more participative democratic practices.

The arenas of regional and local government, and hence the planning system and its practices, are therefore institutional terrains within which significant struggles are being played out about the nature of British government and its democratic form. Introducing 'good practice' in collaborative planning is thus not just a matter of the capability and commitment of those involved in particular practices. Its possibility is encouraged or constrained by the institutional context. Some of this context is rooted in local institutional histories, in the resources of relationships, arenas, discourses and trust which have built up over the years. The rhetoric of central government also makes a difference, interacting with the discourses of policy elites to shape ideas developed locally. But the practices of central government also make a difference, and as long as these combine strong central direction of resource flows and regulatory interpretation with ambiguous support in action for their own rhetoric, the potential of locally-driven collaborative practices will be limited. The power of 'business as usual' to continue is substantial, with collaborative policy development and delivery initiative potentially hijacked by a narrow relational nexus, the 'usual suspects' (see for example, Vigar, Steele et al., 2000).

This suggests that more than rhetoric is needed to change the mindsets and habits of those involved in governance in order to encourage policy attention to the issues arising from the spatiality of complex social relations as they intersect in the places of territory and locale, and to foster policy processes which are more inclusionary, more responsive to multiple stakeholders, more capable of learning new ideas and habits and more accountable. Changes in the 'hard infrastructure' are needed as well. Although there has so far been little discussion in the literature on collaborative planning on how the design of planning systems could facilitate or inhibit collaborative, multiparty place-making practices, the following key systemic institutional parameters have the potential to make a difference in the British context (see also Kitchen's discussion in the following chapter):

• the right to voice in spatial planning processes to all stakeholders;

- the duty on those centrally involved in spatial planning processes to consider the concerns of all other stakeholders;

- the requirement to provide robust justification and reasoning for policy decisions, grounded in discourses of argumentation (collective reasoning) which have been produced through collaborative processes which attend to all stakeholders;

- the requirement to consider qualities of places and the spatiality of development impacts as a criterion, (the idea of *territorial impact assessment* as promoted in recent European planning ideas (CSD, 1999) provides an example), along with other criteria which are defined as of EU or national importance;

- the promotion of the competencies of local and regional levels of governance in articulating planning strategy and policy, and the limitation of central government involvement to a few criteria, aimed to protect and promote matters of wider concern and subject to the same assertion of rights and exercise of duties as for local strategy-builders;

- the provision of resources in ways which cultivate consideration of places and collaborative processes.

The argument of this paper has been that the regulatory relationships embodied in the British planning system and its practices need to change, in order to reconnect the detailed practices of conflict management with the promotion of the qualities of places. This reconnection is needed if the system is to play a positive role in the new politics and practices of place-making which the emerging 'new times' see to demand. Such a reconnection, in the context of present tendencies and pressures, needs to happen in ways which acknowledge the range, variety and political salience of the many stakeholders in what places are like and could become. This paper has stressed that this involves moving away from sole reliance upon a largely aspatial, performance criteria approach to regulation, towards more collaborative and strategic approaches. It has argued that such an approach has the potential to achieve more effective conflict mediation. It also responds to the demands for strategic attention from many stakeholders, concerned about the qualities of places and about providing a more stable strategic framework within which development initiatives and partnership processes can be imagined and taken forward. Collaborative place-making as an approach in a multi-stakeholder society is thus justified because it is more efficient (reducing regulatory transaction costs in the longer term), because it is more politically legitimate, and because it 'adds value' to the ongoing flow of place-making actions, through building shared knowledge and understanding, generating opportunities for creative synergy, and developing the capacity among stakeholders to work together locally to solve common problems.

To develop this approach within the British planning system, however, will require a considerable transformation of the parameters of the current system and its practices. Changing the practices of a government system which has been highly sectoralised and centralised, with deeply embedded habits of paternalist government inherited from the mid-century form of the welfare state and the traditions of imperial administration, will be a long and difficult road, with opportunities for 'capture' by alternative practices along the way. Fifty years ago, new legislation emerged from a rich environment of forward thinking by advocates for planning who sought to design a new system and its practices and who were very aware of the need to position it centrally in the structure and discourses of the newly emerging welfare state. Twenty years ago, Thatcherite neo-liberalism caught planners on the hop. In the next decade, a vigorous effort across those with a stake in the qualities of places will be needed if the mindsets and habits of a more place-focused and participatory re-invention of governance is to evolve.

References

Amin, A. and Hausner, J. (eds) (1996), *Beyond Market and Hierarchy: Interactive Governance and Social Complexity*, Edward Elgar, Aldershot, Hants.

Amin, A. and Thrift, N. (1995a), 'Globalisation, "Institutional Thickness" and the Local Economy', in Healey, P. et al. (eds), *Managing Cities*, John Wiley, London, pp.91–108.

Amin, A. and Thrift, N. (eds) (1995b), *Globalisation, Institutions and Regional Development in Europe*, Oxford University Press, Oxford.

Bailey, N., Barker, A. and McDonald, K. (1995), *Partnerships in Practice*, UCL Press, London.

Blowers, A. (ed.) (1993), *Planning for a Sustainable Environment*, Earthscan Publications, London.

Brindley, T., Rydin, Y. and Stoker, G. (1989), *Remaking Planning*, Unwin Hyman, London.

Bryson, J. and Crosby, B. (1992), *Leadership in the Common Good*, Jossey Bass, San Francisco, CA.

Commission for the European Community (1994), *Europe 2000+: Co-operation for European Territorial Development*, European Commission, Luxembourg.

Committee on Spatial Development (1999), *European Spatial Development Perspective: Towards Balanced and Sustainable Development of the Territory of the EU*, Potsdam, Germany.

Cullingworth, J.B. (1993), *The Political Culture of Planning: American Land Use Planning in Comparative Perspective*, Routledge, London.

Davoudi, S., Healey, P. and Hull, A. (1996), 'Rhetoric and Reality in British Structure Planning in Lancashire: 1993–1995', in Healey, P. et al. (eds), *Making Strategic Spatial Plans*.

Dear, M. (1995), 'Prolegomena to a Postmodern Urbanism', in Healey, P. et al. (eds), *Managing Cities*, John Wiley, London.

Department of the Environment, Transport and the Regions (1998a), *Modernising the Planning System*, DETR, London.

Department of the Environment, Transport and the Regions (1998b), *Modern Local Government: In Touch with the People*, DETR, London.

Department of the Environment, Transport and the Regions (1999a), *Planning Policy Guidance Note 11: Regional Planning: Public Consultation Draft*, DETR, London.

Department of the Environment, Transport and the Regions (1999b), *Planning Policy Guidance No 12: Development Plans*, DETR, London.

Evans, A. (1988), *Urban Economics*, Blackwell, Oxford.

Faludi, A. (1996), 'Framing with Images', *Environment and Planning B: Planning and Design*, Vol. 23 (1), pp.93–108.

Foley, D. (1960), 'British Town Planning: One Ideology of Three?', *British Journal of Sociology*, Vol. 11, pp.211–31 (and in Faludi, A., *Reader in Planning Theory*, 1973, Pergamon, Oxford).

Freeman, C., Littlewood, S. and Whitney, D. (1996), 'Local Government and Emerging Models of Public Participation in the Local Agenda 21 Process', *Journal of Environmental Planning and Management*, Vol. 39, pp.65–78.

Graham, S. and Healey, P. (1999), 'Relational Concepts of Place and Space: Issues for Planning Theory and Practice', *European Planning Studies*, Vol. 7 (5).

Grove-White, R. (1991), 'Land, Law and Environment', *Journal of Law and Society*, Vol. 18 (1), pp.32–47.

Habermas, J. (1993), *Justification and Application*, Polity Press, Cambridge.

Hall, P. (1995), 'Bringing Abercrombie Back from the Shades', *Town Planning Review*, Vol. 66 (3), pp.227–42.

Healey, P. (1983), *Local Plans in British Land Use Planning*, Pergamon, Oxford.

Healey, P. (1988), 'The British Planning System and Managing the Urban Environment', *Town Planning Review*, Vol. 59 (4), pp.397–417.

Healey, P. (1994), 'Development Plans: New Approaches to Making Frameworks for Land Use Regulation', *European Planning Studies*, Vol. 2 (1), pp.38–58.

Healey, P. (1997), *Collaborative Planning: Shaping Places in Fragmented Societies*, Macmillan, London.

Healey, P., Cameron, S., Davoudi, S., Graham, S. and Madanipour, A. (eds) (1995), *Managing Cities*, John Wiley, London.

Healey, P., Khakee, A., Motte, A. and Needham, B. (1997), *Making Strategic Spatial Plans: Innovation in Europe*, UCL Press, London.

Healey, P., McNamara, P., Elson, M.J. and Doak, J. (1988), *Land Use Planning and the Mediation of Urban Change*, Cambridge University Press, Cambridge.

Healey, P. and Shaw, T. (1994), 'Changing Meanings of "Environment" in the British Planning System' *Transactions of the Institute of British Geography*, Vol. 19 (4), pp.425–38.

Innes, J. (1992), 'Group Processes and the Social Construction of Growth Management: the Cases of Florida, Vermont and New Jersey', *Journal of the American Planning Association*, Vol. 58, pp.275–8.

Innes, J. (1996), 'Planning Through Consensus-Building: a New View of the Comprehensive Planning Ideal', *Journal of the American Planning Association*, Vol. 62, pp.460–72.

Innes, J. and Booher, D. (1999), 'Consensus Building And Complex Adaptive Systems: A Framework for Evaluating Collaborative Planning', *Journal of the American Planning Association*, Vol. 65 (4).

Innes, J., Gruber, J., Neuman, M. and Thompson, R. (1994), *Coordination Through Consensus-Building in Growth Management*, report to the California Policy Seminar, Department of City and Regional Planning, University of California, Berkeley, CA.

Klosterman, R. (1985), 'Arguments For and Against Planning', *Town Planning Review*, Vol. 56 (1), pp.5–20.

Lipietz, A. (1992), *Towards a New Economic Order: Post Fordism, Ecology and Democracy*, Oxford University Press, New York.

Lowe, P. and Goyder, J. (1983), *Environmental Groups in Politics*, Allen and Unwin, London.

Marsden, T., Murdoch, J., Lowe, P., Munton, R. and Flynn, A. (1993), *Constructing the Countryside*, UCL Press, London.

Oatley, N. (ed.) (1998), *Cities, Economic Competition and Urban Policy*, Paul Chapman Publishing, London.

Petersen, P. (ed.) (1985), *The New Urban Reality*, Brookings Institution, Washington, DC.

Purdue, M. (1994), 'The Impact of Section 54A', *Journal of Planning and Environment Law*, pp.399–407.

Putnam, R. (1993), *Making Democracy Work: Civil Traditions in Modern Italy*, University of Princeton Press, NJ.

Ravetz, A. (1980), *Remaking Cities*, Croom Helm, London.

Rydin, Y. (1998), *Urban and Environmental Planning in the UK*, Macmillan, London.

Schön, D. and Rein, M. (1994), *Frame Reflection: Toward the Resolution of Intractable Policy Controversies*, Basic Books, New York.

Storper, M. and Scott, A. (eds) (1992), *Pathways to Industrialisation and Regional Development*, Routledge, London.

Sutcliffe, A. (1981), *Towards the Planned City*, Blackwell, Oxford.

Thornley, A. (1991), *Urban Planning Under Thatcherism*, Routledge, London.

Urban Task Force (1999), *Towards an Urban Renaissance*, E and FN Spon, London.

Vigar, G., Healey, P., Hull, A. and Davoudi, S. (2000), *Planning, Governance and Spatial Strategy-Making in Britain: An Institutionalist Approach*, Macmillan, London,

Wakeford, R. (1990), *American Development Control: Parallels and Paradoxes from an English Perspective*, HMSO, London.

Wilkinson, D. and Appelbee, D. (1999), *Implementing Holistic Government*, Policy Press, Bristol.

Williams, R. (1975), *The Country and the City*, Penguin, Harmondsworth.

Wolsink, M. (1994), 'Entanglement of Interests and Motives: Assumptions Behind the Nimby-Theory of Facility Siting', *Urban Studies*, Vol. 31, pp.851–66.

Chapter Thirteen

Shaping Urban Areas into the Twenty-first Century: The Roles of the Planning Process

Ted Kitchen

Introduction

This chapter tries to look at some of the forces that may well affect attempts to shape our urban areas into the next century, and within this in particular it looks at how the planning process might seek to grapple with some of these forces. Since at its heart the planning process is a public activity, within which the key player is the local planning authority, the health and the 'fitness for purpose' of the local planning authorities responsible for our major urban areas must be part of this equation. But local planning authorities are (or ought to be) servants of the communities for which they are responsible rather than dictators to them, and thus the views, attitudes and wishes of customer communities need to play a significant role in shaping the characteristics of individual authorities, perhaps more so than is the case today.

Of itself, this is a very large agenda for a single chapter. In addition, it is inevitable that an attempt to look into the future (notwithstanding the fact that this is what planning is actually supposed to be about!) is both speculative because the future is by definition unknowable and at the same time unavoidably rooted in the present. All of these things mean that the process of tackling the agenda set above must be selective, partial and personal.

Given these characteristics, the chapter commences with a review of what I regard as the key issues facing our major urban areas today. It then looks at some of the key challenges that might affect both our major urban areas and the local planning authorities that seek to shape them over the next few years. More speculatively, it looks at some of the longer-term issues that could have a very significant impact on our major urban areas over the first half of the next century. Finally, it tries to draw some of these threads together into some tentative conclusions.

As well as the texts referred to throughout this chapter, I have drawn quite extensively on two particular recent pieces of my own that have tried to look at different aspects of the future in different ways. The first is my paper to the Newcastle 50th Anniversary Conference (Kitchen, 1996e) which gave rise to this book, where I assumed the alter ego of St Peter's Assistant Planner who had come back to the 100th Anniversary Conference in 2046 and presented a retrospective on the previous 50 years. This tortured device was an attempt to envision the longer-term future and what it might mean for planning systems and processes without being excessively concerned with the present day. The second is my professorial lecture at Sheffield Hallam University (Kitchen, 1997b), where in much more conventional form I tried to look at the prospects for the urban local planning authority looking both backwards on the 50th anniversary of the formative 1947 Town and Country Planning Act and forwards to and beyond the millennium.

What Are the Key Issues?

I have argued elsewhere (Kitchen, 1996b) that the four inter-related major policy challenges facing British urban local planning authorities at present, and therefore likely to determine how successful they are over the next few years, are:

• the need to keep working at securing an economic base for our cities, in the face of constant economic change. Cities came into being on the back of economic change (Briggs, 1982), and they will survive insofar as they can continue to adapt to it. The characters of cities change as their economic bases change, however, as Peter Hall argues when looking particularly at New York, London and Tokyo up to 2010, a period he describes as producing '… the city of the tarnished belle époque' (Hall, 1996, pp.402–22);
• the need to tackle the problem of major concentrations of socioeconomic deprivation in our cities, so that the 20–30 per cent of people (the figure I estimated for Manchester – Kitchen, 1996b) who by contemporary measures are seriously disadvantaged in these terms do benefit from economic change and do participate in the effective governance of our cities. The American alternative of the creation of large and apparently permanent urban 'underclasses' (Kelso, 1994) faces us if we do not tackle this problem successfully, and as Will Hutton has graphically reminded us in his depiction of the 40:30:30 society (Hutton, 1996) we are moving

inexorably in this direction. It is salutary to note in this context that Brian Robson and his colleagues, in their massive overview of what more than 20 years worth of inner city or urban policy had achieved (Robson et al., 1994), concluded that relatively speaking the position of many of the poorest people in our cities had probably deteriorated over this period. It is also worth noting that we actually know very little about the incidence of the benefits of urban regeneration expenditure in these terms (Lawless, 1996), although the 'trickle-down' thesis that dominated much of the thinking about these matters in the 1980s has been widely debunked (see, for example, Deakin and Edwards, 1993);

- the need to find transport policies and programmes that work well for our cities and their people, in the face of ever-rising private vehicle ownership and usage (Royal Commission on Environmental Pollution, 1995) and with a disastrous policy heritage in terms of deregulation that has made it virtually impossible within the current system for anyone to see through to fruition this kind of planning action (Pickup et al., 1991);

- the need to move towards making our cities ever more sustainable places. An immediate challenge in this context will be for our planning systems to take on board the fruits of the commitment to Local Agenda 21 in 70– 75 per cent of local authority areas, which during 1997 is likely to produce a raft of policy statements with widespread commitment to them from amongst the many sectors that have participated in this process. This could be regarded as the greatest public participation exercise in planning yet undertaken in Britain. It has also significantly raised the expectations of participants, however, so unless its fruits are taken seriously and make a noticeable difference to what the mainstream planning system is doing it is an exercise that could quickly reinforce negative images of that system (Young, 1996).

The nature of these issues will vary from place to place, as will the degree of success achieved in dealing with them, but this broad package of issues will be on the table in our cities for many years to come.

The inter-relatedness of these four issues needs to be emphasised. What this actually means in practice is that the stance taken in relation to any one of them is likely to affect all the others. Take for example the question of action to seek to secure the economic base of a city, and whether this is an overriding objective or whether (and if, so, how) it should be constrained by environmental concerns. This was a very major policy debate during the latter part of my period as City Planning Officer of Manchester (Kitchen, 1997a), when the prevailing view of the Council's then political leadership appeared to be that economic base considerations were of overriding concern. Very crudely, the consequence of this view can be traced through the four key issues as shown in Figure 13.1.

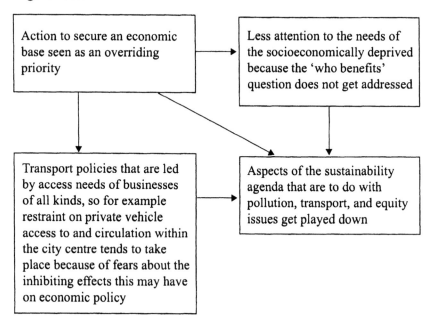

Figure 13.1 Consequences of over-riding economic base considerations

In turn, the consequences of these views could be followed through this policy chain to the point where, for example, environmental conditions in terms of congestion and pollution arising from traffic in central areas are proving to be a disincentive to economic activity in those areas. A policy response to this might then look as follows (Figure 13.2).

This very simple pair of illustrations of how changed policy stances in one field can have knock-on effects throughout this range of key issues should serve to make the point that it is not possible to tackle any one of these issues without such actions affecting the ways in which the others also are handled. Practicalities often determine that issues are handled on a piecemeal basis, but it is important in these circumstances to be aware of what the implications of such actions are likely to be. What all of this requires, as near as possible, is an holistic vision of what we want our places to be, rather than a policy-by-policy perception; and at least, such visions will need to be expressed in the form of ideas about all four of these key issues.

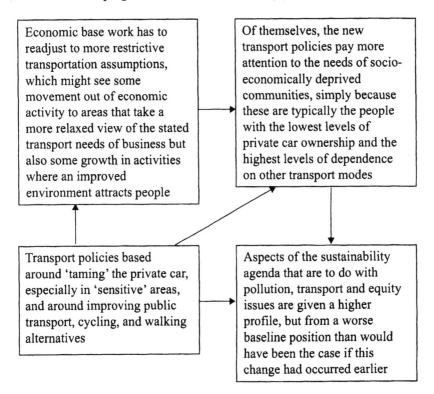

Figure 13.2 Possible policy responses

What Key Changes Might Take Place?

Inevitably, when looking at a question such as this, one is venturing into the realms of speculation. Nevertheless, I have selected six elements of change that I expect will face our major urban areas over the next decade, three of which are essentially about challenges to and opportunities for our places and three of which are about the relationships that are likely to affect the shape that local planning authorities are in when they come to address these matters:

Challenges and Opportunities

• at the regional scale;

• arising from the changing nature of work;

• offered by technological developments.

Relationships

• between elected members and professional officers;

• between local government and central government;

• between local planning authorities and their customer communities.

The challenges and opportunities at the regional scale are likely to depend in part on how far down this road the New Labour government goes in erecting a locally-accountable regional structure of government in England. Scotland and Wales, although they would use language that talks in national rather than in regional terms, may point the way forward here. I hope that in England this encourages some new thinking about what we actually mean by regions. For example, I believe that the case for the coterminous Liverpool, Manchester, Leeds and Sheffield conurbations, an area I have elsewhere described as 'northern heart' (Kitchen, 1996d), to be seen as an entity for some purposes and as a northern England powerhouse able to stand in some senses as a national counterweight to London, has many attractions. Drawing a regional boundary line down the middle of the Pennines, as traditionally we would do, would in all probability discourage any such moves at least for a period of time. But what is also important as part of this process is the attitude that is taken to Europe, and particularly to the European notion of a 'Europe of regions'. We may well have to get used to the idea as the European Union expands eastwards that many areas of Britain that at present benefit from structural funds will no longer do so, even though in all probability there will be a transitional period, since (for example) many areas of the former communist bloc would seem likely to score more highly against the existing EU Objective 1 or Objective 2 criteria or their future equivalent than would some parts of Britain that at present qualify (Williams, 1996, pp.260–62). The scale of this is potentially very considerable. English Partnerships have calculated that European resources from Objectives 1, 2 and 5b over the 6 years 1994–99 inclusive will be available in the parts of England that qualify for these programmes to the tune of £2775 millions (English Partnerships, undated, p.23); European resources from these programmes for Scotland, Wales and Northern Ireland are in addition to this figure. This is a yearly average of just over £460 millions, which for comparative purposes is approximately twice the size of English Partnerships' 1995/96 development programme (English Partnerships, 1996, p.11) and about 60 per cent of the

Single Regeneration Budget resources available for that year excluding earmarked funds (Balchin et al., 1995, p.273). Both English Partnerships and Single Regeneration Budget resources can be applied across a wider range of localities than can EU structural funds by virtue of the latter's qualification rules, so the concentrated effect of EU funding is correspondingly greater. Clearly, therefore, a threat to this level of funding would be a serious matter for British urban regeneration, since it is not immediately obvious that there is a ready-made public or private alternative to this expenditure. Another possible threat arising from the development of the European Union in an easterly direction is that it might emphasise still more Britain's geographical peripherality, and particularly that of those parts of Britain not encompassed within Europe's 'blue banana', such as the Liverpool–Manchester–Leeds–Sheffield agglomeration which is to the north of this area and well to the north of Europe's 'Golden Triangle' (Williams, 1996, p.95). Thus, a return to greater levels of regional polarisation than we have seen in recent years may be possible. The need to think carefully about these kinds of issues puts the coming regional challenge into a rather different perspective from that merely of regional devolution within our own country.

The challenges arising from *the changing nature of work* are relatively easy to describe but are daunting in the extreme to face. Industrial geographers (for example, Hayter, 1997) tell us that Western industrial cities can no longer expect to acquire jobs in the kinds of heavy manufacturing activities that fuelled their growth in the past, but instead may see some growth in fields such as:

• specialist high technology manufacturing, which 'adds value';

• fashion industries, particularly those catering to groups with significant disposable incomes;

• sports, cultural industries and the arts (which can be described as 'industries of collective consumption', since they mainly depend upon significant numbers of people coming to a single location to 'consume' a product they regard as having distinctive or desirable qualities);

• knowledge-based industries, and particularly those utilising links with the higher education and research sectors;

• urban tourism, and perhaps particularly its heritage component;

* green industries of all kinds.

This is a very different list from that which would have been produced 50 years ago, and this ought to make us very cautious about how long such a list might last into the future. One of the interesting characteristics for planning of a list of this kind, whether or not it turns out to be accurate as a forecast of our urban industrial future, is what it implies about the ways in which we set about through planning processes helping to meet industrial needs. Traditional methods saw this in terms of industrial land availability (see, for example, Keeble, 1964, pp.187, 188); this example was suggested in Healey, 1997, pp.132, 133) and starting from a population base, calculated a job need, translated that into a land use need, subtracted the land already occupied by industrial activity, and added a margin of error. One of the most critical components of this calculation was the step involved in jumping from a need for jobs generated by population size to a land need based upon knowledge of average job densities. However heroic these calculations, and whatever difficult assumptions they appeared to make about the spatial relationships between home and work, they have been rendered completely redundant in the case of most of the potential urban employment growth areas listed above by the fact that these do not have a simple relationship with land-take. Indeed, many of them until recently (such as for example cultural industries; Bianchini and Parkinson, 1993) have not been thought about primarily in job-generation terms at all. Thus, a development plan-making process for an urban area 30 years ago may well have gone through such a calculation to establish the need for a quantum of industrial land, but a contemporary development plan-making process which accepted that the above list contained the target fields for employment growth would not see the problem primarily in land-need terms and would not attempt such a calculation at all. Rather, the approach would be likely to be one of trying to understand the conditions and the locations in which such industries might grow, and then seeking to understand how a development plan might encourage such activities alongside a range of other relevant tools.

The challenges to and opportunities for planning processes as a consequence of *technological developments* are potentially enormous, as are the threats they pose to our cities in terms of the locational freedom they confer on many activities (Castells, 1989; Simmie, 1997). It is probably true to say that, as the pace of change in technological developments accelerates, so it becomes harder to see for long periods into the future. Two technologies that already exist have considerable potential to transform planning processes if they are used constructively. The first is the ability of the technology of the transmission of television (be this by cable, digital or other means in the future) to facilitate not merely community involvement in a wide range of processes but also interactive processes generating speedy feedback on issues and choices, if they can be conveyed effectively via this medium. The second is the potential of virtual reality technology to help with development decisions of a kind which raise issues of 'goodness of fit' with the surrounding environment in a design sense, by simulating both that environment and how the proposal would look when slotted into it. Planning Committees and planning consultation processes would no doubt find such a capability helpful, certainly as compared with the widely distrusted 'artist's impressions' that seek to do such a job today. It could also be argued that other developments, such as the extensive use of the Internet, could broaden out communication processes as compared with the patterns visible today, and no doubt for many of the customers of the planning service this will turn out to be true. At the same time, it probably needs to be acknowledged that most new forms of communication technology as well as opening up huge opportunities in these terms also create access barriers for some people, and ways of overcoming these will need to be found. On balance, however, if harnessing the power of technology enables more communicative and more participative planning processes to emerge, better decisions to be taken, and the quality of those decisions (for good or for ill) to be more widely understood than it is today, this can only be to the good of the planning process. The potential undoubtedly exists for local planning authorities to make much fuller use of proven technologies than many do as yet, especially when acceptable unit costs fall as more development work is done on these applications. The question, as ever, will not be whether or not the technology exists but rather how well and how transparently we use it.

The question of *the relationships between elected members and professional officers* in the work of local planning authorities is a very topical issue, and is likely to remain so in the light of the publication of the report by the Nolan Committee on conduct issues in local government (Committee on Standards in Public Life, 1997). Highly publicised difficulties of this kind in North Cornwall (Department of the Environment, 1993), in Warwick (Picking, 1996) and more recently still in Doncaster, for example, have shown what can go wrong when the relationships between elected members and professional officers, and particularly perhaps the respect for each other's roles, break down. My own experiences in Manchester may contribute something to this debate (Kitchen, 1997a). A recent study for the Royal Town

Planning Institute (Zetter et al., 1997) has concluded that the solution to these
kinds of difficulties is essentially to introduce a whole series of procedural
rules. Whilst agreeing with this, North Cornwall's Director of Planning and
Development (Philp, 1997) has argued that effective plans, regular member
training, regular site visits to demonstrate the impacts of decisions, and visible
evidence that external monitors such as the District Auditor and the
Government Regional Office are both watchful and willing to act where
necessary have all played a part in turning that District Council's performance
around. What seems clear in all of this is that these relationships are now
under scrutiny as never before, and if this results in the improved transparency
of local government planning decision-making this would of itself be a
significant contributor to the ability of the planning system to do a better job
in managing change in our cities.

   Relationships between local government and central government have
been a perennial source of difficulty in Britain, exacerbated in recent years by
the 'beauty contest' approach to the allocation of scarce public sector resources
for regeneration (Oatley, 1995), although it could be argued that the election
of a government apparently intrinsically less hostile to local government than
the 1979–97 Conservative governments appeared to be for most of their lives
might allow a new and more stable set of relationships to emerge. If the New
Labour government really means what it appears to be saying about
decentralisation, however, then it is at least possible that we will see a
programme of devolution of responsibility which makes it possible for local
government not only to do the things that are genuinely local but also to do
this in a way which makes sense at the locality level rather than in terms of a
national template. I have argued elsewhere, for example, that development
plans would be much more effective if they were freed from the existing web
of national constraints about process, format, content and language and were
left to evolve in ways that were of the most use in the localities they are
designed to improve (Kitchen, 1996c). We will see soon enough whether
changes of this kind will occur over the life of this new government.

   Arguably the single most important set of relationships being discussed
here is that between *local planning authorities and their customer communities.*
There isn't the space here to go into who these customers actually are and
how these relationships might actually work (but see Kitchen, 1996a and
1997a), but it should be clear without needing to do this that what will be at
the heart of the development of such relationships will be the provision of a
satisfactory service to customers. There are pragmatic reasons for asserting
this, as well as reasons of professional ideology; after all, 440,000 Mancunians

to 110 planners produces odds of 4000:1, and anything that can be done to reduce the potential impacts of these sorts of odds has to be beneficial for the planning service. And these are not atypical figures for Metropolitan Districts. In an as yet unpublished piece of research on the structure and organisation of the planning service in English local government that I carried out during 1996/97, the population mean per authority for the 17 Metropolitan Districts that replied to a postal questionnaire was 314,164 and the average size of planning staff was 73.39, producing a ratio of one member of planning staff for every 4,280 people. Much of the process of trying to improve customer satisfaction with the service provided must be about the way it operates rather than necessarily the outcomes of individual decisions, since many planning decisions have winners and losers as an unavoidable consequence. Whether or not customers see themselves as eventual winners or losers as a result of a planning decision, everyone could have been properly consulted, fairly and courteously treated, and could have had their views accurately reported and systematically taken into account in the processes leading up to that decision; and this is surely a goal to aim for in the management of local government planning services. It can be argued that British society in terms of its expectations of 'officialdom' has changed radically over the past 30 years, and that planning practice and the planning literature have not yet fully caught up with society's changing aspirations in this regard. After all, it is only 30 years ago (and less in some cases) that the inner city areas of most of our conurbations were being torn down and redeveloped with very little if any public consultation, and with a 'we know best what's good for you' attitude (Davies, 1972). It is hard to envisage a large-scale programme being undertaken today, whatever the arguments about need, without very careful thought being given to the processes of discovering the wishes and views of affected communities where they are not already known (Atkinson, 1995). The difference between the redevelopment of Hulme in Manchester in the late 1960s/early 1970s and its second redevelopment in the 1990s illustrates very well how much has changed in these terms over such a relatively short period (Kitchen, 1997a). This trend will continue; I see no evidence that demands for greater community involvement in decisions that affect those communities will suddenly stop growing. This is a major challenge for the planning profession, because it means that to win community support for actions taken in the name of planning we will have to continue to develop our thinking about how to do this against ever-rising expectations. It also means that we will have to tackle the probably conflicting challenges both of opening up our planning processes to greater public involvement and of bringing them to satisfactory conclusions in a reasonable time-frame so that their intended beneficiaries do actually gain some benefit from them. Not only is this not happening, but it could be argued that development plan-making, for example, is slowing down still further (Kitchen, 1996c). Patsy Healey's recent call for a much more communicative and collaborative planning process, whatever difficulties there may be in moving from where we are now to where this model tells us that we ought to be, is likely to be a beacon on this journey (Healey, 1997).

Whilst these critical sets of relationships will undoubtedly heavily influence how effectively local planning authorities manage the process of shaping changes in our cities, another requirement may well turn out to be the need for a degree of structural stability for the authorities themselves. The scale of the changes that have taken place in the recent past in these terms may not be widely appreciated, but the research project referred to above on the structure and organisation of local government planning services in England has illustrated this very clearly, as the following table based upon a 45 per cent sample of these authorities illustrates.

Table 13.1   Changes experienced by English local planning authorities in the two years up to 31 December 1996

Affected by:	All local planning authorities %	Metropolitan Districts and London Boroughs %
changes in the structure of local government	17.2	3.3
changes in committee responsibilities for planning	23.0	26.7
changes in responsibilities between departments	41.5	40.0
changes in the internal organisational structure of the planning service	48.1	46.7
changes in sharing arrangements for scarce staff	7.7	3.9

These changes, over a relatively short period, are on a very large scale. In particular, two in every five local planning authorities have seen responsibilities related to planning move between Departments, and virtually half have seen the internal organisational structure change in a single two year period. Whilst changes of this kind will take place naturally from time to time (Leach, Stewart and Walsh, 1994) and indeed need to in order to prevent ossification, it must be doubted whether a continuation of this pace of change would be desirable simply because the planning system would be in constant turmoil. Indeed, one of the consequences of this sort of situation can be that attention is too heavily concentrated on these internal affairs to the detriment of the major agenda that the service is actually supposed to be dealing with. Thus, a call for a period of relative stability is not merely something that the staff affected would probably wholeheartedly welcome, but is also part of the process of ensuring that the substantive issues affecting our urban areas get the attention they deserve.

What Might Some of the Longer-Term Issues Be?

The great advantage of posing as St Peter's Assistant Planner 50 years' hence (Kitchen, 1996e) as a way of looking at the future was that it offered the opportunity to speculate about what might happen in the long-term without worrying about how well grounded that was in present-day knowledge or about how we might get from where we are now to the states that such 'envisioning' might suggest could materialise. It also freed one from having to argue very much about how likely these views are to materialise, as compared with any other of the multiplicity of futures that one might envision. Thus, I offered the following series of one-shot-views not as forecasts, but as what occurred to me when I tried to look at the next 50 years retrospectively:
Planning System and Process Issues might be relatively stable:

• the case for a strong statutory planning system was widely accepted, and concerns about the quality of the system replaced sniping at it;

• the planning system ceased to be a national planning system at all, but became a series of locally-tailored systems to which a small number of national policy requirements applied;

• the involvement of elected members on Planning Committees could only happen after they had taken a nationally-approved training course and then attended regular refresher courses;

- chief planning officers were given statutory protection in respect of their bona-fide professional advice;

- regional tiers of government continued to fail, and were not repeated after the break-up of the United Kingdom and the collapse of the Euro on the Pacific money markets;

- development plans largely withered away, to be replaced by annual rolling development statements, linked to local political manifestos;

- planning emerged as a secondary school discipline, focusing on the application of logical though processes to problem-solution;

- many planning decisions were informed by community referenda.

Planning Substance Issues are likely to be extremely turbulent:

- cities that failed to attract and develop the sunrise industries of the twenty-first century collapsed, and Urban Undevelopment Corporations had to be established to return them to open space, urban forest and river margin wetlands. Tourism in such areas grew as a consequence;

- after extensive civil disturbances in the inner cities, policies of population dispersal combined with targeted programmes to enable those that stayed behind to be gainfully active on community and environmental service programmes contained the problem, although inner-city residents were still substantially the poorest in the country;

- the ownership of personal transit vehicles ceased to be a right, but became a rarely-granted privilege. Free public transport was provided, but access to it depended upon satisfying a 'need-meter' that a journey was necessary, which administered an electric shock to card-holders if it wasn't;

- the virtual holiday became very popular. No longer was it necessary to travel to destinations for a holiday, but by harnessing the power of communications technology in effect destinations came to you;

- the problems of global warming were not resolved because politicians stumbled over the 'act local' bit of their slogan 'think global: act local'. As a result, the British climate and landscape changed, with the drowning of parts of the East Anglian coastline, permanent water rationing in the South East and the emergence of semi-desert conditions in parts of the South West. The acceptance of the need to take sustainability issues more seriously only became really widespread after these consequences had become inescapable;

- forced community work camps for people found guilty of dropping litter were used to promote the rapid growth of recycling and the generation of electricity as a by-product.

Like most attempts at envisioning what a quite far-distant future might be like, the probability must be that, amongst those 14 sets of propositions, a significant proportion will arrive well before 2046 and a further proportion will never arrive at all. But as a comparison with the previous section of this chapter will readily demonstrate, in truth these are not really separated from the constraints of current knowledge, despite the elaborate assumption of a wraithlike alter ego in order to try to achieve this objective. The single piece of envisioning over this sort of timescale which has probably the greatest chance of turning out to be correct is that the things that will really be shaping planning 50 years' hence are things that we would find great difficulty in imagining today. So the probability must be that urban planning systems by the middle of the next century will be less grounded in our current knowledge and understanding than is this particular piece of envisioning, no matter that some of it is very far removed from where we are today, and will as a consequence have to cope with some changes that are more radical than those described above. Since most of these changes will take place incrementally rather than in one fell swoop, whatever else this will do it will certainly be a challenge to the adaptability of our planning systems and processes and of the people who are role-players in them.

Conclusions – What Might the Prognosis for the Future Be?

The analysis presented above suggests that the planning process in urban areas has both a sizeable and a challenging substantive agenda in front of it. Whilst it would be very difficult to plot a path for dealing with the very long-term possibilities that have been canvassed, the urban agenda of the immediate future is with us today. Indeed, since we always start from where we are, the processes of trying to shape the future of our cities must start with the development of clear and holistic views about how to maintain viable urban economies, how to improve the living circumstances of the most seriously economically and socially deprived residents of our cities, how to generate transport networks that function to the overall advantage of our cities, and how to move towards the goal of urban sustainability. It may well be the case that not all cities will handle these issues equally successfully, and it is more than likely that what appears to work well in one location will not necessarily work as well elsewhere. There are important research questions in this, because understanding why things work or don't work is the key to learning from collective experiences; and as yet, we have done less of this kind of research than would have been desirable.

It is possible that the process of tackling this substantive planning agenda in our cities will be heavily influenced by what was emerging as the key urban issue at the end of the period of Conservative government from 1979 to 1997. This is the question of the location of the 4.4 million extra households expected to form between 1991 and 2016 (Department of the Environment, 1996). If it can be achieved, the successful adaptation of our urban areas to enable them to accommodate the bulk of this household growth as people choose to live in cities is likely to offer a wide range of opportunities to tackle the key issues facing our cities constructively, because the one is likely to be an integral part of the other. But equally, a failure to adapt our cities so that a high proportion of these people choose to live outside them may serve to exaggerate the difficulties in these policy fields that our cities are already facing. The key to this seems to be the notion of what would be needed to make our cities into attractive places where a high proportion of people would choose to live, since it is difficult to see that an approach to this issue which is based either upon a degree of compulsion (even assuming that this would be acceptable in a democratic society) or upon a policy stance which effectively denies alternatives (which is difficult to deliver in a market economy when the loop from consumer demand to political reaction is often a rapid one) has any realistic prospect of delivering the desired outcome. This idea of cities as places where large numbers of people would choose to live may be difficult to credit in the face of a visual inspection of many of Britain's contemporary inner cities, but this is perhaps a measure of the scale of the task rather than a statement as to its impossibility. What we need to know much more about, however, is what it is about cities that people value in making their residential choices, and what sorts of policies need to be pursued to improve people's perceptions of cities in these terms. This is another research challenge that needs to be addressed more emphatically than has been the case to date.

In terms of how effectively the planning process might grapple with all of this in the future, five themes have been touched upon in the course of this chapter and are likely to be of considerable significance. These are:

- the resource base of the planning service;

- approaches to structural and organisation change;

- the need to engage more effectively with the customers of the planning service;

- professional officer/elected member relationships;

- resolving the emerging difficulties with development plans.

The *resource base* of the planning service in urban areas has been under considerable pressure for some time now, and thus it is often no surprise when planners gather together that they can find it difficult to lift their heads above concerns about funding for programmes and about staffing levels. Much of this stems from the rethinking that took place in the 1980s about the respective roles of the public and of the private sectors, with the objective of rolling back the boundaries of the state. (Brindley, Rydin and Stoker, 1989; Blackman, 1995, pp.64–100). Whilst urban local planning authorities were undoubtedly wounded by that process, they have survived it, and arguably (at any rate in some cases) their contribution is much more valued locally than the national and essentially ideological debate ever seemed capable of recognising. I look forward to the time, which I believe will come, when the basic role of the planning service is not at issue in urban areas, when it is recognised that it needs to be adequately resourced in order to do that job, and when attention switches to the quality of the product and the added value that it produces. These things will need to be debated and to be measured; and planners must participate vigorously in these processes, including in the development of effective performance measures that help our customer public not merely to understand what they are getting for their money but also that provide vehicles to enable customers to suggest how the value thereby obtained could be improved.

The obsession with *structural and organisational change* that we continue to see needs itself to be the subject of an intensive comparison of the real costs it incurs and the benefits it generates. I suspect that such an examination in many cases would reveal that real costs are much greater than was anticipated, with actual benefits being rather less than was hoped for even when it was clear at the outset what these were. Part of the explanation for this lies in the fact that structural change is often an easy response to problems that are not at their heart structural. But part of the explanation must also lie in the readily-observable phenomenon that committed and capable professional staff can often deliver good quality and valued services to their customers largely irrespective of the organisational structure within which they work. This is the real challenge for managers in urban local planning authorities; to get the best out of their staff on behalf of their customers by providing the most conducive working environment possible in the circumstances, and only to pursue structural change when it is clear that the benefits of so doing particularly in terms of services to customers will clearly outweigh the costs.

I have argued in several places about *the need to engage more effectively with the customers of the planning service.* This is partly a function of remembering that planning is a public service industry in the first place; partly a function of the rapidly-rising expectations that we have seen over the last 30 years as compared with the largely-passive public of the 1960s; and partly because the feature of the planning service that needs to be emphasised most is its local nature and indeed its local relevance. The available evidence suggests that whilst there are undoubtedly negative views about some aspects of planning services held by people who regard themselves as its customers, this situation is by no means wholly bleak (McCarthy and Harrison, 1995). But this is not mainly a question of trying to improve some negative public reactions to planning, essentially as a public relations exercise. Our urban places belong to their people, and it is up to planners to try to ensure not only that those places are the kinds of places in which people would choose to live out their lives to fullest effect but also that people have ample opportunity of participating in the processes of shaping those places to this end.

This is very much linked to the idea that more light needs to be thrown *on professional officer/elected member relationships* in a democratic local government structure. It is understandable that customers of the planning service should be concerned about how meaningful consultation processes might be when they suspect that political decisions have already been taken about their outcome. Equally, it is understandable that customers may well question the objectivity with which their representations are taken into account in officers' reports when they suspect that those officers have been constrained to reach a preordained conclusion. If decision-making processes are to carry conviction in the planning field, whatever people may feel about the outcome at the end of the day, then basic principles of fairness have to apply to them and the roles and responsibilities of the key players in those processes have to be clarified and respected. The technological scope for improving the volume and the range of public involvement in planning decision-making, as I have already argued, is enormous, but these things will be of little worth unless the issues outlined above are tackled head-on. That is why I welcome the attention that has been given to professional officer/elected member relationships in recent years. I hope this attention bears fruit.

The *need to resolve the emerging difficulties with development plans* is an important issue in its own right, because development plans are arguably one of the two major tools that planners actually have at their disposal for seeking to achieve the things that have been talked about in this Chapter (the other being the development control process). The intention of Section 54A of the Planning Act seems to be to strengthen the hand of the planning system in these terms (Keene, 1993), and even to restore the position to what it could be argued that the authors of the 1947 Town and Country Planning Act had intended in the first place. The difficulty, as has already been noted above, is that in practice the ever-growing demand for consultation and involvement, and the consequential likelihood of formal objections, seems to be making the process take longer without necessarily offering many compensating benefits (Kitchen, 1996c and 1997b). As Macregor and Ross (1995) argue, we need to think about whether the development plan should be seen as the master or a servant, because there is a growing danger that the voracious demands of the plan-preparation process are turning it into the master. And as Ho (1997) argues, the power of the Secretary of State to intervene at a very late stage in the process can give an added but largely unwanted dimension to these difficulties. The risk in all of this is that the development plan will become increasingly discredited both amongst planners and amongst the customers of the service, unless ways and means can be found of accommodating legitimate public desires to be involved in the process whilst achieving a valued product when it is needed. My personal view is that this may prove impossible, because no amount of tinkering with the procedural rules will change the essential conundrum posed by the fact that these tensions are pulling in incompatible directions. Hence the thought that in the longer term we may well see much simpler annual rolling statements, where the process of collaborative planning (Healey, 1997) is essentially continuous but where the responsibility for producing a clear and concise current position statement at regular intervals falls unambiguously to the local planning authority.

Pulling all of this together, I would suggest that the planning process in Britain's urban areas may shortly be moving into a sixth phase, its first 50 years of powerful statutory support having to my mind already been through 5 phases. This unfolding story can be expressed as Table 13.2 shows.

Table 13.2   The history and immediate future of the British urban planning process

Phase	Time period	Key characteristics
Phase 1	1948–mid 1950s	Getting started: 1947 Act Development Plans
Phase 2	mid 1950s–early 1970s	Inner city and city centre redevelopment: informal plans dominant
Phase 3	early 1970s–early 1980s	Uncertainty: slum clearance programmes end: local government reorganisation
Phase 4	1980s	The local state under national attacks of all kinds
Phase 5	1990s	Partnerships: competitive bidding: major financial limitations: the resurgence of development plans
Phase 6	late 1990s–early 21st century	Greater emphasis on the local element: very variable record in dealing with key issues at the local level: waning influence of the development plan

Source: adapted from Kitchen, 1997b.

If the greater emphasis on the local element being suggested here as a characteristic of phase 6 might well be quite widely welcomed, its corollary that Governments might be more willing in the future than in the past to see the local state fail or at any rate in a relative sense significantly under-perform would probably not be. And the suggestion that we may need to develop different kinds of tools as the influence of the development plan as we now know it wanes raises all kinds of issues, both about what these tools might be and about how the urban challenges discussed in this Chapter might be tackled in the interim. But it is important to think about remaking our planning processes in just the same way that it is important to think about remaking our cities. One of the greatest challenge of them all, as Cherry (1996) has argued, may be the need to reinvent tools of the trade that are grounded in views about the nature of the planning process as it was envisaged by the writers of the 1947 Act rather than congruent with the needs of the future.

References

Atkinson, R. (1995), *Cities of Pride: Rebuilding Community, Refocusing Government*, Cassell, London.

Balchin, P.N., Bull, G.H. and Kieve, J.L. (1995), *Urban Land Economics and Public Policy*, Macmillan, Basingstoke.

Bianchini, F. and Parkinson, M. (1993), *Cultural Policy and Urban Regeneration: the West European Experience*, Manchester University Press, Manchester.

Blackman, T. (1995), *Urban Policy in Practice*, Routledge, London.

Briggs, A. (1982), *Victorian Cities*, Pelican Books, London.

Brindley, T., Rydin, Y. and Stoker, G. (1989), *Remaking Planning: the Politics of Urban Change in the Thatcher Years*, Unwin Hyman, London.

Castells, M. (1989), *The Information City*, Blackwell, Oxford.

Cherry, G.E. (1996), *Town Planning in Britain since 1900*, Blackwell, Oxford.

Committee on Standards in Public Life (the Nolan Committee) (1997), *Standards in Public Life – Standards of Conduct in Local Government in England, Scotland and Wales*, HMSO, London.

Davies, J.G. (1972), *The Evangelistic Bureaucrat*, Tavistock, London.

Deakin, N. and Edwards, J. (1993), *The Enterprise Culture and the Inner City*, Routledge, London.

Department of the Environment (1993), *Enquiry into the Planning System in North Cornwall District by Audrey Lees*, HMSO, London.

Department of the Environment (1996), *Household Growth: Where Shall We Live?*, Cm. 3471, HMSO, London.

English Partnerships (1996), *Annual Report and Financial Statements, 1995/96*, English Partnerships, London.

English Partnerships (undated), *Working with our Partners*, English Partnerships, London.

Hall, P. (1996), *Cities of Tomorrow*, Blackwell, Oxford.

Hayter, R. (1997), *The Dynamics of Industrial Location*, John Wiley, Chichester.

Healey, P. (1997), *Collaborative Planning: Shaping Places in Fragmented Societies*, Macmillan, London.

Ho, S.Y. (1997), 'Scrutiny and Direction: Implications of Government Intervention in the Development Plan Process in England', *Urban Studies*, Vol. 34 (8), pp.1259–74.

Hutton, W. (1996), *The State We're In*, Vintage, London.

Keeble, L. (1964) *Principles and Practice of Town and Country Planning*, Estates Gazette, London.

Keene, D. (1993), 'Plans, Policies, Presumptions: How the Law is Approaching the Plan-led System', *Proceedings of the Town and Country Planning Summer School 1993*, Royal Town Planning Institute, London, pp.25–8.

Kelso, W.A. (1994), *Poverty and the Underclass: Changing Perceptions of the Poor in America*, New York University Press, New York.

Kitchen, T. (1996a), 'Roles and Responsibilities in the Delivery of an Effective Planning Service', *Proceedings of the Town and Country Planning Summer School 1996*, Royal Town Planning Institute, London, pp.84–6.

Kitchen, T. (1996b), *The Emerging Urban Agenda*, Department of Planning and Landscape, University of Manchester, Occasional Paper Number 43, Manchester.

Kitchen, T. (1996c), 'The Future of Development Plans: Reflections on Manchester's Experiences, 1945–1995', *Town Planning Review*, Vol. 67 (3), pp.331–53.

Kitchen, T. (1996d), 'The Heart of the North', *Town and Country Planning*, Vol. 65 (1), pp.7–11.

Kitchen, T. (1996e), *2046: The Diaries of St. Peter's Assistant Planner*, paper to the Newcastle Planning School 50th Anniversary Conference: 'Shaping Places', 27 October.

Kitchen, T. (1997a), *People, Politics, Policies and Plans*, Paul Chapman, London.

Kitchen, T. (1997b), *The Urban Local Planning Authority in the 21st Century*, Professorial Lecture, Sheffield Hallam University, 4 June.

Lawless, P. (1996), 'The Inner Cities: Towards a New Agenda', *Town Planning Review*, Vol. 67 (1) pp.21–43.

Leach, S., Stewart, J. and Walsh, K. (1994), *The Changing Organisation and Management of Local Government*, Macmillan, Basingstoke.

McCarthy, P. and Harrison, T. (1995), *Attitudes to Town and Country Planning*, HMSO, London.

Macgregor, B. and Ross, A. (1995), 'Master or Servant? The Changing Role of the Development Plan in the British Planning System', *Town Planning Review*, Vol. 66, (1), pp.41–59.

Oatley, N. (1995), 'Competitive Urban Policy and the Regeneration Game', *Town Planning Review*, Vol. 66, (1), pp.1–14.

Philp, T. (1997), 'North Cornwall Revisited', *Planning*, 7 March, No. 1208, p.18.

Picking, J. (1996), 'Dangerous Liaisons', *Proceedings of the Town and Country Planning Summer School 1996*, Royal Town Planning Institute, London, pp.87–8.

Pickup, L., Stokes, G., Meadowcroft, S., Goodwin, P., Tyson, B. and Kenny, F. (1991), *Bus Deregulation in the Metropolitan Areas*, Avebury, Aldershot.

Robson, B., Bradford, M., Deas, I., Hall, E., Harrison, E., Parkinson, M., Evans, R., Garside, P. and Robinson, F. (1994), *Assessing the Impact of Urban Policy*, HMSO, London.

Royal Commission on Environmental Pollution (1995), *Transport and the Environment*, Oxford University Press, Oxford.

Simmie, J. (1997), *Innovation Networks and Learning Regions?*, Jessica Kingsley Publishers and the Regional Studies Association, London.

Williams, R.H. (1996), *European Union Spatial Policy and Planning*, Paul Chapman, London.

Young, S. (1996), *Promoting Participation and Community Based Partnerships in the Context of Local Agenda 21: A Report for Practitioners*, Department of Government, University of Manchester, Manchester.

Zetter, R., Darke, R. and Mason, R. (1997), *The Role of Elected Members in Plan Making and Development Control*, Royal Town Planning Institute, London.

Index

24 hour city 31

ABC Strategy 118
Aboriginal people 79, 87, 89–92
access 106
access to technology 110, 112, 113, 116, 117,
    129, 130, 134, 136, 142, 143, 151
    social disparity of 130, 151
actant-network theory 73–4, 96
actant-networks 20, 95, 97, 98
*Agence d'Urbanisme de la Communauté
    Urbaine de Lyons* 223–5, 230, 232,
    233
Agence d'Urbanisme de la Région Nîmoise
    233, 226
Agnew, J. 75
Agreement of Wassenaar (1982) 187
Ahearne, J. 32
Alexander, C. 107
American Farmland Trust 245
Appleyard, D. 111
area-based initiatives 154
argumentative approach 178, 183
Art in the City 226
artificial light 31
Atkins, D.J. 62
authentic spaces 33

Bank of America 245
Baudrillard, J. 34
Bauman, Z. 81
Beck, U. 179
Bell, C. 53
Bell, D. 23
Benjamin, W. 32
Berlin 143
Bianchini, F. 42
blueprints 273
Bochum 143
Booher, D. 12, 13, 174, 176
Bosma, K. 150
boundaries 51–62, 64, 66, 67
Bourdieu, P. 42, 44

Boyer, C. 38
Brechtian critical science 181
Bristol 131, 142
Britain 4, 5, 29, 30, 35, 175, 185, 199, 203,
    265, 266, 267, 269, 271, 272, 273,
    274, 276, 278, 279, 289, 292, 293,
    296, 302, 306
Bropho, Mr. R. 78, 89, 90, 91
Bruno, G. 38
business organisation 43, 44

California 240–61
California Resources Agency 245
Callon, M. 72, 73, 91, 97
Capital Web 111
capitalism 25, 32, 38, 42, 43, 44, 45, 46
Capra, F. 247, 260
Carlisle 52
Castells, M. 4
central government control 203, 206
Central Planning Office (CPO) 197
Central Valley, California 245
centralisation 103–6
Cervero 118
Cherry, G.E. 306
Chicago 29, 30, 34
cities
    as 'celebrity' 34
    as collection of artefacts 160
    as repositories of knowledge 42
    embodied 24, 36, 38, 44
    future of 124–7
    in use 24
    learning 38, 42–6
    notion of 147, 149, 157, 302
    spatial trends of 103
classification 59
coalition-building 199
Coleridge, S.T. 23
collaborative approach 175, 267–8, 274,
    277–84
collective action 164–5
collective intelligence 254–5

Collomb, F. 234
Communauté Urbaine, Lyon (COURLY)
    225, 232–3
Communes 223, 224, 225, 232
communication
    content of 28
    corridors 189
    networks 102
    technologies 29, 295
community 125, 134–6, 142, 144, 208, 212,
    216, 295, 297, 300
Compact, Urban, Green 192
complex system 239, 240, 245, 248, 252,
    254, 256, 258
complex systems thinking 240
complexity theory 240, 246, 250–52
concept of localities 55
conflict mediation 266, 274, 277, 283
connectibility of city 35
consensus 179, 187, 252, 254, 257–9
Conservative 203, 296, 302
Cooke, P.N. 53, 56
Coombes, M.C. 7, 20, 51, 52, 58
Corbin 30
Crane, D. 111
cultural theory 192

Dahmann, D.C. 58
dance 40–43
Davis, M. 34
decentralisation 103–5
de Certeau 32, 33
decision-making 69, 70, 97, 172, 174, 179,
    180, 189, 198–9
definition, act of 74
definitions 53–5, 64, 66–7
democratic practice 179, 180, 181
Department of Environment, Transport and
    the Regions 129
despatialisation of activities 155
determinism
    environmental 9, 157
    technological 28, 126
development control 204, 207
development plan 8, 204–8, 215, 217–19,
    294, 296, 298, 300, 303, 305, 306
dialogic democracy 252, 257, 258
Dickens, C. 114, 121

discontinuous change 251–2, 258–9
discourse 183–4
    institutionalisation of 186
    rational technical 77
    planning (Dutch) 189
discursive institutions 172
Douglas, M. 192
Drucker, P. 43, 45
Dryzek, J. 180
Dublin, Temple Bar 133, 145, 146
Duncan, J. 75
Dutch model 187, 189, 200

East Anglia 62
Eco, U. 34
ecological modernisation 185, 186
economic development 2, 10, 13, 14
economic development/environment tradeoff
    239, 255
economic entrepreneurialism (Dutch) 192,
    195, 196, 198
Eder, K. 179, 180, 181, 199
Edge Cities 105, 106
Edinburgh 149
Einstein, A. 159
Eliot, T.S. 114
England 172
English Partnerships 292, 293
environment 171, 174–5
Environment Agency 267
Erickson, B. 21, 102
EU Objective 1 292
EU Objective 2 292
EU Objective 5b 292
Eurocity 229, 234
Europe 3, 14, 105, 106, 116, 126, 137, 138,
    140, 144, 145, 196, 271, 273, 278
European Commission 5, 103
European Metropolis 228–9
European Regionalisation Algorithm (ERA)
    58, 60, 61, 62, 66
European Union 1, 208, 212, 292, 293
everyday life 23, 25, 28, 32
Ewald, F. 179

facts
    brute 158
    institutional 158

Faludi, A. 195
family 33–4, 38
Finch, J. 33
Finnegan, R. 41
fiscal system, fragmented 242
Fitzpatrick, T. 131
Fitzsimmons, J.D. 58
Foley, D. 270
Foucault, M. 11, 36, 42, 75, 182, 185
France 3, 130, 172, 174, 223, 224, 228
Frey, W. 58
Friedmann, J. 4

Garreau, J. 105, 106, 116
GEMESIS project 143
geographical information systems (GIS) 10,
      38, 57, 59
Gibbons, M. 36
Giddens, A. 251, 252, 257
Gilroy, P. 35
Gingrich, N. 136
global space 156–7
good practice 282
Gore, A. 256
Gosling, D. 111
Gottmann, J. 131
governance process 2, 3, 12, 117, 270
government 2, 171, 188
Government Office for the North West 212
Government Office for the West Midlands
      215
Grabher, G. 37
Graham, M. 21, 107
Graham, S. 40,
Grossman, L. 151
Grosz, E. 38
growth 209, 212, 214, 218

Hägerstrand, T. 39, 40, 75
Hajer, M. 8, 12, 14, 172, 173, 176, 178
Hall, P. 52, 53, 288
Handy, C. 45, 251
Harvey, D. 26, 27
Healey, P. 1, 12, 13, 175, 265
Heidegger, M. 44
Hellinga, H. 150
heritage
      Aboriginal 78, 87
      white colonial settler 78, 86, 89, 97

Hill, D. 133
Hillier, B. 107
Hillier, M. 7, 20, 21, 69,
Hirst, P. 183
history 24, 27
Ho, S.Y. 305
Hoch, C. 96
home 75, 79–84, 86
Homer 115
housing 188, 196
Hull, A.D. 1, 172, 173, 203
human
      bodies 38
      creativity 24, 25
      practices 23, 36
Hutchins, E. 249
Hutton, W. 288

identity
      people's 51, 61, 69, 70, 78, 83, 95, 155–6
      place 28, 52, 69, 70, 71–5, 78, 83, 85, 86,
            90, 91, 95, 97, 104, 113–117, 228,
            230
      society's 85
image 70–90, 92, 94–8
imageability 107, 113
indicators 249–61
industrialisation 161
information districts 133, 137, 143, 144, 145,
      148, 150
information economy 127–30
infrastructure 188, 190, 195, 196, 198, 199,
      200
Innes, J. 12, 13, 174, 176, 239
institutional
      change 180, 223, 265
      power 198
      practices 214
      relations 224, 230, 235–6
      terrains 282
integrated metropolis 102, 104, 117–21
intentionality 158, 163
interaction
      different types of 55, 57, 66, 215
      face-to-face 105, 112, 127, 130, 137
interactions
      city/telecommunications 137, 147
      electronic 125, 127, 132, 147

interlinked centres 132
Internet 124, 131–6, 141–3
    metropolitan dominance 127, 134
Inter-Regional Information Society Initiative
    (IRISI) 144
intersection 8, 13, 154, 167–8
investment 208–9, 211–12, 215–16
IT islands 142

Jackson, P. 23
Jacobs, J. 108
Jameson, F. 34
Japan 140
Johnny-come-latelies 92

Kantian perspective 181
Kasparov, G. 248
Kay, J. 45
Kent 203, 207–11, 217
Kirklees 141
Kitchen, T. 12, 14, 175, 287
knowledge 24–38, 40, 42–5, 112–15, 121
    of place 103
    Type 1 36
    Type 2 36
Kuhn, T. 182

Laban, R.V. 40
Labour (*see also* New Labour) 203, 208,
    213, 220
Lancashire 203, 208, 209, 212, 217–18
land use 69, 72–3, 78, 80, 92–3, 160–61
language 164, 173, 278–9
Lash, S. 131, 197
Latour, B. 24–5, 97, 181–2
leadership 252, 254, 258–9
Leeds 52
Leeflang, H. 191
Lefebvre, H. 4, 9, 32, 33, 39, 40
Leibniz, G. 159
Leicester 52
Levitt, T. 45
litigation 242
living circumstances 302
Lloyd-Jones, T. 7, 21, 102
locale, notion of 224
Localities 7, 9, 51–6, 60, 61, 64, 66, 67
localities 208

locality, concept of 53, 55
Local Labour Market Areas (LLMAs) 64, 66
local media 214, 218
local relations 132
London 31, 34, 103, 106, 110, 114, 116,
    120–21, 126
    Brent Cross 110, 116
    Camden Lock 111
    City of 29, 130–31
    Heathrow 106, 121
    Lower Regent Street 111
    New Oxford Street 111
    North Circular 106
    Oxford Circus 111
    Oxford Street 111
    Shoreditch 133
    Soho 146
    West End 130
Los Angeles (LA) 34, 35, 139, 144, 145
    Blue Line TeleVillage 144
Lynch, K. 109, 111, 113, 114
Lyon 13–14, 174, 223–36
    Lyon 2010 225, 229, 234

MacCormac, R. 112
Macregor, B. 305
Madanipour, A. 1, 7, 13, 19, 154
Maitland, R.B. 111
Major, J. 204
management 43–7, 129
management gurus 45
Manchester 141, 143, 145, 151, 175, 288,
    292, 293, 295
    Hulme 297
    Northern Quarter 145
market-oriented planning (Dutch) 188
market thinking 211
Marvin, S. 21, 107
Masser, I. 58
Massey, D. 54, 55, 70, 72
materiality 163
media strategies, city-wide 137, 141, 143,
    144
memory 78, 91
mental maps 109, 111
Merleau-Ponty, M. 39, 44
Metropolitan Area Network ('MAN') 143
metropolitan centre 104, 106–7

Metropolitan Debate (Dutch) 190
metropolitan development 239–41, 246–7,
    249, 250, 252, 254, 259
Metropolitan Statistical Area 58
metropolitan system 244, 249, 254, 256–9
Middlesborough 51
Milton Keynes 41
Mitchell, W. 146
modernists 164
Morgan, G. 45
Moss, M. 134
Moss Kanter, R. 45
Motte, A. 13, 172, 173, 174, 223
Mulgan, G. 124
multiculturalism 156
mythology 91
myths 23, 26, 42

Naisbitt, J. 45
Netherlands 3, 12, 14, 172, 179, 185, 187,
    188, 190, 195, 196, 197, 199
network poverty 136
networks 3, 5, 20, 21, 24, 28, 34, 37, 44
Newby, H. 53
Newcastle 136, 141
new industrial revolution 124
New Labour 203, 205, 267, 268, 280, 281,
    292, 296
New Map 190, 191
Newton, I. 159
Newtonian, mechanistic model 246
New York 29, 30, 34, 133, 135, 145, 288
    Manhattan, SoHo 133
    Manhattan, Tribeca 133
    Silicon Alley 133, 145
Nice, S. 21, 102
Nietzsche, F. 46
night life 31
Nilles, J. 128
NIMBY (not-in-my-back-yard) 217, 219,
    277
Nîmes 13, 174, 223–37
Noir, M. 234
Norwich 52
notions of order 165
Nottingham 141
Nye, D. 31

officers of governance (Australian) (*see also*
    planners) 72, 78–9, 87
Ogborn, O. 23
Ohmae, K. 45
Olds, K. 130
Owen, D.W. 62

Paris 34, 35, 39, 130
    Périphérique 106
participation 72, 76–9, 84, 95–6, 104, 203–7,
    216, 219–20
pattern of development 105, 111, 116, 244–5
patterns of consumption 161
patterns of differentiation 167
Penn. A. 107
perceptual space 129
performance criteria approach 266–8, 274–5,
    278, 281, 283
performance measures 254, 256
perspectives 19, 22, 71, 154–67
Perth, Australia 69, 77, 84, 88, 95
Peters, T. 45
Pile, S. 23
place-focused concerns 266–7
placelessness 29–30
place-making 3, 13, 160, 265–8, 270, 271,
    274, 277–9, 282–4
place meaning 154–65
place/movement 7
places
    interchangeable 29
    shaping 12–14
    vision of future 226–8
place/territory 7
Plan d'Ordonnancement 224, 226, 228, 229,
    230, 233, 236
plan-led system 173, 205, 217, 218, 266, 268
planners 69–71, 74, 76–8, 81–2, 84, 91–2,
    96–7, 178, 183, 189, 191, 195–6,
    265, 272–3, 284
planning 2, 223–5, 229, 232, 234, 236
    cultural (Dutch) 192, 196
    spatial 1–4, 6–13, 171–3, 176, 265–72,
        277–9, 282–3
    welfare (Dutch) 192, 195–8
Planning Act, Section 5A 305
Planning and Compensation Act (1991) 204
planning issues 284

Planning Policy Guidance Note 1 103
planning system 12–14, 173–5, 203, 208,
    215, 218, 220, 265–8, 272, 275–7,
    279–84, 289, 296, 299, 305
Polanyi, M. 44
political planning process 234
Pollock 38
Porrit, J. 128
post-corporatist society 178–81, 189, 200
postmodern analysis 266
postmodernists 164
poultry farming 85
power 72–6, 79, 81, 96–8
    symbolic 149, 151
power differences, structural 77
Pred, A. 70, 75
Probyn 26, 40
professional organisations 190
Projet d'Agglomération 224, 225, 234, 236
property rights 271, 272, 275
Proposition 13, 243, 250
public inquiry 205, 207, 217
public participation 72, 76, 78–9, 95–6, 185,
    195, 197
public realm 103, 110, 112, 119, 120, 121

quality
    of life 203, 211, 245, 265, 273
    of place 156, 196, 208, 266, 278, 281
    spatial 191

Raban, J. 116
Reagan, R. 183, 184
Regional Development Agencies 155, 220,
    280
regional structure 292
relationships
    elected representatives/technical officers
        225, 230, 232–3, 235, 303–5
    local/central government 230, 232, 234
    members/officers 295
    planning authorities/customer
        communities 292, 296
    public-private 161
    regulatory 271, 274, 283
residents
    Aboriginal 89–92

Euro-Australian 88–91, 93
local 70, 75, 78, 79, 82
long-term 88, 92
short-term 88, 92
resource base 303
rhythmanalysis 39
Road Transport Informatics (RTI) 140, 141
Roberts, M. 21, 102
Robson, B. 289
Rose, N. 23
Ross, A. 305
Rossi, A. 109
Royal Commission on Local Government in
    England 52
Royal Town Planning Institute 295
Ruimtelijke Perspectieven (Spatial
    Perspectives Report, 1986) 188

sacred sites 81, 89, 92
Samuel, R. 38
San Francisco 35, 133–4, 250–51, 261
Sassen, S. 104
Satolas airport 229
Savage, M. 30
Schearwater, J. 58
*Schéma Directeur d'Aménagement et
    d'Urbanisme* 223–5, 228–30, 232,
    234, 235, 237
Schipol airport, Amsterdam 106
Schön, D.A. 259
Schwarz, M. 180, 192
Searle, J. 158
Senge, P. 258, 261
SENIM 226
Sennett, R. 40
SEPAL 225, 230, 232
Sheffield, Cultural Industries Quarter (CIQ)
    145
Simmel, G. 31
Single Regeneration Budget (SRB) 293
situ-based sales tax 244
Smart City 143
social-constructivist vein 185
social-democratic agenda (Dutch) 192
social geometries 161
social reality 158, 163, 165
social reflexivity 251–2, 257, 259

social relations 9, 11, 112, 161
society, local 54
socioeconomic
    conditions 209
    deprivation 288
socio-spatial
    approach 11
    process 3, 4
    relations 12
    schema 114
Soja, E. 4
Solihull 216
Soros, G. 259
space 2–14, 19–22, 74–6, 80, 82, 96–8,
    154–62, 164–5, 167, 211
space-time relations 10, 75
spaciousness 84, 97
spatial
    behaviour 158
    focus 188
    strategy 102, 206, 207, 209, 212, 214
    thinking 4
spatiality 4, 6–14
spatial plan 172, 174–5, 203–6, 211, 223, 237
Spatial Planning Act (Dutch) 196, 198
spatial planning agenda 10
Speare, A. 58
Spokane, WA 145
sprawl 245–6, 256, 260
stakeholder interaction 207, 210–18
stakeholders 203–4, 206, 208, 217–19, 224,
    236, 254, 257, 261, 267–8, 270–71,
    273, 274, 277–84
stakeholder society 270, 274, 284
Stark, D. 37
state intervention 2, 3, 5
state-society relations 1, 2
Stockton-on-Tees 51
stories 69, 77–9, 82, 90–91, 92, 94, 96
storylines 184–5, 187, 192
structural change 304
structure plan (*see also* development plan)
    204, 209–13, 218
structure plan inquiry 213
Sudbury 56, 57, 62, 64
sustainability 102, 107, 116, 119, 128, 149,
    157, 175, 212, 239–40, 252–4, 256,
    259, 266, 268–9, 301–2

sustainable
    cities 111, 120, 289
    development 212, 253
    system 241, 255
Swan Valley, Perth, Australia 69, 77–97
synthetic data 59–67
synthetic data method 60
systems thinking 240, 258

technical officer (French) (*see also* planners)
    232–3
technological developments 291, 294
Teesside 51
telecities 144
telecommunications 107, 112, 124, 125–32,
    135, 137–9, 143, 146–51
Telecommunications for Clean Air 137
telecommunications planning, urban 137
telecommuters 138
teleworking 128, 132, 137–9
Thames Gateway 210
Thatcher, M. 183, 184
The Hague 196
Thompson, G. 180, 192
Thompson, M. 183
Thornton, S. 41
Thrift, N. 7, 23, 130, 131, 183
time-geography 39
time-space relationship 26–7, 171
tourism 80, 85–6, 89, 97–8
Town and Country Planning Act (1947) 4,
    288, 305
Town and Country Planning Act (1990) 204
tradition
    Aboriginal 91, 93
    white colonial 93
translation 73–5, 96
transport 103, 105, 107–11, 116–21, 212–14,
    216–17, 289, 300, 302
transport/relecommunication relations
    128–30
travel times 110
Travel-to-Work Areas (TTWAs) 57, 64, 66

Unitary Development Plan 215
United Kingdom (UK) 3, 12, 120, 137, 138,
    139, 140, 141, 142, 143, 146, 207,
    219

United States (US) 3, 12, 29, 30, 45, 58, 105, 116, 128, 131, 132, 133, 134, 136, 137, 138, 140, 142, 143, 144, 145, 239, 245, 256, 261, 277
Urban and Regional Teleworking Initiatives 137
urban
   development process 162
   economies 302
   Internet guides 135
   landscape 150
   management, role of 140
   regeneration expenditure 289
   regeneration funding 293
   structure 106, 109, 111, 121
   televillages 137, 144
Urry, J. 131, 197
utopianism 126

Valentine, G. 23
value
   aesthetic 81, 83, 84, 86, 95
   economic 80, 85, 86, 88, 91, 98
   exchange 5, 6, 10
   heritage 81
   landscape 81
   spiritual 89, 91, 94
   use 4, 5, 10, 80
values 8, 13
Van der Valk. A. 178, 195
Vienna 34
Vigar, G. 172, 173, 203

VINEX 188, 189, 198
VINO 188, 189, 198
VINO/VINEX 189
Virilio, P. 26, 27
virtual
   cities 142
   networks 119
vision 81, 90, 91, 224, 226, 228, 232, 235
viticulture 78, 80, 85, 93

Wakeford, N. 135
Walker, R.A. 35
Warde. A. 30
Warren, R. 126
West Midlands 203, 208, 209, 215, 216
Wilson, E. 115
Winsemius, P. 191
Wirth, L. 31
Wollen, P. 40
working area 79, 80, 83, 85, 86, 88, 97
world
   as machine 247
   as organism 247
World Bank 104
world cities 104
Worpole, K. 31, 42
Wymer, C. 7, 51

Zone d'Aménagement Concerté 226
zoning approach 277
Zurich 34